MICROSOFT®

WINDOWS 2000
SERVER

Nancy Woolridge
Fullerton College
Fullerton, California

Dale Craig
Fullerton College
Fullerton, California

Developmental Editor	Tom Modl
Illustrations	Colin Hayes
Copy Editors	Cheryl Wilms, Gretchen Bratvold
Indexer	Donald Glassman
Cover and Text Design	Joan D'Onofrio, Leslie Anderson
Production	Desktop Solutions
Cover Image	ImageState

Publishing Team—George Provol, Publisher; Janice Johnson, Director of Product Development; Tony Galvin, Acquisitions Editor; Lori Landwer, Marketing Manager; Shelley Clubb, Electronic Design and Production Manager

Acknowledgments—The authors and publisher wish to thank the following reviewers for their technical and academic assistance in testing exercises and assessing instruction:
- April Miller Cripliver, Sawyer College
- Frank Futyma, Columbus Technical College
- Roger Young, Davenport University

Photo Credits—p. 11, Belkin Components, p. 13, top and bottom, Cisco Systems, p. 14, Cisco Systems, p. 15, top and bottom, Cisco Systems.

Library of Congress Cataloging-in-Publication Data
Craig, Dale.
     Microsoft Windows 2000 server / Dale Craig, Nancy Woolridge.
           p. cm.
     includes index.
     ISBN 0-7638-1331-1 (text + CD-ROM)
     1. Microsoft Windows server. 2. Client/server computing. I. Woolridge, Nancy. II. Title.

     QA76.9.C55 C72 2002
     005.4'4769—dc21

                                     2001040237

Care has been taken to verify the accuracy of information presented in this book. However, the author, editor, and publisher cannot accept any responsibility for Web, e-mail, newsgroup, or chat room subject matter or content, or for consequences from application of the information in this book, and make no warranty, expressed or implied, with respect to its content.

Trademarks—Some of the product names and company names included in this book have been used for identification purposes only and may be trademarks or registered trademarks of their respective manufacturers and sellers. The author, editor, and publisher disclaim any affiliation, association, or connection with, or sponsorship or endorsement by, such owners.

Text: ISBN 0-7638-1331-1
Order Number: 01534

© 2002   by Paradigm Publishing Inc.
         Published by **EMC**Paradigm
         875 Montreal Way
         St. Paul, MN 55102

         (800) 535-6865
         E-mail: educate@emcp.com
         Web site: www.emcp.com

Printed in the United States of America
10 9 8 7 6 5 4 3 2 1

TABLE OF CONTENTS

Chapter 4

Disk Management   113

Chapter 5

Printing   157

Chapter 6

Introduction to Domains   201

Chapter 7

Users and Groups   235

Chapter 8

Profiles and Policies   275

Chapter 9

Sharing, Permissions, and the Distributed File System   329

Chapter 10

Microsoft Network Infrastructure   377

Chapter 11

Active Directory   427

Chapter 12

Windows 2000 Security 479

Chapter 13

Performance Monitoring, Backups, and Troubleshooting 517

Chapter 14

Internet Information Services 563

Appendix A

Appendix B

PREFACE

Microsoft® Windows 2000 Server was written to teach students how to install, configure, and administer Microsoft Windows 2000 Server and how to administer a Windows 2000 network. Through teaching Windows 2000 Server classes, we have learned that network administration skills are best taught with a combination of hands-on and Problem Solving Exercises. Hands-on exercises provide students the opportunity to learn how to perform specific network administrative tasks. Problem Solving Exercises provide students with the opportunity to demonstrate critical thinking skills.

Another important component to learning Windows 2000 Server administration is obtaining the background knowledge required to understand the operation of the software. This includes an understanding of basic data communications concepts, how the Windows 2000 Server software works, and other foundational computer concepts.

Text Overview

This book includes features that support all three of these teaching goals: step-by-step exercises, Problem Solving Exercises, and technical background information. Each chapter of this book includes the following:

- A set of step-by-step detailed exercises that take the student through important chapter topics. These exercises contain descriptions and sample screens.
- A set of step-by-step Lab Exercises, located at the end of the chapter, to reinforce and extend concepts presented in the chapter. These exercises include only the steps and not descriptions or figures.
- A set of Problem Solving Exercises that reinforce problem solving skills.
- End of chapter questions to test the student's understanding of concepts presented in the chapter.
- A definition list of terms from the chapter.
- Technical notes that provide background information.

The instructor's materials that will accompany this book will include the following:

- PowerPoint slides for each chapter
- Answers to end of chapter questions

- Teaching suggestions and resources for each chapter
- Sample tests
- A utility that generates scripts documenting student progress in doing exercises on the operating system

A New Approach to Active Directory

Most Windows 2000 Server textbooks present Active Directory in an early chapter. This is a difficult topic for even experienced network administrators, and presenting it too early in a textbook for students can result in more confusion than comprehension. This book delays covering Active Directory until a later chapter and allows students to first become familiar with the basics of Windows 2000 Server. The general progression of topic coverage in this book is—

1. Background information and installation (chapters 1 and 2 – introduction and installation)
2. Configuring and managing a single server (chapters 3, 4, and 5 – hardware and software management, disk management, and printing)
3. Connecting to a domain and managing domain resources (chapters 6, 7, 8, and 9 – introduction to domains, users and groups, profiles and policies, shares and permissions)
4. Preparing for, designing, and installing Active Directory (chapters 10 and 11 – network infrastructure and Active Directory)
5. Windows 2000 topics (chapters 12, 13, and 14 – security, Internet Information Services, and performance monitoring and troubleshooting)

Although Active Directory is briefly covered in chapter 6, this is done so that students can connect to a domain. This chapter also presents a very quick overview of DNS and other infrastructure topics necessary to understand domains. Active Directory is covered in more detail, including design issues, in chapter 11. Before covering the Active Directory chapter it is necessary to present various networking infrastructure topics, such as TCP/IP and DNS, in chapter 10.

Topics by Chapter

Chapter 1 – Introduction: Provides an overview of Windows 2000 Server and covers basic networking concepts, such as the OSI and DOD network models. It also contains information about the MCSE program.

Chapter 2 – Installing Windows 2000: Includes the steps for installing Windows 2000 Server and includes topics related to installation such as selection of the server hardware and purchasing of software licenses. Topics also include using the Sysprep command to install Windows 2000 Server from an image file.

Chapter 3 – Server Hardware and Software Management: Includes topics on installing and configuring hardware and software on a server. These are commonly performed tasks that require knowledge of how Windows 2000 Server uses drivers, how to use an MSI file, and how to make changes to the Registry.

Chapter 4 – Disk Management: Includes disk management topics such as formatting and mounting drives, compressing and converting drives to NTFS, and using RAID drives. The CD that comes with this book includes simulations for selected exercises that give students the option of practicing modifying disk configurations without physically changing the drives.

Chapter 5 – Printing: Includes topics related to installing, sharing, and managing network printers. This includes configuring shared printers and printing across the Internet.

Chapter 6 – Introduction to Domains: Teaches students how to connect a server to a domain and how domains work. Topics include a quick overview of DNS and name resolution and using DCPROMO to install a domain. These topics are covered in greater detail in chapters 10 and 11.

Chapter 7 – Users and Groups: Topics in this chapter include creating and managing users and groups within a domain. Students learn how to create users and groups, how to configure user and group accounts, and how to modify such accounts.

Chapter 8 – Profiles and Policies: Teaches students how to create and manage user profiles and policies at the domain level. This includes using policies with organizational units, policy inheritance and overriding, and using policies to automatically install software.

Chapter 9 – Sharing, Permissions, and the Distributed File System: Topics in this chapter include sharing network resources and using share and file permissions. This chapter also presents topics with the distributed file system and includes exercises on setting up this system within a domain.

Chapter 10 – Microsoft Network Infrastructure: Presents topics related to installing and configuring network infrastructure services such as DNS, DHCP, and WINS. In addition, this chapter presents the basic concepts of TCP/IP, IP addressing, and subnetting.

Chapter 11 – Active Directory: Includes topics on designing and managing an Active Directory network. (Installing Active Directory was covered in chapter 6.) Students learn how Active Directory works with DNS, how Active Directory is replicated across the network, the FSMO roles played by selected servers, and how to configure Active Directory sites.

Chapter 12 – Windows 2000 Security: Presents topics related to network security. These include the Kerberos security system, how public/private key systems work, using the IPSec services to protect network traffic, file and folder encryption, and using security templates.

Chapter 13 – Internet Information Services: Topics in this chapter include installing, configuring, and managing Internet Information Services. Students will learn how to create a Web site, how to set Web site security, and how to use Windows 2000 Terminal Services.

Chapter 14 – Performance Monitoring, Backups, and Troubleshooting: This chapter includes topics on monitoring the performance of a Windows 2000 server, backing up a server, and troubleshooting problems. Students learn how to use the Performance Monitoring tool to gather information and how to interpret the information for troubleshooting purposes.

Computer Configurations

The exercises in this book assume students have access to a computer running Windows 2000. This book was written using Windows 2000 Advanced Server, but can be used with Windows 2000 Server, including the 120-day trial version of Windows 2000 Server. This book cannot be used with Windows 2000 Professional.

When installing Windows 2000 Server you must give each computer a unique computer name and static IP address (do not use dynamic IP addresses because Windows 2000 Server will not correctly run Active Directory or DNS). In a computer lab, the name assigned to each system might be based on location. For example, R1C3 would be assigned to the third computer in the first row. When assigning static IP addresses, consider using non-routable addresses. The exercises in this book use addresses in the range 192.168.XXX.XXX. Remember to assign addresses within the same subnet so pairs of systems can communicate with each other. For example, two paired computers might be given the following settings:

> Computer A
> Name - R1C3
> IP Address - 192.168.100.10
>
> Computer B
> Name - R1C4
> IP Address - 192.168.100.11

Lab Configurations

Some of the exercises in this book require two networked computers on the same subnet. Exercises that must be done on one of the paired computers include an identification of the computer on which they are to be performed. The minimal requirements to complete the exercises in this book are two networked computers running Windows 2000 Server, but another common configuration is a computer lab containing multiple systems. Configuring computers in a lab is no different than configuring pairs of systems. Make sure that each system has a unique name and unique static IP address. If the computer lab is on a single subnet the IP addresses can be set to a non-routable number and placed within the same subnet.

Windows 2000 can be installed on a computer that also contains Windows 9x. This can be done by creating two partitions on a hard drive (the partition that will hold Windows 2000 Server should be at least 600 Megabytes) and formatting these partitions with DOS. Install Windows 9x on the first partition and then install Windows 2000 Server on the second partition. During installation of Windows 2000 a boot manager will be installed that allows dual booting between Windows 9x and Windows 2000.

Windows 2000 can also be installed by using a disk image program. This is done by first running SYSPREP on an installed copy of Windows 2000, creating a disk image, and installing the image. When Windows 2000 is first run after SYSPREP, it will automatically install itself. Chapter 2 contains instructions for using SYSPREP and a sample INF file that can be used to automatically install Windows 2000.

Acknowledgements

Nancy Woolridge: I would like to thank all of the people that made this book possible: my parents who taught me how to work and learn, my husband for support, patience and numerous babysitting hours, my co-author for guidance. I never could have done this alone.

Dale Craig: I wish to thank all those who helped in the production of this book and especially my wife Jane for her support and encouragement in face of late nights and missed dinners. I also would like to thank my co-author for her seemingly boundless patience and constancy.

We both wish to thank those people who were instrumental in helping make this book a reality. The editors at EMCP did a fantastic job on this highly technical material, making it look easy with a great deal of work. Thanks also go to our colleagues at Fullerton College, Nora Spencer and Richard Smead, for allowing us to test our chapters on their students. Special thanks go to Richard Smead for his valuable technical insights in networking and Microsoft Windows. Very special thanks go to Forsythe.com and to Steve Siedschlag for invaluable technical assistance. Finally, we dedicate this book to our students.

INTRODUCTION TO NETWORKS AND WINDOWS 2000 SERVER 1

Performance Objectives

After completing this chapter you will be able to:

- Explain the concept of a network operating system
- Discuss the operation of a computer network
- Identify the parts of the OSI network model
- Identify the major parts of Windows 2000 Server
- Contrast the differences between Windows NT 4 and Windows 2000 Server
- Specify the hardware and networking resources necessary for Windows 2000

Introduction

Windows 2000 represents the latest and best effort by Microsoft to create a **network operating system** (**NOS**) powerful enough for very large enterprise networks yet easy to install and manage and easy to integrate with non-Microsoft network operating systems.

Before learning to install and administer Windows 2000, it is important to review some foundational concepts in data communications. This chapter contains a review of data communications concepts as well as an outline of how Windows 2000 works. How information is passed across a network, the role of network protocols, and the types of hardware found on a computer network will be reviewed. The concepts presented in this chapter will be applied in later chapters when you install and configure Windows 2000 Server.

Windows NT and Windows 2000

The precursor to Windows 2000 was Windows NT. One of the goals of the Windows NT design team was to create a robust and enterprise-level network operating system that had the Windows user interface. One of the primary requirements placed on the NT design team was to make Windows NT compatible with legacy Microsoft software applications. The result was Windows NT 3.51, which was later upgraded to Windows NT 4.

Although Windows NT 4 was widely adopted as the network operating system of choice by many companies, it had some significant shortcomings, such as—

- Incomplete support for Windows software and standard hardware
- Difficulties managing very large networks
- Nonstandard networking components
- High network administrative costs

Microsoft has addressed all these concerns in Windows 2000. Windows 2000 supports a wider range of software packages and works better with existing hardware than Windows NT does. The most significant improvement in this area for Windows 2000 is the addition of **Plug and Play**. This feature allows the operating system to automatically recognize and install hardware components and thus reduces problems associated with incompatible drivers.

Windows NT was not designed to easily support very large networks. The number of network accounts stored on a single server was limited by the physical size of the registry. Windows NT 4 had problems when the number of accounts in a domain reached about 20,000 users. In order to support more users, an NT network had to be broken into pieces and links between the pieces manually created and maintained. In contrast, Windows 2000 includes a component called *Active Directory* that is used as the repository and security boundary for network accounts and resources. Active Directory can easily support very large numbers of network users and devices. In simulations at Compaq a single Windows 2000 domain was successfully loaded with more than 100 million objects.

Windows NT worked well on networks that included only computers running Windows 95/98 or Windows NT. This was a problem for companies that had a heterogeneous networking environment. Integrating Windows NT Servers and UNIX servers on the same network was difficult at best. To solve this problem, Microsoft includes several key industry standard technologies in Windows 2000. These include the **Kerberos** security system, directory access using the **Lightweight Directory Access Protocol** (**LDAP**), and support for a standard resource look-up system, also known as a **domain name system** (**DNS**). These features allow Windows 2000 to be more easily integrated into a network that includes computers running non-Microsoft operating systems.

One of the major problems with Windows NT was that many network resources required administrative support. Windows NT 4 DNS records had to be manually updated, and user accounts across domains had to be managed. Microsoft designed Windows 2000 to make such tasks much easier. *Dynamic DNS* removed the requirement that domain name system records be manually updated, while Active Directory removed the necessity of manually establishing trust relationships between domains.

Many other features in Windows 2000 make it a major improvement over Windows NT 4. For these reasons, Windows 2000 is a safe choice for new networks and should be seriously considered as an upgrade for existing Windows NT 4 networks.

Network Operating Systems

Before learning how to install and manage a Windows 2000 network, it is helpful to understand the following general functions of a network operating system:

- Resource management
- Network access management
- User account management and security

These features are found in most network operating systems, including Windows, UNIX, Novell Netware, and SUN OS.

Resource management involves making various network resources available, including servers, printers, scanners, and other devices that will be shared by network users. Network access management includes setting the access rights to such network resources. These rights might include which users can access the resource, how the resource can be used, and when the resource can be used. User account management and security involves creating user accounts and defining the level of access to the network resources for each user.

The Client/Server Model

One way to understand the operation of a network operating system is through the **client/server** model. This model describes the relationship between different parts of a network. A client is a computer or software application that makes requests of a server. The server is the computer or software application that responds to requests from clients. The client instigates the contact by sending a request to the server. The server cannot predict when or if it will receive client requests. A server waits for client requests and responds to the requests as they are received. Most servers can handle multiple client requests, but clients normally only send requests to one server at a time.

This model can be used to describe a computer network. Client computers are connected to the network and send requests to a server. The server responds to client requests as they are received. For example, when logging into the network a user enters an account name and password. Information based on this user input is sent to a server for verification. If the account name and password match, the client computer is given the right to use the network. The server that issues this authorization may be receiving requests from and responding to multiple clients at the same time.

Computer Networks

The environment for a network operating system is a computer network. The network provides the pathway through which clients can communicate with servers. A computer network consists of the following elements:

- Network connection software
- Network connection hardware
- Network computers

Network connection software consists of the software and protocols necessary for information to move across the hardware components. The network connection hardware consists of the physical components that make up the network These include the device that connects the computer to the network, the hardware connections between computers on the network, and any hardware necessary to interconnect segments of the network. Network computers are the systems connected to the network and using the network to communicate with other systems.

Network Connection Software

Network connection software provides a way for computers to communicate across the physical network. This coordinated communication is not an easy task because most networks are made up of hardware components from many different vendors. Providing a common communication language is the primary purpose of connection software. This language is called network **protocols**.

The term *protocol* was originally used to describe an agreed-upon activity performed by people in specific situations (for example, bowing when brought before the Queen of England). With computer networks the term is used to describe an agreed-upon networking language and/or process. Protocols define the language used by network components and network software for communication.

Standard protocols are important because they facilitate communication between different kinds of network components and network software. For example, a protocol named Ethernet is used to transfer data across a physical network. This protocol defines the structure of the data bits and how devices should send and receive these bits. Once such a standard protocol has been defined and agreed upon by networking vendors, components can be created that, when they correctly implement the protocol, can easily communicate with components created by other companies.

OSI and DOD Network Models

Because of the complexity of network communication software, it is helpful to use an abstract model to represent the structure of the network protocols. Such models make it easier to understand how information passes across a network as well as providing a framework for networking standards. Two commonly used network models are the **Open Systems Interconnect** (**OSI**) network model and the **Department of Defense** (**DOD**) network model.

Each of these models abstractly describes communication across a computer network as a series of layers, with each layer performing a different communication function. A layer can only send information to the layer above or below itself. When a network message moves across the network it may pass through several different layers. Each sublayer hides complexity from an upper layer. A simple message at an upper layer may, in order to be sent across the network, be broken into a complex data structure at a lower layer.

To use an analogy, consider what happens when sending a package with a courier service. You fill out a form and write the address of the recipient on the package. The courier service then adds its own internal code number to the package so it can be tracked. This code number may include the ID number of a local destination courier site or the number of an outgoing airline flight. Once placed into the courier system, the package is tracked only by the assigned ID number and not the destination address.

When the package arrives at a local courier office, it is given to a driver who then uses a conventional address to make the final delivery. Up to this point, only the internal courier ID has been used to identify the destination of the package.

Network protocols work in much the same way. A mail message will include the e-mail address of the recipient, but this destination address may be converted into a network number address at some lower level. E-mail programs are not concerned with network number addresses, leaving this detail to a lower layer protocol.

The OSI Model   The **International Organization for Standardization (ISO)** developed the OSI model illustrated in Figure 1.1 It is made up of seven interconnected layers.

FIGURE **1.1**   *Open Systems Interconnect (OSI) Network Model*

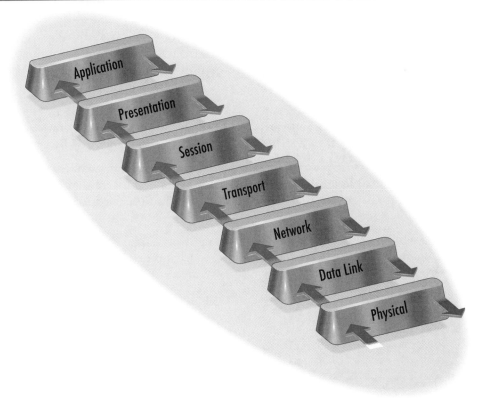

- The **application layer** is where specific network programs and protocols operate. These programs perform tasks such as sending e-mail and transporting Web pages from computer to computer. In order to send or receive data, this layer relies on software at the presentation layer.

- The **presentation layer** consists of the software necessary to format the network data for the application layer programs. It receives messages from the application layer, formats the data, and sends it on to the session layer. It can also receive messages from the session layer, format the message to make it suitable for the application layer, and then send the message up to the application layer.

- The **session layer** consists of the software necessary to maintain a connection between computers on a network. It receives formatted messages from the presentation layer and starts to send them across the network. However, in order to make the connection, it needs the help of the transport layer to locate the destination computer.

- The **transport layer** consists of the software used to locate computers on the network. Software at this layer responds to requests from the session layer to find a computer on the network. Once the computer is located, the transport layer needs the assistance of the network layer to move data across the network hardware.

- The **network layer** software is responsible for negotiating the data flow between computers on the network. It attaches the computer location, derived from the transport layer, to each message. However, the network layer software needs the assistance of the data link layer software to create a series of frames in which the data must reside.

- The **data link layer** software collects the bits of information flowing across a network into a structure. This structure is recognized by the physical layer network hardware.

- The **physical layer** consists of the hardware and software that converts data from 0s and 1s to their physical representation, such as voltages moving across a cable.

The DOD Model   Another commonly used network model is the one developed by the **Department of Defense (DOD)**. This model also describes a communication session over a computer network, but has fewer layers (Figure 1.2).

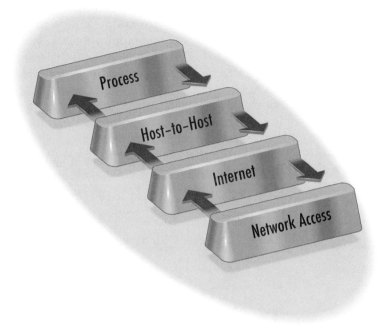

- The **process layer** includes the application, presentation, and session elements of the OSI model. Software in this layer manages, formats, and sends data between computers. In order to send data, the software at this layer needs to locate the computer on the network through the host-to-host layer software.

- The **host-to-host layer** corresponds to the transport layer in the OSI model. In this layer, software locates computers across the network. After locating a computer, the message must be moved across the network to the other computer. This is done by the Internet layer.

- The **Internet layer** corresponds to the network layer in the OSI model. Software in this layer negotiates the data flow between computers. Before data can be sent, it needs to be formatted and reduced to a physical media through the network access layer.

- The **network access layer** corresponds to the data link and the physical layers in the OSI model. This layer consists of the software that structures the raw network data and converts it into the physical media, such as cable voltages.

How the Models Work

Both the OSI and the DOD models abstractly describe communication over a computer network. The bottom layers are closer to the hardware, such as network cabling, while the top layers are closer to the network operating system. Each layer is independent of the others in the sense that communication takes place only between adjacent layers. It allows network software and hardware from different vendors to work more easily together as long as standard rules for interfacing with adjacent layers are followed.

To illustrate how the models work, consider an Internet server hosting a Web site. Client computers connect to the server over the Internet and request Web pages. (The user enters a Web address in a browser and presses the Enter key.) Because the Internet is a network, the process by which the requested Web page is delivered to the client can be described in terms of a networking model (see Figure 1.3).

FIGURE **1.3** *Sending Data Through a Web Server*

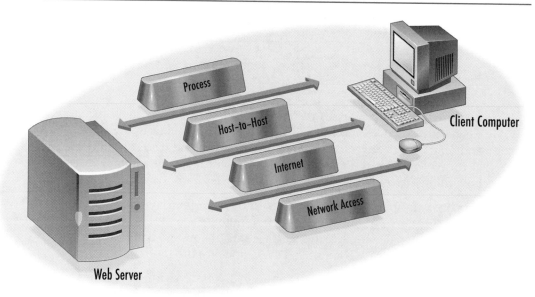

- **Process Layer**   The Web client uses the Hypertext Transfer Protocol (HTTP) to send a message to the server requesting a Web page. The server, which also uses HTTP, receives the address of the client computer along with the page request. The server formats the Web page information and sends it to the client. However, although HTTP can be used to format Web page data, it cannot, by itself, send the data across a network. This is done by software at a lower layer.

- **Host-to-Host Layer**   The software in this layer consists of the Transmission Control Protocol (TCP). This protocol software takes the Web page information created by HTTP and converts it to message packets. These packets are sent to the client computer that requested the Web page. TCP has the ability to verify that all of its packets are received by the client and will resend missing packets. However, like HTTP, the TCP protocol cannot by itself move packets across the network. This task is done by software at the next lower level.

- **Internet Layer**   At this layer, the Internet Protocol (IP) moves packets created by TCP across the network. IP has a simple function: sending packets. It cannot ensure delivery or resend missing packets. In order to perform these tasks, IP passes information back to the TCP layer and receives instructions from TCP about delivery and resending packets. Although IP is responsible for sending packets over the network, it does not directly communicate with the network hardware. The only information that moves across network cable is in bits (0s or 1s). IP needs the assistance of software at a lower layer to convert the packets into bits and then into electrical signals.

- **Network Access Layer**   At the bottom layer in the DOD model, software converts high-layer messages into bits (0s or 1s) and then into electrical signals. The software at this layer is usually burned into chips that are installed in hardware devices such a network cards. An example of software and hardware at this layer is Ethernet.

The DOD model is sometimes preferred over the OSI model because it more closely describes a network that uses the TCP/IP protocol.

Data Communications Protocols

Most protocols work only within a single layer of the networking model. The Ethernet protocol is found at the physical or networking layer. Other protocols, such as TCP/IP, are found at higher layers. Table 1.1 lists just a few of the common protocols and the networking layers with which they are normally identified.

T A B L E 1.1 *Protocols for the Various Networking Layers*

Networking Layer	Protocol
Process	TELNET FTP SMTP HTTP SMB
Host-to-Host	TCP OSPF SPX
Internet	IP ICMP IPX ARP NETBT
Network Access	Ethernet NDIS ATM FDDI ISDN Token Ring SDLC

A network administrator must deal with protocols and understand where they fit in the networking model. For example, when installing Windows 2000 the administrator must choose which protocols will be used to communicate with the rest of the network. If the wrong protocol is selected, the server cannot participate in the network.

Network Hardware

Networks include both software and hardware. The software consists of the network operating systems running on the servers and the various software protocols used to move data across the network. Network hardware consists of the computers attached to the network, the cabling, the **network interface cards** (**NICs**), and other more specialized items. Network administrators often find themselves installing and troubleshooting network hardware as often as software. It is helpful to understand how such hardware functions.

Network Cables Network cables are the physical media over which network messages travel. The most common type of network cables are **unshielded twisted-pair** (**UTP**). These contain copper metal strands and resemble common telephone wire, but are capable of transmitting the electrical signals used for network data.

UTP cable comes in different categories (see Figure 1.4). Each category identifies the maximum amount of data and the distance the data can be carried. Table 1.2 lists UTP categories along with their data capacity and distance rates.

TABLE 1.2 *UTP Rates and Distances*

UTP Category	Maximum Data Transfer Rate (in millions of bits per second, or Mbps)	Maximum Distance (in meters)
1	1	90
2	4	90
3	10	100
4*	16	100
5	100	200

* Shielded twisted-pair

FIGURE **1.4** *UTP Cable*

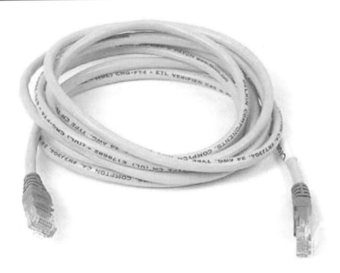

Another commonly used network connection is **fiber optic cable** (**fiber**). Such cable is thinner than UTP and consists of glass or plastic strands through which optical, rather than electrical, signals pass. Fiber is capable of transmitting more data than UTP and at much greater distances. However, fiber is most often used as a network backbone rather than to connect desktop computers. One of the reasons fiber is only used for the network backbone is that it is more difficult to deploy than UTP and is more expensive.

Strictly speaking, a network does not require physical cables and might include connections by way of radio, infrared, or microwave. Although most networks still rely on physical cable, wireless networks are becoming more feasible. The speed and reliability of wireless connections has greatly increased and within the next three to five years a majority of networks may be wireless. The IEEE has established the wireless protocol 802.11b. Many devices now implement this protocol, which makes affordable 11-megabit wireless home networks possible.

Network Interface Cards   The **network interface card** (**NIC**) is the device that physically connects a computer to a network (see Figure 1.5). The NIC contains a unique **media access control** (**MAC**) number, which is used to identify the NIC and the associated computer. Most NICs are installed inside a computer, but others come on PCMCIA cards or USB devices and can be used with portable computer systems.

Different types of NICs are capable of sending and receiving data at different speeds. A network that uses Category 5 UTP, which supports data rates of 100 megabits per second, should use a NIC on the server that can send and receive information at this speed. The server NIC should also use a PCI connection on the motherboard to maximize data throughput.

FIGURE 1.5 *Network Interface Card*

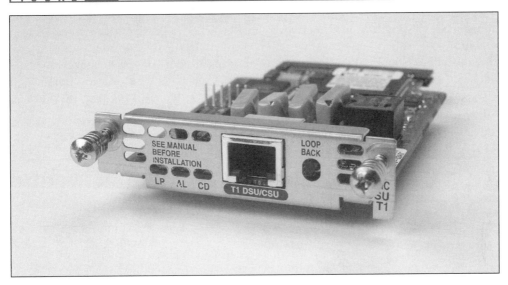

Hubs Depending on the network configuration, various hardware components will be used to connect clients and servers. A **hub** is a device that interconnects a group of client PCs by providing a central conduit for the network connections. Hubs are boxes that contain a set of plugs for network cables. Once a group of PCs are connected to a hub, network messages can pass between any connected PCs. Network messages are passed between the connections without restriction. Hubs may amplify signals, but they don't examine the message (see Figure 1.6).

FIGURE 1.6 *HUB*

Switches   From the outside, a switch may look much like a hub, but it is much more capable. **Switches**, like hubs, interconnect a group of computers, but a switch does more than just pass messages. Switches examine messages and decide the appropriate destination. Each network cable attached to a switch is connected to a switch port. When a message arrives at the switch, the destination address of the message is examined and sent to the appropriate port. If the message contains damaged packets, the switch will discard the packets. If the destination port is busy, a switch may save the message in a memory buffer until the port becomes available (see Figure 1.7).

FIGURE **1.7** *Switch*

Bridges and Gateways   Most large networks are segmented into smaller subnetworks. These segments may be located on different floors of a building or in different buildings. One type of hardware device used to connect network segments is called a **bridge**. Bridges stand between network segments and forward messages. When a message arrives at a bridge, the destination address is examined and, if the address is within the destination segment, the bridge forwards the message. If the address is within the network segment from where the message originated, the message is discarded. Bridges will only interconnect network segments that use the same network protocol.

A **gateway** works much like a bridge by standing between network segments and forwarding network messages (see Figure 1.8). The difference is that gateways are used to connect networks that do not use the same protocol. A gateway must not only forward messages but also translate messages from one protocol to another protocol. Sometimes a gateway is nothing more than a stand-alone computer with two NICs, each connected to different network segments, which runs protocol translation software.

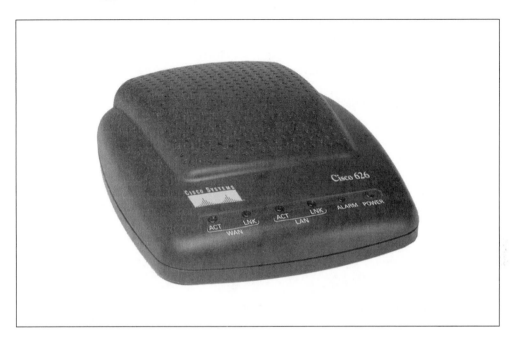

Routers **Routers**, like bridges and gateways, move network messages from place to place (see Figure 1.9). The difference is that routers do not just forward messages but select the best path for the messages. Routers contain an internal map of the surrounding network environment and use this map to send messages. When a router receives a message, it inspects the destination address and chooses the best path for the message. If one path becomes inoperable, the router will, if possible, choose another. Routers play an important role in TCP/IP networks and will be discussed in more detail in a later chapter.

F I G U R E **1.9** *Network Router*

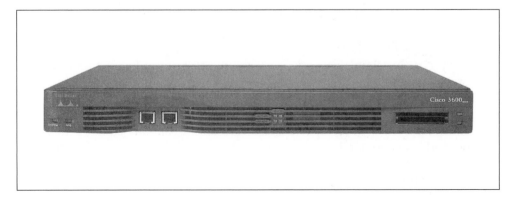

Network Design

A complete discussion of network design is beyond the scope of this chapter. However, network administrators must understand the different types of network designs and how such designs affect the network operating system. The design of a network consists of the physical layout of the clients, servers, and network hardware. A typical and simple network design is illustrated in Figure 1.10.

FIGURE **1.10** *Simple Hub-Based Network*

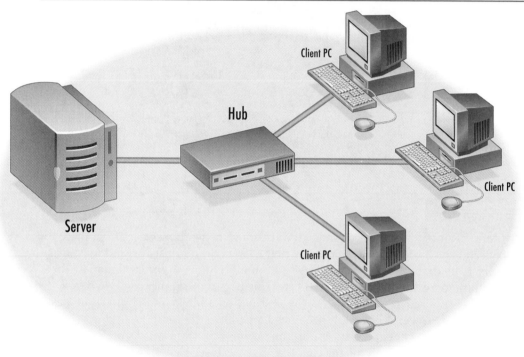

In this design, several client computers and a single server share access through a hub. The server may be connected to an outside network or to the Internet. The network message traffic is local and all client computers share access to the outside network through the server.

For simple networks, such a design usually proves adequate. Problems arise when the server in such a simple network is called upon to perform too many tasks, such as hosting a database program or being used as an applications server.

Figure 1.11 illustrates a more complex network design. In this design, a router is used to connect a network to an outside network or to the Internet. This design does not force a network server to act as a conduit for communication with the outside world. The router, which is designed for such tasks, is more efficient than most servers. This network also has additional specialty servers used to host database applications and to provide print services.

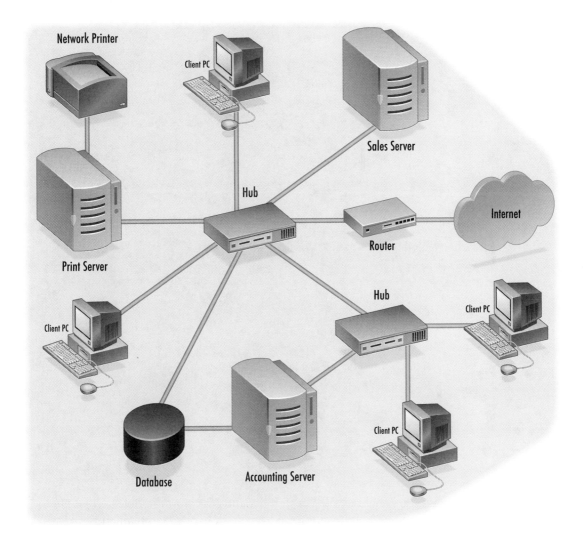

The network illustrated in Figure 1.12 is often found in large corporations. When network message traffic becomes too heavy, networks are broken into segments. Each segment has a router or switch that provides access to the rest of the network. Message packets destined for computers within the same segment are blocked by the router or switch from reaching other parts of the network, thus reducing overall network traffic.

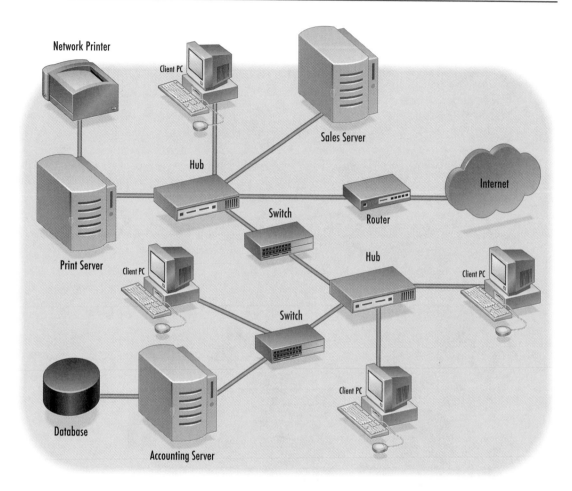

Choosing an optimal network design depends on a number of factors. How many client computers will be connected to the network? How much network traffic will be going across the network? What types of applications and services will the network servers be hosting? Many of these questions must be answered before deciding on a network design.

Windows 2000 Architecture

Most network administrators need to understand the basic parts of the Windows 2000 operating system in order to troubleshoot various problems. In a later chapter you will learn more about the internals of Windows 2000 in order to monitor the performance of a network server. This section presents a basic overview of the different parts of the Windows 2000 operating system.

The developers who created Windows 2000 had several design goals. The main ones were to create a multiprocessing operating system that had the power to support a large number of network users and was robust enough to not require constant care. The way these goals were accomplished in Windows 2000 was to divide the operating system into subsystems. These subsystems are illustrated in Figure 1.13 and include the following:

- Executive services
- OS kernel
- Hardware abstraction layer (HAL)

FIGURE 1.13 *General Subsystem Structure*

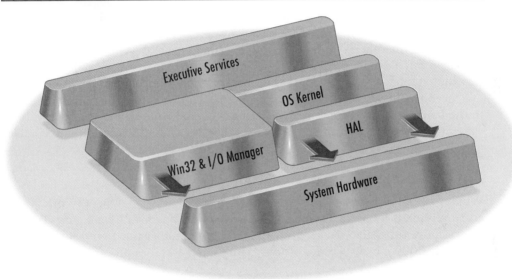

Figure 1.13 illustrates the relationship between these subsystems. The **executive services** subsystem performs tasks such as memory management and security processing. The **OS kernel** includes the software drivers for the hardware, such as disk drives and video. Most of the processes in the executive services subsystem use the kernel subsystem to accomplish tasks.

Below the executive and kernel is the **hardware abstraction layer** (**HAL**). The HAL consists of a set of "virtual" hardware objects. These HAL objects represent the actual hardware devices connected to the computer running Windows 2000. Rather than have the executive and kernel processes directly access hardware components, Windows 2000 forces these subsystems to use the HAL hardware objects. Device driver code found in the HAL translates the commands from the executive and kernel into direct hardware commands. Any problem that develops with the hardware request submitted to the HAL by the executive or kernel is caught at the HAL level.

Using a hardware abstraction layer has two benefits and one drawback. The benefits are cross-platform compatibility and stability. Theoretically, to create a version of Windows 2000 that works on different hardware platforms involves only changing the HAL, because the only hardware interface is through this subsystem. In fact, things are not this easy. Some processes in the executive directly communicate with the hardware and completely bypass the HAL.

The second benefit derived from HAL is stability. A common problem with Windows 95/98 is that some application programs directly access the hardware. When a Windows 95/98 program sends bad instructions to a hardware component, it can crash the entire operating system. This situation is unacceptable for a network server. With the HAL, software applications never directly access the hardware and must always work with a virtual hardware device.

The drawback to using the HAL is that software processes can run slower. If every request for a hardware resource must be first passed through the HAL, performance can suffer.

Some of the other Windows 2000 subsystems, such as Win32 and the I/O Manager, can also talk directly to the hardware. They are allowed to do this so that they can have high-speed access to the hardware. For example, the I/O manager may need to directly access the storage system in order to move data from memory to the hard disk. The Win32 system includes components that must directly communicate with the video hardware and the printer in order to provide acceptable performance.

Rings

Windows 2000 was designed to be a stable operating system. One way this is accomplished is by protecting the hardware behind the HAL. Keeping processes in the executive subsystem separate from each other is another way to provide stability. Windows 2000 creates a series of four "**rings**" and confines processes to specific rings (see Figure 1.14).

FIGURE 1.14 *Rings*

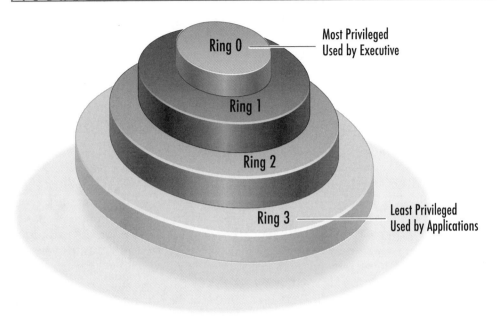

Windows 2000 only uses ring 0 and ring 3 (to maintain compatibility with non-Intel microprocessors). Only executive processes are run within ring 0, while regular application processes are run within ring 3. When a regular application process needs a service from the operating system, it must communicate with an executive process running in ring 0. Only processes in ring 0 can communicate with the hardware. This design prevents an application from bringing down the entire operating system.

Multitasking

Windows 2000 is a **multitasking** operating system. This means that even though only a single *central processing unit* (*CPU*) may be in use, multiple processes can be executed at the same time. Because a CPU can only execute one instruction at a time, the operating system must manage a queue of instructions and data and pass them to the CPU in the correct order.

The two main types of multitasking are cooperative and preemptive. Cooperative multitasking allows each process an equal share of the CPU time. Preemptive multitasking allows an executive service to interrupt a process in order to allow other processes a chance to execute. Preemptive multitasking is more efficient than cooperative multitasking and more secure. A process could go out of control and hang the system unless it is under the control of an external process like the executive. Think of a roundtable discussion where each person has a turn to speak. One person might monopolize the conversation. In a preemptive-type of meeting, a moderator could cut short a long-winded monologue.

Memory

Because Windows 2000 is currently a 32-bit operating system, it can directly access 2^{32} bytes of memory, which is about 4 gigabytes (GB). The operating system divides this memory into 2-GB sections. Operating system processes use the upper 2-GB section, and application processes use the lower 2-GB section. The Windows 2000 operating system will not use more than 2 GB of memory.

Most servers do not have 4 GB of physical memory, so Windows 2000 includes a **virtual memory manager** (**VMM**). The VMM fools applications, and even the operating system itself, into believing they have more memory than is physically available. This trick is accomplished by mapping memory addresses to a hard disk file. Such mapped memory is called **virtual memory**.

For example, if an application needs 50 megabytes of memory, but only 20 megabytes (MB) of physical memory are available, the VMM moves some of the contents of physical memory to a special file located on the server's hard disk. The application is then given the newly freed memory. When a second application needs more physical memory, the first application's information is moved to the hard disk. This scheme works because Windows 2000 switches between applications very quickly and, like a juggler, manages to keep all the memory addresses in the air at the same time. The special file used by the VMM to store the contents of physical memory is called a paging file. In Windows 2000 this file is named PAGEFILE.SYS.

Operating system processes, along with application processes, use virtual memory. The most important parts of the operating system are the kernel processes. Some of these kernel processes are so important that the VMM keeps them in nonpaged memory (memory that is not swapped to a disk), while other kernel processes are maintained in paged memory. The amount of nonpaged memory allocated to kernel processes is based on available physical memory, but it cannot exceed 128 MB, while the paged memory limit for kernel processes is 192 MB.

The Registry

The final piece of the Windows 2000 software subsystems, the registry, is one of the most important. The **registry** is a database maintained by the Windows 2000 operating system that contains a great deal of operating system-related information including—

- Types of hardware installed on the server
- Location of the software driver files
- Installed applications and their configurations
- Names and types of hardware ports
- Names and identifications of all software components

When Windows 2000 boots, it opens the registry and uses the information found there to install hardware drivers, start processes, and connect users.

In a later chapter you will explore the registry in greater depth and learn how to safely edit registry entries. Sometimes the network administrator must change registry entries but should take great care when doing so. If the registry is damaged, Windows 2000 will not boot and may have to be completely reinstalled.

Sometimes a server will appear to run out of memory when the kernel memory, either paged or nonpaged, is used up. This can happen if the registry, which is maintained in memory, grows too large. It was a problem in Windows NT 4, but Windows 2000 has moved elements normally saved in the registry to another location.

Server Hardware

One of the most important jobs of a network administrator is managing the hardware components attached to the server. This hardware likely includes a hard disk drive, network interface card, monitor, keyboard, and mouse. It might also include a printer or scanner. Understanding how Windows 2000 supports hardware is useful when trying to fix hardware-related problems.

In general, it is not a good idea to attach too many hardware devices to the server. The job of the server is to make resources available to users on the network, not to be used to play computer games or print posters.

As has been illustrated, hardware is protected by the HAL. Processes that wish to use a hardware device must instead use the virtual hardware object presented by the HAL. At a lower level, hardware devices require a way to communicate with the CPU. This type of communication uses Interrupts. An **Interrupt** is a special signal to the CPU. When the CPU receives an Interrupt signal, it stops what it is doing and performs a predefined action, analogous to a worker sorting mail. Whenever the worker sees a red flag, he or she stops sorting mail and retrieves a new bag of unsorted mail. The red flag is the Interrupt signal and the predefined action is to get another bag of mail. In the same way, a print device might send an Interrupt to the CPU indicating that the paper bin is empty. The CPU stops its current tasks and performs a predefined set of routines, perhaps sending an on-screen message to the operator. Each Interrupt is identified by a unique number that prevents, for example, the print device Interrupt from being mistaken for an Interrupt from a different hardware component.

The two kinds of Interrupts recognized by the CPU are software Interrupts and hardware Interrupts. Software Interrupts are sent by processes that require the attention of the CPU. Hardware Interrupts are sent by a hardware device connected to the computer. Each Interrupt, both software and hardware, comes with a defined Interrupt service routine. This routine consists of the instructions the CPU must follow when it recognizes a particular Interrupt.

The CPU can handle only a limited number of Interrupts. If two hardware devices that use the same Interrupt are connected to the computer, one or both may not work correctly. In the mailroom example, if a red flag is used to tell the mail sorter to get a new bag of mail and also is used to signal lunchtime, the mail sorter will not know what to do when presented with a red flag.

To solve the problem of limited and misconfigured Interrupts, computer makers and hardware component manufacturers agreed upon a standard interface between hardware devices and computers: the Plug and Play standard. A complete discussion of Plug and Play is beyond the scope of this chapter, but you will learn to install and troubleshoot Plug and Play devices in a later chapter.

Briefly, a Plug and Play device is capable of using different Interrupts and can be told what Interrupt to use by the computer. When such a device is installed in a computer, a set of BIOS routines burned into the system's motherboard negotiates with each attached Plug and Play hardware device and assigns each its own Interrupt number. When a new Plug and Play hardware device is later attached, the system BIOS will find an unused Interrupt number and tell the device that it must use this number.

Hardware Requirements for Windows 2000 Server

One of the many critical decisions often made by a network administrator is the selection of the server hardware. Selecting a home computer is likely done based on price and features, but selecting a computer system that will be used to run a company becomes a much more complex decision. The first step when selecting a Windows 2000 server is to check the **Hardware Compatibility List** (**HCL**). This list, maintained by Microsoft, consists of hardware components certified to work with Windows 2000. The list is posted on the Microsoft Web site at www.microsoft.com/hcl and updated as new hardware becomes certified. When selecting a server, make sure the server and server components, such as network cards and hard drives, can be found on the HCL.

In addition to being listed on the HCL, server components must also use Microsoft-designated software drivers, and these drivers must be used under the configuration tested by Microsoft. Windows 2000 will work with a wide variety of hardware and software configurations, but Microsoft will not provide technical support on systems that do not appear on the HCL and do not use authorized drivers. Perhaps the easiest way to make sure that a server can successfully run Windows 2000 and meet the Microsoft requirements is to locate the server on the Microsoft HCL.

Microsoft awards a Windows 2000 logo to computers that are certified to run Windows 2000. However, the logo is sometimes awarded before the HCL Web site is updated. Even if the server you want to use is not listed in the HCL, the vendor may already have a Microsoft logo.

The following server components are critical to Windows 2000:

- The CPU type and speed
- The system BIOS and the Plug and Play BIOS
- The system memory type, speed, and amount
- The mass storage components such as disk and tape drives
- The video components
- Networking components such as the network interface card

CPU   The central processing unit (CPU) is the first element to consider when selecting a Windows 2000 server. The important CPU features are—

- The CPU type
- The CPU speed
- The amount of installed L2 cache memory

Until recently, the only company making Windows-compatible CPU chips was Intel. However CPU chips from other manufacturers have become available. The best of the compatible chip makers is Advanced Micro Devices (AMD).

Missing from the list of Windows 2000-supported CPU chips is DEC/Compaq. The DEC Alpha chip, which was supported by Windows NT 4, is not supported by Windows 2000.

The minimum configuration required to run Windows 2000 is a Pentium-class CPU running at 133 megahertz (MHz). This configuration is the minimum; in the real world a faster CPU would be required. The recommended configuration is for a Pentium III running at 500 MHz.

An important element in the selection of a CPU is the onboard cache memory. CPU chips have two types of on-chip memory, L1 and L2. The L1 memory is on the CPU and L2 memory is directly accessible from the CPU. Windows 2000 makes heavy use of the L2 cache memory, and if a CPU has inadequate amounts of L2 memory, performance will lag. Windows 2000 needs a minimum of 128 KB of L2 cache. A good rule of thumb is that L2 cache memory should be 1/1000 the amount of main memory. For example, if main memory is 256 MB, L2 cache should be 256 KB.

When choosing hardware the rules are not consistent. The L2 cache runs at half-speed on most Intel CPUs, but at full speed on the high-end Pentium IIIs. This factor should be considered when choosing a CPU.

Many servers now come configured with multiple CPUs. Windows 2000 was designed to support multiple CPUs, but not an infinite number. Windows 2000 Professional can support two CPUs, Windows 2000 Server can support four CPUs, Advanced Server supports eight CPUs, and Windows 2000 DataCenter Server supports 16 CPUs. (With OEM configurations, Windows 2000 DataCenter can support up to 32 CPUs.) A custom HAL is required in order to use Windows 2000 on a server with multiple CPUs. This custom HAL should be supplied by the computer system manufacturer and created specifically for the computer.

To summarize the factors in selecting a CPU—

1. Select a CPU that has sufficient speed. A Pentium III with a minimum 500 MHz is suggested.
2. Select a CPU with sufficient L2 cache. The L2 cache should be at least 128 KB and should be 1/1000 of the amount of main memory. L2 cache with 256 KB is suggested.
3. For servers with multiple CPUs, make sure the HAL is supplied by the computer vendor.

System BIOS   The **basic input/output system** (**BIOS**) consists of the read-only software burned into chips on the motherboard of a computer. This software is used to perform low-level system functions. Windows 2000, unlike previous versions of Windows NT, is much less forgiving of a computer's BIOS. One of the reasons for this is that Windows 2000 supports the **advanced configuration and power interface** (**ACPI**) hardware standard. The ACPI standard is an extension to the BIOS that allows the operating system more control over the hardware.

One of the most common problems Windows 2000 encounters with the BIOS is inadequate Plug and Play support. Windows 2000 uses Plug and Play to locate and configure hardware. This feature only works when the BIOS and the hardware peripherals support the same type of Plug and Play software. Before installing Windows 2000, check the system BIOS and make sure Plug and Play is enabled.

If you have problems during setup, disable ACPI from the system BIOS and make sure Plug and Play is enabled.

System Memory   Network operating systems require the server to have enough memory to run the operating system itself and to run the applications hosted by the server. The absolute minimum amount of memory necessary just to start Windows 2000 Server is 64 MB. Microsoft recommends a minimum of 128 MB. A more realistic minimum is 256 MB, which will handle the operating system and some simple server applications. If the system will be running programs such as Microsoft SQL Server or the Oracle database program, the amount of memory should be doubled to 512 MB.

Because Windows 2000 makes use of a memory address that may not be used by Windows 95/98, bad memory components are more likely to be discovered when running Windows 2000. A computer that worked with Windows 95/98 may not work with Windows 2000. Many failed installations of Windows 2000 are the result of bad memory components.

Video Components   Selecting a video card may seem like a trivial decision, but Windows 2000 can make it a major problem. Windows 2000 does not hide the video processing subsystem behind the HAL very well. Applications, such as the video drivers, can get direct access to the hardware. A bad video driver that is not compatible with Windows 2000 can bring down the entire operating system. Make sure the video card and drivers are on the HCL.

Mass Storage Devices   A server will live or die based on its hard disk system. A server can have the fastest CPU on the market and be liberally stocked with memory, but it will still run slowly if it has a substandard hard disk. The three main features to consider when selecting a hard disk system for a network server is the size of the hard disk drive, the type of hard disk drive, and the data transfer rate.

The capacity of hard disks has been growing at an almost exponential rate. Most new computers are sold with 50-GB hard drives as standard equipment. (For some perspective, 15 years ago a 10-MB hard disk drive was state-of-the-art technology and cost more than a thousand dollars.) The size of the hard drive should be based on the role of the server. A print server will not require a hard drive as large as a database or file server.

The second feature to consider when selecting a hard drive is the drive type. Typical hard disk drives are **integrated drive electronics (IDE)**, also known as intelligent drive electronics, and **small computer system interfaces (SCSI)**. IDE drives are most commonly found on lower-end servers because the drive is less expensive. SCSI drives are found on higher-end servers because their performance is better than IDE drives. The problem with SCSI hard disk drives is that special drivers are sometimes required and those drivers may not be compatible with Windows 2000.

When choosing a hard disk drive, two features will affect the performance of Windows 2000: disk speed in revolutions per minute (rpm) and data transfer rate. The disk speed is measured by how fast the hard disk platters rotate, which affects how fast information is read or written to the hard disk. The data transfer rate is the amount of data per millisecond that can be moved from the hard disk to the computer's main bus. Depending on the purpose of the server, it is better to select a SCSI hard disk drive. SCSI drives generally have faster disk seek times and data transfer rates than IDE drives. However, if the server will not need high-speed disk access, then a regular IDE drive will be sufficient.

Networking Components   The primary server networking component is the network interface card (NIC). Because Windows 2000 uses Plug and Play to configure components, the server NIC selected should be listed on the Microsoft HCL and should be Plug and Play. The NIC should be a bus-mastering PCI card because this allows the computer to move data to the network at increased speeds.

Server Hardware Recommendation Summary

Table 1.3 includes the Microsoft minimum hardware configuration necessary to run Windows 2000 Server and the suggested configuration.

TABLE 1.3 *Minimum and Suggested Hardware Configuration*

Microsoft Minimum Configuration	Suggested Configuration
133 MHz Pentium	300 MHz Pentium III with 128 L2 Cache
128 MB of memory	256 MB of memory
Hard disk space: 850 MB plus 2 MB for each MB of memory (With 128 MB of memory the hard disk should be 1.1 GB.)	4 GB hard disk drive. (Disk should be ultra IDE or ultra wide SCSI.)
Bootable CD	Bootable CD
NIC card	PCI-based bus-mastering NIC card
Standard video	Standard video with 800 x 600 resolution
Keyboard and mouse	Keyboard and mouse

Microsoft Certification Program

As computer technology rapidly changes, companies face a common problem when hiring new employees—how to determine if the employees have the skills necessary to perform the job. Most big companies use standardized screening tests, along with technical interviews, to evaluate the applicant's ability. To help meet this requirement to screen applicants, Microsoft has created a networking certification program. This program consists of a set of Microsoft-created exams designed to test for the knowledge and skills necessary to administer a Windows 2000 network. When someone passes the required set of exams, Microsoft awards them a certificate.

Microsoft Certified Systems Engineer (MCSE) is the most commonly sought certificate. In order to get an MCSE you must complete five core exams and two elective exams. Table 1.4 outlines the required exams and the exam numbers.

TABLE 1.4	**Requirements for Microsoft Certified System Engineer Certification**		
Exam Name	**Exam Number**	**Required for MCSE**
Installing, Configuring, and Administering Windows 2000 Professional	70-210	Yes
Installing, Configuring, and Administering Windows 2000 Server	70-215	Yes
Implementing and Administering a Microsoft Windows 2000 Network Infrastructure	70-216	Yes
Implementing and Administering a Microsoft Windows 2000 Directory Services Infrastructure	70-217	Yes
*One of the following core exams must be completed.		
Designing a Windows 2000 Directory Services Infrastructure	70-219	Yes*
Designing Security for a Microsoft 2000 Network	70-220	Yes*
Designing a Microsoft Windows 2000 Network Infrastructure	70-221	Yes*
Designing Highly Available Web Solutions with Microsoft 2000 Server Technology	70-226	Yes*
Two of the following elective exams must be completed.		
Implementing and Supporting Microsoft SNA Server 4.0	70-085	Elective
Implementing and Supporting Microsoft Systems Management Server 2.0	70-086	Elective
Designing and Implementing Data Warehouses with Microsoft SQL Server 7.0	70-019	Elective
Designing and Implementing Databases with Microsoft SQL Server 7.0	70-029	Elective
Designing and Implementing Databases with Microsoft SQL Server 2000 Enterprise Edition	70-229	Elective
Administering Microsoft SQL Server 7.0	70-028	Elective

(cont'd)

Exam Name	Exam Number	Required for MCSE
Installing, Configuring, and Administering Microsoft SQL Server 2000 Enterprise Edition	70-228	Elective
Implementing and Supporting Web Sites Using Microsoft Site Server 3.0	70-056	Elective
Installing, Configuring, and Administering Microsoft Exchange 2000 Server	70-224	Elective
Implementing and Supporting Microsoft Proxy Server 2.0	70-088	Elective
Installing, Configuring, and Administering Microsoft Internet Security and Acceleration (ISA) Server 2000	70-227	Elective
Implementing and Supporting Microsoft Internet Explorer 5.0 by Using the Microsoft Internet Explorer Administration Kit	70-080	Elective
Migrating from Microsoft Windows NT 4.0 to Microsoft Windows 2000	70-222	Elective
Installing, Configuring, and Administering Microsoft Clustering Services by Using Microsoft Windows 2000 Advanced Server	70-223	Elective
Designing and Deploying a Messaging Infrastructure with Microsoft Exchange 2000 Server	70-225	Elective

Microsoft has designed the Windows 2000 MCSE certification program for working professionals who are already managing a network. Microsoft recommends that before taking the exams the candidate have at least one year of experience implementing and administering a network with the following characteristics:

- 200 to 26,000 supported users
- Up to 150 physical locations
- Network services that include file, print, database, messaging, firewall, dial-in server, desktop management, and Web hosting

In addition, Microsoft recommends that the test candidate have one year's experience doing the following:

- Interconnecting different network operating systems
- Designing a network infrastructure
- Working with a desktop operating system

CHAPTER summary

➤ Windows 2000 is a network operating system designed for both small and large-scale networks. It was developed to make it easier for network administrators to administer large and complex networks. Windows 2000 was also designed to be stable and robust.

➤ Computer networks are made up of software communication components, hardware networking components, and network servers. Software communication components are called protocols. They are used to facilitate communication across a network by dividing up the work into layers. Each layer performs a specific function and only communicates with layers above or below itself.

➤ Network hardware consists of the physical cable connections (or wireless connections) and various specialized computers used to connect network segments. Network design involves planning the placement of the servers and the various hardware connection components.

➤ The Windows 2000 internal architecture was developed to provide a stable operating system. The internal software was divided into subsystems, each of which plays a defined role. Direct access to the hardware by application programs is impossible. Application programs access hardware through a software subsystem.

CHAPTER terms

ACPI	Advanced configuration and power interface: A standard hardware BIOS used to control different aspects of a computer.
Application layer	The OSI layer that consists of application programs.
BIOS	Basic input/output system: ROM-based software used to control basic hardware operations.
Bridge	A network component that connects two or more similar network segments together.
Client/server	A relationship between computers on a network. The client sends requests to a server and a server responds to requests from clients.
Data link layer	The OSI layer that collects bits of data into a structure.
DNS	Domain name system: A standard name resolution software system used in Windows 2000.

DOD model	The network model developed by the Department of Defense that divides network communication software into four levels with each level performing clearly defined tasks and only communicating with levels above and below itself.
Executive service	A software subsystem in Windows 2000 that performs system level tasks.
Fiber optic cable	A type of network cabling that transmits data through glass or plastic strands.
Gateway	A network component that connects two or more network segments that do not use the same protocol.
HAL	Hardware abstraction layer: A software subsystem in Windows 2000 that interfaces with the system hardware devices.
HCL	Hardware Compatibility List: A list of Windows 2000-compatible hardware components and systems maintained by Microsoft.
Host-to-host layer	The DOD layer that locates computers on the network.
Hub	A network component used to interconnect a group of PCs and a server without restrictions.
IDE	Integrated drive electronics: A type of hard drive used in personal computers.
Internet layer	The DOD layer that negotiates the data flow between computers on a network.
Interrupt	A technique whereby the CPU is caused to stop processing and respond to an event in the system.
ISO	International Organization for Standardization.
Kerberos	A standard security software system implemented in Windows 2000.
LDAP	Lightweight Directory Access Protocol: A standard directory access software system used in Windows 2000.
MAC address	Media access control: A unique number burned into an NIC that allows the computer using the NIC to be uniquely identified.
Multitasking	The ability of an operating system to perform more than one task at a time.
Network layer	The OSI layer that negotiates the data flow between computers on the network.
Network access layer	The DOD layer that formats and converts the data from binary to voltages.

NIC	Network interface card: A card that plugs into a computer and allows the computer to be connected to the network.
NOS	Network operating system: A multi-user, multitasking software application that manages network resources and users.
OS kernel	A software subsystem in Windows 2000 that contains hardware drivers.
OSI model	The network model developed by the ISO that divides network communication software into seven levels with each level performing clearly defined tasks and only communicating with levels above and below itself.
Physical layer	The OSI layer that converts data from 1s and 0s to voltages.
Plug and Play	A hardware standard used to automatically configure devices.
Presentation layer	The OSI layer that formats network data.
Process layer	The DOD layer that formats and sends data between computers on a network.
Protocol	An agreed upon method of communication between software components.
Registry	A Windows 2000 database that contains system configuration data.
Rings	A method of dividing Windows 2000 software systems so that only certain subsystems can interact with other systems.
Router	A network device that maintains a network map and that can decide the destination of network traffic.
SCSI drive	Small computer system interface: A type of hard drive used in personal and large computers.
Session layer	The OSI layer that maintains connections between computers.
Switch	An intelligent network component used to interconnect a group of PCs and a server that can be programmed to move data from place to place.
Transport layer	The OSI layer that locates computers on the network.
UTP	Unshielded twisted-pair: A type of network cable that looks like telephone wire.
Virtual memory	A technique whereby physical memory is mapped into a disk file, allowing applications to use more memory than is physically installed in the computer.
VMM	Virtual memory manager: The software subsystem that manages virtual memory.

CONCEPTS review

Multiple Choice

1. Windows 2000 was designed to improve Windows NT 4 by:
   a. Supporting very large networks.
   b. Reducing administrative costs.
   c. Providing easier hardware installation and configuration.
   d. All of the above.

2. The most important part of network resource management is:
   a. Making network components available on the network.
   b. Connecting different hardware components together.
   c. Installing new computers on the network.
   d. Installing software on the network.

3. In the client/server model:
   a. The client can send messages to multiple servers.
   b. The server responds to clients.
   c. The server instigates a response from a client.
   d. All of the above.

4. Network connection software is used to:
   a. Configure selected hardware devices.
   b. Allow network computers to communicate with each other.
   c. Install software applications on clients.
   d. Install software applications on servers.

5. A protocol is:
   a. An agreed-upon method of communication between computers.
   b. An applications installation language.
   c. A network hardware standard.
   d. A network cabling standard.

6. Which of the following layers is *not* in the OSI network model?
   a. Application
   b. Data link
   c. Internet
   d. Session

7. The Internet layer in the DOD network model corresponds to what layer in the OSI model?
   a. Network
   b. Application
   c. Data link
   d. None of the above

8. A message sent using HTTP is identified with what layer of the OSI model?
   a. Network
   b. Data link
   c. Application
   d. Transport

9. The term *UTP* means:
   a. Universal transport protocol.
   b. Unshielded twisted-pairs.
   c. Unshielded transport Pairs.
   d. None of the above.

10. The purpose of the MAC number is to:
   a. Register a NIC with a computer.
   b. Allow the NIC BIOS to boot.
   c. Allow the NIC BIOS to connect with the server's BIOS.
   d. Uniquely identify the NIC.

Short Answer

1. List the minimum hardware requirement necessary for a server to host Windows 2000.
2. List the layers found in the DOD network protocol model.
3. Give two benefits to using the hardware abstraction layer in Windows 2000.
4. List three problems commonly found with Windows NT 4 that are solved by Windows 2000.
5. List three hardware devices that might be found on a network and used to interconnect network segments.

LAB exercise

Using the Microsoft HCL on the Microsoft Web site, list the components of three systems that would meet the recommended hardware requirement listed in this chapter.

PROBLEM SOLVING exercise

Using the Microsoft HCL on the Microsoft Web site, write the hardware requirements for three servers that will perform the following operations:

Server 1: Used to store user accounts and login scripts for a 1,200-person network.

Server 2: Used to run an SQL Server database that will store approximately 50 GB of data and be used by 150 people on a daily basis.

Server 3: Used as a print server to send print jobs to five network printers.

INSTALLING WINDOWS 2000 2

Performance Objectives

After completing this chapter you will be able to:

- Plan an installation of Windows 2000
- Check the hardware and software required for an installation of Windows 2000
- Discuss the licensing requirements for installing Windows 2000
- Create an installation checklist
- Perform an attended install of Windows 2000
- Discuss an unattended install of Windows 2000
- Use the Sysprep utility
- Discuss installing Windows 2000 on multiple computers

Introduction

Correctly installing Windows 2000 Server is the first step in building a successful network. Unlike installing an application program such as Microsoft Office, installing Windows 2000 requires careful planning. Selecting the wrong option during the installation process can affect the entire network. In this chapter you learn how to plan for and perform a Windows 2000 installation. You will learn the different ways Windows 2000 can be installed on a single server and how it can be installed on multiple servers. You will also learn about Microsoft licensing policies and how to select the best licensing options for your network.

Planning to Install Windows 2000

Before installing Windows 2000, the network administrator needs to create an installation plan and an installation checklist. The installation plan should reflect the particular situation within a company and should include the following tasks:

- Verify that the target server has the hardware necessary to run Windows 2000
- Verify that the hardware and applications software to be run on the server are compatible with Windows 2000
- Verify that the server has the most current BIOS updates
- Verify that adequate client licenses have been purchased for the server
- Back up information on the server (if upgrading an existing server)

- Schedule downtime for the server and ensure the tasks performed by the server are covered by other servers (if upgrading an existing server)
- Develop or use an existing computer-naming policy
- Create a checklist that contains all the information necessary to successfully install Windows 2000

The last item in the installation plan is the creation of an installation checklist. This task is important because during the installation process of Windows 2000, the administrator will often need specific configuration information. This information, such as the computer name, should be listed on the installation checklist.

As with the installation plan, an installation checklist will vary depending on the situation. A basic checklist should include the following items:

- The location of the install files, the location of the install temp files, and the destination of the operating system
- The location of any hardware driver files that may be required during the installation
- The name that will be assigned to the computer
- The default administrator password
- The type and number of client licenses
- Network connection information
- A list of networking components to be installed
- The name of the domain or workgroup to be joined

You should compile this checklist prior to beginning the installation.

Hardware Requirements

Part of the installation plan includes verifying that the target server has the hardware necessary to run Windows 2000. Table 2.1 lists the minimum and suggested hardware required in order for a server to run Windows 2000.

TABLE 2.1 *Windows 2000 Hardware Requirements*

Microsoft Minimum Hardware Configuration	Suggested Hardware Configuration
133 MHz Pentium	300 MHz Pentium III with 128 L2 Cache
128 MG of memory	256 MG of memory
Hard disk space: 850 MB plus 2 MB for each MB of memory (with 128 MB of memory the hard disk should be 1.1 GB.)	4 GB hard disk drive (Disk should be ultra IDE or ultra wide SCSI.)
Bootable CD	Bootable CD
NIC card	PCI-based bus-mastering NIC card
Standard video	Standard video with 800 x 600 resolution
Keyboard and mouse	Keyboard and mouse

Of course, the suggested hardware configuration will vary depending on how the server will be used and the application programs the server will be running. For example, if a Windows 2000 server will operate as a database server, the amount of hard disk space and memory will likely need to be increased. One of the safest ways to ensure that the hardware is appropriate for Windows 2000 is to purchase a server from a well-known manufacturer such as Compaq. Such companies verify that their hardware will work with Windows 2000.

Windows 2000 Hardware Compatibility

Another important part of the installation plan is verifying that the hardware and software to be run on the server are compatible with Windows 2000. The hardware includes the basic server components, such as the motherboard, BIOS, hard drive, and video, along with peripherals such as tape drives and external storage devices. The software includes the drivers necessary to operate the hardware and application programs that will be run on the server.

Hardware compatibility can be checked several ways—

- Check the Microsoft hardware compatibility list Web site (www.microsoft.com/hcl)
- Check with the hardware manufacturer
- Run the Windows 2000 install program WINNT32 with the /checkupgradeonly option

The Microsoft Web site hardware compatibility list contains a list of hardware and software verified by Microsoft to be compatible with Windows 2000. This site is not always completely up-to-date, and if the target server is not on the Microsoft site, you need to check with the manufacturer.

Another way to check the hardware (and software) on a system is to run the WINNT32 program with the /checkupgradeonly option. To use this option, open a command window, select the *I386* folder on the Windows 2000 Install CD, and key **WINNT32 /checkupgradeonly**.

This command will cause the Windows 2000 setup program to examine the computer's hardware and software and create a printable report of all incompatible components. If the server hardware or software is reported incompatible by the WINNT32 program, it does not mean that the manufacturer does not have a compatible version. Always check with the manufacturer of the hardware or software.

The two important components that can make a server incompatible with Windows 2000 are the **basic input/output system** (**BIOS**) and the hard disk storage system. The BIOS is a set of low-level software routines burned into a ROM or PROM chip located on the motherboard. If the BIOS is outdated, it may not work with Windows 2000. In addition, Windows 2000 supports the advanced configuration and power management interface (ACPI). If the BIOS on the target server does not include ACPI support, Windows 2000 may not install correctly.

Upgrading the BIOS is relatively simple in most cases. A BIOS upgrade program can be downloaded from the server vendor's Web site and run to upgrade the BIOS.

Make sure you know the current BIOS version before upgrading to a new version. The version can be checked by watching the screen when the server boots (during the memory check process). Pressing the Pause or Break key during the initial boot process will freeze the screen and allow you to record the BIOS version number.

Another common area of incompatibility is the server hard disk storage system. Most middle to high-end servers now come with multiple hard drives configured as a disk array. In order for Windows 2000 to properly work with a system that uses disk arrays, you may need to update the disk controller BIOS or replace the controller itself. Check with the manufacturer for Windows 2000 compatibility.

Windows 2000 Software Compatibility

Software compatibility is another area of concern for a network administrator installing Windows 2000. Most programs written to work with Windows 95/98 will also work in Windows 2000. However, some programs written for Windows NT may not work correctly in Windows 2000. Microsoft changed the device driver model in Windows 2000, making it more compatible with Windows 95/98. Older programs, written for Windows NT 4, used the Windows NT driver model and are likely incompatible with Windows 2000. If in doubt, check with the software company for an update of the application.

Some application programs will not work with Windows 2000 Server at all. For example, software used to create CD-ROMs typically will not work with Windows 2000 Server but only work with Windows 2000 Professional. Make sure that the application specifically indicates it will work with Windows 2000 Server.

Licensing Requirements

As with any other software application, Windows 2000 Server requires a license (about $1,000 for Windows Server and about $4,000 for Windows Advanced Server). However, because Windows 2000 is a network operating system the licensing requirements are more complex than they are for a stand-alone operating system. To use Windows 2000 Microsoft requires—

- a server license
- Client access licenses (CALs)

The server license comes with the purchased copy of Windows 2000. It allows you to install the software on a single server. In order for multiple users to connect to the server you must also purchase a set of **client access licenses** (**CALs**) (about $40 each, in quantity). In this case a "user" is defined as a logged-in user, a device (such as a printer), or an application running on a client computer that connects to the server.

CALs can be purchased either as per-seat or per-server. The per-seat option assigns a CAL to each user on the network. Once a CAL has been purchased for a user he or she can connect to any Windows 2000 server on the network. The per-server option assigns a set number of CALs to a single server. When the number of users connected to the server equals the number of per-server CALs, additional connections are blocked.

You will be prompted to select a type of CAL license during installation and so must understand the benefits and drawbacks to each type. Depending on how the network will be used, either a per-seat or per-server CAL licensing option will be more appropriate. As an example, consider Company A that has three Windows 2000 servers and 100 employees who use the network.

Per-Seat CAL Option The per-seat CAL licensing option requires a CAL to be purchased for each client or application that access a Windows 2000 server. In the case of Company A, 100 CALs would need to be purchased. Assuming a standard cost of $1,000 for each server license and $40 per CAL, the total cost would be:

3 servers at $1,000	$3,000
100 CALs at $40	$4,000
Total	$7,000

Additional CALs can be purchased as new employees are added to the company.

One problem with this option is keeping track of each CAL and purchasing new CALs. It sometimes costs more to generate the paperwork necessary to purchase a CAL than the CAL is worth. Additionally, someone must make sure that every employee using the network is covered by a CAL. This means tracking employees who leave and new employees who are hired. Such an activity is easier for small companies than for larger companies. The benefit to the per-seat option is that only the CALs necessary for the users need to be purchased.

Per-Server CAL Option The per-server CAL licensing option requires that a set of CALs that corresponds to the maximum number of users who can simultaneously connect to the server be assigned to each Windows 2000 server. In the case of Company A, a per-server licensing option might look like the following:

3 servers at $1,000	$ 3,000
100 CALs per server at $40	$12,000
Total	$15,000

The per-server CAL licensing option is more expensive, assuming that each server is licensed for a maximum number of connections. In reality, not everyone in the company will be logged onto each server at the same time. This licensing fee might be reduced by assuming that each server will, at most, have 20 simultaneous connections.

3 servers at $1,000	$3,000
20 CALs per server at $40	$2,400
Total	$5,400

The problem is that now only 20 connections *can* be made to each server at the same time.

A general rule of thumb when choosing a CAL licensing option is that a small company with a single or few Windows 2000 servers and static growth is better off with the per-server licensing option. A larger company with many servers will find the per-seat licensing option easier to implement. A block of CALs for new employees can be purchased, avoiding the overhead of buying single CALs. However, the licensing option chosen will depend on a number of factors, including the cost of tracking per-seat CALs. It is sometimes less expensive to pay for additional CALs on the server than hire personnel to track the per-seat CALs.

Computer-Naming Policy

During the Windows 2000 installation process, the server must be assigned a name. This name will be one of the ways the server is identified on the network. In small networks, with few servers, names can be informally chosen. However, in larger networks with multiple servers a naming policy should guide the choice of a server name. One tradition names servers after Shakespearean and various cartoon characters (Othello, Snoopy, Troll, and so on). These names may be cute, but are not really useful in conveying information to the administrator and user. Using the location of the server as part of the name is also not a good idea. A server named RM317-08, which is located in building 317 room 08, is good only as long as the server is not moved. The server name should describe the purpose of the server or the department or area associated with the server. For example, backupDB or SalesSrv might be appropriate names. The server name must be unique and cannot be longer than 15 characters. The name cannot have embedded spaces and should not include special symbols.

Administrator Password

Security is an area of concern on networks. During the installation process an administrator password must be selected. This password can be changed after Windows 2000 has been installed, but too often it is not. Large companies often have a password policy that guides the selection of passwords for network administrators and users. The reason such a policy is important is that the most vulnerable part of a network is its passwords, and without a policy many users choose passwords like "password" or "pass" or just repeat their login name.

Administrator passwords should be especially secure because a compromised administrator account can lead to major problems. Administrator passwords should follow a basic policy, such as one with the following characteristics:

- Be at least six characters long
- Contain both numeric and alphabetic characters
- Should not be a dictionary word or a variation on the login ID

Installation Checklist

Once the installation plan has been created and reviewed, the network administrator should next create an installation checklist. The checklist will contain all the information necessary to install Windows 2000. It will include the network addresses of the server and other systems on the network. It will also contain a list of items that should have been completed before starting the installation process.

Table 2.2 presents a typical installation checklist.

T A B L E 2.2 *Typical Installation Checklist*

Item	Value or Status
Server IP address	192.168.100.100
Server name	AccountBackup
Domain or workgroup name	AccountDomain.local
DNS Servers IP addresses	192.168.100.05
WINS Servers IP addresses	192.168.100.05
Gateway IP address	192.168.100.1
Administrator password	account65pass30
Computer BIOS checked	Yes/No
Hard drive BIOS checked	Yes/No
Disk mirroring disabled	Yes/No
UPS disconnected	Yes/No
Licensing option	Per-user/Per-server
Number of CALs purchased	XX
Server backup date	XX
Old NT 4 disks available	Yes/No

Windows 2000 servers will almost always have a static IP address. As you will learn, an IP address is a way to uniquely identify a computer on a network. Although most computers are automatically given an IP address from a pool of IP addresses when they connect to the network, servers should have a static IP address. In a training situation it is best to isolate the lab computers that will be running Windows 2000 from the rest of the campus network. This isolation is accomplished by assigning **nonroutable IP** addresses to the servers. Routers and switches will not pass network packets that contain these special nonroutable IP addresses.

Any of three sets of nonroutable IP addresses can be used in this situation. They are—

10.0.0.0	to	10.255.255.255
172.16.0.0	to	172.31.255.255
192.168.0.0	to	192.168.255.255

This book will use the 192.168 range of IP addresses.

Ways to Install Windows 2000

Once the installation plan and installation checklist have been created, it is time to install Windows 2000. Installing Windows 2000 on a server can be done several different ways—

- Install from a set of Windows 2000 boot disks

- Boot DOS and run the WINNT program from the *I386* folder on the Windows 2000 CD or a network share

- Boot Windows 98 and run the WINNT32 program from the *I386* folder on the Windows 2000 CD or a network share

- Run the Windows 2000 Setup Wizard through Windows 95/98

The method selected depends on several factors.

- If the server is new and has an unformatted hard disk or the hard disk will be reformatted during install, it is best to use boot disks or the Install CD (if the server has an Autostart CD drive).

- If the server hard drive has been formatted but is otherwise blank, the WINNT or WINNT32 programs in the *I386* folder on the Install CD should be run or the boot disks can be used.

- If the server's hard drive has been partitioned into two logical drives and Windows 2000 will be installed alongside Windows 95/98, then the Setup Wizard on the Install CD can be run. (A **partition** is an area on a hard disk that can be used to install an operating system.)

- If the server already contains a copy of Windows NT, any of the install methods can be used.

The most common method of installing Windows 2000 is by running the WINNT or WINNT32 program located in the *I386* folder. These programs can be run with a number of parameters that can be used to customize the installation process. An unattended installation requires the use of the WINNT or WINNT32 programs. If possible, you should always install Windows 2000 by running either WINNT or WINNT32.

WINNT and WINNT32

The WINNT and WINNT32 programs are used to install Windows 2000 on a target computer and are located in the *I386* folder on the Windows Install CD. The WINNT program must be used from a DOS prompt. The WINNT32 program is used if the computer has been booted in Windows 95/98 or Windows NT. These programs are run from a command window or from a DOS boot disk and the options are placed after the program name, as in—

```
WINNT32 /option
```

Table 2.3 and Table 2.4 list the options for both the WINNT and WINNT32 programs.

T A B L E 2.3 *WINNT Options*

WINNT.EXE Options	
/s [:sourcepath]	Specifies the location of the Windows 2000 files. You can use a disk drive letter or a network path. For example WINNT /s:x:\i386 or WINNT /s:\\DIST1\SETUP
/t [:drive letter]	Specifies the disk drive for the temp folders Windows 2000 creates during setup. For example WINNT /t:q:\. If a disk drive is not specified, Windows 2000 attempts to find space on the primary partition.
/u [:answer file]	Performs an unattended setup using an answer file. This option also requires the /t option.
/udf:id[, UDF file]	This option is used with an unattended install and modifies entries in the answer file. The identifier specifies an entry in a UDF file to be used in the install script.
/r [:folder]	Specifies a folder to be installed along with Windows 2000. This folder will remain after setup completes.
/rx [:folder]	Specifies a folder to be copied, which will be deleted after setup finishes.
/e	Specifies a command to be executed at the end of the GUI setup process.
/a	Enables accessibility options.

T A B L E 2.4 *WINNT32 Options*

WINNT32.EXE Options	
/s [:sourcepath]	Specifies the location of the Windows 2000 files. You can use a disk drive letter or a network path. For example WINNT32 /s:x:\i386 or WINNT32/s:\\DIST1\SETUP.
/tempdrive [:drive letter]	Specifies the disk drive for the temp folders Windows 2000 creates during setup. For example WINNT32 /tempdrive:q:\. If a disk drive is not specified, Windows 2000 attempts to find space on an existing drive.
/unattend [num] [:answer file]	Performs an installation in unattended mode using the specified answer file. The number of seconds after copying files and before restarting the computer is specified by num.

(cont'd)

WINNT32.EXE Options	
`/copydir:folder name`	Specifies a folder to be copied along with the Windows 2000 setup files. This folder will be placed in the default install folder for Windows 2000. For example, `WINNT32 /copydir:helpfiles` will place the folder *helpfiles* under the default installation folder.
`/cmd:command line info`	Instructs the setup program to run a command from the command line before the last phase of setup (after the computer has restarted twice).
`/debug [level] [:filename]`	Creates a debug file of the specified level and places debug information into the file. For example `WINNT32 /debug2:d:\errors2.log` would create a file named errors2.log on drive D. The debugging levels are: 0 – severe errors, 1 – errors, 2 – warnings, 3 – information, 4 – detailed information. Each level includes the levels below it.
`/udf:id[,UDF file]`	Indicates an entry in a uniqueness database file (UDF) that modifies an answer file used in an unattended install. It must be used with the /unattend option. For example, `WINNT32 /unattend5:setup12.txt /udf:ADM_usr,setupfile.udb` performs an unattended install using the answer file setup12.txt, but specifying the changes identified by the id `ADM_usr` found in setupfile.mdb.
`/syspart:drive letter`	This option specifies that setup copies setup files to the disk drive and stops. You can then install the disk drive into another computer and it will continue with the setup.
`/checkupgradeonly`	Used to check hardware and software compatibility of an existing operating system with Windows 2000. A report is generated indicating problems with installing Windows 2000 on the target computer.
`/cmdcons`	Adds a recovery console option to the setup process.
`/makelocalsource`	Copies all necessary installation files to the hard disk. It is used when you want to remove the CD and continue with the installation.
`/noreboot`	Prevents setup from rebooting the computer after the file copy phase of the setup procedure.

These options can be combined when running one of the programs. For example, to run the WINNT32 program and have it read the setup files from the location x:\w2k\i386, and also have it use disk drive J as the temp drive, you would key

```
WINNT32 /s:x:\w2k\i386 /tempdrive:j
```

When to Use WINNT and WINNT32   Which and how each of these programs is used will depend on the installation situation. For a small company with a single or few Windows 2000 servers, Windows 2000 can be installed from the Install CD. A DOS boot disk can be created and used to format the hard drive of the target computer. If the target computer has an autoboot CD-ROM, the Install CD can be inserted in the CD-ROM drive and the system rebooted. The setup wizard will start the installation.

However, if a company is installing Windows 2000 on multiple computers company wide, a more efficient installation method must be used. Normally, a network boot disk is created and used to connect to a shared network drive. On this shared drive is placed a copy of the *I386* folder from the Windows 2000 Install CD. The network administrator runs the WINNT program in the *I386* folder on the shared drive to install Windows 2000 on the target computer.

Phases of a Windows 2000 Installation

Before actually installing Windows 2000 it is important to understand the different installation phases. Three phases make up the setup process—

1. Text mode
2. Graphical mode
3. Initial login

During the text mode installation phase, Windows 2000 prepares the disk drive to receive the software, makes an initial inventory of the hardware installed on the server, and copies the files necessary for the graphical setup phase.

The hard disk can be formatted and repartitioned during the text mode setup phase. Windows 2000 inspects the hard disk, determines the drive's format and capacity, and prompts for the location of the system files. If the hard disk already has an operating system, Windows 2000 will change the boot sector and add a menu that allows the user to select the old operating system during system startup.

Windows 2000 will also reformat any old **NT file system** (**NTFS**) partitions it finds. Windows 2000 will not allow old NTFS disk partitions (found in Windows NT 3.51 and early versions of Windows NT 4) to exist with copies of Windows 2000. If you want to keep an existing version of Windows NT 4 on the same disk as Windows 2000 you must upgrade Windows NT 4 to the latest service pack.

Because Windows 2000 relies on the Plug and Play standard to detect hardware, the process of inspecting server hardware is more complex. During the text mode setup phase Windows 2000 runs the NTDETECT.COM program that inspects the server hardware (you see the message *Setup is inspecting your computer's hardware configuration*) and builds an initial hardware abstraction layer (HAL) database. The graphical mode setup program will use this database as a starting point for a much more exhaustive detection effort.

Once the text mode phase has completed, the server is rebooted and the graphical mode phase starts. During the graphical mode the remainder of the Windows 2000 software is installed, the server tested for Plug and Play capability, and network information collected from the user. On initial logon final settings are made.

Creating a DOS Boot Disk   In order to install Windows from a DOS prompt, a boot disk must be created. A DOS boot disk can be used to install Windows from a network share or from a local non-autostart CD-ROM drive. Table 2.5 lists the files that must be installed on a DOS boot disk to be used on a Network Share and on a CD-ROM drive.

TABLE 2.5   *Files to Be Installed on a DOS Boot Disk*

DOS Network Share Disk	DOS CD-ROM Disk
System files: Format a disk with the /s option	System files: Format a disk with the /s option
Network driver files: These files will be network specific	CD-ROM DOS driver files: [CDROMDriver.sys] and MSCDEX.EXE from the Windows folder (you may have to download the [cdromdriver.sys] file from the computer maker's Web site); HIMEM.SYS from the Windows folder.
SMARTDRV.EXE from the Windows folder	SMARTDRV.EXE from the Windows folder
Config.sys may contain the network drivers	Config.sys should contain the following lines: device = HIMEM.SYS device = [cdromdriver.sys] /D:CDROM1
Autoexec.bat should contain the network driver program to be automatically run and the SMARTDRV program	Autoexec.bat should contain the following lines: SMARTDRV MSCDEX /D:CDROM1

Installing Windows 2000

In the following exercises you will install Windows 2000 on a target computer that has a formatted hard drive partition. The first part of an installation will be different depending on how it was started. Installing through Windows 95/98 will be different from installing from a DOS boot disk. The main difference is the initial process of copying files and entering the Windows 2000 CD key. Once this part has been done, the remainder of the installation process is similar. The following exercises cover both these possibilities.

Exercise 1a assumes you are installing Windows 2000 on a computer that already has Windows 95/98 and you are using a CD-ROM or network share. Exercise 1b assumes you are installing Windows 2000 from a DOS disk. The steps in Exercise 1c will be the same (with some minor differences) if you started with either Exercise 1a or Exercise 1b. Depending on your lab configuration you will start with either Exercise 1a or Exercise 1b and then finish with Exercise 1c.

Exercise 1a

INSTALLING WINDOWS 2000 FROM WINDOWS 95/98

In the following exercise you will install Windows 2000 on a computer that already has the Windows 95/98 operating system. This target computer must have a formatted partition on the hard drive that is large enough to hold the Windows 2000 files (about 1.8 GB). During this exercise, Windows 2000 will install a boot manager program on the target computer so that when the system boots the user can choose either Windows 95/98 or Windows 2000. This feature is useful in lab situations where a single computer may be used for different purposes.

1. After starting Windows 95/98, make sure that no antivirus programs are running. If an antivirus program is running you will see an icon on the taskbar. Right-click the icon and click STOP or EXIT. If the Windows 2000 Installer finds an antivirus program in memory it will stop the installation.
2. Insert the Windows 2000 Install CD. You may see the window shown in Figure 2.1.

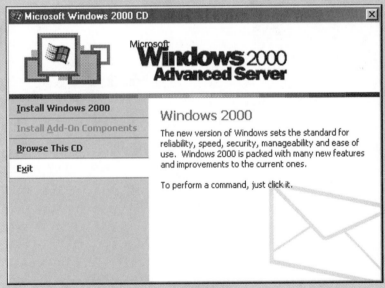

Figure 2.1

3. Open a DOS window (click Start, <u>P</u>rograms, MSDOS Prompt) and locate the *I386* folder on either the Windows 2000 Install CD or on a network share. Set the *I386* folder as the default folder in the DOS window.

4. In the DOS window enter the command:

   ```
   WINNT32
   ```

   You will see the wizard dialog box in Figure 2.2

Figure 2.2

5. Make sure the *Install a new copy of Windows 2000* option is selected and click <u>N</u>ext to start the Wizard. You will next see the license agreement dialog box in Figure 2.3.

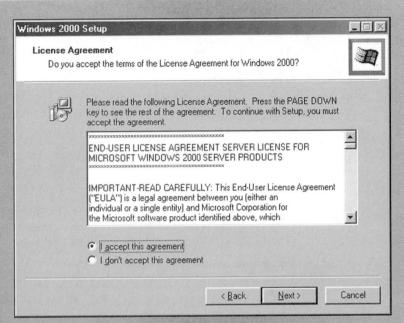

Figure 2.3

6. Click *I accept this agreement* and click <u>N</u>ext. You see the Product Key dialog box in Figure 2.4.

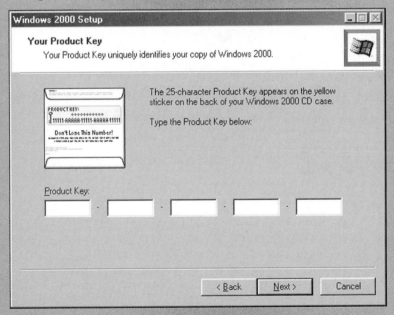

Figure 2.4

7. Enter the product key found on the Install CD and click Next. If the key entered is invalid you cannot proceed. If the key is valid you will next see the Select Special Options window in Figure 2.5.

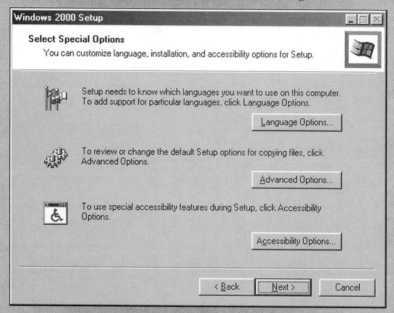

Figure 2.5

8. This dialog box allows you to change language options, set custom installation options, or use accessibility options during setup. Click the Advanced Options button to view setup options. You see the Advanced Options dialog box in Figure 2.6.

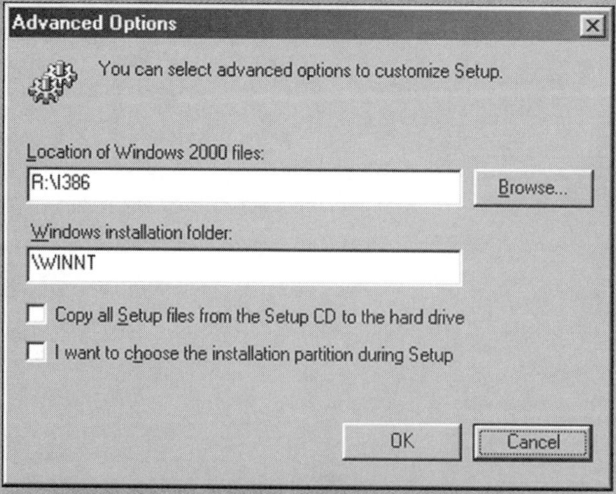

Figure 2.6

This dialog box allows you specify where the Windows 2000 files are to be installed on the target computer and the name of the installation folder. You can also choose to copy the entire setup file from the Install CD to the hard drive, which allows you to remove the CD after this step. You can also select an option in this dialog box to manually choose the installation partition during setup. If you are installing from a network share, you should click the Copy all Setup files option because when the computer reboots into text mode, it cannot find the files necessary to continue the setup process.

9. Click the OK button to leave this dialog box and return to the Select Special Options dialog box.
10. In the Select Special Options dialog box, click the Next button to start the setup process.

The setup files are copied to the hard drive and the target computer will reboot. The next phase of the setup process is text mode (Exercise 1c).

Exercise 1b

INSTALLING WINDOWS 2000 FROM A DOS BOOT DISK

In the following exercise you will install Windows 2000 by using a DOS boot disk. You may be given a boot disk or you may have to create one yourself. A DOS boot disk can be used to install Windows 2000 from a network share or from a CD-ROM. If Windows is to be installed from a network share, the boot disk must have network drivers. If you will install from a local CD-ROM drive, the disk must have the CD-ROM drivers.

1. Boot the DOS disk.
2. From the DOS prompt enter the command SMARTDRV to run the smartdrv program (if it is present).
3. From a DOS prompt, locate the *I386* folder on the Install CD or on a network share, change the default drive to the *I386* folder, and enter the command:

    WINNT

4. You see a screen confirming where the setup files are located. It should be the *I386* folder. Press Enter to continue.

The setup program will next spend several minutes copying files to the hard drive, and you will see a progress bar indicating the file copying status. If you have not loaded the smartdrv program, this process may take a long time. At the end of this process the computer will reboot and the text mode setup part will start (Exercise 1c).

Exercise 1c

TEXT MODE SETUP

During this part of the setup process, Windows 2000 will perform a number of tasks. These tasks include preparing the hard drive and copying the files necessary for the graphical mode portion of the setup program.

1. Once the text mode portion of setup has started, you see a screen like Figure 2.7. Press the Enter key to continue.

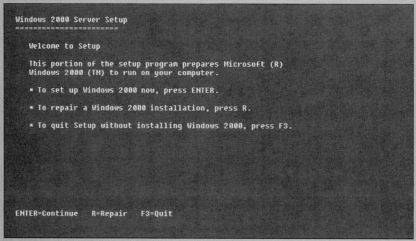

```
Windows 2000 Server Setup
========================

    Welcome to Setup

    This portion of the setup program prepares Microsoft (R)
    Windows 2000 (TM) to run on your computer.

    * To set up Windows 2000 now, press ENTER.

    * To repair a Windows 2000 installation, press R.

    * To quit Setup without installing Windows 2000, press F3.




ENTER=Continue    R=Repair    F3=Quit
```

Figure 2.7

2. If you started with the DOS disk installation (Exercise 1b) you will see the licensing agreement page. If you started from the Windows 95/98 install (Exercise 1a) you will not see the licensing agreement page. Press the F8 key to accept the agreement.

You will next see a screen listing the hard drive resources. Your screen will look different from but similar to Figure 2.8.

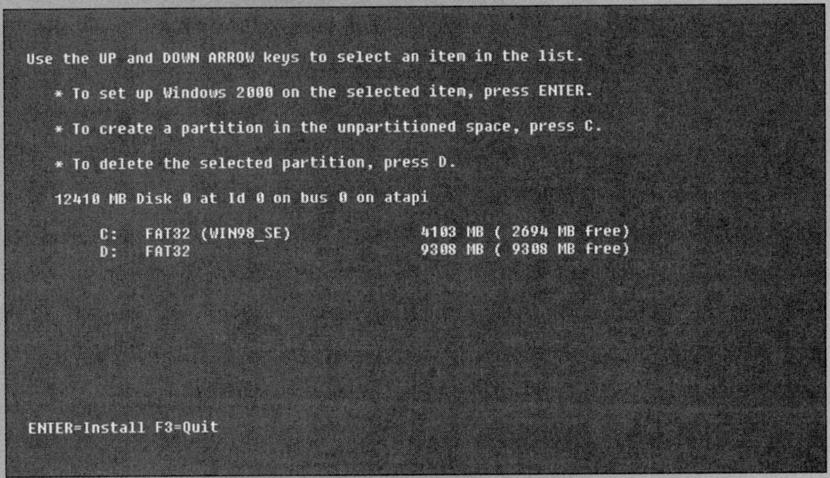

```
Use the UP and DOWN ARROW keys to select an item in the list.

   * To set up Windows 2000 on the selected item, press ENTER.

   * To create a partition in the unpartitioned space, press C.

   * To delete the selected partition, press D.

   12410 MB Disk 0 at Id 0 on bus 0 on atapi

        C:   FAT32 (WIN98_SE)            4103 MB ( 2694 MB free)
        D:   FAT32                       9308 MB ( 9308 MB free)




ENTER=Install F3=Quit
```

Figure 2.8

Any unpartitioned space on the hard drive would also be listed. The Windows 2000 setup program can create and remove partitions.

3. Select the disk drive onto which Windows 2000 will be installed and press Enter. You will next see a screen giving you the option to format the selected partition (Figure 2.9).

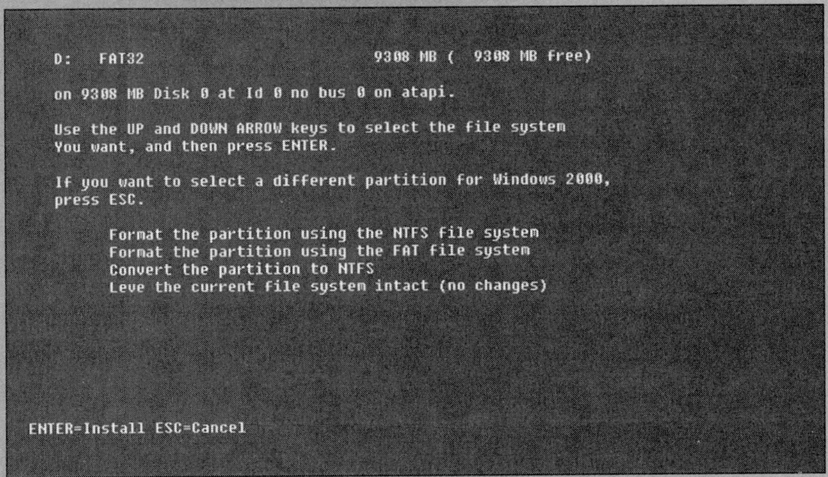

```
   D:   FAT32                       9308 MB ( 9308 MB free)

   on 9308 MB Disk 0 at Id 0 no bus 0 on atapi.

   Use the UP and DOWN ARROW keys to select the file system
   You want, and then press ENTER.

   If you want to select a different partition for Windows 2000,
   press ESC.

        Format the partition using the NTFS file system
        Format the partition using the FAT file system
        Convert the partition to NTFS
        Leve the current file system intact (no changes)




ENTER=Install ESC=Cancel
```

Figure 2.9

The partition can be formatted as FAT or NTFS or can be converted to NTFS. It is best to always install Windows 2000 on an NTFS partition.

4. Select *Format the partition using the NTFS file system* and press Enter.

5. You see a screen indicating that the files on this partition will be deleted. Press the letter F to continue. Formatting may take a few minutes. After formatting, setup files are copied to the selected partition. After copying files, the setup program reboots the computer and starts the graphical setup mode.

Once the setup program has completed the text mode it reboots into graphics mode.

Exercise 1d

GRAPHICAL MODE SETUP

1. Once the computer has rebooted into graphical mode, click the Next button to start the wizard. At this point, Windows 2000 inspects the hardware of the target computer and identifies all Plug and Play devices. This detection phase may take several minutes and you will see a progress bar indicating the status.

Once the hardware inspection phase has completed, you see the Regional Setting dialog box that is used to customize Windows 2000 for a different language or keyboard.

2. At the Regional Settings dialog box, click Next.
3. At the Personalize Your Software dialog box, enter your name and an organization name and click Next.
4. If you started from a DOS disk you will be prompted to enter the Product Key. If you started from the Windows 95/98 setup you will not be asked for the key. If asked, enter the Product key and click Next.
5. The next dialog box is used to set the licensing mode to per-server or per-seat. In this lab situation, select the per-server option and set the number of CALs to 25. Once done, click Next.
6. You will next be asked for a name to be given to the target computer and for the administrator's password. Each computer name must be unique and you should check with your instructor for a computer name. Key the word **classroom** in the administrator password text box and in the confirm password text box. Click Next when done.
7. The next dialog box allows you to add components to this installation of Windows 2000. They can be added later, so at this point you can accept the default values. Click Next to continue.
8. You see the Date and Time Setting dialog box. Make sure the date, time, and time zone are correct, and then click Next.

The setup program will next install the networking components. The Windows 2000 setup program installs them by listening to the connected network and determining which protocols to install. Often, the default setup for network components is unacceptable. For example, the setup program will, by default, use dynamic IP addresses, which are not appropriate for servers. These options can be changed after Windows 2000 has been installed.

9. You see the Network Setting dialog box where you can customize the network installation. Accept the default values and click Next. The next dialog box is used to designate how this computer will be connected to a network. A Windows 2000 computer can either be a member of a local workgroup or a member of a domain. This designation can be changed after setup.

10. Select the Workgroup option and use the workgroup name "Workgroup." At this point, the Windows 2000 setup program will copy the remaining setup files and customize the system. This process may take several minutes.

11. Click the Finish button to complete the setup. The system will reboot.

Exercise 2

INITIAL LOGIN SETTINGS

Accepting the default values makes the setup process quick and easy. However, the default setup values may not be appropriate, especially the networking components. In this exercise you will log on to Windows 2000 and reset some of the network components.

1. At the opening screen in Windows 2000 press the Ctrl-Alt-Delete keys. You see a logon screen.

2. For the administrator password key **classroom** and click OK.

3. You see the Configure Your Server window. Click *I will configure this server later* and then click Next.

4. Close the Configure Your Server window. You will next view the network components installed during setup and change the IP address.

5. Click Start, click Settings, and then click Network and Dial-up Connections. You see the screen in Figure 2.10.

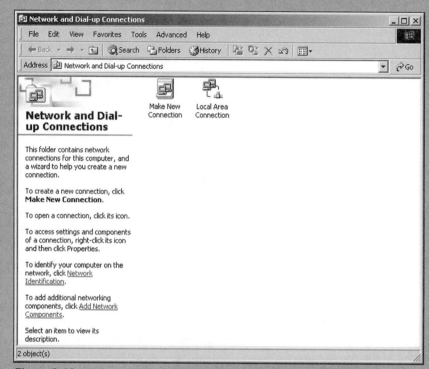

Figure 2.10

6. Right-click the *Local Area Connection* icon and click Properties. You see the Local Area Connection Properties dialog box in Figure 2.11.

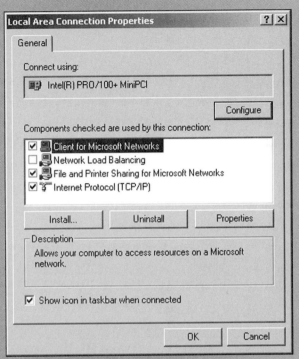

Figure 2.11

7. Click the Internet Protocol option and click Properties. You see the Internet Protocol dialog box in Figure 2.12. The default setup option is to obtain an IP address automatically.

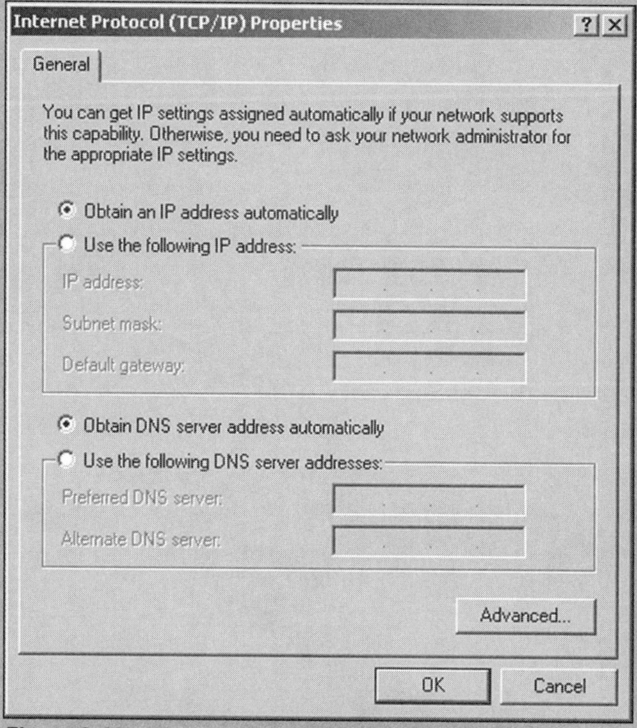

Figure 2.12

8. If you are told to change the IP address by your instructor, click *Use the following IP address* and enter an IP address. You must also enter a DNS server address and (possibly) a gateway address.
9. After entering the IP address information, click the OK button and then click the OK button on the Connection Properties dialog box.

Dual Booting Windows 2000

When Windows 2000 is installed on a computer that already has Windows 95/98, the files necessary to host both operating systems on the same computer are automatically installed. These files allow the computer to boot into either Windows 2000 or into Windows 95/98. This capacity is called **dual booting.** Although this configuration is not recommended for production servers, it is often implemented in lab situations when a single computer must serve multiple users.

Windows Boot Process In order to manage a dual boot system it is helpful to understand the Windows 2000 boot process. The following steps make up the Windows 2000 boot process:

1. During the **power on self test** (**POST**), the computer hardware BIOS routines perform initial checks. This process will vary from system to system, but it usually ends with the computer locating a bootable drive and starting the boot process.

2. Once the POST has located a bootable drive (usually the hard drive), the **bootstrap-loading** step is initiated. During this step the **master boot record** (**MBR**) is located on the hard drive and the contents are loaded into memory. The MBR contains information about the hard drive that allows the BIOS routines to locate the boot sector. Once located, the contents of the boot sector are loaded into memory and executed. The code in the boot sector is designed to locate and load a secondary bootstrap loader program. In Windows 2000 this program is named **NTLDR**. If the NTLDR file cannot be found, an error message is displayed and the boot process stops.

3. The NTLDR file, once loaded and executed, looks for a file named **BOOT.INI**. This file is used when dual booting Windows 2000 with Windows 95/98. As you will see, the BOOT.INI file contains information about the operating systems on the hard drive. NTLDR will also look for the Windows 2000 kernel program file (**NTOSKRNL.EXE**), the hardware abstraction layer file (**HAL.DLL**), and the video driver file (BOOTVID.DLL). If these files are found, they are loaded but not executed.

4. Before initializing the Windows 2000 kernel, the NTLDR file performs an initial hardware detection phase by running a program named NTDETECT.COM. This program performs a basic survey of the computer's hardware and builds a data structure in memory to allow the Windows 2000 kernel to boot correctly.

5. At this point in the boot process, the computer's screen is in DOS mode and displays a progress bar along the bottom of the screen. NTLDR reads the Windows registry file and starts loading services that have been marked as starting when Windows 2000 boots.

6. Once the boot services have been started, the NTOSKRNL program is executed and the Windows 2000 kernel loaded into memory. The screen switches to graphics mode.

7. The final steps in the boot process involve building a paging file, running additional services, and running the **WINLOGON.EXE** program, which prompts the user to enter an ID and password.

The BOOT.INI File   During the boot process, at step 2, the BOOT.INI file is examined. Boot problems can often be traced to an incorrect BOOT.INI file. The BOOT.INI file is a text file that contains information about the location of the operating systems on the hard drive. NTLDR builds a DOS menu from the BOOT.INI file and allows the user to select an operating system.

A typical BOOT.INI file appears as follows:

```
[boot loader]
timeout = 30
default = multi(0)disk(0)rdisk(0)partition(3)\WINNT

[operating systems]
multi(0)disk(0)rdisk(0)partition(3)\WINNT = "Microsoft
    Windows 2000 Server" / fastdetect
C:\ = "Microsoft Windows"
```

Each of the two sections to this BOOT.INI file is identified by a name enclosed in square brackets []. The [boot loader] section contains the number of seconds the boot menu will be displayed before the default operating system is loaded. The [operating systems] section lists the operating systems installed on the computer.

If you want the BOOT.INI menu to never timeout, replace 30 with –1.

The location of an operating system is identified by the **advanced RISC computing path** (**ARC path**). The format of an ARC path is:

```
diskcontroller()disk()relativedisk()partition()\systemroot
    = "Menu display string"
```

In the sample BOOT.INI file the ARC path is:

```
multi(0)disk(0)rdisk(0)partition(3)\WINNT = "Microsoft
    Windows 2000 Server" / fastdetect
```

The diskcontroller() section identifies the type of disk controller found on the computer. The number identifies the controller, starting with zero. The possible values are as follows:

multi() identifies IDE controllers and SCSI controllers with a local BIOS.

scsi() identifies older SCSI controllers without a local BIOS and is not used in Windows 2000 but remains for backward compatibility.

signature() identifies controllers that do not follow the standard INT13 configuration.

The disk() section is used with the scsi() controller type for older drives. This section is always disk(0).

The relativedisk() section identifies the physical hard drive location of the boot files. If a computer has two hard drives and places the Windows 2000 boot files on the second hard disk (the slave hard drive), then the value of this section would be—

```
rdisk(1)
```

If the boot files are located on the master hard disk drive then the value of this section would be—

```
rdisk(0)
```

The partition() section identifies what partitions on the selected hard drive contain the boot files. Partition numbers start with 1 rather than 0. If the boot files are on the second partition the value would be—

```
partition(2)
```

The \systemroot section identifies the folder containing the operating system files, which is \WINNT by default. Microsoft strongly discourages changing this value.

The final section ="Menu Display" is used to set the message displayed by the NTLDR program when it reads the BOOT.INI file.

Given the preceding information, we can "decode" the BOOT.INI file listed previously as follows:

```
[boot loader]
timeout = 30
        (wait 30 seconds before loading the default operating system)

default = multi(0)disk(0)rdisk(0)partition(3)\WINNT
        (the ARC path of the default operating system)

[operating systems]
multi(0)disk(0)rdisk(0)partition(3)\WINNT = "Microsoft
        Windows 2000 Server" / fastdetect
        (Windows 2000 is installed on an IDE controller on the first hard
        drive and in the third partition with the system files located in the
        \WINNT folder.)

C:\ = "Microsoft Windows"
        (The Windows boot files are located on drive C.)
```

Changing the BOOT.INI file should be done with care. If the BOOT.INI file is damaged or erased the system will not boot. It is sometimes a good idea to copy the BOOT.INI file to a disk.

The BOOT.INI file can be changed by using a simple text editor or by using a command under the *My Computer* icon. It is safer to change the BOOT.INI file by way of My Computer.

Exercise 3

CHANGING THE BOOT.INI FILE

1. After booting Windows 2000, right-click the *My Computer* icon and click Properties. You see a dialog box like Figure 2.13.

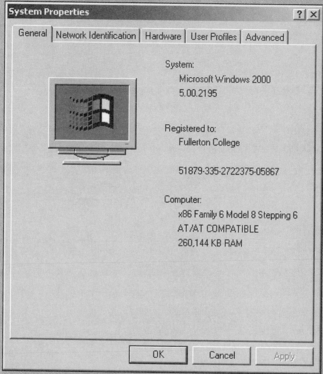

Figure 2.13

2. Click the Advanced tab and then click the Startup and Recovery button. You see the dialog box in Figure 2.14.

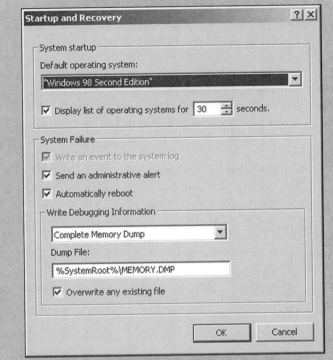

Figure 2.14

3. Change the number of seconds to display the operating system to 45 and click OK.
4. Click OK again to leave the System Properties dialog box.

Installing Windows 2000 on Multiple Computers

Installing Windows 2000 Server and Professional on multiple computers presents special challenges to network administrators. During the install process the hardware is examined, Plug and Play devices queried, and a security ID (SID) created. The SID must be unique to each server or workstation.

The three ways to quickly install Windows 2000 on multiple computers are as follows:

1. Disk cloning
2. Using remote installation services
3. Creating automated installation scripts

Each method has particular benefits and drawbacks.

Disk Cloning

Disk cloning involves using a third-party program, such as Norton Ghost™ or Drive Image™, to create a bit copy of a hard disk, save this bit copy to a network drive or CD-ROM, and use the third-party program to "clone" the disk image to a new computer. The two main problems with using this method to create Windows 2000 computers are the hardware configuration and SID.

During a Windows 2000 installation, the hardware on the server is examined in detail. If the hardware, such as network interface cards, are Plug and Play compliant, the software automatically configures their settings. Cloning computers will only work if they have the same hardware. When a cloned computer starts up, it compares the installed hardware with its own internal list. Differences can cause the system to fail. The first requirement for using the disk cloning method is to only clone computers that are identically configured.

The second problem with disk cloning is the SID. During installation, Windows 2000 creates a unique SID, which is partly based on hardware features. If two computers on a network have the same SID, various Windows 2000 operations will fail. Various third-party programs can be used to dynamically change the SID after a computer has been cloned, but Microsoft does not support these programs. A Microsoft product called SIDWALKER can be used to change the SID on a computer, but it is an OEM product and not easy to use.

The way to install Windows 2000 systems by using disk cloning is through the Sysprep program, which is supplied on the Windows 2000 setup CD. To use the Sysprep program, take the following steps:

1. Install and configure a Windows 2000 system as you want it duplicated.

2. Copy the SYSPREP.EXE and SETUPCL.EXE files from the Deploy.cab file located in the *\Support\Tools* folder on the Windows 2000 Install CD to a folder named *sysprep* on the system drive. For example, if Windows 2000 were installed on drive D, then you would create a folder named *sysprep* under drive D and copy these two files into this folder.

3. Click Start, then <u>R</u>un, and then key **SYSPREP.EXE**.

4. After Sysprep has completed configuring Windows, you will be prompted to shut down Windows.

5. After shutting down Windows you can use a third-party disk-cloning program to make a copy of the hard drive.

6. After the clone has been copied to a new system, boot the new computer. Windows will start up and automatically regenerate the hardware configuration and the SID.

To completely automate the process you can create a file named sysprep.inf that contains configuration information and place this file either in the *sysprep* folder or on a floppy disk. When Windows 2000 first boots after the sysprep command, it looks for the sysprep.inf file in the *sysprep* folder on the system drive or looks for this file on the floppy drive. Windows uses the information in this file to perform the install. Once the mini-install has completed, the *sysprep* folder and its contents are removed.

The reason that *sysprep* is useful is that the complete setup program is not run, as it is when a regular unattended install is performed. Creating a disk image of an already installed system after running Sysprep runs a mini-setup program that only prompts for selected configuration information. This minimal amount of information can be saved in the sysprep.inf file and automatically added.

Exercise 4

USING SYSPREP

1. Create a folder under the system drive named *sysprep*.
2. Copy the files SYSPREP.EXE and SETUPCL.EXE from the Deploy.cab file on the Windows 2000 Install CD into the *sysprep* folder.
3. Open Notepad and key the following lines:

```
[Unattended]
;Prompt the user to accept the EULA.
OemSkipEula=Yes
[GuiUnattended]
;Skip the Welcome screen when the system boots.
OemSkipWelcome=1
OemSkipRegional=1
Timezone=004
AdminPassword="classroom"
[UserData]
;Prepopulate user information for the system.
FullName="Your College Name"
OrgName="Your Department"
;ComputerName="CompName"
ProductID="XXXXX-XXXXX-XXXXX-XXXXX-XXXXX"
[Networking]
InstallDefaultComponents=Yes
[LicenseFilePrintData]
Automode=PerServer
AutoUsers=50
[Identification]
JoinWorkgroup=Workgroup
```

4. Save this file on a disk with the name sysprep.inf.

Notice that the ComputerName section is commented out with a semicolon before the option. This means that when Windows 2000 mini-setup runs you will be prompted for a computer name. Commenting out other sections of the INF file results in more prompting.

5. Reboot the computer and start Windows. Make sure the floppy disk containing the sysprep.inf file is available. When the sysprep copy first starts, it looks for the *sysprep* folder in the system root drive. If it does not find the *sysprep* folder it looks at the floppy disk for the sysprep.inf file.

Remote Installation Services and Install Scripts

Both remote installation services (RIS) and installation scripts use scripts to install Windows 2000. The difference is that RIS can be installed on a server and set to automatically download and install Windows 2000 Professional (but not Server). In both cases, Windows is installed from a script file, but the RIS can only install Windows 2000 Professional.

The idea behind an install script is that the input requested of the user during the installation process can be represented as a series of commands in a file. Forcing the Windows setup program to read responses from a script file rather than wait for user input will make the install process easier.

Using Install Scripts

A scripted installation of Windows 2000 is done by creating an Answer file and running the WINNT or WINNT32 program with an option to read information from the Answer file. For example, to install Windows 2000 where the setup files are on drive D and the script file is on drive A you would use the following commands:

```
WINNT /u:a:\unattend.txt /s:d:
```

or

```
WINNT32 /unattend:a:\unattend.txt /s:d:
```

The script file containing setup information is named unattend.txt.

A script file is just a text file that contains specific sections. Figure 2.15 contains a minimal unattended script file.

FIGURE 2.15

```
[Unattended]
UnattendMode = FullUnattended
TargetPath = WINNT

[UserData]
ComputerName = "The Computer Name"
FullName = "Administrator Name"

;make sure this is changed
[GuiUnattended]
AdminPassword = default admin password
TimeZone = "002"

[LicenseFilePrintData]
AutoMode = "PerServer"
AutoUsers = "30"

[Networking]
InstallDefaultComponents = Yes

[Identification]
JoinWorkgroup = workgroup name
```

A document outlining the complete script file parameters is included on the Windows 2000 Install CD.

CHAPTER summary

➤ Before installing Windows 2000 it is necessary to create an installation plan, check the hardware and software requirements, choose the software licensing options, and create an installation checklist. Windows 2000 licensing involves purchasing the server software and purchasing a client access license (CAL) for each client that will be using the server. Microsoft allows you to choose a per-server or per-client licensing option. A per-server option means that you must purchase a CAL for each connection to the server. A per-client option means that you purchase a CAL for each network client.

➤ Windows 2000 can be installed from the Install CD by running the WINNT or WINNT32 program. Once installed, the IP address must be set. Automated installations are normally performed when installing Windows 2000 on a group of servers.

CHAPTER terms

ARC path	A string found in the BOOT.INI file that is used to represent the location of a bootable operating system on a hard disk.
BIOS	Basic input/output system: The name given to the chip-based software that is a part of the computer system. The BIOS system is used in hardware configuration.
BOOT.INI	A text file that contains information about the location of the operating systems on the hard drive. The NTLDR program uses this file.
Bootstrap loading	Boot process that progressively loads parts of the boot software by locating the initial boot code on a predetermined place on the hard drive.
CAL	Client access license: A single user license to connect to a Windows 2000 server. In quantity, it costs about $40 each.
Dual booting	Installing Windows 2000 on a computer that already has Windows 95/98. A boot menu that allows selection of the operating systems on the drive is automatically added.
HAL.DLL	Part of the Windows 2000 operating system that handles hardware interfaces. Application and operating system programs use the HAL.DLL file to access the system hardware.

MBR	Master boot record: An area on the hard drive that contains information about the operating system boot information.
Nonroutable IP	An IP address that will not allow messages to be passed across a router or switch.
NTFS	NT file system: The name of the file system used in Windows 2000; also used to describe the type of disk formatting.
NTLDR	Part of the Windows 2000 operating system that handles the initial boot. This program reads the BOOT.INI file.
NTOSKRNL	Part of the Windows 2000 operating system that contains the basic kernel.
Partition	An area on a hard disk that can be used to install an operating system.
POST	Power on self–test: A process by the hardware BIOS that initializes computer hardware.
WINLOGON.EXE	The program that prompts the user with a login screen and processes the login information. After Windows 2000 has been loaded, this program is automatically executed.

CONCEPTS review

Multiple Choice

1. In order to run Windows 2000, a computer must have:
   a. A computer BIOS from Microsoft.
   b. A hard drive with at least 1 GB free.
   c. A video card with no less than 800 x 600 resolution.
   d. All of the above.

2. The Microsoft hardware compatibility list is used to:
   a. List problems with non-Microsoft hardware.
   b. List systems and components that will work with Windows 2000.
   c. List Windows 2000 updates to third-party hardware devices.
   d. None of the above.

3. The WINNT32 program option to check the hardware and software compatibility of a target computer is:
   a. /checkhardware.
   b. /checksystem.
   c. /checkcomputer.
   d. /checkupgradeonly.

4. A client access license (CAL) is:
   a. Part of the Windows 2000 setup files.
   b. A component installed after Windows 2000 has been set up.
   c. A communications protocol that allows connections to a server.
   d. None of the above.

5. When installing Windows 2000, an administrator password:
   a. Is optional.
   b. Must be at least six characters long.
   c. Must contain at least three numbers and five letters.
   d. Must be entered at least three times.

6. Which of the following is a nonroutable IP address?
   a. 172.12.0.0
   b. 192.233.0.0
   c. 172.20.0.0
   d. 192.166.0.0

7. Why would you run WINNT rather than WINNT32 to install Windows 2000?
   a. You initially booted from DOS.
   b. You initially booted from Windows 95 or 98.
   c. You initially booted from Windows NT 4.
   d. You initially booted from a non-Microsoft operating system.

8. The three phases to the Windows 2000 setup process are:
   a. Boot mode, text mode, initial login.
   b. Text mode, install mode, initial login.
   c. Text mode, graphical mode, initial login.
   d. None of the above.

9. During setup, the purpose of the NTDETECT.COM program is to:
   a. Look for previous operating system files on the hard drive.
   b. Look for a previous version of Windows 2000 and, if found, delete the files.
   c. Inspect the server hardware components.
   d. Inspect the server and client hardware components.

10. During installation the computer name:
    a. Is optional.
    b. Must be at least 12 characters.
    c. Must be unique.
    d. None of the above.

11. The purpose of a DHCP server is to:
    a. Supply an IP address when requested by a computer.
    b. Supply an Internet address when requested by a computer.
    c. Supply Windows 2000 setup files when requested.
    d. Perform an automated installation of Windows 2000.

12. The purpose of the POST is:
    a. To initialize computer hardware devices.
    b. To connect to the network.
    c. To install software.
    d. None of the above.

13. During a Windows 2000 boot process the bootstrap loading happens:
    a. At the very end of the boot process.
    b. At the very beginning of the boot process.
    c. After the operating system kernel has been loaded.
    d. Before the operating system kernel has been loaded.

14. The ARC path text string identifies:
    a. The hard drive controller.
    b. Which hard disk the operating system is installed on.
    c. Which partition the operating system is installed on.
    d. All of the above.

15. Disk cloning *cannot* be used to install Windows 2000 on multiple computers if:
    a. The computers have identical hardware.
    b. The computers have the same size hard drive.
    c. The computers have the same BIOS.
    d. None of the above.

Fill In

1. The suggested CPU speed for a computer that will host Windows 2000 is _____.

2. The suggested hard disk size for a computer that will host Windows 2000 is _____.

3. The Microsoft hardware compatibility list is located at the Web site _____.

4. The WINNT and WINNT32 programs are located in the _____ folder on the Windows 2000 Install CD.

5. If you are installing Windows 2000 on a server that does not have a formatted hard disk you must create a set of _____ disks.

Short Answer

1. The _____ option is used with WINNT32 to examine the Windows 20000 hardware and software compatibility.
2. The _____ licensing option allows the purchase of a single license giving a user access to multiple servers.
3. According to common security policy, an administrator password should be at least _____ characters in length.
4. During the _____ mode of the Windows 2000 installation process, hard drive partitions can be formatted.
5. When a computer is set for _____ boot mode, multiple operating systems can be accessed from an initial start menu.

LAB exercises

Exercise 1 – Install at a DOS Prompt from a Network Share

1. Boot to a DOS prompt.
2. Change to the Windows 2000 setup folder *I386*.
3. Run WINNT with the parameters for the source drive and path. For example, WINNT /s:D:\I386 will install from drive D.
4. During the install process, format the target drive with NTFS.
5. Install Windows 2000 with default values. Set the administrator password to *classroom*.
6. Ask your instructor for the computer name.
7. During the install on the networking screen, select the TCP/IP protocol properties and either set the IP address to a static number or allow Windows to get an IP dynamically. Ask your instructor for the information at this step.

Exercise 2 – Create an Unattended Install Script

1. Using the Windows 2000 Install CD, double-click the *Support* folder.
2. In the *Support* folder, double-click the *Tools* folder.
3. In the *Tools* folder, double-click the file named DEPLOY.CAB (you may not see a file extension).
4. Copy the following files into the *WINNT* folder on the hard drive:

       SETUPMGR.EXE
       SETUPMGX.DLL
       UNATTEND.DOC

5. After copying the files, click Start, then <u>R</u>un, and then key **SETUPMGR** and press Enter. You see the Setup Manager program.

6. Click the Next button.
7. Click *Create an answer file that duplicates this computer's configuration* and then click Next.
8. Click *Windows 2000 unattended installation* and click Next.
9. Click *Windows 2000 Server* and click Next.
10. Click *Fully Automated* and click Next.
11. Click the License Agreement checkbox and click Next.
12. Enter your name and organization and click Next.
13. Select per-server licensing, set the number of clients to 100 and click Next.
14. Type the computer name, click Add, and then click Next. (You may need to get the computer name from your instructor.)
15. Key **classroom** in the *password* and *confirm password* fields, and click Next.
16. Select the defaults for the display and click Next.
17. Click *Typical Settings* for the network options and click Next.
18. Click either *Workgroup* or *Domain* (you may have to ask your instructor for the correct value) and click Next.
19. Select the default time zone and click Next.
20. Click *Do not edit the additional settings* and click Next.
21. Click *No, this answer file will be used to install from a CD* and click Next. (You may be prompted. If so, click Yes.)
22. Save this file on a disk with the name unattended.txt and click Next.
23. Click Finish.

PROBLEM SOLVING exercises

Exercise 1

You are responsible for installing Windows 2000 on three servers. Five hundred people in the company will be connecting to the servers. The company works in three 8-hour shifts and one-third of the people work each shift. Assuming that 10 percent of the employees will be working across shifts (working longer than their shift hours), compute the most cost effective Windows 2000 licensing option, per-seat or per-server. Assume the server license is $1,500 and the CALs are $50 each.

Exercise 2

You are responsible for installing Windows 2000 on 50 servers at your company. You will have approximately 120 users for each server with an annual employee turnover rate of 10 percent per year. Each time you purchase one or a set of CALs it costs Purchasing about $100. In order to track individual CALs per employee you must use part-time office personnel at a cost of $12,000 per year. Assuming the server licenses are $1,200 each and the CALs can be purchased at $30 each, calculate the cost of using per-server and per-seat licensing.

Exercise 3

Select a server at your company or at school and get the manufacturer name and hardware specifications of that server and as much information as possible about the server components. Using the Microsoft HCL Web site and the manufacturer Web site, write a memo indicating whether the server is appropriate for hosting Windows 2000.

Exercise 4

Using a server at your company or at school, write an installation plan and create an installation checklist detailing an installation of Windows 2000. Make sure your plan contains information about expected server downtime, number of licenses required, network information needed for the installation, computer name, and administrator password. From your installation plan create an installation checklist.

Exercise 5

Your server has two IDE hard disk drives, and the Windows 2000 system files are on the second partition of the second drive in a folder named *WINNT*. Write the ARC path that would be found in the BOOT.INI.

SERVER HARDWARE AND SOFTWARE MANAGEMENT 3

Performance Objectives

After completing this chapter you will be able to:

- Discuss the issues with installing hardware and software in Windows 2000
- Discuss how Plug and Play works with Windows 2000
- Describe and discuss the options found in the Control Panel
- Install a new hardware device
- Install new software and upgrade Windows components
- Remove hardware and software
- Discuss the purpose and function of the Windows 2000 registry
- Open and view the contents of the registry

Introduction

Once a server has been installed, the next step is to customize the installation. Customization often involves installing and configuring additional hardware and software. Many tools in Windows 2000 can help with this process, including tools located in the Control Panel, the Administrative Tools menu, and the Microsoft Management Console (MMC). In order to install and configure hardware and software you need to understand how these tools work and how Windows 2000 saves and uses configuration information. Such information is saved in the registry database. This chapter teaches you how to install and configure hardware and software on a network server, how to troubleshoot such installations, and how to use the Windows 2000 registry.

General Hardware and Software Installation Issues

Although Microsoft has worked hard to make installing hardware and software under Windows 2000 easy, it can still prove challenging. The main issues with installing hardware and software are—

- Assigning resources to hardware devices
- Installing correct hardware device drivers
- Resolving hardware conflicts
- Installing and configuring software
- Removing hardware devices and uninstalling software

Installing and Configuring Hardware

Resources must be allocated to newly installed hardware devices before they can be used. These resources include things such as Interrupt Requests (IRQ), I/O ports, direct memory addresses (DMA), and other system-level settings. When hardware devices are installed under Windows 2000, the operating system must correctly configure these resources within itself while the hardware device must be configured with compatible settings. For example, if a hardware device requires the use of IRQ 12, Windows must be configured so it assigns this resource. If IRQ 12 is not available, then the setting on both the hardware device and Windows must be changed.

An **Interrupt Request** (**IRQ**) is a special signal sent to the CPU requesting attention. When a hardware device or a software program wants to get the CPU's attention it sends a signal on a predetermined Interrupt channel. The CPU listens on a set of Interrupt channels and responds to signals. The reason for this Interrupt architecture is so that while the CPU is processing another task it can always be interrupted.

For example, the print device (the physical printer) commonly uses IRQ 7. If you attempt to print a document from a word processing program and the printer is out of paper, the print device will signal the CPU on IRQ 7. The CPU will suspend the current program (the word processing program) and query the print device.

A common problem with Interrupts is their limited number and the fact that different hardware devices sometimes want to use the same Interrupt channel. This simultaneous usage is unacceptable because Windows will associate only a single Interrupt with a designated hardware device. To resolve this problem the hardware device and the device drivers (see below) must be set with a new Interrupt. This is one of the tasks performed by the Plug and Play part of Windows 2000.

I/O ports and **direct memory addresses** (**DMA**) are channels through which hardware devices communicate with the CPU. Like IRQs, these must be reserved.

In order to use a hardware device, such as a printer or scanner, Windows must have a compatible software driver loaded. These software programs are called **device drivers** and are normally packaged with the hardware device. When the hardware device is installed the associated device driver must also be installed. Windows 2000 contains a large library of common hardware device drivers, which it can use for new hardware devices. However, it is always best to use the most current driver that ships with the hardware device.

When a hardware device requests specific configuration settings, such as a specific Interrupt number or I/O port, it may conflict with other devices. Resolving hardware conflicts involves inspecting the requested resource information and, if necessary, adjusting the parameters. For example, if both a network card and a modem attempt to use the same Interrupt, neither will work correctly. The network administrator must locate the conflict and adjust one of the Interrupt parameters.

Installing and Configuring Software

Software is more flexible than hardware and thus easier to install. Despite this flexibility, installation problems can also arise with software. The main set of problems related to software installations involves the supporting files necessary for the software to run. Most software applications use files already installed in the operating system. For example, many older applications use a file named MFC42.DLL. This file contains a set of low-level C++ library routines that are called by application programs. In order to work, an application program must have access to this file. The application installation program may copy this file to an operating system folder. The problem is that other already installed programs may also use this file. If the MFC42.DLL file is a different version, it could break currently installed applications.

For example, most software applications are installed by running a setup program. This setup program copies the application files and any required support files and inserts configuration information in the registry. If the setup program was not written correctly it could damage other already installed programs by overwriting information in the registry. If an application setup program copies an old version of the MFC42.DLL file and replaces a current version, other programs that rely on the later version of MFC42.DLL will break.

Plug and Play Hardware and the Software Manager

Plug and Play was developed to simplify the process of installing hardware and make hardware installations as easy as software installations. New hardware devices such as printers or scanners are designed to be Plug and Play aware. This capability means that the devices have chip-level-embedded software that can communicate with a Plug and Play software manager. The Plug and Play manager is a program running on the computer that performs the following tasks:

- Allocates system resources such as IRQ and I/O ports
- Loads the device drivers required by the hardware device

Plug and Play devices communicate with the Plug and Play manager in Windows 2000, which negotiates with the operating system for resources such as IRQs and I/O ports. The Plug and Play manager attempts to automatically locate and load the associated device driver software. This loading usually happens after the device is connected to the computer and the computer and device are powered up.

Driver Signing

Although the Plug and Play system can reduce hardware device resource conflict problems, it cannot check for badly written device drivers. A hardware device must use a device driver to communicate with the operating system, and the hardware vendor usually writes these device drivers. Poorly written device drivers are a major cause of system crashes in both Windows 95/98 and Windows NT.

In an attempt to prevent problems with device drivers, Microsoft developed the **Driver Signing** program. In this program hardware vendors submit their device driver code to the Microsoft **Windows Hardware Quality Lab** (**WHQL**). The device driver is tested and verified by Microsoft. If it passes the Microsoft tests, the software is given a digital signature, which is a special software-based key attached to the driver code. When Windows 2000 loads a device driver it checks for this digital signature. If the driver does not have this signature, Windows displays a warning message indicating that this driver may not work with the operating system (Figure 3.1).

FIGURE **3.1** *Microsoft Warning Message for Digital Signature*

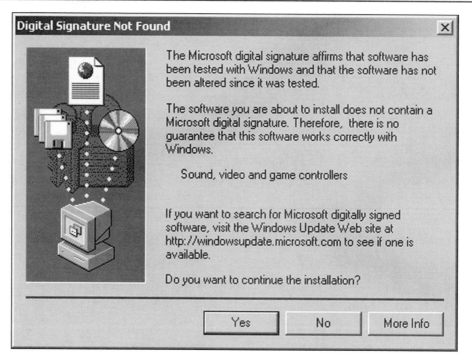

You can still install the driver, but Microsoft warns you that the driver may not work. By default, Windows 2000 warns before installing an unsigned driver. You can set an option so that Windows either ignores unsigned drivers and just installs them anyway, or refuses to install unsigned drivers. The option to allow or reject unsigned drivers can be set from the System option in the Control Panel. The default setting, which warns about unsigned drivers but allows them to be installed, is the middle ground. Any hardware manufacturer that wants to sell products will likely seek a Microsoft digital signature.

To check your installed driver files for this digital signature you can run the program SIGVERIF by clicking Start, then <u>R</u>un, then keying **SIGVERIF**, and then pressing Enter. This program will scan your system for unsigned files and save the results in a log file.

The Control Panel

The Control Panel is used to configure the hardware and software on the server. More complicated network and server configurations will be done through the Administrative Tools menu or in a Microsoft Management Console. A typical Control Panel window is displayed in Figure 3.2.

FIGURE 3.2 *Control Panel Window*

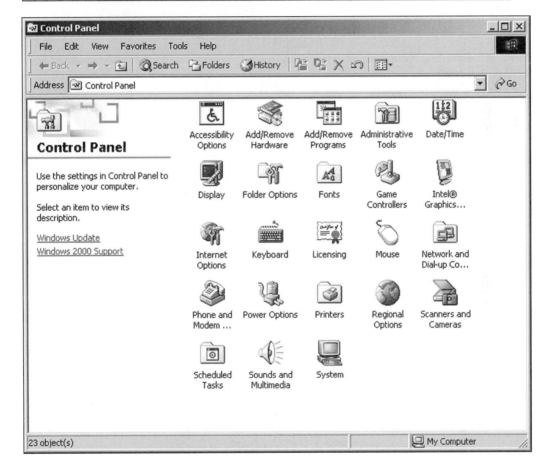

Your Control Panel may have fewer or additional icons than what is displayed in the figure. Some application programs add their own controls to the Control Panel. Table 3.1 contains the most common Control Panel items and indicates their basic functions.

TABLE 3.1 *Typical Control Panel Options*

Common Control Panel Items	
Accessibility Options	Sets options in Windows 2000 for physically challenged individuals, including setting keystroke options so multiple key command (such as Shift-Alt) can be performed one key at a time.
Add/Remove Hardware	Adds and removes hardware devices.
Add/Remove Programs	Adds and removes application programs and Windows operating system options.
Administrative Tools	Displays a set of program icons used to manage the operating system.
Date/Time	Changes the system date and time.
Display	Changes the display options such as the window colors, desktop background, and display resolution.
Folder Options	Changes how folders display information (as icons, text listings, and so on).
Fonts	Adds, removes, and displays fonts installed on the system.
Game Controllers	Adds and configures a game controller.
Internet Options	Sets options for Internet Explorer such as the connection type, security, and history list.
Keyboard	Sets options on the keyboard such as the language characters and the keystroke rate.
Licensing	Adds and removes client access licenses (CALs) and sets the type of licensing option (per-seat or per-server).
Mail	Sets network mail account options.
Mouse	Sets options with the mouse such as the double-click rate and the mouse button assignments.
Network and Dial-up Connections	Displays information about the current network or modem connections and is used to make new connections. These options can also be accessed directly from the Settings menu along with the Control Panel.
Phone and Modem Options	Sets options for an attached modem or telephone such as area code.
Power Options	Sets power options for both desktop and laptop computers. Windows 2000 can communicate with hardware that is compatible with the advanced power management system, including "Green" monitors and CPUs that automatically reduce their power when not in use.

Common Control Panel Items	
Printers	Creates and manages printers.
Regional Options	Sets regional settings such as the language, numbering system, and time and date system being used.
Scanners and Cameras	Configures scanners and cameras.
Scheduled Tasks	Adds and removes scheduled tasks. Windows 2000 comes with a task scheduler program that can be used to automatically run a program at a specified time.
Sounds and Multimedia	Configures sound and multimedia devices connected to the system and sets the sounds used when Windows performs tasks such as closing windows.
System	Displays and sets system-level information such as the location of the Swap file, sets environment variables, and sets options in the BOOT.INI file. This option can also be selected by right clicking the *My Computer* icon and clicking Properties.

Many of the items found in the Control Panel are similar to those found in Windows 98 and will probably be used more in a Windows 2000 Professional environment than on a 2000 Server. (Hopefully no game controllers will be located on the servers!) Three of the options will be discussed in this chapter because they are often used to configure a server after installation.

- Administrative Tools
- Add/Remove Hardware
- Add/Remove Programs

Administrative Tools

Almost all the options in the Control Panel are used to manage the local computer. Administrative Tools contains options for managing a network server. You will learn to use these tools in later chapters. The most common options in Administrative Tools are listed in Table 3.2. They will vary depending on which Windows 2000 options have been installed.

TABLE 3.2 *Control Panel Administrative Tools Options*

Component Services	Manages COM+ applications. These programs use distributed software components located on a server.
Computer Management	Opens an MMC that contains various options for the local server.
Configure Your Server	Runs the Configure Your Server Wizard, which contains a set of management wizards.

Data Sources (ODBC)	Defines and configures data source links on the server. Typically, developers and database administrators use it.
Distributed File System	Manages the Windows 2000 distributed file system.
Event Viewer	Displays system event messages that may be sent by processes and applications.
Internet Services Manager	Manages the Internet Information Services program that is automatically installed with Windows 2000.
Licensing	Manages the licensing server in Windows that monitors CALs and other Windows product licensing.
Local Security Policy	Manages the local security policies and rights on the computer.
Performance	Runs the Performance Monitor program, which is used to view the status of system resources.
Routing and Remote Access	Configures the routing and remote access services in Windows 2000.
Services	Displays a list of services running under Windows 2000.

Adding and Removing Hardware

Installing a Plug and Play device is almost easy. The steps for the process include—

- Physically installing the hardware device according to the manufacturer's directions
- Restarting the server
- Watching as Windows 2000 configures the device and installs the device driver software (you may be prompted to insert the CD or disk that accompanied the hardware device)

Things get a little trickier if you attempt to install a device that is not Plug and Play compatible. Windows 2000 will not automatically find the hardware device and will not automatically load the device drivers. Installing this type of hardware device requires the Hardware Wizard. This wizard is run from the Add/Remove Hardware option in the Control Panel. The basic steps in using the Hardware Wizard include—

- Connecting the hardware device and starting the wizard
- Locating the device to be installed by manufacturer and name from a list, or opening a device driver install file (an **INF file**)
- Installing the device driver software

Exercise 1

INSTALLING THE MICROSOFT LOOPBACK NETWORK ADAPTER

In this exercise you will install a "virtual" hardware device named the Microsoft Loopback Network Adapter. This non-Plug and Play network adapter is used for testing purposes.

1. Click Start, Settings, and then Control Panel.
2. Double-click the *Add/Remove Hardware* icon to start the Hardware Wizard. You see the initial wizard screen.
3. Click Next to start the Wizard. You see a dialog box prompting you to add or troubleshoot a new device or remove a device (Figure 3.3).

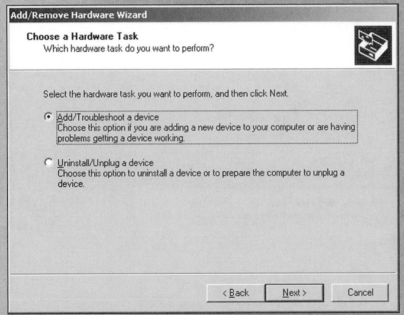

Figure 3.3

4. Accept the Add/Troubleshoot option and click Next. At this point Windows will search for new Plug and Play hardware to install. If the hardware is found, it is automatically installed. If Windows does not find any new Plug and Play hardware it presents a list of installed devices (Figure 3.4).

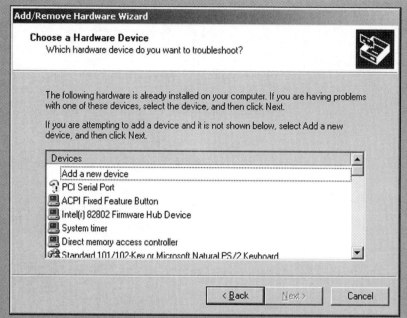

Figure 3.4

5. Click the generic *Add a new device* and then click <u>N</u>ext. The wizard will prompt you to search for new hardware (Figure 3.5).

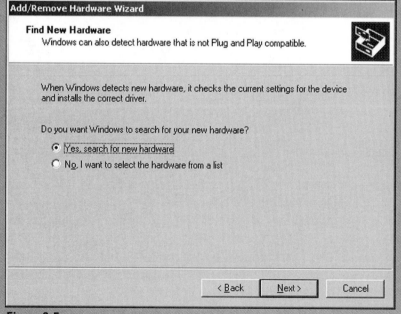

Figure 3.5

At this point you can let Windows examine all connected non-Plug and Play hardware devices and compare them to an internal list of installed devices. The other option allows you to select the specific device from a list or to directly open the device driver INF file.

6. Click *No, I want to select the hardware from a list* and click <u>N</u>ext. You see a list of devices.
7. Scroll down to and select *Other devices* in this list (Figure 3.6) and click <u>N</u>ext.

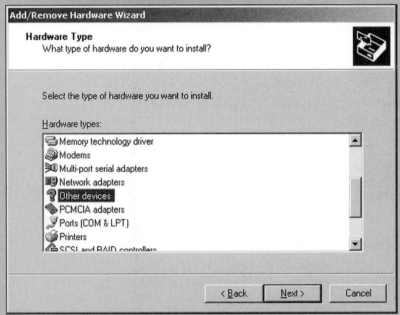

Figure 3.6

You see a list of device drivers sorted by manufacturer and then model.

8. Scroll down to and click *Microsoft* and then click the model *Microsoft Loopback Adapter* on the right side of the dialog box (Figure 3.7).

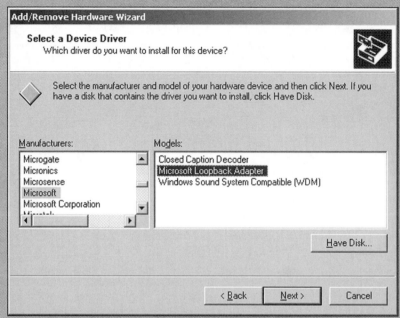

Figure 3.7

If you could not find the hardware manufacturer or the model, and you had the hardware device driver software on a disk or CD, you could click the Have Disk button and select the INF file for the device driver software.

   9. Click the Next button. You see a screen indicating that the default values of the Microsoft Loopback Adapter will be used.

  10. Click Next to start the installation. When the installation is done, click the Finish button. The Loopback Adapter is now installed.

Viewing Hardware Configurations   Windows 2000 builds and maintains a database listing each installed hardware device along with information about the associated device driver. This information can be used when a piece of hardware is incorrectly installed, in case of a driver conflict, or if you want to update the device driver.

Exercise 2

VIEWING HARDWARE RESOURCES

In this exercise you will display information about the Loopback Adapter installed in Exercise 1 and you will attempt to update the device driver for this hardware component.

1. Click Start, Settings, and Control Panel.
2. Double-click the *System* icon. You see the dialog box in Figure 3.8.

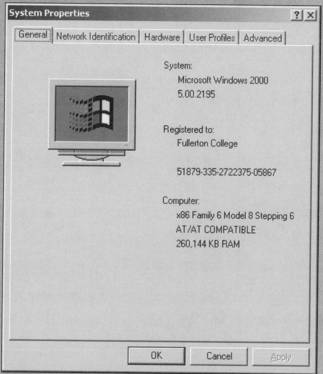

Figure 3.8

3. Click the Hardware tab, which gives you the dialog box in Figure 3.9.

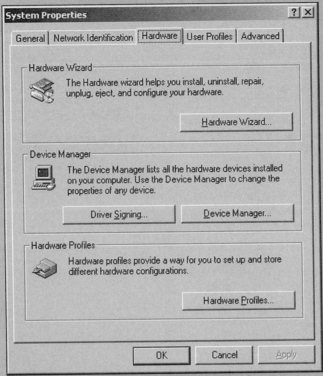

Figure 3.9

4. Click the Device Manager button. This command displays a list of hardware categories, under which are listed the components installed on your computer (Figure 3.10). Your list may look different from the one pictured. If a device is not working, it is displayed with a small yellow question mark icon.

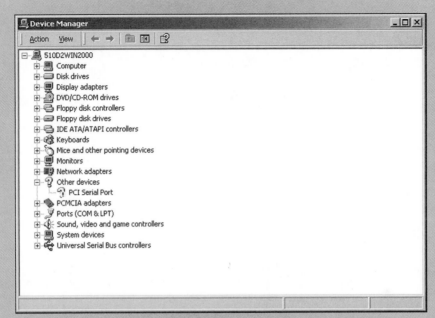

Figure 3.10

5. Click the plus symbol next to *Network adapters*, which displays the details of this category (Figure 3.11).

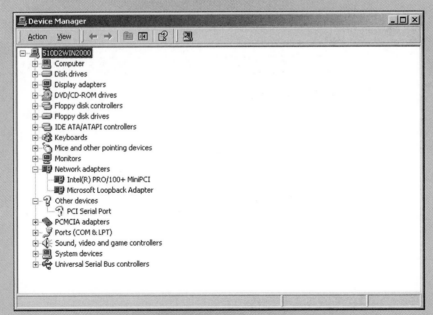

Figure 3.11

6. Double-click *Microsoft Loopback Adapter*. A dialog box then appears containing information about this device (Figure 3.12). A device that is not working correctly can be turned off and on by using the Device usage list.

Figure 3.12

7. Click the Driver tab. It opens a dialog box shown in Figure 3.13, which contains options for displaying the driver files, uninstalling the device, and updating the hardware device drivers.

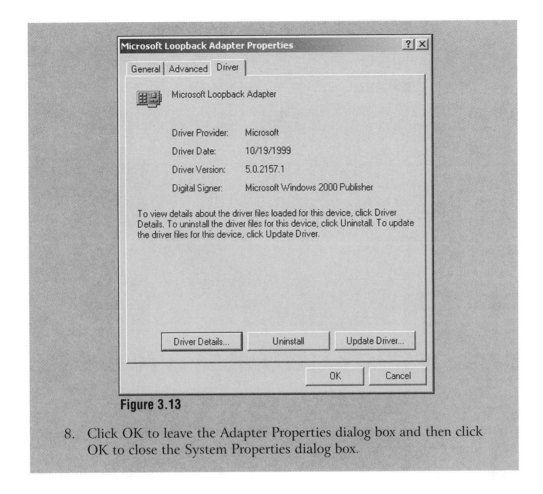

Figure 3.13

8. Click OK to leave the Adapter Properties dialog box and then click OK to close the System Properties dialog box.

Removing Hardware   Because most hardware requires Windows to maintain a list of allocated resources, removing hardware should be done through the Add/Remove Hardware Wizard. This process allows Windows to adjust its resource allocation lists. The Add/Remove Hardware Wizard can be accessed from the Control Panel or from the *My Computer* icon in the desktop. When the Add/Remove Hardware Wizard is run and used to remove a piece of hardware, Windows will update the list of resources allocated to installed hardware.

Exercise 3

REMOVING THE LOOPBACK ADAPTER

In this exercise you will remove the Loopback Adapter installed in a prior exercise. Rather than use the Control Panel option, you will use the *My Computer* icon.

1. From the desktop right-click *My Computer* and click Properties. You see the System Properties dialog box in Figure 3.14

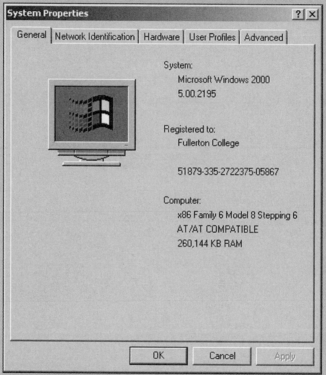

Figure 3.14

2. Click the Hardware tab to display the various hardware options for the system (Figure 3.15).

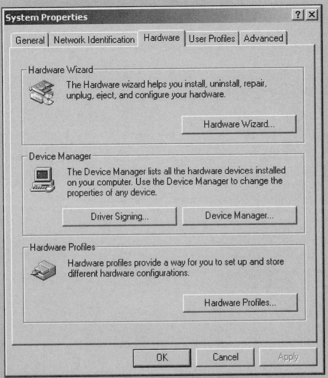

Figure 3.15

The options in this dialog box allow you to run the Hardware Wizard to add or remove devices, set the driver signing options, view the hardware device manager, or setup different hardware profiles to be used during system startup.

3. Click the Hardware Wizard button to start the Hardware Wizard.
4. Click Next.
5. Click the Uninstall/Unplug a device option and then click Next.
6. Click the Uninstall a device option and then click Next. You see a list of installed devices (Figure 3.16).

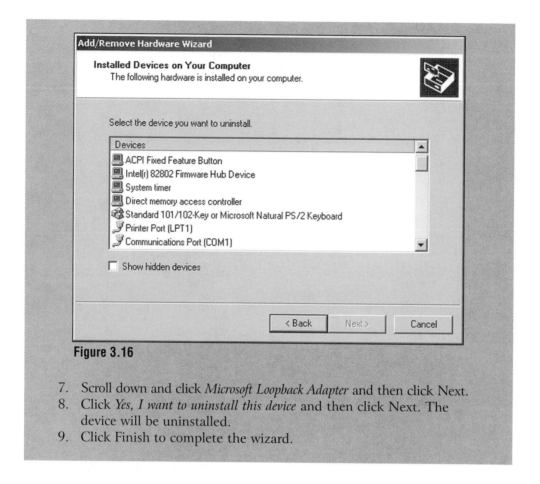

Figure 3.16

7. Scroll down and click *Microsoft Loopback Adapter* and then click Next.
8. Click *Yes, I want to uninstall this device* and then click Next. The device will be uninstalled.
9. Click Finish to complete the wizard.

Adding and Removing Software

Adding and removing software is similar to adding and removing hardware and is accomplished by using the Control Panel option named Add/Remove Programs. This option can be used to both install new programs and remove existing programs. This option is also used to add and remove Windows components. A Windows component is a support program that is part of the Windows operating system.

Installing software under Windows 2000 is normally done by running a special setup program. This setup program generally performs the following tasks:

- Copies the application files into a folder (creating the folder if necessary)
- Copies and/or updates support files as needed
- Adds the program to the Start menu and/or desktop
- Writes configuration information about the program to the Windows registry
- Provides a way to uninstall the program

If a setup program is badly written it may replace files that other programs need or damage the system registry file, which could result in Windows not working correctly. To prevent these kinds of problems Microsoft developed the Microsoft Installer program by which application programs can safely install themselves under Windows.

Microsoft Installer

The Microsoft Installer program is part of Windows 98 and Windows 2000. It is used to install and automatically maintain application software. When a setup program is written following the Microsoft Installer format, the setup program is given the file type *MSI*. When this MSI file is run, the Microsoft Installer program on the hard drive reads the install steps in the MSI file and performs the installation. The installer program also remembers the location of the setup MSI file and saves this location in the Windows registry. If the application files are erased or become damaged, the installer will automatically rebuild the application using the MSI file.

This feature of automatically rebuilding an application is useful in a network environment. If the MSI setup files are installed from a network drive and are maintained on the network drive, users will always have access to the application setup files. If some of the application files on the client are deleted or damaged, the installer will automatically reload the required files from the original setup MSI file located on the network.

Exercise 4

INSTALLING AN APPLICATION

In the following exercise you will install a simple application that uses the Microsoft Installer technology.

1. Copy the setup program named happysad.msi from the book CD to your desktop.
2. Double-click this program to start the installation. You see an initial setup window.
3. Click Next to start the setup.

You see a screen allowing you to select the installation folder. The default folder is named *happysad* and is located in the *Program Files* folder (Figure 3.17).

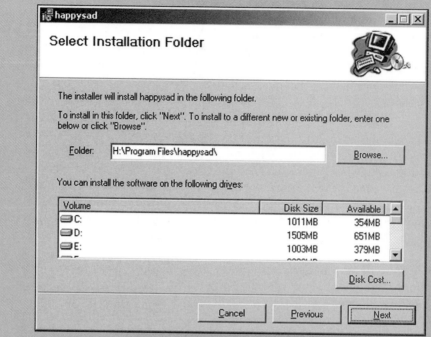

Figure 3.17

4. Click <u>N</u>ext to accept the default location of the application.
5. Click <u>N</u>ext to start the installation.
6. When the installation is complete, click the <u>C</u>lose button.
7. Click the Start button. You should see an icon on the Start menu.
8. Select the happysad program and click the Happy and Sad buttons a few times. (This program has a limited capability.)
9. When done with the happysad program, close the program window.

This exercise may seem a bit trivial, but more is happening than what appears on the surface. Windows has marked the location of the setup file happysad.msi. If part of the application is deleted, Windows will automatically reinstall the application from this setup file.

Exercise 5

BREAKING AND REPAIRING AN APPLICATION

In the following exercise you will delete a file in the HappySad application and then try to run the program from the Start menu.

1. From the desktop, double-click My Computer and double click the drive icon that contains the operating system files.
2. Double-click the *Program Files* folder.
3. Double-click the *happysad* folder. You should see a single file in this folder named HappySad.exe.
4. Right-click this program file and select Rename.
5. Change the application name to Happy.exe and press Enter.

Once an application has been renamed it is no longer linked to the shortcut added to the Start menu. When the shortcut on the Start menu is selected, Windows will try to repair the program.

6. Click Start and choose the HappySad shortcut. You will see a new copy of the renamed application installed in the *happysad* folder.

Exercise 6

REMOVING SOFTWARE

Removing software is done by selecting the Add/Remove option from the Control Panel. When a program is installed with the Microsoft Installer, uninstall information is saved in Windows. When a program is removed the files, folders, and registry entries should also be removed. In this exercise you will remove the HappySad program installed in a prior exercise.

1. Click Start, then Settings, and then Control Panel.
2. In the Control Panel, double-click the *Add/Remove Programs* icon. You see the Add/Remove Programs screen in Figure 3.18.

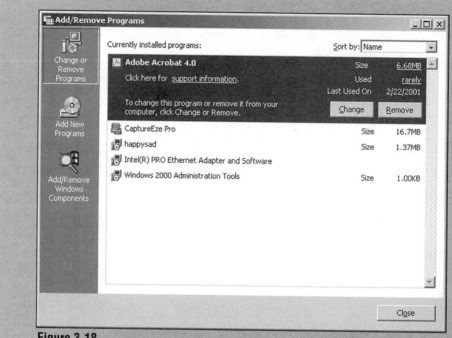

Figure 3.18

The left side of the window contains a list of options for changing or removing programs, adding new programs, or adding and removing Windows components. The first option in the left-hand window displays a list of installed application programs including the happysad program.

3. Click *happysad* and then click the <u>R</u>emove button. The program and program files, including the folders, will be removed.

4. Once the program has been removed, click the Cl<u>o</u>se button to exit the Add/Remove Programs window.

The Windows 2000 Registry

The Windows 2000 registry is a database used to store hardware and software configuration data. Both application programs and Windows 2000 use it to store information. The registry is a core part of Windows 2000; if the registry becomes damaged, Windows 2000 may not even boot. Because the registry is so important to the operation of Windows 2000, network administrators should understand how the registry works, the overall structure of the registry, and how to use registry editing in Windows 2000. In a later chapter you will learn how to back up the registry along with other critical system-related information.

The registry grew out of the early Windows **INI files**. These files had the file name extension *INI* and contained configuration information about the computer system. Application programs used these INI files to configure and locate resources. The problem with INI files was that they were easily changed and were not in a structured (database) format. In Windows 95/98 and Windows NT, Microsoft created a registry database to take the place of INI files.

An example of an INI file is displayed in Figure 3.19.

FIGURE **3.19** *Sample INI File*

```
; for 16-bit app support
[drivers]
wave=mmdrv.dll
timer=timer.drv

[mci]
[driver32]
[386enh]
woafont=dosapp.FON
EGA80WOA.FON=EGA80WOA.FON
EGA40WOA.FON=EGA40WOA.FON
CGA80WOA.FON=CGA80WOA.FON
CGA40WOA.FON=CGA40WOA.FON
```

Windows 2000 still contains INI files. You can find such files in the *WINNT* folder. These files are still present because older programs cannot use the registry and expect to find an INI file.

Registry Logical Structure

The registry is opened when Windows 2000 boots and is used while the operating system is running. Information is both read from and written to the registry. The registry is a hierarchical database and is structured like the file system found in Windows 2000. The registry database is a series of keys. A key, like a folder in the Windows 2000 file system, can contain other keys (folders) or can contain a value (a file).

There are six **root keys** (also called subtrees) in the registry with each root key containing a different set of information. The root keys are—

- HKEY_USERS
- HKEY_CURRENT_USER
- HKEY_CLASSES_ROOT
- HKEY_LOCAL_MACHINE
- HKEY_CURRENT_CONFIG
- HKEY_PERFORMANCE_DATA

Although these root keys appear as separate items when viewed with registry editing software, some of the keys are actually links. A link is a key that appears at the top level of the key structure but in fact points to a subkey located in another key structure. For example, HKEY_CURRENT_USER is a link to a subsection of the HKEY_USERS key structure.

Along with the six root keys, the registry also has a set of hives. A **hive** is a section of the registry structure that is located under a root key containing a set of keys and subkeys. Hives are stored as separate files within Windows 2000. Table 3.3 lists the hives in Windows 2000 and the location of the hive files.

T A B L E 3.3 *Registry Hives and Locations*

Hive Registry	Hive File Path
HKEY_LOCAL_MACHINE\SAM	\winnt\system32\config\sam
HKEY_LOCAL_MACHINE\SYSTEM	\winnt\system32\config\system
HKEY_LOCAL_MACHINE\SOFTWARE	\winnt\system32\config\software
HKEY_LOCAL_MACHINE\SECURITY	\winnt\system32\config\security
HKEY_LOCAL_MACHINE\HARDWARE	Hive dynamically created in memory
HKEY_LOCAL_MACHINE\SYSTEM\Clone	Hive dynamically created in memory
HKEY_USERS\[SID of user]	\documents and settings\[user name]\ntuser.dat
HKEY_USERS\[SID of user]_Classes	\documents and settings\[user name]\Local settings\Application Data\Microsoft\Windows\Usrclass.dat
HKEY_USERS\DEFAULT\	\winnt\system32\config\default

Reportedly, the term *hive* comes from the fact that the data in the hive files are stored in B-Tree format.

Figure 3.20 shows five of the six root keys displayed in the Regedit32 program window. (The HKEY_PERFORMANCE_DATA key is not shown.)

FIGURE 3.20 *Registry Editor with Root Keys*

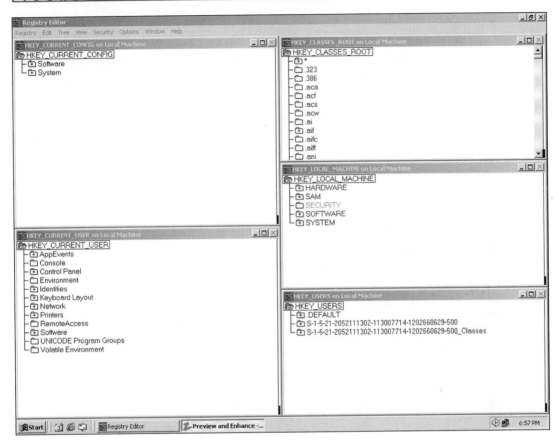

Registry Root Keys

To understand the registry you must understand the kinds of data stored in each root key.

HKEY_USERS This key contains information about the users on the local computer, including user-specific software settings, profiles, and other user-related information. When someone logs on to the local computer, information in this key is used to configure user-specific settings such as system colors. Subkeys located under this root key are identified by a Windows 2000 SID (security ID). This unique number is created by Windows and assigned to user accounts.

HKEY_CURRENT_USER This link is a subsection of the HKEY_USERS key. Information in this key represents the user currently logged on to the system while the information in the HKEY_USERS area contains information about all local users. This key makes it easier for software programs to modify the settings for the user currently logged on.

HKEY_CLASSES_ROOT When an application is installed in Windows 2000, it associates a file type with a program. This kind of information is stored in this root key. For example, when Microsoft Office is installed on a computer it associates a file type, such as *.doc* or *.xls* with an Office application program. When the user double clicks a file with one of these types, the associated program is run and the selected file automatically loaded into the program. The associations between file types and programs are stored in this key.

HKEY_LOCAL_MACHINE This key stores computer configuration information and includes the names and locations of device drivers, network connections, protocols, installed software, and other information Windows needs to operate. Without this key Windows will not even boot.

HKEY_CURRENT_CONFIG This key stores hardware and software configuration information at the current point in time. As changes are made to the system, the information in this key is automatically updated by Windows 2000.

HKEY_PERFORMANCE_DATA This key is used to hold performance data. The information in this key is never really written to disk and is gathered while Windows 2000 runs.

Working with the Registry

Because the registry files are so important to Windows 2000, working with the registry should not be done casually. Damaging part of the registry could result in having to completely reinstall Windows 2000. For this reason, two rules should be followed when working with the registry—

1. Only modify the registry when absolutely necessary, and know *exactly* what you are doing.

2. Back up the registry (along with other parts of Windows 2000) on a regular basis.

A later chapter will cover the steps for backing up and restoring the registry. In the following exercises you will view and change the registry. These exercises will have you work with an unsaved copy of the registry files. BE CAREFUL!

Viewing the Registry

The two programs used to edit the registry are REGEDIT and REGEDT32. The REGEDIT program is found in earlier versions of Windows while REGEDT32 is found in Windows NT and Windows 2000. REGEDIT displays the registry in a single window while REGEDT32 displays the root keys in separate windows. The REGEDIT program is often used to make quick changes to the registry. The main difference between REGEDIT and REGEDT32 is that REGEDIT has a feature that allows you to search for both keys and values while REGEDT32 can only search keys. Because of the simplified display, you will use the REGEDIT program in the following exercise.

Exercise 8

VIEWING AND EDITING THE REGISTRY

In this exercise you will use the REGEDIT program to view the registry, locate a specific key, and delete the key.

1. Click Start, click <u>R</u>un, key **REGEDIT**, and press Enter. You see the REGEDIT screen in Figure 3.21.

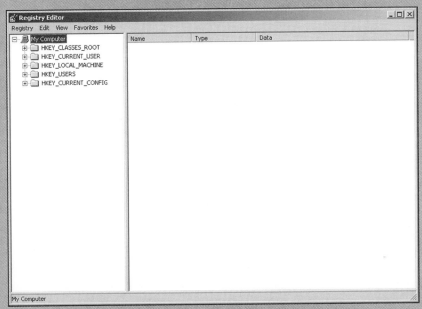

Figure 3.21

The five root keys are displayed as folders, much like Explorer displays folders on the hard disk.

2. Click the plus symbol next to the key *HKEY_LOCAL_MACHINE*. You see subkeys that represent hives (*HARDWARE, SAM, SECURITY, SOFTWARE, SYSTEM*).
3. Click the plus symbol next to the *SOFTWARE* hive. You see a list of keys used by the applications installed on the computer.
4. Scroll down until you see the key named *Savannah Software*.

The happysad program you installed in a prior exercise added this key. When you removed this program, the happysad uninstaller failed to remove its own key from the registry. (Some badly written programs will fail to clean up after themselves.)

5. Click the *Savannah Software* key. In the right side of the window the key value is displayed. This key does not have a value. (See Figure 3.22.)

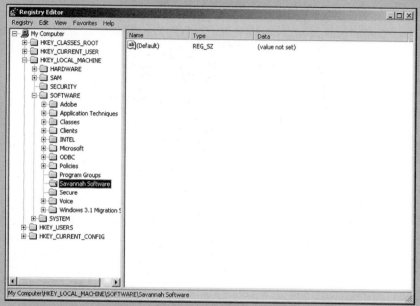

Figure 3.22

6. Make sure the *Savannah Software* key is selected, press the Delete key on the keyboard, and click Yes when asked if you are sure you want to delete. This will remove the key from the *HKEY_LOCAL_MACHINE* root key. The REGEDIT program deletes the key from the registry. **Note:** There is no UNDO key.
7. This key is also stored under the *HKEY_CURRENT_USER* root key and must be removed from both places. Click the plus sign next to *HKEY_CURRENT_USER* and then click the plus sign next to *Software*.
8. Locate the *Savannah Software* key and delete it.
9. Click the registry menu and click Exit to leave the program.

CHAPTER summary

> ➤ In this chapter you learned how to install hardware and software under Windows 2000. Installing hardware often involves loading device drivers. Windows 2000 has simplified this process by using Plug and Play. However, at times you will need to use the Hardware Wizard to manually update drivers. Most current software is installed under the Microsoft Installer. It allows developers to create a script that is run by the Installer program on Windows 2000. The benefit of the Installer program is that if an application has files erased or damaged, Windows will automatically restore the files from the application setup program.

> ➤ The final section of this chapter introduced the Windows registry. This database is used to store various hardware and software configuration information as well as user information. Information is stored in six root keys and saved in a set of hives. Data consists of keys and values, which can be edited or deleted by using the REGEDIT or REGEDT32 programs.

CHAPTER terms

Device drivers	Software used by the operating system to communicate with a hardware device.
DMA	Direct memory addresses: A memory identification used by hardware to communicate with the system.
Driver Signing	A program from Microsoft to ensure that hardware device drivers will work on Windows 2000. A digital signature is issued to acceptable drivers and checked by Windows 2000 prior to installing the driver.
Hive	A section of the registry that is saved as a disk file. Windows 2000 contains eight hives.
I/O port	A number indicating where a hardware device can listen and send data to the system.
INF file	A file that contains instructions to Windows on loading a device driver.
INI files	Text files that contain configuration data used with older versions of software but are not used with current operating systems.
IRQ	Interrupt Request: A hardware/software identification used by devices to get the attention of the CPU.
Root key	One of six keys in the registry that does not contain any parent keys.
WHQL	Windows Hardware Quality Lab: A group at Microsoft that verifies third-party device drivers and issues digital signatures.

CONCEPTS review

Multiple Choice

1. The purpose of an IRQ is:
   a. To allow the user to log on to Windows.
   b. To display colors on the screen.
   c. To communicate with the CPU.
   d. None of the above.

2. A device driver is normally:
   a. Used by Windows to communicate with a hardware device.
   b. Installed along with the hardware device.
   c. Shipped with the hardware device.
   d. All of the above.

3. The Plug and Play system in Windows 2000:
   a. Allocates system resources to hardware devices.
   b. Changes the screen display resolution.
   c. Formats the system hard disk drive.
   d. None of the above.

4. The purpose of driver signing is to:
   a. Allow only Microsoft-written drivers to be used in Windows 2000.
   b. Verify that Microsoft has tested a driver.
   c. Verify that a driver has a current date.
   d. Load a driver more quickly.

5. The organization at Microsoft responsible for driver signing is:
   a. WQL.
   b. WDQL.
   c. WRQL.
   d. WHQL.

6. The following is *not* commonly found in the Windows 2000 Control Panel:
   a. Accessibility Options
   b. Folder Options
   c. Game Controllers
   d. Optimize Hardware

7. The purpose of the Event Viewer in Administrative Tools is to:
   a. Send messages to other computers.
   b. Receive messages from other computers.
   c. Schedule tasks to take place at scheduled times.
   d. None of the above.

8. For what reason should the Add/Remove Hardware Wizard be used to remove hardware?
   a. It is faster than removing by hand.
   b. It removes drives and reallocated resources.
   c. It is the only way to remove hardware.
   d. None of the above.

9. The file type associated with the Microsoft Installer is:
   a. EXE.
   b. MSI.
   c. MIS.
   d. CFG.

10. If an application used the Microsoft Installer to install itself to the system, deleting a critical application file results in:
    a. A message that the application will not run.
    b. A prompt for the user to reinsert the install disk.
    c. The application being uninstalled.
    d. The application being reinstalled.

11. Early precursors to the registry are files with the file type:
    a. CFG.
    b. MSI.
    c. INI.
    d. EXE.

12. In the registry, a key can contain:
    a. Keys and values.
    b. Keys only.
    c. Values only.
    d. Folders only.

13. What is the relationship between HKEY_CURRENT_USER and HKEY_USERS?
    a. HKEY_CURRENT_USER is contained within HKEY_USERS.
    b. HKEY_USERS is contained within HKEY_CURRENT_USER.
    c. They are identical keys.
    d. They are not related.

14. To protect the server from problems, the registry should be:
    a. Deleted and rebuilt on a regular basis.
    b. Set read-only.
    c. Backed up on a regular basis.
    d. All of the above.

15. The registry key HKEY_PERFORMANCE_DATA:
    a. Is not displayed in the registry editing programs.
    b. Is not written to disk.
    c. Holds system performance data.
    d. All of the above.

Fill In

1. The organization at Microsoft that signs drivers is named the
   _____.

2. The Control Panel option used to display information about the current network settings is _____.

3. The type of file containing driver information is
   _____.

4. The registry key that contains information about the hardware installed on the computer is called _____.

5. The two programs used to edit the registry are named
   _____ and _____.

Short Answer

1. List three of the resources Windows 2000 is likely to manage for hardware devices.
2. List three actions Windows 2000 can be set to perform when it finds an unsigned device driver file.
3. List five options that are commonly found in the Control Panel.
4. List the six root keys found in the Windows 2000 registry.
5. Briefly explain the purpose of the HKEY_CURRENT_USER registry key.

LAB exercises

Exercise 1 – Install the Loopback Adapter and Update the Device Driver

1. Right-click My Computer in the desktop.
2. Click the Hardware tab.
3. Click the Hardware Wizard button.
4. Using the Hardware Wizard, add a new device.
5. Select the hardware from a list.
6. Choose the hardware category Network Adapter.
7. Click *Microsoft* from the list of manufacturers and click *Loopback Adapter*.
8. Finish the Hardware Wizard.
9. Open the My Computer Properties dialog box and choose Device Manager.
10. Click *Loopback adapter just added* and then click Properties.
11. Under the Driver tab click the Update Driver button.
12. Start the wizard and display a list of known drivers.
13. Select the loopback driver and install it.

Exercise 2 – List Information for the COM, KEYBOARD, and CPU Devices

1. Click Start and then click Run.
2. In the Run text box key **mmc \winnt\system32\devmgmt.msc** and press Enter.
3. Find the communications port device (under Ports).
4. Write down the port settings and the resources for this device.
5. Locate the keyboard device and write down the resource settings.
6. Locate and write down the date and driver version for the direct memory access controller device.

Exercise 3 – Install the RGB Program and Then Uninstall It

1. Copy the RGB.MSI program to your desktop from the CD that comes with this book.
2. Install the program RGB.MSI.
3. Run the program to ensure it is installed correctly.
4. Rename the setup file from RGB.MSI to RGB.OLD.
5. Run the program again to make sure it works.
6. Locate the program folder *RGB* in the *Program Files* folder.
7. Rename the program RGB.EXE to RGB.OLD.
8. Try to run the program from the Start menu.
9. When done, rename the file RGB.OLD to RGB.MSI in the desktop.
10. Run the program one final time.

Exercise 4 – Locate the RGB Program Information in the Registry Using REGEDT32

1. After performing exercise 3, locate the key for this program in the registry.
2. Delete the program key from the registry (*SampleKey RGB*). Make sure you delete it from the two locations where it will be stored.

PROBLEM SOLVING exercises

Exercise 1

Install the happysad program from your boot drive, delete the happysad program file, and rename the happysad .msi file. Try to run the program. What happened? Why? How can this be fixed?

Exercise 2

Find the Loopback Adapter program in the registry. Where would it be located? What data does Windows save about this device? Print the registry information about the loopback adapter.

Exercise 3

Your company now requires *all* drivers to be signed. How can you enforce this policy? What are the ramifications?

DISK MANAGEMENT 4

Performance Objectives

After completing this chapter you will be able to:

- Describe basic disk terminology
- Mount drives
- Format drives
- Convert between file systems
- Compress files
- Describe dynamic disk terminology
- Upgrade basic disks to dynamic disks
- Use volumes
- Identify and discuss RAID disk drives
- Perform disk maintenance

Introduction

Disk management is a necessary but sometimes frustrating task for network administrators. Because the operations of the disk drives on the network server are so critical, the drives must be carefully configured and maintained. Even though much of Windows 2000 disk management will look familiar to Windows NT 4 veterans, some new tools in Windows 2000 will prove helpful. They include a disk management tool that centralizes most of the administrative tasks and makes it possible to manage disks on remote systems, to compress and encrypt files and folders, and to use dynamic disks.

The primary tool used to manage disks under Windows 2000 is the disk management tool. This tool can be accessed through the Computer Management window or as a snap-in to a custom Microsoft Management Console (MMC). In this chapter you will use this tool through the Computer Management window. Creating a custom MMC will be discussed in a later chapter.

Windows 2000 supports two types of disks: basic and dynamic. Basic disks are backward compatible with older operating systems such as Windows 95/98 and older versions of Windows NT. Dynamic disks are a new type of disk that provide extra capabilities but are only available to Windows 2000 systems. Basic disks are the default setting for new installations of Windows 2000 and upgrades from Windows NT. Such systems can be reconfigured later to support dynamic disks. This chapter initially covers basic disks and later discusses dynamic disks.

Basic Disk Concepts and Terminology

In order to perform disk management you need to understand how hard disks work and know some of the terminology. The most fundamental unit of disk management is the **physical disk,** which is the actual piece of hardware installed on a computer system. Physical disks are purchased with a certain storage capacity that cannot be changed. One way to increase the amount of storage on a server is to add additional physical disks.

When a physical disk is formatted it is divided into **tracks** and **sectors**. A track is a section of the physical disk on which data is stored. Tracks are subdivided into sectors. Each track and sector is identified by a number, which the operating system and physical disk read/write software use to read and write data. Each sector is assigned 512 bytes. The allocation unit will consist of one or more sectors. (See Figure 4.1.)

FIGURE 4.1 *Tracks and Sectors*

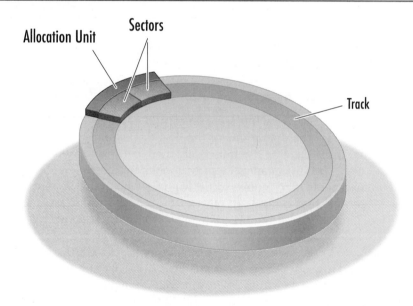

When using basic disks, the physical hard drive can be logically divided into areas called **partitions**. If the disk were a house, the partitions would be the rooms in that house. The process of creating partitions on a hard disk generates a **master boot record** (**MBR**) and a **partition table**. The master boot record is located in the first sector of the first track of the hard disk. When the computer boots, the system basic input/output system (BIOS) software looks at the MBR to get enough information to access the disk. The MBR contains the partition table, which is like a table of contents for the disk. This table contains information about how many partitions the disk has and their size and location.

Primary, Extended, and Active Partitions and Logical Drives

Two types of partitions can be created on a physical disk: *primary* and *extended*. A **primary partition** is a partition that can boot an operating system. Windows 2000 automatically creates a primary partition when it is installed. The size of the primary partition can be set when the disk is formatted. Up to four primary partitions can be created. This enables you to have multiple operating systems such as OS/2, Linux, DOS, and Windows 2000 loaded on the same hard disk at the same time. In order to boot different operating systems you would need a program that would allow you to change which primary partition was the *active* partition. The **active partition** is the partition that will be automatically used during the boot process.

If you do not have the maximum amount of four primary partitions and you have additional space on your physical disk that is not assigned to a primary partition, you can use the space to create a second type of partition called an *extended partition*. An **extended partition** cannot be used to boot an operating system and you can only create one extended partition on each physical disk. However, you can divide an extended partition further into logical drives. Logical drives can be very handy in helping you to organize your data. For example, you could keep the company payroll data on one logical drive and the marketing data on another.

Figure 4.2 illustrates a physical disk with two primary partitions and an extended partition divided into two logical drives.

F I G U R E **4.2** *MBR, Active Partitions, and Boot Manager*

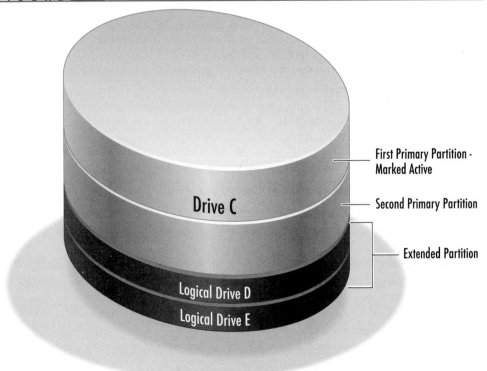

First Primary Partition - Marked Active

Second Primary Partition

Extended Partition

Drive C

Logical Drive D

Logical Drive E

Windows 2000 comes with a simple boot manager that allows multiple Windows operating systems to boot from a single primary partition. When Windows 2000 is installed on a computer that has Windows 95/98, this boot manager is automatically installed and a simple boot menu created. During subsequent boot processes, a DOS menu allows the user to select which operating system to boot from. To create a multiboot computer with Windows 95/98 and Windows 2000, you need to take the following steps:

1. Format the hard drive with two logical drives C and D by using the DOS Fdisk command. (Or use two physical hard drives if they are available.)
2. Install Windows 95/98 on the first drive.
3. Install Windows 2000 on the second drive. During the installation process, Windows 2000 will automatically add the boot manager and create a BOOT.INI file on drive C. The format of the BOOT.INI file is detailed in Chapter 2.
4. After installing Windows 2000 and rebooting, you will see the boot manager menu prompting you to select either Windows 2000 or Windows 95/98.

System and Boot Partitions

Microsoft calls the primary partition where the boot files for Windows 2000 are stored the **system partition**. Although the boot files for Windows 2000 must be stored on the primary active partition, the majority of the operating system files for Windows 2000 can be located either on the same partition as the boot files or on a different partition. The partition that holds the operating system files is called the **boot partition**. (This labeling may seem a bit backward—the system partition holds the boot files and the boot partition holds the system files!) If the system and boot files are located on the same partition, that partition is both the system *and* the boot partition.

Disk Management Tool

The disk management tool is used to manage disks and disk partitions. This tool is found in the Disk Management menu and gives you the ability to view information about a disk partition, mark partitions as active, format partitions, and delete partitions. Although the disk management tool contains some built-in safeguards, it can still be dangerous. Always double-check before performing tasks with the disk management tool.

Exercise 1

CREATING AN EXTENDED PARTITION

In this exercise you will use the Create Partition Wizard in the disk management tool to create an extended partition. *(Note: To complete the following exercise you must be using a computer with unallocated hard disk space.)* Once the extended partition has been created, you will create a logical drive in the next exercise.

1. Open the computer management tool by clicking Start, Programs, Administrative Tools, and Computer Management.
2. Click the plus sign next to the *Storage* icon if the storage tool is not already expanded.
3. Double-click the *Disk Management* folder. You will see a screen similar to what is shown in Figure 4.3. (If this is the first time the disk management tool has been run you may be taken into a wizard. Click Cancel to leave the wizard.)

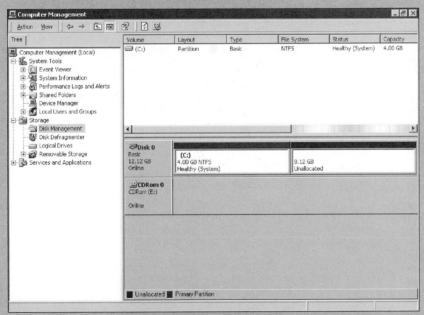

Figure 4.3

4. Right-click the unallocated space block and select the drop-down menu option Create Partition. (The unallocated space block has a black border and the words "Unallocated.")
5. Click the Next button to start the Create Partition Wizard (Figure 4.4).

Figure 4.4

6. Click *Extended partition* and then click Next (Figure 4.5).

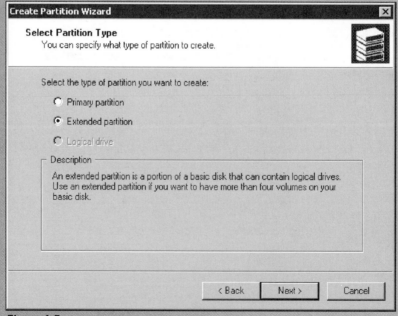

Figure 4.5

The extended partition is that area of the disk on which additional drives can be created. The primary partition, which you do not want to create, holds the operating system files.

7. Key the amount of disk space you wish to include in the extended partition. Note that the amount of space to allocate must be less than or equal to the amount available that is unallocated. Click Next after entering this number (Figure 4.6).

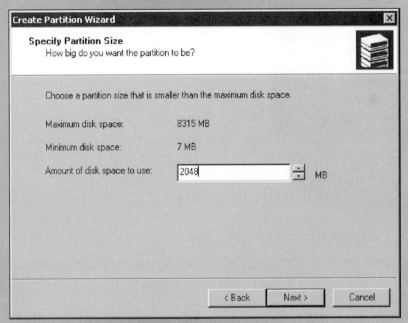

Figure 4.6

8. At the Completing the Create Partition Wizard screen, you should see the details about the partition you just created (Figure 4.7). Review the statistics. If something is wrong you can use the Back button to return to the proper screen and correct the error. If everything is correct, click Finish.

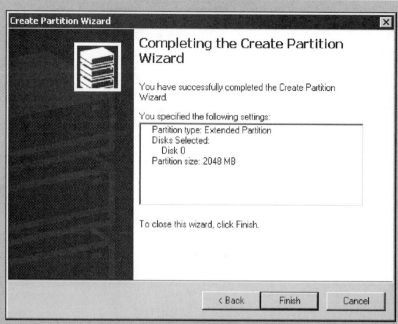

Figure 4.7

In the Computer Management screen you will now see the new partition designated as Free Space (Figure 4.8).

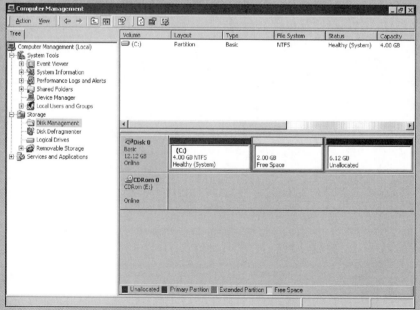

Figure 4.8

In Microsoft terminology *free space* refers to space contained in an extended partition that does not have logical drives; it is not simply unused space. *Unallocated space* is space that does not belong to a partition.

Now that you have created an extended partition, you can proceed to create logical drives within that partition. These drives can either be assigned drive letters or mounted. The next section will show you how to mount a drive.

Volume Mount Points and Mounting Drives

In previous versions of Windows, whenever a partition or logical drive was created it had to be assigned a drive letter in order to be accessed. For example, the primary partition on most personal computers is called the C drive. Without the drive letter this part of the hard disk could not be accessed. Network drives also had to be given a drive letter before they could be used. The limitation of this system lies in the fact that the Roman alphabet contains only 26 letters.

Windows 2000 allows you to map a network drive, or removable drive such as a zip disk, to an empty folder instead of requiring the use of a drive letter. This capability is achieved by using a volume mount point. A **volume mount point** allows you to make a disk volume appear as a local folder. Application programs that use folders to save and read data will continue to work correctly, but the data going into the folder is actually being stored on the disk volume.

For example, suppose you want to centralize the financial data with which your network users work. The application programs (such as Excel) store data into a local folder named *Finance*. A volume mount point for a disk volume on a network server could be created and attached to the *Finance* folder. (The folder must be empty before creating a volume mount point.) The *Finance* folder will appear to be a regular local folder, but all activity in that *Finance* folder will actually be directed back to the disk volume on the network server. Copying a file into the *Finance* folder results in the file being stored on the server instead of on your local drive.

Exercise 2

MOUNTING A DRIVE

In the following exercise you will create a logical drive and a volume mount point for the drive. (This can be done for new drives or for existing drives. An exercise to mount an existing drive can be found at the end of this chapter.) In this exercise you mount the Budget logical drive to an empty folder named *Finance* located on the C drive of your local machine. In a large network it is more likely that you would mount the Budget logical drive to a folder on a different machine.

You first create an empty folder for mounting a drive.

1. Open your computer management tool. (Click Start, Programs, Administrative Tools, Computer Management.) Minimize your Computer Management screen by clicking the minus sign in the top right corner of your screen.
2. Double-click the *My Computer* icon to open it.
3. Double-click the *Local Disk (C:)* icon (or whatever local drive you are using) to open it.
4. Click File, New, and Folder.
5. Rename the newly created folder *Finance*. The C drive of your local machine will now appear as it does in Figure 4.9.

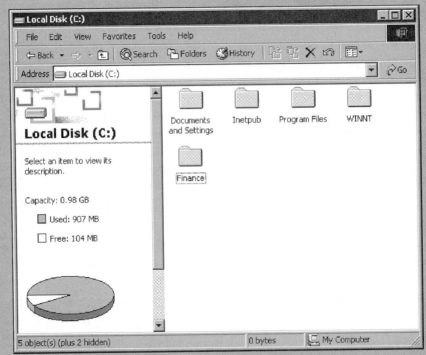

Figure 4.9

You will now use the Computer Management window to begin creating your logical drive.

6. Open the Computer Management window by clicking on the Computer Management tab on the toolbar and then click the *Storage Management* folder under the Storage option.

7. Right-click the bar representing the newly created free disk space (created in the previous exercise) and click the Create Logical Drive option.

8. Click Next at the Create Partition Wizard. (No, you are not actually creating a new partition; it is just how the welcome screen appears!)

9. *Logical drive* should be the only available option. Click Next to continue.

10. Accept the default of using all of your disk space for the partition and click Next. Your screen will now look as it does in Figure 4.10.

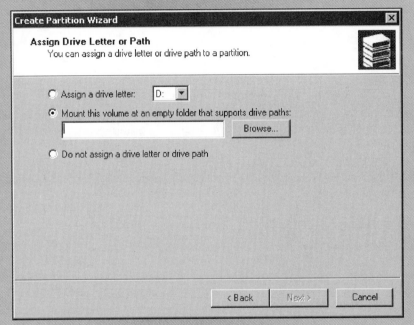

Figure 4.10

11. You are given the option of mounting this newly created disk partition to a specific folder. Click *Mount this volume at an empty folder that supports drive paths*.

12. Click the Browse button and locate the empty *Finance* folder on the C drive (Figure 4.11), and then click OK to select this folder.

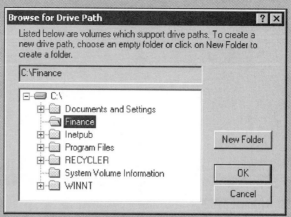

Figure 4.11

13. At the Create Partition Wizard screen click Next to continue.
14. You will now be presented with the Format menu. Accept the default to format this partition with NTFS and default allocation unit size.
15. Key **Budget** as the volume label and click Next.
16. Review the summary information and then click Finish. The space is now designated as a logical drive instead of free space in the Computer Management window. It may take several minutes for the format to complete.
17. Once the format is complete, open My Computer by clicking the folder tab on the taskbar. Your *Finance* folder now appears as a drive (Figure 4.12). This indicates that the object is a volume mount point.

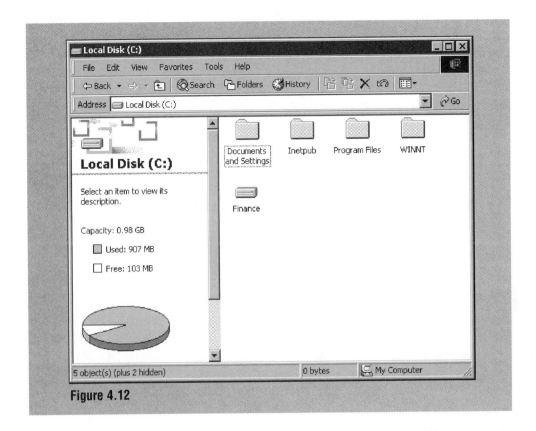

Figure 4.12

Formatting and File Systems

As you progressed through the wizard to create and mount a logical drive, you chose to format the drive with the NTFS file system. Before a partition or volume can be used it must be formatted. It can either be formatted when it is created or at a later time. Before formatting a disk partition, you must first decide what file system to use. Windows 2000 supports the FAT16, FAT32, and NTFS file systems. The many advantages to using the NTFS file system on a Windows 2000 computer include the following:

- File and folder compression
- Encryption (discussed in detail in the security chapter)
- Additional security for data (discussed in the security chapter)
- Disk quotas
- More efficient use of disk space

Also, NTFS keeps a log, called a *change journal*, of actions performed on the disk. The change journal is used to rebuild disk information. It helps to prevent volume corruption when power is lost or the server comes down without going through a proper shutdown process.

All three file systems support fault-tolerant options such as disk mirroring and stripe sets with parity. All three file systems are also supported on both basic and dynamic disks.

With all the advantages of NTFS, you would probably only choose a FAT file system (FAT16 or FAT32) if you were dual booting with another operating system and both operating systems had to utilize the same disk space. DOS and all of the Windows operating systems can read FAT16. Windows 95 OSR2 and Windows 2000 can read FAT32. Windows NT and versions of Windows previous to Windows 95 OSR2 will not read FAT32. If you are not sure about what format to use, select the FAT file system. You can, if necessary, always convert to NTFS at a later time.

If performance is an issue on your machine you may want to move your swap file to a FAT partition. The swap file is more efficient on a FAT partition. Moving a swap file will be discussed in the chapter on performance tuning, disaster planning, and recovery.

Formatting a Disk Drive

The actual format process is simple and can be accomplished in several ways. In Exercise 2 you formatted a logical drive during creation, but you could have also chosen not to format the drive until a later time. In either My Computer or Explorer, when you right-click on a disk you see the Format option on the pop-up menu. This option allows you to format the drive. If you attempt to access a drive that has not been formatted you will be prompted with the dialog box in Figure 4.13 to format the drive.

FIGURE 4.13 *Format Dialog Box*

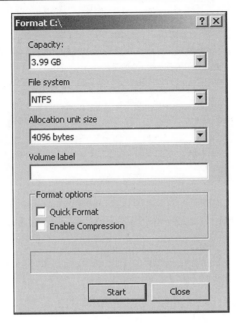

The default values are as follows:

- Capacity: how much data the volume can hold

- File system: type of file system to be written to the volume

- Allocation unit size: fixed size to make the sectors when formatting

- Volume label: a name to be applied to the volume up to 11 characters when formatting with FAT16 or FAT32 and up to 32 characters when formatting with NTFS

- Quick Format: removes files from a previously formatted volume and does not check for bad sectors

- Enable Compression: compresses the files on the volume and is only available when using NTFS

Most of the format options have default values. Capacity is determined from the physical disk, and the default allocation unit size is determined by selecting the size that results in the most efficient use of the disk, depending on the size of the disk and the file system selected. The user can enter the volume label. Both regular formatting and using the Quick Format option will erase all data currently on the disk, but a Quick Format will not check the disk for bad sectors. Performing a full format is recommended.

The allocation unit size is the smallest amount of disk space that can be used to store a file. Therefore, when information is written or read from the disk, it is done within this fixed amount of space. For example, if the allocation unit size is set to 4096 bytes and a file is only 256 bytes, an entire allocation unit is reserved to store the file, even if the file does not fill the space. Also, when information is read from the disk, it is done in allocation unit sizes. Therefore larger allocation units speed up disk reads. Different allocation unit sizes will affect how the disk is used. If the disk will hold many small files, then the allocation unit size should be set low. If the disk will hold database records the allocation unit size should be set high so that applications will read more information from each disk sector.

To format a disk from a command prompt, you would use the following command:

```
Format driveletter /fs:filesystem /v:volume name /q
/a:sector size /c /x
```

The *filesystem* option must either be FAT, FAT32 or NTFS. The *volume name* is the name to be assigned to the volume. The **/q** option performs a quick format. The *sector size* option sets the fixed size of the disk sectors. The **/c** option sets the volume as compressed. The **/x** option unmounts the volume first before formatting.

For example:

```
Format d: /fs:fat32 /v:DiskD
```

formats drive D with the FAT32 file system and with the label *DiskD*.

```
Format e: /fs:ntfs /v:AppsDiskE /a:512
```

formats drive E with NTFS, sets the disk label to *AppsDiskE,* and sets the sector allocation size to 512 bytes.

Converting between File Systems

Given the benefits of NTFS, it is preferable to run Windows 2000 on a disk with this format. A new disk can be formatted with the NTFS file system, but it is sometimes necessary to convert from a FAT16 or FAT32 file system to NTFS, which can be done without losing data by using the Convert utility. However, you cannot convert back from NTFS to FAT16 or FAT32. Make sure you really want to convert before you do it!

A disk can be converted from FAT16 or FAT32 to NTFS only from the command prompt:

```
convert driveletter: /fs:ntfs
```

For example, to convert disk drive D from FAT32 to NTFS you would open a command prompt and key:

```
convert D: /fs:ntfs
```

If you are attempting to convert the drive on which the system files are located you will need to reboot your system to finish the conversion.

The NTFS file system included with Windows 2000 is NTFS version 5 and is different from NTFS version 4, which is included with Windows NT 4. These two versions of NTFS are not perfectly compatible. If you are trying to dual boot Windows NT 4 and Windows 2000 it can get messy. Windows 2000 will automatically upgrade any NTFS 4 partitions it finds to Windows 2000 NTFS partitions. It will not ask if you want to upgrade, nor will it give you a chance to stop the upgrade. The problem is that the original Windows NT 4 cannot read the Windows 2000 version of NTFS. Only if Windows NT 4 Service Pack 4 has been loaded can Windows NT 4 access Windows 2000 NTFS volumes. Even with Service Pack 4, however, problems remain. Windows NT 4 will not be able to read encrypted files or mounted volumes on Windows 2000, nor will it pay attention to disk quotas. In addition, actions preformed by Windows NT 4 on the Windows 2000 disks will not be tracked by the change journal.

To set up a Windows 2000 and Windows 95/98 dual boot system and still use NTFS you can partition your drive into pieces. The primary active partition needs to be FAT16 or FAT32 because it is shared by both operating systems. Therefore, you should first install Windows 95/98 before installing Windows 2000. During the Windows 2000 install process, the partition on which Windows 2000 will be installed can be formatted for NTFS.

File Compression

Another important disk management option in Windows 2000 is compression. Windows 2000 supports file and/or folder compression under the NTFS file system. A file compressed on a Windows 2000 system will be slightly larger than the same file compressed on a Windows 95/98 system, but the compression algorithm works much faster under Windows 2000. Once you have turned on compression for a particular file, that file will be automatically compressed each time it is saved and decompressed each time it is opened. If you choose to set compression on a folder, all the files created in or copied to that folder will be automatically compressed. However, any files that already existed before compression was applied to the folder will remain uncompressed. By default, file or folder compression is turned off.

Compression is a property that can be set for files and folders by right-clicking the file or folder and clicking Properties. Compression can also be done from the command line. To compress from the command line use the compact command. Key **compact** /? at a command line to see help for this command. If you simply key **compact** with no parameters, you will see the current status of the drive with reference to which files and folders are compacted.

Exercise 3

COMPRESSING A FILE

In this exercise you compress a file by setting the file property.

1. Create a directory on your NTFS drive called Compressed Files.
2. Copy the files Prairie Wind.bmp, Santa Fe Stucco.bmp, and Soap Bubbles.bmp from the *WINNT* folder (or the CD that comes with your textbook) to the *Compressed Files* folder.
3. Right-click the Prairie Wind file and click Properties. You see the dialog box in Figure 4.14.

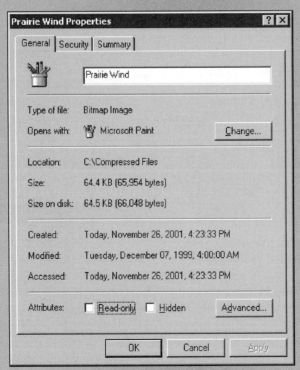

Figure 4.14

4. Make sure you have the General tab selected and note the size of the file. Click the Advanced button to open the Advanced Attributes dialog box shown in Figure 4.15.

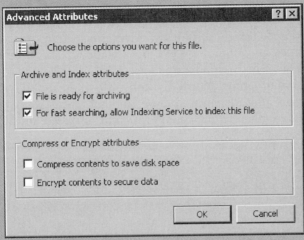

Figure 4.15

5. Click the *Compress contents to save disk space* check box and click OK to close the Advanced Attributes dialog box.
6. Click OK to close the Properties dialog box and wait a minute for the file to compress.
7. Right-click the Prairie Wind file again and click Properties.
8. Make sure you have the General tab selected and note the new size of the file. The Size and the Size on disk numbers should be different. Size lists the actual size of the file and Size on disk lists the compressed size.

This same procedure can be used for folders. Right-click the folder, click Properties, and then click the Advanced button within the General tab. You will see the option *Compress contents to save disk space* is selected. All existing files in the folder are *not* compressed, but new files saved to, copied to, or moved to the folder are automatically compressed.

Dynamic Disks

Windows 2000 supports two types of disks: basic and dynamic. **Basic disks** are backward compatible with older operating systems, such as Windows 95/98 and prior versions of Windows NT. When installing Windows 2000 or upgrading an old NT system, the default type of disk will be the basic disk system. Basic disks can be upgraded to dynamic disks.

To this point in the chapter you have been working with basic disks. Functions such as formatting, compression, and mounting drives work in the same manner for both basic and **dynamic disks**. However, the terminology used with dynamic disks is different from that used with basic disks. The definition of a physical disk is the same but, instead of partitions, dynamic disks only have volumes.

Working with volumes has several advantages over working with partitions and logical drives. Once partitions and logical drives are created, their size cannot be changed without deleting all data on the drive, while volume sizes can be increased without deleting data. Also, partitions and logical drives are limited to a single physical disk. In contrast, volumes are logical divisions, which means that a single volume can be created across multiple physical disks. Another advantage of dynamic disks is the ability to create fault-tolerant volumes such as mirrored and RAID5 volumes.

If you upgrade a system that has volume, mirrored, or stripe sets created in an older version of Windows NT, those sets will continue to function on a basic disk in Windows 2000.

Upgrading Basic to Dynamic Disks

If you want to fully use the fault-tolerant features of Windows 2000 you will need to upgrade from basic disks to dynamic disks. Fault-tolerant features, such as disk mirroring and RAID (see page 137), become easy to manage with dynamic disks. During conversion from basic to dynamic disks, the logical drives and partitions are converted to volumes. After conversion, logical drives and the primary partitions become simple volumes, volume sets become spanned volumes, and the various RAID sets become RAID volumes.

Before converting to dynamic disks you need to consider the following ramifications to make sure you are making the right choice for your situation:

- Dynamic disks really only provide an advantage when you have multiple disks.

- Dynamic disks cannot be used, or even seen, with operating systems other than Windows 2000. You will not want to upgrade a dual-boot system.

- You cannot upgrade a Windows NT 4 system partition that contains NT4 RAID volumes.

- You cannot extend volumes that were originally created on a basic disk. Only volumes that were created on dynamic disks can be extended.

- You cannot install Windows 2000 on a disk that was originally set as dynamic. Windows 2000 can only be installed on a basic disk or a basic disk that has been converted to a dynamic disk.

- Not all drives can be converted to dynamic disks. (Laptops and removable drives are not supported as dynamic disks without an unsupported registry change.)

- Dynamic disks can be converted back to basic disks but only after deleting all volumes. The data on these volumes will be lost. To keep data, back up volumes before doing this type of conversion.

- You cannot convert a disk that does not have at least 1 MB of free space.

Once you have decided to change to dynamic disks, the conversion process is simple. The following simulation illustrates this conversion process.

Exercise 4

CREATING A DYNAMIC DISK

This exercise should only be performed on a computer that can be reformatted. Use the Chapter 4 Simulation of this exercise from the CD that comes with your textbook if you are using a computer that cannot be reformatted.

1. Open the *Disk Management* folder in the Computer Management tool (Figure 4.16).

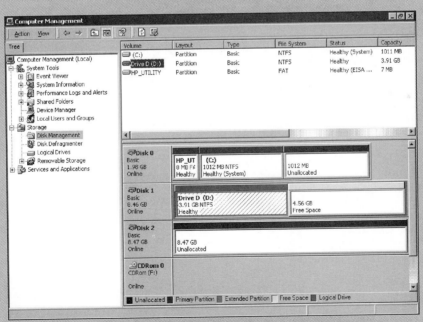

Figure 4.16

2. Right-click the gray rectangle on the left side of the bar that identifies the disk number you wish to convert, and then click Upgrade to Dynamic Disk (Figure 4.17).

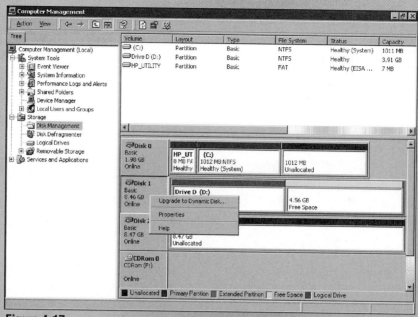

Figure 4.17

3. You will see an Upgrade to Dynamic Disk dialog box that shows the disks in the system. Make sure the box is checked next to the disk number you wish to upgrade and then click OK (Figure 4.18).

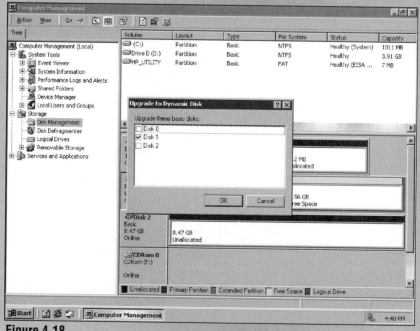

Figure 4.18

4. If partitions or logical drives are present on the disk, you will see a detailed view of the disk. Click Upgrade to continue. (If no partitions or logical drives are present the upgrade will take place immediately with no other steps necessary.)
5. When you receive a warning message, click Yes to acknowledge that older versions of Windows will not be able to use the dynamic disk.
6. Click Yes to acknowledge that all mounted volumes will be disconnected. Your drive will now be labeled Dynamic. Any free space will be changed to unallocated, and logical drives will be converted to simple volumes. If you upgrade a disk that has open files, such as system files, the upgrade will not complete until the next time you boot your computer.

Disk Volumes

A **volume** in a dynamic disk replaces partitions and logical drives in a basic disk. The two types of volumes that can be created on a dynamic disk are simple volumes and spanned volumes. A *simple volume* resides on a single physical disk. A *spanned volume* can reside on more than one physical disk.

Consider a server with two 4-GB physical drives installed. On the first drive, 3 GB are used by the operating system and 1 GB is used as a simple volume to hold payroll data. On the second drive the marketing group uses 1 GB of space and the remaining 3 GB are unallocated (Figure 4.19).

FIGURE **4.19** *Two Drives Not Spanned*

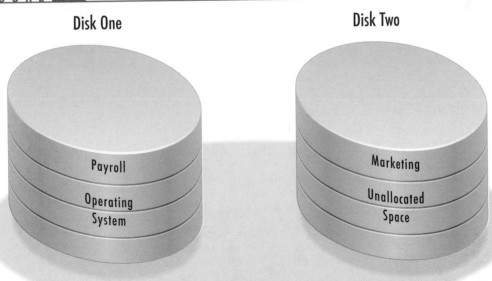

Disk One · Disk Two

Payroll · Operating System

Marketing · Unallocated Space

The company changes payroll systems and needs 4 GB of space for the new software. The second drive has only 3 GB left, so the options are to buy another hard disk or create a volume. A volume will logically join the unallocated space on the second disk with the 1 GB of payroll data on the first disk to give you the needed 4 GB of space. The payroll application and the users accessing the volume will not be aware that the payroll data is technically located on two different physical disks (Figure 4.20).

FIGURE 4.20 *Spanned Volume*

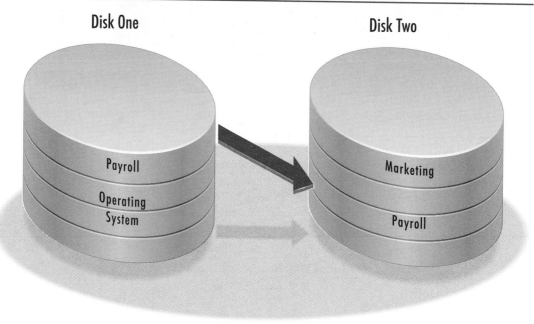

Disk One   Disk Two

Payroll

Operating System

Marketing

Payroll

The disadvantage of using a volume is the lack of fault tolerance. In this example, if one of the two disks crashes, all the payroll data would be lost. Up to 32 disks can be included in a volume, but the more disks that are included the more likely the chance that one will go bad and the entire volume will be lost. Also, a volume does not significantly increase read or write times because the disk heads are being used consecutively, not concurrently. Each disk is filled with data before anything is written to the next disk.

Simple and spanned volumes can be created on either FAT or NTFS partitions; however FAT volumes cannot be expanded. If you want to expand an already existing FAT volume, you must convert the partition to NTFS. Also, volumes cannot be reduced in size.

RAID

If you have more than one disk on your system you may employ storage options such as mirror sets and stripe sets, also known as different levels of RAID. **RAID** stands for **redundant array of inexpensive disks** or **redundant array of independent disks** (depending on whom you ask). It is a standard disk storage format supported by the computer industry. RAID allows the use of multiple disks in different configurations to improve fault tolerance, access times, space utilization, or some combination of the three. RAID actually has six levels, but levels 0, 1, and 5 are the most commonly used and the only levels supported by Microsoft. RAID 1 and RAID 5 are fault tolerant, while RAID 0 is not fault tolerant.

> The reason RAID levels 2, 3, and 4 are not supported is because each is a subset of RAID 5. RAID 5 has all of their features plus more capabilities.

RAID 0 is also known as a stripe set without parity. (**Parity** is the process of using a data bit to verify other data bits when they are written to a hard disk.) A **stripe set** works exactly the same way as a volume, which was discussed earlier. Like volumes, stripe sets consist of combined sections from different disks, but only disk sections that are the same size. In the earlier example a 1-GB volume was combined with a 3-GB space to get a 4-GB volume. A stripe set under the same conditions would be only a 2-GB stripe set, because the stripe set could only use 1 GB of the 3-GB space. The size of the stripe must be the same on all disks.

A second difference between stripe sets and volumes is access times. The entire stripe on one disk does not need to be full in order for the stripe set to write to the second disk. It means that all disk heads are working more of the time. Like a volume, however, RAID 0 is not fault tolerant.

RAID 1 is also called *disk mirroring*. It is the first level of RAID that provides fault tolerance. Whole disks or partitions on a disk can be mirrored using RAID 1. Mirroring works with pairs of disks or partitions. Whatever is written to the first disk or partition also is written automatically to the second. This feature results in two complete copies of information at all times, so if one disk stops working a copy of the data from the second disk can be used. Disk mirroring also speeds up read requests because the read heads for both disks will search for the requested information and the first one to find it will return the data. The disadvantage of disk mirroring is that you must purchase twice as much disk space.

Disk mirroring still has the potential for a single point of failure. If the two disks share a controller and the controller fails, you will not be able to retrieve data until the controller is replaced. Even though the data will not be lost, you will lose time. To solve this problem, each disk should be placed on a separate controller. Even if one controller fails, the system will continue to work. This method of disk mirroring is called *disk duplexing*.

RAID 5 is disk striping with parity. This option is similar to RAID 0 but includes fault tolerance. To use RAID 5 the computer needs at least three different disks or partitions. RAID 5 works by including not only data on the disks but also a code that allows it to recover from the loss of a single disk in the RAID 5 array. Table 4.1 shows a simplified example of how RAID 5 works. Assume the system is using even parity, that is, the sum of all data bits must be an even number. (Odd parity means the sum of the data bits is odd.)

T A B L E 4.1 *An Example of RAID 5*

	DISK 1	DISK 2	DISK 3
Stripe A	1 data	1 data	0 parity
Stripe B	1 data	1 parity	0 data
Stripe C	0 parity	1 data	1 data

As data is written, it is written across all the disks in the stripe set. In stripe A the data bits are written to disk 1 and disk 2 and the parity bit is written to disk 3. Because the system is running even parity and the data bits add up to be an even number (2), the parity bit on disk 3 is set to 0. On stripe B the data bits are written to disk 1 and disk 3. Because the data bits add up to an odd number (1), the parity bit must be a 1 to maintain the even parity. (1 bit on disk 1 plus 0 bit on disk 3 is odd so the parity bit on disk 2 must be set to 1 to make the addition of all three data bits even.) On the C stripe, disks 2 and 3 both hold a data bit of 1, so a 0 parity bit is written to disk 1.

If disk 3 were to fail and be replaced, the RAID system would go through calculations to figure out what data the failed disk contained. Stripe A has 2 data bits left so no data was lost from stripe A. Stripe B has 1 data bit and 1 parity bit, which equals 2, an even number, which means that the data bit lost on disk 3 had to be a 0. If it had been a 1 the total of the row would have been 3, which is an odd number, and not allowed in even parity. Stripe C has a remaining 0 parity bit and 1 data bit, meaning the lost data bit must have been a 1. RAID 5 will then convert the parity bits on the working disks to their appropriate data values and the system will continue to function.

You can include as many as 32 disks in a RAID 5 array. The more disks you include the less space is wasted on the overhead of parity bits. If you have three disks you will lose one third of your space to parity, if you have four disks you will lose only one fourth. Like RAID 0, the pieces of disk included in a RAID 5 array must be the same size.

Exercise 5

CREATE A RAID VOLUME

In the following exercise you will format a disk for RAID 5. To complete this exercise you must have three disks or partitions and unallocated space on each disk or partition.

1. Click Start, Programs, Administrative Tools, Computer Management.
2. Click the plus sign next to the *Storage* icon to expand it.
3. Double-click the *Disk Management* icon.
4. Right-click *Unallocated space on Disk 0* and then click Create Volume.
5. At the Welcome to the Create Volume Wizard, click Next.
6. Click the button for RAID-5 Volume and click Next.
7. At the select disk window, click *Disk 1* and *Disk 2* to highlight them and then click Add.
8. Note what amount of space will be used on each disk and click Next.
9. Accept the default drive letter D and click Next.
10. Select the option to format the volume using the NTFS file system and default allocation unit size; label the volume *RAID 5* and click Next.
11. Check the Summary for accuracy and then click Finish.
12. After several minutes spent formatting, your RAID 5 array should appear up and healthy.

In a RAID 5 system it is important to pay attention to the hard disks. If more than one disk fails, all the information on the entire stripe set will be lost. Make sure to replace failed disks and rebuild the RAID array as soon as possible. Many servers will have colored lights on the front panel that indicate the health of the disks; the lights will go from green to red when there is a failure.

Because the RAID array will continue to function with one failed disk, you may not notice that a disk has failed.

The status of the disk volumes can also be checked using the disk management tool. Sometimes a problem with a volume indicates a problem with the disk. A bar representing the disk contains a status message. Table 4.2 lists the possible status messages and what they mean.

Healthy	The volume is performing normally with no problems.
Healthy (At Risk)	The dynamic volume is performing normally; however, the disk itself is experiencing I/O errors. (Basic disks will not display this warning.)
Failed Redundancy	The volume is functioning but no longer fault tolerant. The usual cause is a failed or offline disk.
Failed Redundancy (At Risk)	The dynamic volume is functioning but no longer fault tolerant, and I/O errors have been detected on one of the remaining functioning disks. (Basic disks will not display this warning.)
Failed	The volume is not functioning.
Missing	A dynamic disk is offline or corrupted.
Regenerating	The process of repairing a failed fault-tolerant configuration is taking place after the damaged disk is replaced.

All of the RAID levels discussed in this chapter can be handled by the Windows 2000 operating system. When such disk management options are installed they are called *software RAID*. The operating system creates and maintains the RAID volumes, meaning that the system or boot partitions cannot be included in either a stripe set or a stripe set with parity when using software RAID. Because a mirror set includes a complete copy of the operating system for Windows 2000 to boot from, the system and boot volumes can be included in a mirror set.

Because using the Windows 2000 software RAID limits your fault tolerance options and also puts a load on the operating system, it is preferable to use hardware RAID. *Hardware RAID* consists of a special disk controller and associated controller firmware that perform RAID functions.

Firmware is software that is part of a hardware device. It is burned into EPROM chips that are part of a hardware device, such as a disk controller.

Many of today's servers can use such hardware RAID for mirroring and striping at the hardware level, so the operating system does not need to be involved. This method of implementing RAID allows you to include both system and boot files in the RAID array. It also removes the strain of maintaining fault tolerance from the operating system. Using RAID-capable hardware is more expensive than using the operating system for software RAID, but it is worth the money. If you purchase a server that has hot-swappable disks in a RAID array, and one of the disks goes bad, all you need to do is pull the damaged disk out and replace it with a new disk. A hot-swappable RAID system will automatically rebuild the RAID array and your server will never be out of commission.

Disk Maintenance: Check Disk

Several tools included with Windows 2000 help keep your disks working efficiently. These tools do not deal with actual hardware problems but with issues surrounding the way data is stored on those disks. The first tool has been around since the early days of DOS. It is called *Chkdsk*, which is short for check disk. The Chkdsk program has changed over the years, and earlier versions of Chkdsk for other operating systems will not work on Windows 2000. However, the function of the program is basically the same. When run, Chkdsk makes several passes over the disk and does the following:

- Tests each sector, determining whether the sector is good and can be used for data storage
- Determines whether each directory in the directory structure is properly documented in the master file table (MFT); the MFT is similar to the table of contents of a book, with each directory having an entry
- Verifies where each file is located on the disk
- Determines whether each user file is properly documented in the MFT

If you are using the NTFS file system on a Windows 2000 computer, you have the advantage of a transaction log. The transaction log maintains the structure of the volumes, such as the mirrored volumes or striped volumes, but it does not maintain user data. Here is where the Chkdsk program is used.

The following exercise illustrates how to use the Chkdsk program from the *My Computer* icon. You may also run this program from Windows Explorer.

Exercise 6

USING CHKDSK

1. From the desktop, double-click the *My Computer* icon.
2. Right-click the *C* drive icon (or the icon of your boot drive) and then click Properties. You see the Properties dialog box (Figure 4.21).

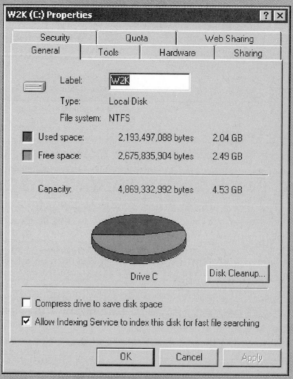

Figure 4.21

3. Click the Tools tab. You see the Tools dialog box (Figure 4.22).

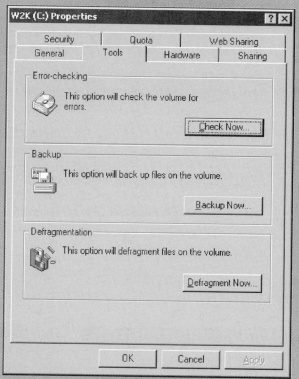

Figure 4.22

4. Click the <u>C</u>heck Now button in the Error-checking section. You see a dialog box requesting you to start the scan (Figure 4.23).

Figure 4.23

5. Check the box to *Scan for and attempt recovery of bad sectors.* (Chkdsk cannot automatically fix file system errors on a drive that currently has files open. If you select this option the Chkdsk program will not run until the next time you reboot your machine.)

6. Click Start. The Chkdsk program will start.
7. When the disk scan is completed, a dialog box displays indicating that the scan is done without giving an actual report of what it did. Click OK.
8. Click OK to close the Properties window.

Chkdsk can also be run from a command line. By running this program from the command line you have the advantage of using several different options, as well as receiving a report at the end of the Chkdsk program showing the results. To run from a command line, use the following format:

```
chkdsk driveletter: /option
```

The same command as you ran above from the *My Computer* icon would be

```
Chkdsk c: /r
```

The /r is the option to check for bad sectors. To see other available options, open a Command window and key

```
Chkdsk /?
```

Disk Maintenance: Disk Defragmenter

A second tool that is available to help maintain disks is the Disk Defragmenter that comes with Windows 2000. You may notice, over time, that your disks seem to slow down. This slowing occurs because, with use, files become fragmented. A new disk has plenty of room to write files in a contiguous manner. When a file is contiguous, the read/write head of the disk does not have to do much searching to find all the pieces of the file. However, as files are added and deleted not enough contiguous space may be left on the disk for new files. As a result, these new files become split up over many different areas of the disk when they are written and consequently the read/write heads will spend much more time both writing the file and searching for all the pieces of a file when it is read. (See Figures 4.24 and 4.25). The Disk Defragmenter will put pieces of files back together on the disk.

FIGURE 4.24 *Before Defragmentation*

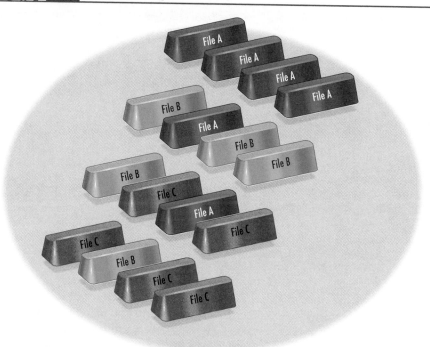

FIGURE 4.25 *After Defragmentation*

Exercise 7

USING THE DISK DEFRAGMENTER

1. Double-click the *My Computer* icon.
2. Right-click the *C* drive icon and then click Properties.
3. Click the Tools tab.
4. Click the Defragment Now button.
5. Click an NTFS formatted drive and then click the Analyze button.
6. When the analysis is complete, click View Report.
7. Click Close after viewing the report.

Defragmentation could take a long time and you might not want to wait for it at this moment. Also it is best to make a backup before defragmenting a disk.

Disk Quotas

A new and popular feature in Windows 2000 is the ability to set disk quotas. Disk quotas allow the administrator to control the amount of disk space taken up by users. The term *disk quota*, however, is somewhat misleading because quotas are set by volumes and not by disk. If the hard disk is comprised of a single volume then the term *disk quota* is accurate, but if a hard drive has been divided into several volumes, disk quotas would need to be set up and configured separately on each volume. In addition, disk quotas can only be set up on volumes that are formatted with the NTFS.

Quotas can be set up simply to warn the user that he or she is getting close to or has exceeded his or her limit. Or quotas can be set with a strict limit that will block users from saving any more information once they have reached their quota. The administrator can also set the event log to record when a user has reached his or her limit.

By default the disk quotas feature is turned off. To turn on disk quotas you need to open My Computer or Windows Explorer and right-click the volume that will be set with quotas. One of the tabs on the Properties menu is called Quota. When you select the Quota tab you will see a dialog box that looks like Figure 4.26.

FIGURE **4.26** *Quota Dialog Box*

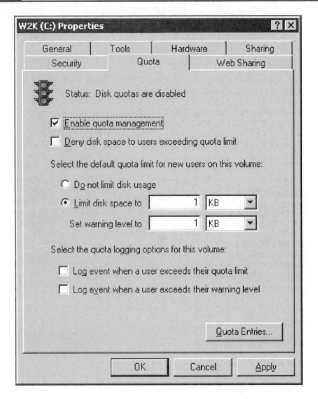

The Quota dialog box has the following elements:

- The *Enable quota management* check box turns disk quotas on and allows them to be configured.

- The *Deny disk space to users exceeding quota limit* check box will prevent users from taking any more disk space once they have hit their limits. If this box is not checked, a user can continue to consume disk space on the volume after exceeding his or her limit.

- The *Limit disk space to* section allows you to set the actual amount of disk space the user can have and the amount of usage at which a warning should be generated. If you choose not to check the *Deny disk space to users exceeding their quota limit* check box you can still generate a warning. The warning can appear in two places; by default it will appear in the Quota Entries window.

- The Quota Entries button displays the Quota Entries window, which lists users. A yellow warning appears under the status column for any users who have hit the warning limit but not yet exceeded the quota, while a red icon indicates those who have exceeded their quota.

Notice that administrators are not subject to disk quotas.

The log event check boxes can be selected to set logging so that events will appear in the event log when users try to exceed their warning or quota level. The event log is a tool that records the state of the applications and system. Many error messages and warnings will show up in the event log, so an administrator will find it a handy tool for troubleshooting problems. The event log will be discussed in more detail in the performance-monitoring chapter.

Do not set up disk quotas that deny disk space to users exceeding the limit on the volume that holds the system files. The main user of this partition is the Windows 2000 system and the machine may fail to boot if the system cannot write to the drive. It is always a good idea to keep user data and the Windows 2000 system files on separate volumes so you can set limits on the user volume without limiting the system.

Remote and Removable Storage

A new feature in Windows 2000 is support for remote and removable storage. Remote storage is defined as hard drive information saved to an offline system such as a tape drive. Removable storage consists of storage devices that may be attached and removed from a server, such as read/write CD-ROM media. Windows 2000 supports both remote and removable storage in different, but related, ways. Windows 2000 includes application programming interface (API) routines that allow third-party hardware vendors to use Windows to manage remote and removable storage devices.

Removable storage can include single-server devices such as a zip drive or read/write CD-ROM drive, and multiserver devices such as an automated tape or CD library. In either case, Windows 2000 can track the devices and the information on the devices in the following ways:

- Mounting and dismounting drives
- Identifying and inventorying removable media
- Pooling remote storage devices across the network

For remote storage devices such as tape drives, Windows 2000 provides the tools to automatically move selected files to tape, while keeping links to the files on the server. When someone attempts to access the file through the link, the file is automatically restored from the tape library.

CHAPTER summary

➤ Disk management includes formatting, configuring, and maintaining the server's hard disks. Windows 2000 includes a large set of disk management tools that allows the administrator to create and format partitions, mount a disk drive to a folder, and change the format of an existing disk partition. Windows 2000 includes a new feature called dynamic disks that allows disk volumes to be resized and combined without erasing the data on the disk. Windows 2000 also includes the ability to create spanned disks and to use fault tolerance features such as RAID.

➤ Folders and files can be compressed, which results in a more efficient use of the hard drive. Other disk tools available in Windows 2000 include the Chkdsk program and a Disk Defragmenter program that brings scattered file pieces together.

CHAPTER terms

Active partition	The primary partition from which the computer will boot.
Allocation unit size	The smallest unit of space that can be written to, consisting of one or more sectors.
Basic disk	Standard disk format (not a dynamic disk).
Boot partition	The partition that contains the Windows 2000 system files.
Dynamic disk	A method of managing disks that allows a logical volume to span physical disks.
Extended partition	A logical subdivision of a disk after a primary partition has been created.
Logical drive	A partition designated with a letter that represents a usable part of the hard drive.
MBR	Master boot record: A data structure residing on the hard drive, used by the operating system to store disk information and to store boot programs.
Parity	Using a data bit to verify other data bits when they are written to a hard disk.
Partition	A logical subsection of a hard drive, normally the section used to divide operating systems on a single hard drive.
Partition table	A data structure that contains structural information about a partition.
Physical disk	The physical hard drive that is part of a computer system.

Primary partition	A partition on a hard drive used to store boot information.
RAID	Redundant array of inexpensive (or independent) disks: A multidisk configuration that allows for mirroring and disk striping.
Sector	Part of the hard disk on which data is stored.
Stripe set	A method whereby data is written to multiple disks at the same time. It is often used in RAID.
System partition	The partition that contains the Windows 2000 boot files.
Track	A section of the hard drive on which sectors are stored.
Volume mount point	A disk drive that is labeled as a local folder.
Volume	A logical division of a hard drive used by the dynamic disk feature in Windows 2000.

CONCEPTS review

Multiple Choice

1. A master boot record (MBR) is:
   a. Located on the last track of the hard disk.
   b. Used to store Windows 2000 disk quota information.
   c. Used to store the hard disk extended partition.
   d. None of the above.

2. The active partition on a hard disk is:
   a. The partition that only holds operating system files.
   b. The partition that can boot an operating system.
   c. The partition that must contain disk quota information.
   d. The last partition created when formatting a hard disk.

3. The allocation unit size can be used to:
   a. Determine the size of the disk sectors.
   b. Determine the size of the disk tracks.
   c. Determine how much physical space a file will take on the hard disk.
   d. All of the above.

4. An extended partition:
   a. Cannot be placed on the same drive as a primary partition.
   b. Cannot hold operating system files.
   c. Cannot be used with the Chkdsk program.
   d. None of the above.

5. The FAT32 file system:
   a. Can be read by Windows 98, Windows 2000, and Windows NT.
   b. Can be read by Windows 2000.
   c. Can be read by Windows 98.
   d. Both b and c.

6. When you compress a folder:
   a. Only the folder is compressed but not any files in the folder.
   b. Only the files in the folder are compressed and not the folder.
   c. Only the folder is compressed along with any new files added to the folder.
   d. Both the folder and files are compressed, but any new files added to the folder will not be compressed.

7. Among the benefits to dynamic disks are:
   a. The ability to easily create and manage RAID disks.
   b. The ability to span volumes across physical disks.
   c. None of the above.
   d. Both a and b.

8. Parity is used to:
   a. Verify the integrity of data written to a disk.
   b. Format data for dynamic disks.
   c. Combine disk sectors together.
   d. None of the above.

9. One way to improve the performance of disk mirroring is:
   a. Increase the size of each disk volume.
   b. Place each hard drive on a different controller.
   c. Add additional hard disks.
   d. All of the above.

10. The purpose of the Disk Defragmenter is to:
    a. Move file sectors closer together.
    b. Set the amount of hard disk space that can be used.
    c. Format the MBR.
    d. None of the above.

Fill In

1. A _____ is identified by a letter of the alphabet and a colon (:).

2. The _____ is used to store the structure of the hard drive and also contains boot information.

3. The _____ contains the size of each disk sector.

4. Sectors are stored on a _____.

5. The _____ is used by the hardware BIOS to boot the computer.

6. By _____ drives, you associate a disk drive with a folder.

7. A(n) _____ is the logical disk structure found in dynamic disks.

8. The _____ file system can not be accessed by Windows NT.

9. A _____ set are a pair of physical disks that have the same information written to each during operation of the server.

10. The RAID level _____ disks use striping with parity to save data.

Short Answer

1. Briefly explain the difference between a basic disk and a dynamic disk.
2. Briefly explain the difference between a primary partition and an extended partition.
3. Explain how parity works on a striped disk.
4. Explain the purpose of the Chkdsk program.
5. Explain how a hard disk gets fragmented.

LAB exercises

Exercise 1 – Mounting a CD-ROM Drive

The chapter discussed mounting a logical drive when it is created. You can also mount existing drives. This exercise will walk you through mounting a CD-ROM drive to a folder.

1. Double-click the *My Computer* icon and open your NTFS partition.
2. Right-click on a blank space inside the partition and click New, Folder from the menu.
3. Name the folder *CD Mount Point*.
4. Minimize the local disk window.
5. Open the Computer Management tool and double-click the Disk Management tool.
6. Right-click the CD-ROM drive.
7. Click the Change Drive Letter and Path option. What drives are listed?
8. Click Add.
9. Click *Mount in this NTFS folder* and click Browse.

10. Browse to find the *CD Mount Point* folder and click on the folder to select it.
11. Click OK.
12. Click OK at the Add New Drive Letter and Path dialog box.
13. Right-click the CD–ROM again.
14. Click the Change Drive Letter and Path option. Now what drives are listed?
15. Click Close to exit the Change Drive Letter and Path dialog box.
16. Close the Computer Management dialog box.
17. Maximize the Local Disk window. What has happened to the *CD Mount Point* folder?

Exercise 2 – Compressing Folders

1. Locate the folder you created on your NTFS drive called *Compressed Files.*
2. Make sure it contains a copy of Santa Fe Stucco.bmp, and Soap Bubbles.bmp from the WINNT directory in the folder. (You can delete the Prairie Wind.bmp file that you compressed earlier.)
3. Right-click each file and click Properties on the drop-down menu.
4. Note the size on disk of each of the files.
5. Make a copy of Soap Bubbles.bmp and place it at the root of your NTFS drive. Name the copy Soap Bubbles1.bmp.
6. Close the *Compressed Files* folder.
7. Right-click the *Compressed Files* folder and click Properties from the menu.
8. Make sure you have the General tab selected and click the A<u>d</u>vanced button to open the Advanced Attributes dialog box.
9. Click so a check mark appears in the *Compress contents to save disk space* check box and click OK to close the Advanced Attributes dialog box.
10. Accept the default option of Apply changes to this folder only by clicking OK.
11. Click OK to close the Properties dialog box.
12. Right-click each of the files, click Properties, and note their size on the disk. Were they compressed?
13. Copy the SoapBubbles1.bmp file into the *Compressed Files* folder and note its size on disk. Was it compressed?

Exercise 3 – Setting Up Disk Quotas

1. Double-click the *My Computer* icon to open it.
2. Right-click the *C* drive icon and click Properties from the drop-down menu.
3. Click the Quota tab.
4. Click the check box called *Enable quota management.*
5. Make sure that *Deny disk space to users exceeding the quota limit* is NOT checked.
6. Set *Limit disk space to* at 5 KB.

7. Set the warning level to 2 KB and click the <u>A</u>pply button.
8. Click OK to accept the warning message and wait until the status stop sign at the top of the page returns to green and says *Disk quota system is active*.
9. Click the Quota entries button. Record the entries you see.

Exercise 4 – Removing Disk Quotas

1. Click *Enable quota management* to remove the check mark and click the <u>A</u>pply button.
2. Click OK to accept the warning message. The status stop sign at the top should now show that the disk quotas are disabled.
3. Click OK to leave the Quotas window.

Exercises 5–10 should only be performed on a computer that can be reformatted. Use the Chapter 4 Simulations of these exercises from the CD that comes with your textbook if you are using a computer that can't be reformatted.

Exercise 5 – Simulation Reverting Back to Basic Disk

1. Right-click the gray box next to Disk 1. Notice there is not an option to revert back to a basic disk.
2. Right-click the Drive D volume and click Delete Volume from the drop-down menu.
3. Acknowledge that all data will be lost by clicking Yes.
4. Once the volume has been deleted, right-click again on the gray box next to Disk 1. Click Revert To Basic Disk from the drop-down menu.
5. Your disk will now show as a basic disk of unallocated space.

Exercise 6 – Simulation of Creating a Stripe Set

1. Right-click the Unallocated space of Disk 1 and click Create Volume from the drop-down menu.
2. At the wizard click Next.
3. Click *Striped volume* and click Next.
4. At the Select Disks screen, highlight *Disk 2* and click Add.
5. Click Next to continue.
6. Accept the default drive letter D and click Next.
7. Key **Drive D** for the Volume label and accept the rest of the defaults by clicking Next.
8. View the summary and then click Finish.

Exercise 7 – Simulation of Creating a Mirror Set

1. Right-click *New Volume on Disk1* and click Add Mirror from the drop-down menu.
2. At the Add Mirror window, highlight *Disk 2* and click Add Mirror. It will take several minutes to generate the mirror set.

Exercise 8 – Simulation of Breaking a Mirror Set

This process allows you to keep the data on both disks, but they will no longer be mirrored.

1. Right-click either of the mirrored volumes, and then click Break Mirror.
2. Click Yes to confirm you want to break the mirror. Now each drive will contain its own simple volume. Notice each half of the original mirrored volume now has its own drive letter.

Exercise 9 – Simulation of Removing a Mirror Set

This process should be used when you only want to keep one copy of the data.

1. Right-click *Disk 2* and click Remove Mirror from the drop-down menu.
2. In the Remove Mirror dialog box, make sure that *Disk 2* is highlighted and click Remove Mirror.
3. Click Yes to confirm removing the mirror. The half of the mirror that was removed will now be unallocated space.

Exercise 10 – Simulation of Creating a Spanned Volume

1. Right-click *Disk 1* and click Extend Volume from the drop-down menu.
2. At the Extend Volume Wizard, click Next.
3. Click *Disk 2* and click Add.
4. Click Next to continue.
5. At the summary click Finish. (Notice that all drives have been converted to dynamic disks.)
6. Right-click *Unallocated space on Disk 0* and click Create Volume from the drop-down menu.
7. At the wizard, click Next.
8. Click *Disk 1* and *Disk 2*, click Add, and then Click Next.
9. Click Next at the Assign Drive Letter or Path window to accept the default drive letter and continue.
10. At the Format Volume screen make sure that *NTFS* is selected, accept the default allocation unit size, and label the volume *RAID 5*. Click Next to continue.
11. Review the summary for accuracy and click Finish. After a few moments your RAID 5 volume will be established.

PROBLEM SOLVING exercise

Write down the steps and procedures you would use to solve the following problem.

You have a server with four disks with the following configuration:

Disk 1: 800 MB, 400 MB with system files and 400 MB of unallocated space.

Disk 2: 800 MB of accounting data.

Disk 3: 800 MB of unallocated space.

Disk 4: 800 MB, 400 MB of finance data and 400 MB of unallocated space.

You want to provide the accounting department with faster access and the most possible space. You want to provide fault tolerance for the finance department. How should you configure these disks using basic or dynamic disk volumes?

PRINTING 5

Performance Objectives

After completing this chapter you will be able to:

- Describe the Windows 2000 printing model
- Plan a network printer configuration
- Install a local printer
- Configure printer ports
- Share printers on a network
- View printer status
- Troubleshoot printer problems

Introduction

Installing, configuring, and maintaining network printers can be one of the more frustrating jobs in store for network administrators. Most networks have shared high-speed printers that are used constantly. When a user cannot print, even if the printer is unplugged and disassembled, the network administrator gets a telephone call. Correctly configuring and maintaining network printers can prevent a great deal of ire from your users. Managing network printing involves developing a network printing strategy, installing the print devices, configuring the print devices to minimize problems, and administrating the print devices. These topics are covered in this chapter.

Microsoft Printing Terms

In order to develop a network printing strategy, it is necessary to understand the terms used to describe network printing. A **print device** is the physical printer. For example, a Hewlett-Packard LaserJet 8100N printer would be called a print device. The software interface between the computer and the print device is called the **printer**, or *logical printer*. A named printer is what users select when they choose the print option from an application program. The **printer driver** is the software, often supplied by the print device manufacturer, that converts print jobs into the low-level print language understood by the print device. The conduit through which print information reaches the print device is called the **port**. A port can refer to a physical connection on the server, such as a parallel or serial port, or it can refer to a software conduit. A **print server** refers to the computer whose primary purpose is to receive, manage, and redirect print jobs to print devices.

Windows Printing Model

Along with the official terms, it is also useful to understand the Windows printing model. The printing model describes the software elements involved in processing a print job. Figure 5.1 illustrates this model.

FIGURE 5.1   *Windows Printing Model*

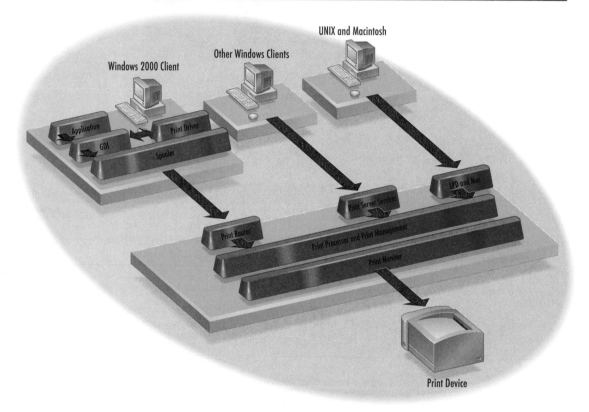

Information is not sent directly from an application, such as Microsoft Word, to a print device. Printers have a built-in printing language that is used by the print device to render the text and graphics that appear on the physical page. Hewlett-Packard print devices use the printer control language (PCL), while other print devices use the PostScript language. Text and graphics created in an application must first be converted into the printer language before being processed by the print device.

The conversion to the printer language takes place in a software subsystem named the graphical device interface (GDI). This subsystem is responsible for rendering information into a graphical format that can be displayed on the monitor or sent to a printer. The GDI, in order to convert text and graphics into a suitable format, must communicate with another piece of software called the printer driver. The printer driver software determines which format to use when the GDI converts the information. After the GDI has converted the text and graphics into a suitable format, it sends the resulting file to the Spooler software subsystem. The Spooler software system is responsible for sending the information to the print device or to a remote print server.

When printing to PCL printers, the GDI uses the enhanced metafile format (EMF). This format allows the GDI to include precise font and graphic information and allows the print job to spool more quickly to the server. Software subsystems on the print server can work directly with EMF files. Windows 2000 uses the Raw format when printing to PostScript printers.

The print server contains two different software subsystems that receive print jobs from clients. Print jobs sent from a Windows 2000 client are received by the print router subsystem. Print jobs sent from non-Windows 2000 clients are received by the print server service, and jobs sent by UNIX and Macintosh clients are received within the print server service by the LPD and Mac service.

Non-Windows clients do not have the GDI system to create print jobs. These non-Windows clients must rely on the print server services running on the server to receive and process print jobs. Windows 2000 includes print service software for several different kinds of clients. UNIX clients use the line printer daemon (LPD) service and Apple Macintosh clients the AppleTalk service. Non-Windows clients must send their print jobs to the server in Raw print format.

Once a print job has been received by the print router, the printer server services, or another non-Windows print services subsystem, the job is passed to the local print provider subsystem, which is also running on the server. This second subsystem holds print jobs at the server, checks for print device access rights, creates separator pages, and performs other management tasks. From the print provider, the job is next passed to the print monitor subsystem. This final piece of software directly communicates with the print device and sends the print job files to the physical printer.

To summarize:

1. The Print command is selected in an application.

2. For Windows 2000 clients, the GDI, along with local client printer drivers, converts the information into an EMF file, spools it, and sends it to the remote print server. For non-Windows clients, the information is converted to a Raw format file and sent to the appropriate printer service running on the print server.

3. The print router on the print server receives jobs from Windows 2000 clients and the printer services software receives jobs from non-Windows clients.

4. Print jobs are then passed to the local print provider. This subsystem sends the jobs to the print processor and other printer management software subsystems.

5. The print processor passes the formatted print job to the print monitor. The print monitor software subsystem communicates directly with the ports and sends and receives information over the ports.

This process may seem needlessly complex, with all the software subsystems passing print jobs back and forth. However, each piece of this process serves a purpose and ensures that print jobs are successfully and reliably printed.

Selecting a Network Print Device

A network printing strategy involves selecting appropriate print devices and installing the devices where they will be appropriately used. Selecting a network print device is different from selecting a print device to be used on a single computer. Because network print devices are used heavily, they should have the capacity and speed to handle a large number of print jobs in a reasonable amount of time. Such print devices should have a low mean time between failures and be easy to maintain.

When choosing a network print device, the network administrator should use the following guidelines:

- How many users will be sending print jobs to the print device?

- What types of print jobs will be sent to the print device? Will print jobs include graphics, color, or require nonstandard paper sizes and types?

- Will users routinely print a large number of copies of single print jobs?

If a network hosts a large number of users who require access to print devices, or users who generate large print jobs, then the most appropriate print device would be a high-speed laser. Many manufacturers make network-ready print devices that are designed to handle a large volume of print jobs.

If users require special paper or color output, the most appropriate print devices are color lasers or high-end color inkjet devices. A color laser prints color prints faster than an inkjet, but requires more expensive cartridges. Inkjet print devices are slower, but are often easier to maintain and more reliable.

If network users routinely print multiple copies of single jobs, a network digital copier should be considered. These devices work like regular copiers, but can also be connected to a network. They have the speed of a copier and the ability to receive print jobs from the network. Although such devices are more expensive than laser print devices, they can also be used as regular office copiers.

Along with the printing capability of network print devices, it is also important to consider the way these devices physically connect to the network. Most network print devices include a built-in network connection that allows the print device to be plugged into the network and to receive print jobs directly from clients, without the requirement of a print server. To the network administrator, this solution to network printing may seem simple and trouble-free, but for a number of reasons, a print server should still be used. Print jobs sent directly to a network print device are uncontrolled and cannot be managed. It may be difficult to stop a 10,000 page print job that was sent directly to a network print device. It is also impossible, with a directly connected network print device, to redirect print jobs to secondary print devices.

Exercise 1

DEVELOPING A NETWORK PRINTING PLAN

Given the following description of the Computer Marketing Company's printing needs, create a network printing plan that includes the following information:

- The number of network print devices required

- A description of each print device that includes capability (color or black and white), speed (pages per minute), and paper handling (size of input tray, paper size, single or double sided)

- The location of the print devices

The Computer Marketing Company has offices in a three-story building. The administrative and personnel offices are located on the ground floor, the sales department located on the second floor, and the marketing department located on the top floor. The administrative and personnel offices contain 12 people who print memos and reports on a weekly basis. The 18 people in the sales department print long and complex sales reports on a twice-weekly basis. These reports include graphics and text, with about 10 percent of the pages printed in color. The marketing department includes 22 people who create color marketing pieces. Each person sometimes prints multiple copies per day.

Compose the printing plan as a word processing document, and name it *xx* network printing, with your initials instead of *xx*.

Printer Ports

Before proceeding to the printer installation steps, it is useful to review the ways a print device can be connected to a print server. A local print device is defined as a print device directly connected to a computer through a parallel, serial, universal serial bus (USB), infrared, IEEE 1394 (Firewire), or wireless connection. Each of these connections must have a corresponding port. Although the term *port* is often used to describe a hardware connection on a computer, it also describes a software conduit through which Windows 2000 sends data to a print device. A print server can create a port without possessing the corresponding physical connection.

When Windows 2000 is installed, several standard local ports are automatically created. These local ports include parallel (LPT1 to LPT3), serial (COM1 to COM4), and FILE (print to a file). In addition, Windows has a set of predefined ports that can be added. Table 5.1 lists the standard local printer ports that can be defined.

T A B L E 5.1 *Windows Standard Print Device Ports*

Port Name	Port Type
LPT1, LPT2, LPT3	Parallel printer ports
COM1, COM2, COM3, COM4	Serial printer ports
IrDA	Infrared printer port
C:\output\filex	Output file; all print jobs are sent to the indicated file; each print job overwrites the contents of the file
\\computer\printername	Printer share name (illustrated in a later exercise)
USB	Sends the print job to the general USB bus; specific USB printers, when attached to the computer, will automatically install their own port
1394	Sends the print job to the general 1394 port (often called "Firewire")
NUL	Tests network printing connections and automatically deletes all received print jobs

The USB and IEEE 1394 ports are automatically installed when a Plug and Play print device with one of these ports is connected to the server.

USB version 1.0 ports can support faster data rates than parallel ports, but are slower than Firewire (IEEE 1394) ports. However, USB version 2.0 ports are faster than Firewire. Windows 2000 requires special drivers to support USB version 2.0 connections.

Installing Local Printers

Before a network print server can receive print jobs and send the jobs to a print device, it must have one or more local printers installed. Remember, a printer is defined as the software interface to a physical print device. When a Plug and Play print device is connected to a Windows 2000 server, the printer software is installed automatically. If this automatic process fails or the printer is not Plug and Play, you can use the steps spelled out in Exercise 2 to install the printer software.

Exercise 2

INSTALLING A LOCAL PRINTER

For this exercise it is assumed that you do not have a print device attached to the server. You will practice manually installing printer software from within the *Printers* folder.

1. Click Start, click Settings, and then click Printers.
2. Double-click the *Add Printer* icon in the *Printers* folder to start the Add Printer Wizard.
3. Click the Next button to start the wizard. You see the window in Figure 5.2

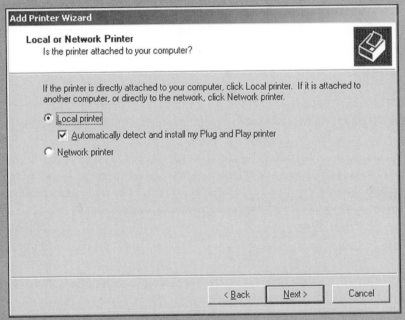

Figure 5.2

You can choose to add either a local or a network printer. A local printer is located on and can be controlled directly from your machine, while a network printer is located on and controlled from another machine.

4. Click *Local printer* and make sure *Automatically detect and install my Plug and Play printer* is checked. Click the Next button to proceed.
5. You see a screen indicating that Plug and Play printers were not found. Click Next to continue with the wizard. You are next presented with a list of printer ports (Figure 5.3). From this list you can choose which port you want your local printer to use.

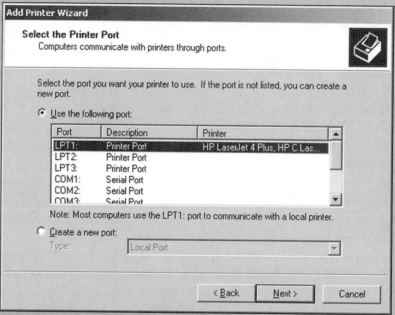

Figure 5.3

6. Click the port *LPT2* and click the <u>N</u>ext button. Because you will be installing only the printer and will not have a print device, you can assign it to a port that is likely not physically attached to the computer. The next screen presents a list of printers (Figure 5.4).

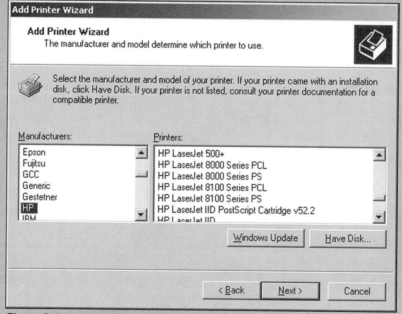

Figure 5.4

7. In the Manufacturers section, click *HP*, and then click *HP LaserJet 8100 Series PCL* in the Printers section. Click Next to proceed.

Windows will locate the driver for this printer. If a printer driver was not located, you will be prompted to insert the printer driver diskette, which was likely packaged with the print device. If the server finds an already installed printer driver for the selected printer, you will be prompted to keep or replace the existing driver.

8. You next see a window prompting for a printer name (Figure 5.5). This name will be used locally to identify the printer.

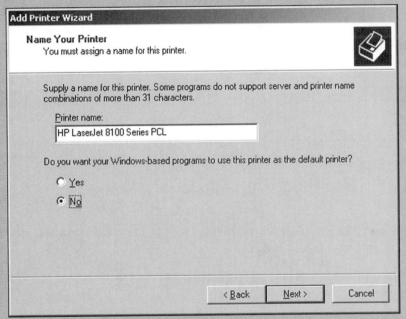

Figure 5.5

9. In the Printer name text box, key the name **HP 8100 PCL**.

When naming a printer, try and select a name that describes the print device. Don't include the port in the printer name because ports can be changed. The printer name can contain up to 220 characters, but it is not a good idea to use long printer names.

10. Click the Yes option for making this printer the default printer and then click Next to proceed.

The next window prompts you to share this printer (Figure 5.6). Sharing means that other people on the network could connect and send print jobs to this printer. A default share name is suggested.

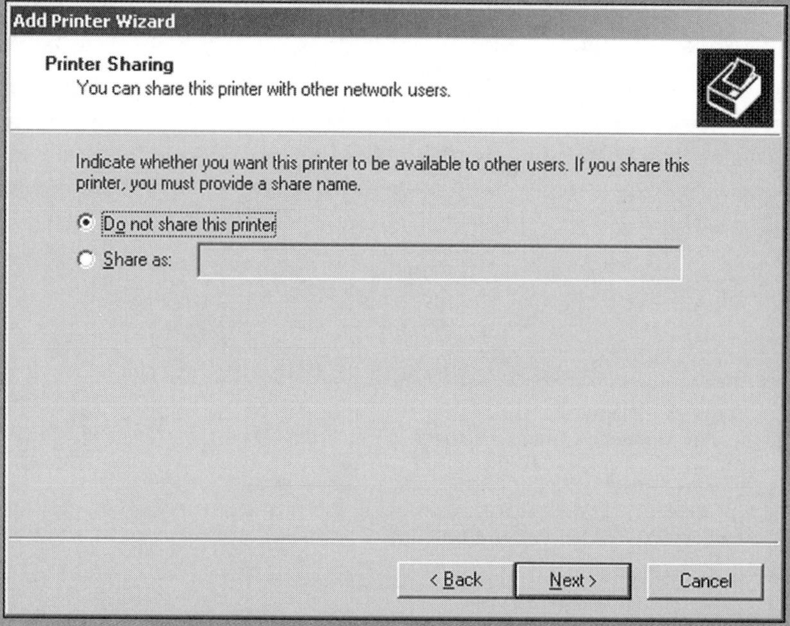

Figure 5.6

Windows 2000 Server assumes, by default, that you want to share local printers. Windows 2000 Professional assumes, by default, that you don't want to share local printers.

11. Click *Do not share this printer* and then click <u>N</u>ext to proceed.
12. The next screen prompts you to print a test page. A test page is a good idea because it allows you to check the connection. In this case, click the No option and then click <u>N</u>ext.
13. The last screen presents a summary of the printer information. Click Finish to complete the wizard. The driver files for the printer are copied to the system and the printer is installed.

The *Printers* folder displays an icon representing the printer just installed. If the printer is set as the default, a small black check mark is placed next to the printer icon. If the printer icon displays a hand below the printer, it means that the printer is shared. A local printer that is not shared can only be used from the local computer. A local printer that is shared can be used by network clients.

Configuring a Local Printer

Once a printer has been installed, it can be managed from the *Printers* folder. A number of printer options can be selected from this folder, including setting the paper size, the graphics resolution, and the default input paper tray. Other options include setting how the printer will be shared, who can manage print jobs for the printer, and what times of the day the printer is available.

Some of the printer options are only applicable to specific printers. A black and white laser printer will not display options for color printing. Setting specific printer options is done through software supplied by the printer manufacturer. During the installation of printer drivers, Windows 2000 also installs unique print management software for the specific printer. When the Printing Preferences option is selected, the specific printer software is run.

Exercise 3

CONFIGURING A LOCAL PRINTER

In the following exercise you will configure the printer you just installed.

1. If the Printers window is not already open, click Start, Settings, and Printers.
2. Right-click the icon for the LaserJet printer just installed and click Properties. You see the dialog box in Figure 5.7.

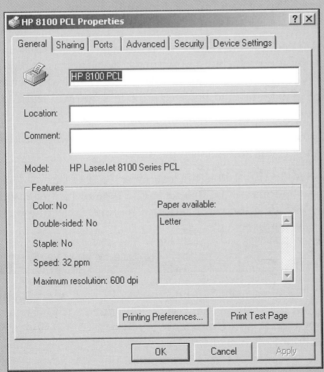

Figure 5.7

3. Click the General tab and key in the Location text box the text **Accounting/Room 518**
4. In the Comment text box, key **Only accessible for Accounting department users.**
5. Click the OK button to close the Printer Properties dialog box.

The options displayed on the Properties menu include setting the selected printer as the default, pausing and canceling print jobs, sharing and using the printer off-line, and renaming, deleting, and creating a shortcut to the printer.

The tabs on this dialog box are general to most printers but, for some printers, additional tabs may be displayed. For example, a color printer would have a tab for Color Management.

The following tabs are found in the Printer Properties dialog box:

General: Contains options used to set the printer name, location, and other information associated with the printer.

Sharing: Contains options used to share the printer over the network and to install additional printer drivers.

Ports: Displays options used to configure an existing port or to add new ports for the printer.

Advanced: Presents options used to set various management options for the printer, including the times the printer is available, the print job priority, how to manage spooled jobs, and whether a separator page is to be printed before a print job. You will learn to use these options in a later exercise.

Security: Displays options used to designate who has rights to print to the printer and manage print jobs.

Device Settings: Presents a summary page of print device options. These options will be unique to the type of printer installed. They may include options for substituting fonts, selecting the input tray, and setting paper size.

Configuring Ports

A port is the destination to which print jobs are directed. Once a printer has been installed, its output port can be changed or configured without reinstalling the printer driver software. A port can refer to a physical connection or it can refer to a software connection.

Most computers come with several standard physical ports: parallel, serial, and USB ports. Each physical port has different features, data transfer rates, and protocols. In terms of speed, serial ports are the slowest and USB ports the fastest.

In most cases, the administrator does not have to be concerned about configuring these types of standard ports. Settings for parallel and serial ports should be unchanged and the USB port will be configured automatically when a USB device is connected to the computer.

Two ports that are sometimes useful to set are the FILE and NULL ports, which are used to send a print job to a disk file and to send a print job into nowhere. Why would anyone set a null port? Because it is often used to test a network shared printer without wasting paper.

A port that is often used with network printers is the TCP/IP printer port. Many network printers have built-in network connectors that can be assigned an IP address. By creating a TCP/IP port and assigning the port the IP address of the print device, you can direct print jobs to this IP address over a network. Depending on the type of network printer, the print job may be held by the print device or directly printed. Connecting to print devices through a TCP/IP port is to be preferred over serial or parallel connections. Printing across the network is much faster than printing to a parallel connection.

Exercise 4

CREATING A TCP/IP PORT

In the following exercise you will define a TCP/IP port and connect the just installed printer to this port.

1. Click Start, Settings, and Printers to display the Printer window.
2. Right-click the printer icon for the printer named HP 8100 PCL and click Properties.
3. Click the Ports tab to display the port options. The printer should have the LPT2 port selected (Figure 5.8).

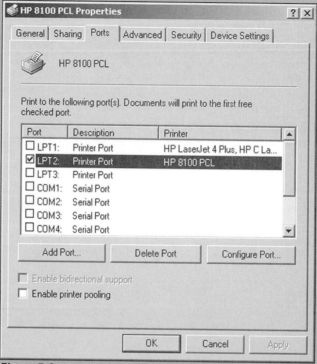

Figure 5.8

Because the TCP/IP ports are not automatically installed, you must first add a new port to this list before connecting the printer to the port.

4. Click the Add Port button to add a new port. You see a list of available ports in Figure 5.9.

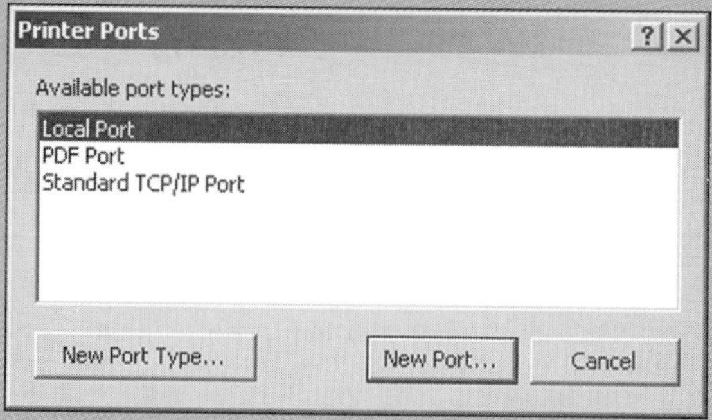

Figure 5.9

Two of the choices are *Local Port* or *Standard TCP/IP Port*. The buttons on this menu allow you to create a new port or create a new port type.

5. Click *Standard TCP/IP Port* and then click the New Port button to create a new TCP/IP port. You will see the TCP/IP Port Wizard.

Before creating a new TCP/IP port, make sure the device to be attached is connected to the network and has power. When the wizard creates the connection, it will send a message to the networked print device requesting information. The network printer will respond with information about itself, which the wizard will use to perform the installation.

6. Click the Next button to continue with the wizard. You see the screen in Figure 5.10.

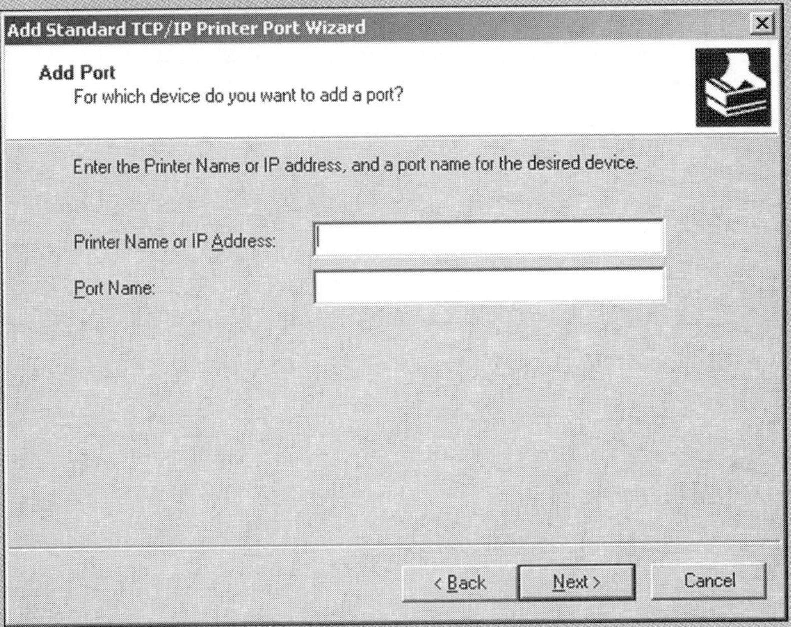

Add Standard TCP/IP Printer Port Wizard

Add Port
For which device do you want to add a port?

Enter the Printer Name or IP address, and a port name for the desired device.

Printer Name or IP Address: |

Port Name:

< Back   Next >   Cancel

Figure 5.10

In this screen you must enter the IP address of the networked printer and give the port a name.

7. If you have a network print device available in your lab, use the IP address for this print device. If you do not have access to a network print device, key the loopback IP address **127.0.0.1**.

The wizard will suggest an appropriate port name. This name will be used for the port only and is not used to identify the printer. It is a good idea to use the IP address as the port name to make it easier to troubleshoot printing problems (Figure 5.11).

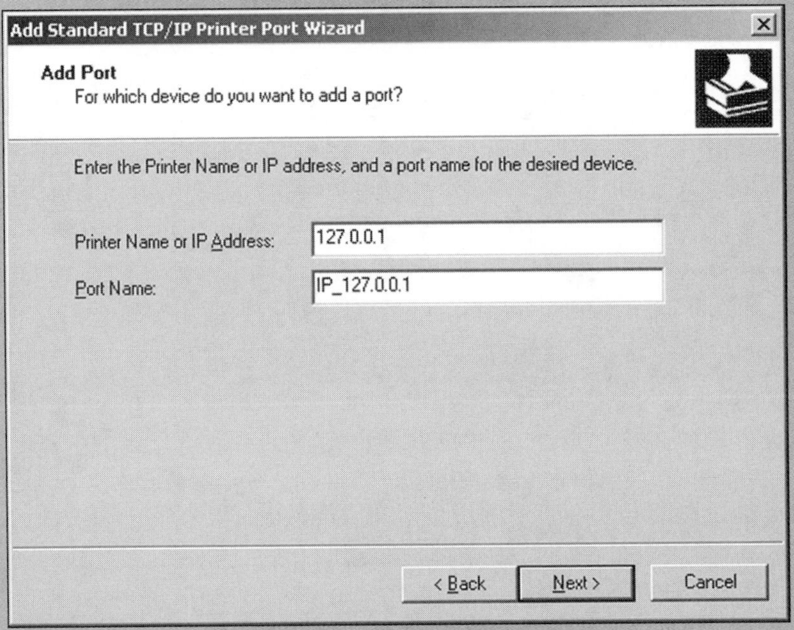

Figure 5.11

8. Click the Next button to proceed with the wizard. The wizard may pause for several seconds at this point.

The wizard will try to contact the print device using the IP address just supplied and query the print device for additional information. The print device should respond to this request from the wizard with information about itself, which can then be used to complete the installation.

If you are using the loopback IP address, nothing will respond to the request from the wizard. If you are using a network print device IP address and do not receive a response, the IP address could be invalid or the print device being contacted is not bright enough to respond to messages from the wizard. If the wizard does not receive a response from the network print device, the screen in Figure 5.12 is displayed.

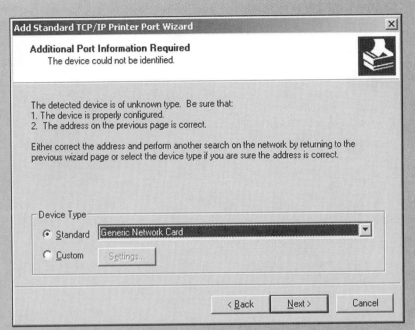

Figure 5.12

At this point, a specific network connection can be selected from the drop-down list or a custom connection can be defined. The default selection is *Generic Network Card*.

9. If you are using the IP loopback address, click the <u>N</u>ext button to accept *Generic Network Card* as the device type. The wizard may again delay for a few seconds.

10. The final screen displays information about the TCP/IP port connection. Click Finish to complete the wizard and close all windows until you see the Printer window.

11. Click the Close button on the Add Port screen. You should see the new port added to the list of existing ports (Figure 5.13).

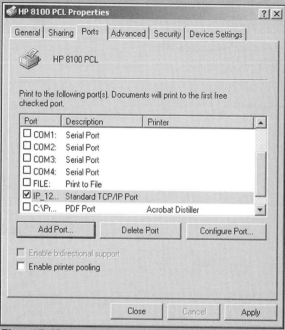

Figure 5.13

Once the port has been created, it can be configured.

12. Click the Configure Port button. You see the dialog box in Figure 5.14.

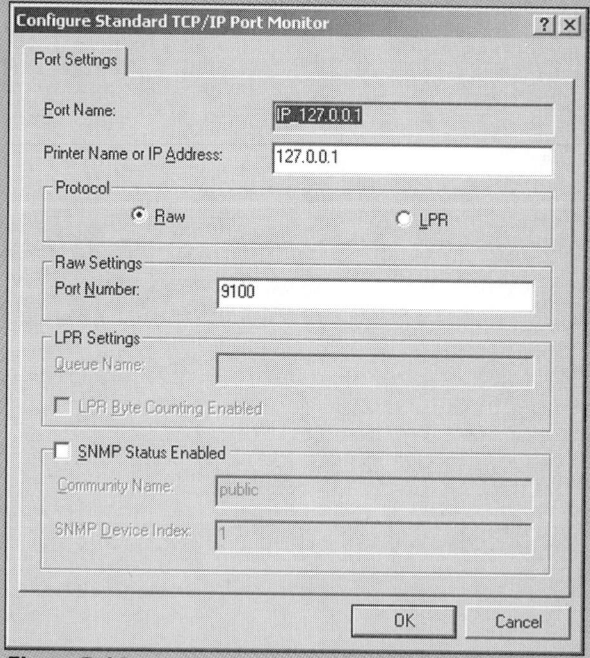

Figure 5.14

Notice the two protocol options are Raw and LPR. The LPR option, which stands for line printer remote, is used to send print jobs to a UNIX computer. Port Number refers to the network port used by the printer on which to listen for print jobs.

13. Write down the port number, close the configuration window and close Properties.

It is possible to add a port that redirects printer output to a software application. When Adobe Acrobat is installed on a Windows 2000 computer, it creates and attaches a special port called a PDF Port. Printing from an application to this special port creates an Adobe Acrobat file. The printer output is directed into a program that automatically formats the data into an Acrobat file.

To complete the next exercises you must have two computers within the same workgroup or domain. One computer must have a shared printer and the other computer will act as a client and access the printer. You will also need a copy of the Windows 95/98 printer drivers for the printer to be installed (HP8100 PCL). You can download a copy of these printer drivers from www.hp.com and save them to a folder located on the server. When prompted for the printer drivers, the shared folder can be selected.

Installing Network Printers

You have created a local printer by connecting the printer driver with a port. In the next exercise you will share an installed printer, and in the following exercise you will connect to the shared printer. Remember that a printer is a logical device and a print device is the physical piece of hardware that produces output. In most cases, Windows 2000 servers will not have any printers defined as only local printers. The purpose of a print server is to allow network clients to print. Although network clients can directly connect to a TCP/IP print device, it is better to connect the print server to the TCP/IP print device and then have network clients connect to the server.

In order for printers to be used by network clients, the printer must be shared. It involves setting a property on the printer and choosing a share name. The share name is used to identify the printer to network clients and is different from the name used to identify the printer in the Printers window.

The name selected for the printer share should be part of an overall network plan. As you will learn in a later chapter, Windows 2000 Active Directory can store the share name as well as information about the type of printer and the printer capability. When selecting a simple printer share name you should follow these guidelines:

- The share name cannot be longer than 8 characters for DOS and Windows 3.1, cannot be longer than 12 characters for Windows 95/98, cannot be longer than 15 characters for Windows NT 3.51, and cannot be longer than 255 characters for Windows NT 4 or Windows 2000.

- The share name should indicate what type of printer is being shared, for example, HPJL8100 or HPDJ2500.

- The share name might also include the location of the print device. For example, a print device located in building A, room 12 would have the share HP5-A-12.

- When using some older applications, make sure the combination of the server name and the printer share name does not exceed 31 characters. For example, on a computer named ACCOUNTINGMARKETRESEARCH the share might be:

        \\ACCOUNTINGMARKETRESEARCH\HPLJ8100

Before installing a shared printer, it is helpful to understand how client computers will use the share. In order for a client computer to use a shared printer the client must have a way to connect to the server that is sharing the printer and must have a local copy of the printer driver. If the client does not have a local copy of the printer driver for the shared printer, it cannot use the printer.

One way to make sure client computers have the appropriate printer drivers is to install the printer on each client and then create a new port that is linked to the server shared printer. The problem with manually installing printers on each client is one of effort. If there are several printers to be shared on the network server and a large number of clients, then manually installing client printers quickly becomes the network administrator's full-time job.

A better way to share a printer is to automatically copy the drivers for the shared printer down to the client when the client creates a printer share. This copy can be made through Windows 2000.

Exercise 5

SHARING A LOCAL PRINTER

In the following exercise you will share the printer installed in a previous exercise.

1. Open the Printers window (Start, Settings, Printers).
2. Right-click the printer just installed (*HP 8100 PCL*) and click Properties.

3. Click the Sharing tab. You see the dialog box in Figure 5.15.

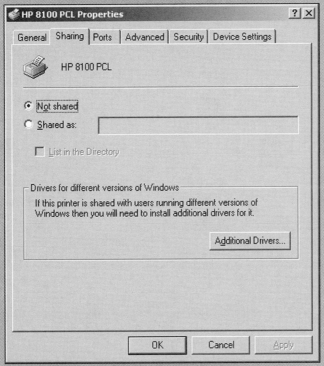

Figure 5.15

4. Click *Shared as*. The printer name is used as the default share name.
5. Key **HP8100A** as the share name for this printer. This name will be used by the clients to locate and attach to this network printer.

In order to cause the printer drivers for this printer to be automatically downloaded to the client, you must use the Additional Drivers option.

6. Click the Additional Drivers button. You see the dialog box in Figure 5.16.

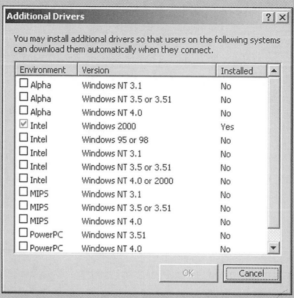

Figure 5.16

This dialog box lists the types of clients that can have printer drivers automatically downloaded and installed. Because the printer has already been installed on the Windows 2000 server, this client option is already selected.

7. Click the check box for *Windows 95 or 98* and then click OK.

Windows 2000 will attempt to locate the printer drivers. You will be prompted to insert the Windows 2000 Install CD or to select the location of the printer driver files. Your instructor will indicate the location of the printer driver files.

8. Click the OK button to search for the printer drivers.
9. You see a dialog box requesting the location of the files. Key **C:\LJ353** (or whatever disk drive your copy is installed on) and click OK. You can also click the Browse button to locate the printer driver files. You will be looking for a file with the type *.INF*.
10. Once you have selected the location of the printer driver files, click OK.
11. You will be prompted to select a printer by name. Select the appropriate printer and click OK. The printer files are copied into a folder located on the server in \WINNT\SYSTEM32\SPOOL\DRIVERS\W32X86.
12. Once the drivers have been copied, exit the Printer Properties dialog box. In the Printers window a small hand indicates that this printer is now shared and can be used by network clients.

Connecting to a Shared Printer

Clients can connect to a shared printer in several ways, depending on the client type. Clients can redirect a local port to a shared printer, install a shared printer from the Printers window, or install a shared printer from the Internet. In the following exercises you will use all three of these methods.

Redirecting a Port

Once a printer and printer drivers have been installed on the client, the printer port can be redirected to a network share. If the client is running DOS or Windows 3.1, it is the only way to use a network printer. The benefit of using this method for accessing network printers is that the client can easily select what network printer to use for print jobs. Different printers can be assigned to different output ports (LPT1, LPT2, COM1, and so on). (Network administrators will likely find this option a drawback rather than a benefit. When users start changing how they use network resources, the network administrator's job gets much more difficult.)

A drawback to using this method for accessing a network printer is that the printer drivers must first be installed on each client and then the port redirected to the network printers. This process can involve a great deal of manual effort by the network administrator. It is preferable to have printers and printer drivers automatically installed.

Exercise 6

REDIRECTING A PORT

In this exercise you will install a printer on LPT3 and then use the command line to redirect this port to a network printer. Your Windows 2000 server will be acting as a client.

1. Open the Printers window and double-click the *Add Printer* icon.
2. Using the wizard, install a Hewlett-Packard LaserJet 5P printer on port LPT3. Name this printer HP5MKT. Make sure you do not make it the default printer, do not share the printer, and do not print a test page.

An easy way (and the only way in DOS) to redirect a port is by using the NET USE command. This command is used to redirect local resources such as disk drivers and ports to resources on a network server. The name of the network printer is given in the universal naming convention (UNC) format. This format consists of two left slashes, the name of the computer, a single slash, and the name of the resource. For example:

```
\\COMPUTERNAME\HP8100A
```

where *COMPUTERNAME* is the name of the server and *HP8100A* is the share name of the printer.

3. Click Start, click Accessories, and then click the Command prompt. You see a Command window open (Figure 5.17).

Figure 5.17

4. At the DOS prompt, key the command

```
NET USE LPT3 \\COMPUTERNAME\HP8100A
```

using the name of your local computer. The NET USE LPT3 part of the command runs the NET program and tells it to redirect anything going to the port LPT3 to the specified network resource. If the command was successful you will see the message *The command completed successfully* in the Command window (Figure 5.18).

Figure 5.18

The local port LPT3 has now been redirected to the shared network printer. It means that any printer using this port, even if the computer does not physically have a third parallel printer port, can print to the network printer.

Another way to connect an existing printer to a client is to use the Properties dialog box and create a new port that redirects to the network printer share. This redirection can be done through the following exercise.

Exercise 7

CREATING A SHARED PORT

1. Click the HP5MKT printer just created and open the Properties dialog box.
2. Click the Port tab to display the available ports. This printer should be set to LPT3.
3. Click the Add Port button to create a new port.
4. Click *Local Port* and then click *New Port*. You see a dialog box requesting the name of the new port.
5. For the port name, key the network printer share in the UNC format:

   ```
   \\computername\HP8100A
   ```

6. Click the OK button. The port for this printer is now redirected to a network shared printer. All print jobs sent to this printer will be spooled locally and then forwarded to the server hosting the shared printer.
7. Exit the Ports dialog box and exit the printer's Properties dialog box.

The problem with locally installing printer drivers and then redirecting ports is the amount of manual effort required. A better way to connect clients to a network printer is by creating the printer and defining the share in one step. In this case, the printer drivers are automatically downloaded from the server and installed on the client.

If the client is running Windows 2000 or Windows NT, each time a print job is sent to a shared printer, a check is made for newer printer drivers. If the print server has installed newer client printer drivers, they are automatically updated. If the client is running Windows 95/98, printer drivers are not automatically updated but are automatically installed when the network printer is first defined.

Exercise 8

INSTALLING A NETWORK PRINTER

1. Open the Printers Window and double-click *Add Printer*.
2. Click Next to start the wizard.
3. Click *Network Printer* and click Next. You see the Locate Your Printer window (Figure 5.19). Your dialog box will NOT have the option *Find a printer in the Directory*. This option is found on domain controllers.

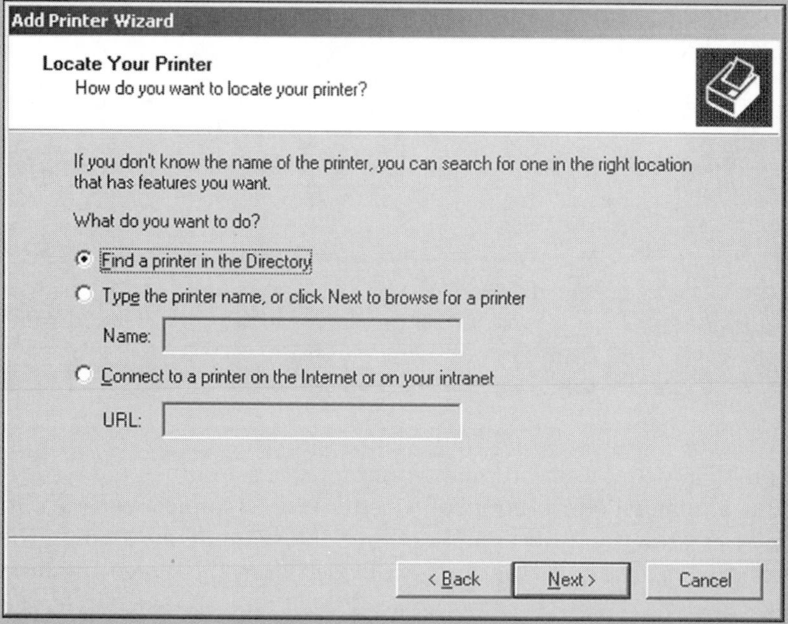

Figure 5.19

You will be asked to specify the name of the network printer by entering the name of the printer in UNC format. Leaving this field blank and clicking the Next button displays a list of known network resources.

4. Click *Type the printer name*, but leave the printer name field blank and click the Next button. You see a screen that looks like Figure 5.20. (If you do not see a list of shared printers, click the computer server icon to display a list of printers.)

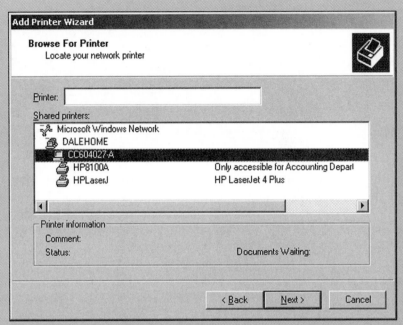

Figure 5.20

A list of shared printers and network servers is displayed. Each shared printer has a small printer icon and each server a computer icon. The small + next to the server icon indicates subentries below the server.

5. Click once on one of the shared printers. The UNC name is automatically placed in the Printer text box.
6. After you have selected a printer, click Next. At this point, the printer drivers will be automatically downloaded if necessary. If you have already installed a printer that uses the same drivers, you will be prompted to keep the existing drivers.
7. The wizard will next prompt you to set this printer as the default. Click No and then click Next.
8. Click Finish to complete the wizard. The Printer window now displays a printer icon with a small network cable to indicate that the printer is located on another computer.

The final way to connect to a printer, which is new in Windows 2000, is by using the Internet Printing Protocol (IPP). This protocol uses standard HTTP to send print jobs across a network. Because the Internet uses HTTP to pass information, printers can send print jobs to a server connected to the Internet running Web server software, such as Internet Information Server.

Most network administrators are not comfortable allowing their print servers to receive print jobs from the Internet. This type of configuration is more natural for an Intranet than for the open Internet. If such a configuration is used, consider having the print jobs received by the Web server and forwarded to the production print servers. If the Web server crashes, external Internet users will not be able to print, but internal network users will still have access to the production print servers.

Either of two ways can be used to connect to a printer using IPP. One way is to specify the name of the printer as a Uniform Resource Locator (URL) during the Add Printer Wizard. This process is much like connecting to a printer using the UNC name. A second way is to use the Internet Explorer browser (version 5 or later) and perform the connection over the Internet.

Exercise 9

USING THE ADD PRINTER WIZARD AND A URL

1. Open the Printer window and double-click the *Add Printer* icon.
2. Start the wizard with the <u>N</u>ext button and then click *Network printer*.
3. Click the second (or third) option in the Locate Your Printer window to specify a URL.

In order to connect to a print server with a URL, the print server must be running Internet Information Server Web hosting software, or Web Services in the case of Windows Professional. If the computer does not have an entry in the DNS server, you cannot specify a server name. However, you can use the IP address of the server. In this exercise you will use the local loopback address.

4. In the URL text box, key:

        http://127.0.0.1/printers/hp8100A/.printer

Make sure you enter this URL correctly. When a printer is shared, Windows 2000 automatically makes it available to Internet Information Server under the printers share. The name entered in the URL is the share name of the printer. You must also include `/.printer` or the URL will not work.

5. You may be asked to enter the server login and password. Enter your login name and password. This security check is performed because the printer request is going over an Internet connection.

At this point, the printer drivers will be downloaded automatically over an Internet connection and installed.

6. Click <u>N</u>ext to keep from setting this as the default printer, and then click Finish to complete the wizard.

You see a printer icon in the Printers window indicating you have just connected to a shared printer. When you send print jobs to this printer, the print jobs will be converted to IPP and then sent over a regular HTTP connection.

In exercise 9, you used the loopback IP address of your own server, but if you had the URL name or IP address of the print server, you could use that name. For example, a server named Marketing in the domain Company.com with a shared printer named HP8100A would be accessible as:

http://Marketing.Company.com/printers/HP8100A/.printer

A second way to install a network printer on the Internet is to use a Web browser. This method is a bit friendlier than using the Add Printer Wizard. A link to installing a printer can be placed on a company Web page for users.

Exercise 10

INSTALLING A PRINTER ACROSS THE NETWORK

1. Open Internet Explorer from the desktop.
2. Key the URL of the network server that will be hosting printing in the format:

```
http://servername/printers
```

In this exercise you will use the IP loopback address, but you can enter a valid server name or the IP address of a server.

3. Key the following URL:

```
http://127.0.0.1/printers
```

4. You may be asked to enter your user name, password, and the name of the server to which you are trying to connect. Enter this information and click OK.
5. You see a Web page listing all the shared printers on the server (Figure 5.21).

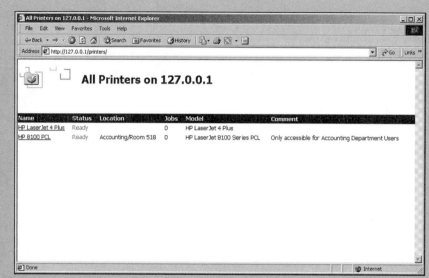

Figure 5.21

This Web page displays the name of the printer, the number of queued jobs, and the printer status.

6. Click the link under the printer name *HP8100 PCL*. You see more information about this printer. In the Printer Actions area, you see a Connect link. (Note: You may not see a Connect link if you are using the loopback address. You may have to use the URL of another server with a shared printer.)
7. Click the Connect link. It will prompt you to add the printer. Clicking <u>Y</u>es will install the printer driver files and add the printer. It may take several minutes because the information is going through HTTP.
8. Once the printer has been installed, you will see a link to view the *Printers* folder. Click this link to make sure the printer has been installed.

Once you have installed a network printer in this manner, you can send print jobs to the printer and manage the printer across the Internet.

Managing Printers

Managing a directly connected printer is easy. Make sure the print device has enough paper and either toner or ink, and that it is plugged into the computer and into a power outlet. Unfortunately, managing shared network printers is not so easy. The network administrator must also consider the following issues:

- How should documents be spooled to the printer from the server?
- What priority level is the printer using?

- Is the user notified when the print job has completed?
- When and who can access to the printer from the network?
- How can long print jobs be handled correctly?

Managing network printers is done from the print server. Most of these options can be set from the printer properties dialog boxes.

Managing Printer Documents

When users send print jobs to a shared network printer, each job is spooled to the server and then forwarded to the printer. As the print job is being forwarded to the printer, its status can be viewed in the Printer window. Print jobs can be canceled, resent, or rescheduled.

Exercise 11

MANAGING PRINTER DOCUMENTS

1. Open the *Printers* folder and double-click the default printer. You see the window in Figure 5.22. This window will display print jobs spooled to this printer.

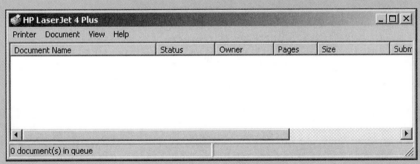

Figure 5.22

To test document management, you will first pause the printer itself.

2. Click the Printer menu in the Printer window and click Pause Printing. This command will keep the printer from receiving any print jobs.
3. Click Start, Programs, Accessories, WordPad. Key your name, and then print the document. Make sure you select the printer being used for testing.
4. Minimize WordPad and look at the Printer window. You will see a listing for the document just printed. The information listed will be the document name, the owner of the document (the user that sent the document to print), how many pages the document has, the document size, and when the document was submitted.

5. Select the document entry by clicking it once and then click the Document menu in the printing window.

The options under the Document menu allow you to pause this specific document, resume printing, restart the document printing from the first page, or cancel the document.

6. Click Printer and then Properties. You see the Properties dialog box.

From the Properties dialog box you can set the print job priority and the scheduled print time. To move a print job ahead of other print jobs, change its priority level. To defer printing a long document until after hours, you can set the schedule.

7. Change the priority for this print job to *50*.
8. Click *Only from* and set the permissible print times from 5:30 p.m. to 11:00 p.m.
9. Click the Separator Page button to select a job separator page. You see a dialog box prompting you for the document name of a separator page file.

This special page is automatically printed by the print server and placed between print jobs. This page is used to organize print jobs and make them easy to locate. The separator page should contain direct printer codes. Windows 2000 has four default separator pages to be used for different kinds of printers. These are located in the *\WINNT\SYSTEM32* folder and are:

PCL.SEP	Used with Hewlett-Packard PCL printers such as LaserJet models. Prints the user name, date, and job number.
PSCRIPT.SEP	Used with PostScript model printers. Puts a printer in PostScript mode, but does not print a separator page. It is used when sending PostScript print jobs to a dual mode printer.
SYSPRINT.SEP	Prints a separator page on a PostScript printer.
SYSPRTJ.SEP	Prints a separator page on a PostScript printer, but includes Japanese fonts.

10. Key the separator file name **PCL.SEP** and click the OK button.
11. Click OK to close the Properties dialog box.
12. Select the print job, click Document, and then click Restart. This print job will not be printed until after the start of the allowable print times.

User Access to Printers

Not everyone should have complete access to all printers. If a company has high-resolution color printers that cost $20 a page in supplies to use, then not everyone on the network should have access. The administrator of the print server can set access rights through the Security dialog box. In a later chapter you will learn how to manage users and user rights, but the following exercise presents the basics of setting user rights to a network printer resource.

Exercise 12

SETTING USER PRINTER ACCESS RIGHTS

1. Open the *Printers* folder, right-click the default printer, and then click Properties.
2. Click the Security tab on the Properties dialog box. You see the dialog box in Figure 5.23.

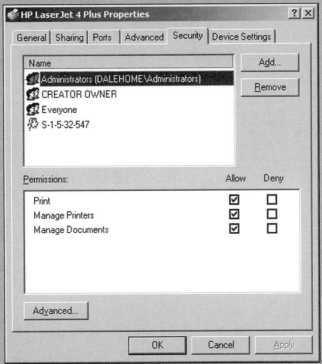

Figure 5.23

The upper section lists the names of groups and individuals who have access to the selected printer. The lower section lists the kinds of rights assigned to the selected group or individual.

As you will learn in a later chapter, a group is a defined set of rights that can be associated with individual users. A user can be placed in, for example, the Power Users group and so inherits all the rights assigned to this group. Everyone with an account is automatically placed in the Everyone group. Members of the Administrators group should have complete access to all resources on the server, including the printers.

3. Click the *Administrators* group name in the upper section. The rights for this group are displayed in the lower section. Administrators have complete rights to the printer.

The three rights assigned to printers are Print, Manage Printers, and Manage Documents. Those users with Print rights can send print jobs to the printer. Users with Manage Printers rights can configure the printer, and users with Manage Documents rights can manage documents in the printer spool.

4. Click the *Everyone* group name and look at their rights. Individuals in the Everyone group can only send print jobs to the printer and cannot manage printers or documents.

It is a good idea to change the default setting for printer security by removing the Everyone group and adding the Users group. Even if you want everyone to use the network printers, only users with a domain account should be able to print. (In a later chapter you will learn how to manage groups and users on a Windows 2000 server.)

5. Make sure the *Everyone* group is selected and click the Remove button. This command removes this group from the selected printer.
6. Click the Add button to add a new user or group. You see a list of users and groups in Figure 5.24.

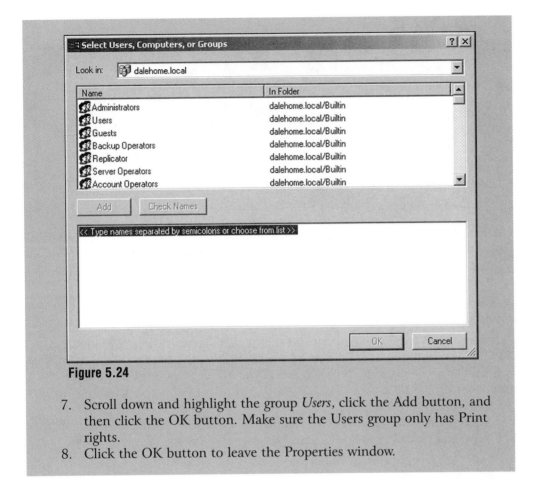

Figure 5.24

7. Scroll down and highlight the group *Users*, click the Add button, and then click the OK button. Make sure the Users group only has Print rights.
8. Click the OK button to leave the Properties window.

Print Pools and Changing Ports

Although computers were supposed to usher in the paperless office, the amount of printing in a typical office is greater than ever. Even with high-speed print devices, it is not uncommon to see multiple jobs queued to a single printer. One way to alleviate such problems is to create a print pool by assigning a single printer (the software drivers and job manager software) to multiple print devices. The printer can have multiple ports attached. When a print job arrives at the printer, Windows 2000 directs the job to the first idle port. The requirement is that all pooled print devices are capable of using the same printer drivers. It also helps if the print devices are in the same physical location.

For example, suppose a company has three Hewlett-Packard LaserJet 8100 printers. Each printer has a TCP/IP card and its own IP address. On the print server, three TCP/IP ports were created and assigned to three different printers. To convert this configuration into a printer pool, two of the printers would be removed and all three TCP/IP ports listed under a single printer.

Exercise 13

CREATING A PRINTER POOL

1. Open the *Printer* folder and right-click the printer *HP8100A*.
2. Click Properties and then click the Ports tab in the Properties dialog box. The printers should have an attached port.
3. Click the Enable Printer Pooling check box. This option allows you to attach additional ports to this printer.
4. With the default port selected, scroll up and click the *LPT2* port. This printer is now connected to both ports.
5. Click the OK button to close the printer Properties dialog box. The HP8100A is now connected to two ports. When a print job arrives, the server print manager will direct it to the first idle port.

Managing the Print Spooler

Windows 2000 starts and runs a process that manages print jobs arriving from clients. This process is called the print spooler. When a job arrives, the print spooler directs it to the proper printer and generally manages print jobs. Sometimes, the print spooler hangs. When it does, printing stops and the network administrator must restart the print spooler.

Because the print spooler is a Windows 2000 service, it must be selected from the Services menu. This menu lists the services running on Windows 2000.

Exercise 14

USING THE PRINT SPOOLER

1. Click Start, Programs, and Administrative Tools, and then click Computer Management. You see the management console in Figure 5.25.

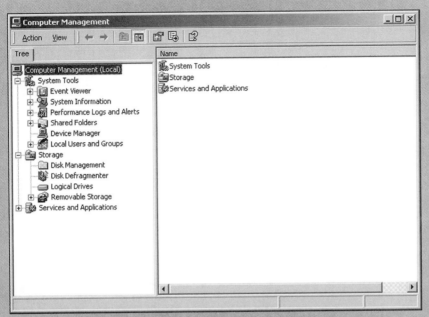

Figure 5.25

2. Click *Services and Applications* in the left frame and then double-click *Services* in the right frame. You see the services for Windows 2000 listed (Figure 5.26).

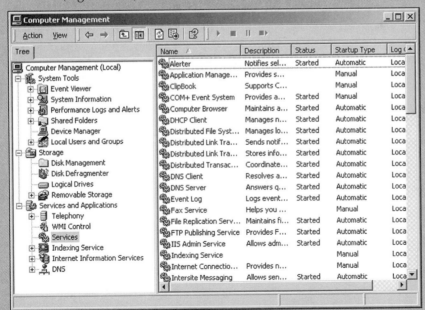

Figure 5.26

3. Locate the service named *Print Spooler* and double-click the service name. You see the Print Spooler Properties dialog box in Figure 5.27.

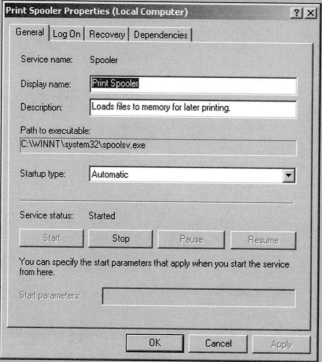

Figure 5.27

4. In the General tab are buttons used to stop and start the service. If print jobs are not printing, the print spooler service can be stopped and restarted.
5. Click the Stop button to stop the service.
6. Once the Start button becomes active, click the Start button to restart the print spooler.
7. Click OK to close the Print Spooler Properties dialog box.

CHAPTER summary

➤ The Windows printing model outlines the steps by which a print job is processed. Windows clients use the GDI and printer drivers to create a printable file. This file is then sent to a print server to be processed by the print processor before being sent to the print device.

➤ Selecting a network print device involves balancing the needs of the users with the speed and capability of the print device.

➤ Windows 2000 installs a number of default printer ports, which can be used to connect a local print device.

➤ When selecting a share name for a network printer, use a name that describes the capability and location of the printer.

➤ Clients can use a network printer by redirecting a local port, using a shared printer, or installing the printer from the Internet.

➤ Print jobs can be deleted, held, redirected, and changed in priority by using print management commands.

CHAPTER terms

Print device	The physical printer.
Printer	The software interface between a computer and a print device.
Printer driver	The software that converts print jobs into a format understood by the print device.
Port	A conduit through which print jobs travel to a print device.
Print server	A computer whose primary purpose is to receive, manage, and redirect print jobs.

CONCEPTS review

Multiple Choice

1. In the Windows printing model, the print router receives print jobs from:
   a. Windows 2000 clients.
   b. Windows 95/98 clients.
   c. Unix clients.
   d. All clients.

2. When printing, the enhanced metafile format (EMF) is used to:
   a. Format only PostScript print jobs.
   b. Format only PCL print jobs.
   c. Format only Raw print jobs.
   d. None of the above.

3. The line printer daemon (LPD) is used to:
   a. Manage Windows 3.1 print jobs.
   b. Only spool print jobs to serial printers.
   c. Only spool print jobs from Macintosh printers.
   d. None of the above.

4. Predefined printer ports do not include:
   a. USB.
   b. Firewire.
   c. NUL.
   d. TCP/IP.

5. A small black check mark next to a printer icon in the Printer window means:
   a. The printer is the default printer.
   b. The printer is currently spooling print jobs.
   c. The printer is out of service.
   d. None of the above.

6. Setting the times of the day when the printer can be used is done from which of the following Printer Properties pages?
   a. Security
   b. Advanced
   c. Sharing
   d. None of the above.

7. Setting which users on the network can access the printer is done from which of the following Printer Properties pages?
   a. Security
   b. Advanced
   c. Sharing
   d. None of the above.

8. When creating a share name for a printer that will be viewable by DOS and Windows 3.1 clients, it is necessary to make the name no longer than:
   a. 9 characters.
   b. 8 characters.
   c. 12 characters.
   d. 15 characters.

9. Which of the following protocols is used by Windows 2000 to send print jobs over the Internet?
   a. Internet Transfer Protocol
   b. Internet Printing Protocol
   c. File Transfer Protocol
   d. None of the above

10. The purpose of a printer pool is to:
    a. Share a single printer for multiple users.
    b. Share a single port for multiple users.
    c. Share a single printer driver for multiple users.
    d. None of the above.

11. A print device is the name given to:
    a. The print drivers.
    b. The physical printer.
    c. The print port.
    d. None of the above.

12. The printer is identified by an IP address when setting up a:
    a. TCP/IP port.
    b. PCL port.
    c. Shared network port.
    d. All of the above.

13. The software most often supplied by the printer manufacturer is the:
    a. Printer port.
    b. Printer.
    c. Printer driver.
    d. None of the above.

14. A local printer:
    a. Can be created on a network server.
    b. Must be installed before it can be shared.
    c. Can be managed through the *Printers* folder.
    d. All of the above.

Fill In

1. A _____ is the name given to the physical printer.

2. _____ software is most often supplied by the printer manufacturer.

3. The _____ is the name give to the conduit through which print jobs reach the printer.

4. On the print client, the _____ subsystem uses the printer drivers to create a printable file before sending it to the server.

5. Clients that use Windows 95/98 send print jobs to the _____ service subsystem.

6. The _____ subsystem on the server manages the physical connection to the local port.

7. The _____ port and the _____ port are automatically installed when a printer that uses these ports is connected to the server.

8. The _____ port automatically discards print jobs and is used to test print settings.

9. When setting up a TCP/IP port, an _____ address is used to identify the printer.

10. A _____ is used to direct print jobs to the first available printer.

11. The Web URL to view installed printers on a server is http://[server name]/_____.

12. Documents are converted to the printer format _____ by Windows 2000 when printing to PCL-based printers.

13. Documents are converted to the printer format _____ by Windows 2000 when printing to PostScript-based printers.

14. The _____ software subsystem on the print server communicates directly with the output port.

15. The _____ port is used to send print jobs to a disk file rather than to a print device.

LAB exercises

Exercise 1 – Add a Local Printer

1. Open the *Printer* folder.
2. Install a LaserJet 4siMX to the parallel port LPT3.
3. Name the printer Sales P1.
4. Do not print a test page.

Exercise 2 – Add a TCP/IP Port

1. Open the *Printer* folder and select the printer created in the previous exercise.
2. Open the Printer Properties menu and add a new port.
3. Add a standard TCP/IP port.
4. Use the TCP/IP address 127.0.0.2.
5. Assume a generic network card.

Exercise 3 – Add a Shared Printer

1. Open the *Printer* folder.
2. Create a new local printer and install the LaserJet 5siMX drivers.
3. Share this printer as Sales P3.
4. Specify the printer location as Sales.
5. Do not print a test page.

Exercise 4 – Set Printer Properties

1. Open the Properties page for the printer created in the previous exercise.
2. Make the printer available only from 12:00 a.m. to 6:00 a.m.
3. Set the printer priority to 3.
4. Insert a separator page named Sales Heading.
5. Set the security for this printer so the local user group Everyone can manage documents.

PROBLEM SOLVING exercises

For each of the following problems, write down the steps that must be taken by the network administrator to arrive at a solution.

1. Your company has two general types of network users: office personnel who typically print single copies of memos and reports, and graphic designers who print high-resolution color proofs of their work. The percentage of user population is 20 percent designers and 80 percent office users. Of the office users, about 15 percent print multiple copies of 50+ page reports on a weekly basis. Given that this company has about 300 users, list the number and types of printers you would recommend management purchase.

2. Design a printing strategy given the following information.

   You are the network administrator charged with developing a printing strategy. Your company has offices on three floors of the building. The top floor has the art department that needs specialized color printers. These color printers are expensive to operate. The second floor has the marketing department that needs access to high-speed laser printers. The volume of print jobs from marketing means that under all circumstances a printer should be available. Sometimes, marketing people need access to printing resources when they are out of the office on travel. The bottom floor contains the management and personnel offices. These offices need occasional access to the high-speed laser printers on the second floor, but also have several regular laser printers.

   Your printing strategy should include the types of printers, how the printers should be configured, and what special options should be set for each printer.

INTRODUCTION TO DOMAINS 6

Performance Objectives

After completing this chapter you will be able to:

- Discuss the concepts behind Domain Name System (DNS)
- Identify public and private DNS roots
- Identify fully qualified domain names
- Discuss name resolution in DNS
- Identify recursive and iterative queries
- Discuss the concepts and organization of Active Directory
- Explain becoming a domain controller
- Troubleshoot the DCPromo program
- Discuss the difference between native and mixed mode domains
- Discuss multimaster replication
- Discuss the purpose of organizational units
- Use the Microsoft Management Console (MMC) to create an organizational unit

Introduction

Up to this point you have been working with a single stand-alone server. A single-server environment is fairly simplistic and in many ways no different from working on a Windows 2000 Professional machine. However, Windows 2000 was designed to be part of a networking environment. In this type of environment the power of the Windows 2000 Server operating system is fully displayed. In this chapter you learn how to configure Windows 2000 as a server in a networking environment. You will also learn how the Domain Name System (DNS) works under Windows 2000 and be introduced to Active Directory. Your instructor will assign another student to be your partner for these exercises.

A major innovation found in Windows 2000 is organizational units. An organizational unit is a container for network objects such as users and computers. Organizational units can be used to organize resources and security within a domain. Because of the distributed nature of Windows 2000 domains, organizational units are a necessity. In this chapter you will learn how to create organizational units. In the users and groups chapter you will learn how to place users in organizational units, and in the Active Directory chapter you will learn how to design a network with organizational units.

Domains

The term **domain** is used to identify two different but related entities found in Windows 2000 and in DNS. You must understand which entity is referred to when this term is used.

- In Windows 2000 a domain refers to a security boundary around a group of computers. Users and network resources are associated with a domain.

- In DNS a domain refers to a set of records used to identify and locate computers and services.

As you will learn in this chapter, these two entities, each referenced by the term domain, are related.

A computer can participate in a Windows 2000 domain by connecting to the domain with a valid user ID and password or by being a domain controller. A **domain controller** is a server that helps manage the security structure that makes up the domain. In order to create a domain or become a domain controller in a previously created domain, two important pieces of the network must be in place, DNS and Active Directory.

Introduction to Domain Name System

DNS is not a new concept that arrived with Windows 2000. DNS has been around since 1984 when it was invented as a way to resolve names on the Internet. In a TCP/IP network, such as the Internet, each computer must have a unique IP address in order to communicate with other systems. Current IP addresses are a set of binary digits, but are normally formatted as four sets of three numbers separated by dots, such as:

```
192.216.189.166
```

In order to communicate with a machine on the Internet you need to know its IP address, just as you need to know the street address of a house in order to send mail. Although numeric addresses are fine for communication between computers, it is easier for people to remember names rather than numbers. An Internet address that uses text rather than an IP address is called a Uniform Resource Locator (URL). An Internet address such as www.pepsi.com is simply a way to locate a computer on the Web without knowing the IP address of the machine that hosts that site.

The problem with URLs is that the network messages must use the IP address. When a URL is typed into a browser, it must have some way for the text to be converted into a numeric address so that it can be used by the computer to communicate with another computer. **DNS** is the system that performs this conversion through a DNS server. A DNS server is a computer that converts or matches host names (URLs) to their corresponding IP addresses.

For example, the URL www.loc.gov identifies the Library of Congress. The corresponding IP address is:

```
140.147.249.7
```

You can verify this reciprocal identification by opening a browser and entering this IP address in place of the URL.

A DNS server contains lists of IP addresses and computer names and will look up an IP address when given a name (and will, if configured, look up a name when given an IP address). This process of locating information is called name resolution. Because maintaining a DNS server requires time and effort, it was often easier, with previous versions of Microsoft Windows, to rely on an external DNS server for name resolution rather than create and maintain a local DNS server. Most Internet service providers and people who provide connections to the Internet maintain DNS servers that perform these tasks.

Because DNS is based on a set of network standards, DNS servers can be hosted on different kinds of operating systems. It is not uncommon to find a Windows NT network using a DNS server that is running a version of UNIX.

Windows DNS

The strategy of using an external DNS server for name resolution will likely change with the advent of Windows 2000. Most Windows 2000-based networks will use a locally installed DNS server running the Windows 2000 version of DNS. Two main reasons for using a local Windows 2000 DNS server are—

- DNS is required in order to use Active Directory and so should be managed by the local network administrators.

- The Windows 2000 version of DNS was developed to work best with other Windows 2000 components.

Some of the advantages of the Microsoft implementation of DNS are:

- **Dynamic Updates**: In the past, any time a machine was added to the network, its name and IP address had to be manually entered into the DNS server by an administrator. With a Windows 2000 DNS server, names and addresses can be added to the DNS server by the computers as they boot onto the network.

- **Active Directory Integration**: As you will learn, Active Directory is a distributed object database that replicates itself across the network. Traditionally, no good fault-tolerant scheme has been available to maintain DNS records if a DNS server fails. By integrating DNS into an Active Directory database, the information from the DNS server is replicated to multiple machines. Active Directory can also query DNS to resolve names, and the two can be managed from a central point.

- **WINS Integration**: Windows 2000 DNS works nicely alongside WINS with down-level clients on the network.

- **Unicode Support**: Standard DNS supports the basic ASCII character set. Microsoft DNS supports Unicode, which is an extended character set that allows for most foreign languages.

If Microsoft DNS needs to work in conjunction with standard DNS you will not be able to use the extended features provided by Microsoft DNS.

The DNS Tree

A DNS server contains a list of IP addresses and their associated names, called the DNS namespace. When given a name, the DNS server locates the associated IP address. A DNS namespace can be pictured as an upside down tree. The root of the tree is represented by a dot with branches coming out from the root. The root branches into top-level domains, which branch further into subdomains. (These DNS domains are not the same as Windows domains.) At the very ends of the branches are the individual servers, or leaves. An example of a **DNS tree** is shown in Figure 6.1.

F I G U R E **6.1** *DNS Tree*

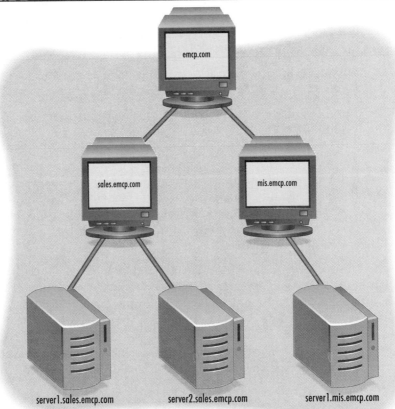

In this figure the root is represented by emcp.com and a period. Under the root are two subdomains, mis.emcp.com and sales.emcp.com. Under the sales.emcp.com branch are two more subdomains, server1.sales.emcp.com and server2.sales.emcp.com. Under the mis.emcp.com is the single subdomain server1.mis.emcp.com.

Fully Qualified Domain Names

Each computer entry within a DNS namespace must have a unique name. This name is called the **fully qualified domain name** (**FQDN**). In Figure 6.1, you see two servers named Server1, but the FQDN of each of those machines is different. The FQDN is read from left to right with the leaf name on the left and the root name on the right. The FQDN of the three servers in the Figure 6.1 namespace are server1.sales.emcp.com, server2.sales.emcp.com, and server1.mis.emcp.com.

Public versus Private DNS Roots

The root of a DNS namespace is where the DNS server starts looking for matches to an IP address. But what about the Internet, which is owned and hosted by no single company? In this case, a public DNS root is used to access computers on the Internet. At the root of the public DNS tree are the following 13 root servers that are **authoritative**, or responsible for the top-level domains:

com	org	net	mil
edu	gov	int	aero
biz	coop	info	museum
name	pro		

A DNS server is identified as authoritative over a namespace when it contains the namespace records and can change the information in the namespace.

Most people are now familiar with some of the common top-level DNS domains because they are seen at the end of URLs. A company would probably have a .com at the end of their URL and a nonprofit organization would have an .org. Below the top-level domains are subdomains assigned to companies, organizations, or individuals. In order for a company, organization, or person to have a domain name at this level, it must register it with an authorized domain name registration organization. The InterNIC, which is a governing body that administers domain names on the Internet, authorizes these registration organizations. At the time of registration, the applicant must provide the TCP/IP addresses of two DNS servers that will be responsible for handling the company's domain. Below this level the organization is welcome to set up as many subdomains as desired.

For example, EMCParadigm Publishing wanted to secure the Internet domain name emcp.com, they would need to set up two different local DNS servers and send the IP addresses of these servers to the registering organization. The registering organization would then add an entry to the top-level root DNS server that consisted of the name "emcp.com" and the two IP addresses. When someone on the Internet enters www.emcp.com, the request is sent to the local servers located at EMCParadigm's company headquarters.

At times a company may not want to use the public DNS root servers, but instead set up a private DNS root server. This arrangement will always be the case if an organization does not have a connection to the Internet or wants to keep the company network behind a barrier to the Internet. In this case a private DNS root must be established in order for DNS to work. A private DNS root would also be appropriate if a company was connected to the Internet through a proxy server.

Name Resolution Using DNS

Now that you understand the structure of the DNS namespace, let's see how a client computer, also called a **resolver**, can use DNS to locate a Web site. In order to use DNS, the resolver must be configured with the IP address of a DNS server. In this example the resolver knows that the IP address of its company's local DNS server, which is named emcpsdns.com, is 192.168.100.56. The resolver is attempting to locate the computer named server1.sales.emcp.net. In order to connect to this server, the resolver must find the IP address associated with the computer name. This process is illustrated in Figure 6.2 and summarized in the following steps:

Step 1: The resolver first contacts emcpsdns.com and asks for the location of server1.sales.emcp.net. Because the emcpsdns.com DNS server only controls its own emcp domain it does not know the address for server1.sales.emcp.net. (It does not have this information in its namespace.)

Step 2: Because the emcpsdns.com DNS server does not know the requested address it attempts to locate another DNS server that may know the address. Emcpsdns.com does know the address of one of the root servers and proceeds to ask the root server, "Where is server1.sales.emcp.net?" The root server does not know where all servers in the emcp.net tree are located, but it does know the IP address for the server responsible for the net domain. The root server sends this IP address back to the emcpsdns.com DNS server.

Step 3: Emcpsdns.com now performs a second query to the net server with the same question: "Where is server1.sales.emcp.net?" Once again, the net server does not know the answer, but it does provide the IP address for the emcp.net domain.

Step 4: Emcpdns.com now does a third query to the emcp.net server, asking, "Where is server1.sales.emcp.net?" Because emcp.net is the authoritative DNS server that is responsible for the emcp.net domain, it contains the records for this server and knows the IP address of server1.sales.emcp.net. The IP address is returned to emcpsdns.com.

Step 5: Having finally learned the address of server1.sales.emcp.net, emcpsdns.com returns the IP address to the resolver who originally asked the question.

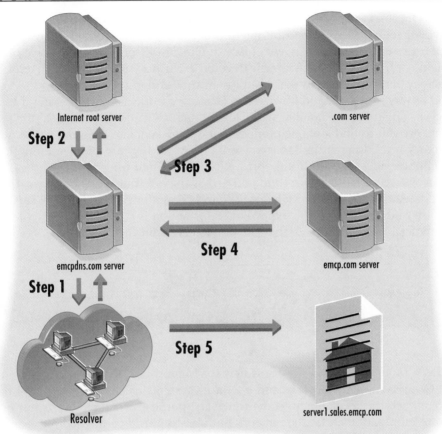

Recursive and Iterative Queries

The preceding steps illustrate two different types of queries, recursive and iterative. By default in Windows 2000, the resolver does a **recursive query**. With a recursive query, when the resolver asks the DNS server for an IP address it expects to receive a complete address as the answer. The resolver will not perform more queries to find the correct IP address. This is what happened in the sample DNS query. The resolver sent a request to the DNS server and received back the IP address of server1.sales.emcp.net.

The emcpsdns.com server illustrates an iterative type of query. In an **iterative query**, the answer does not have to be the requested address, but can be the address of another DNS server. The emcpdns.com DNS server asks the root server for the address of server1.sales.emcp.net but does not receive the complete answer. Instead it receives part of the answer in the form of an IP address of another server to query (Step 2 where the root server returns the address of the net server). Because emcpsdns.com performed an iterative query, it expects that it will have to perform multiple queries in order to receive the final answer, which is exactly what happens.

Introduction to Active Directory

Active Directory is one of the most important and complex parts of Windows 2000. Active Directory needs to be running in order to create network domains. This chapter presents a basic overview of Active Directory from the perspective of a domain controller. A later chapter is devoted exclusively to the topic of Active Directory and explains how it is used in network design.

One way to understand how Active Directory works is by comparing it to a directory you are more familiar with. The phone book is organized as a directory and allows you to find a phone number if you know a name. Windows 2000 Active Directory is used much the same way on a network. Because the main functions of computer networks are to support multiple users and provide those users with resources, users need a way to find and access these resources. The information stored in **Active Directory** includes user and computer names, network services, and other information of this type. This information is stored as objects and automatically replicated to Active Directory servers on the network.

The Active Directory database is held in a file called NTDS.DIT, which is located in the *\winnt\ntds* folder.

Even though Active Directory is new for Microsoft, directory services are not new. Other computer networks and operating systems (such as Novell) have had directory services available for some time. The purpose of a directory is not only to store information about the network but also to provide a method for users to find resources on the network by querying the directory. For example, a user may want to know which printer is available on the second floor of the building and would query Active Directory for this information.

Review of Windows NT Domains

To understand Active Directory domains it is helpful to review how domains were implemented in Windows NT. Starting with Windows NT, the basic administration unit was called a domain. A domain was just a grouping of servers. Servers assigned to a domain do not have to be physically located together in a common geographic area because domains are a logical grouping on the network. For example, servers in a domain named *Manufacturing* might be located in different cities, where the manufacturing plants for a company are located. Although the servers in this domain are located miles apart, they could still be administered as a single unit.

Consider a company that has five servers that belong to a single domain. Instead of having to create a separate account for a user on each of the five servers, a single account could be created within the domain. One server, designated as the primary domain controller (PDC), holds a changeable copy of the user database that contains security information about the user. This user database is called the *SAM*. In order to make a change to the SAM, such as adding a user or changing a password, the PDC must be up and functional. After information in the SAM was changed, the SAM database on the PDC would be replicated to the other servers in the domain that were designated as backup domain controllers (BDCs). After replication all the domain controllers would have a copy of the updated SAM and know about the new user account. This replication process allowed the administrator to create the account only once for the user in order for the user to be able to log on to all five servers.

The SAM database also contains a list of user rights within a domain. One example is the right to back up files and directories on servers. If a user is given the right to back up files, this information is placed in the SAM database and replicated to the other domain controllers. The user can then back up files on any server that belongs to the domain. Basically a Windows NT domain allowed an administrator to centrally manage user accounts and rights.

Organization of the Active Directory

In Windows 2000 the Active Directory database and system takes the place of the NT4 SAM database. (However, the SAM database is still around and used when Windows 2000 deals with older Windows NT servers.) Active Directory has more capabilities and is much more expandable than the old SAM database. It is also much more complex than the SAM system used in Windows NT and requires more planning before being implemented. Before installing a network or converting a Windows NT 4 network to Windows 2000, you need to decide how your Active Directory should be organized. Active Directory can be set up many different ways, and the design selected should be based on a number of geographical, organizational, and other factors. You will learn about Active Directory design in a later chapter.

The following sections discuss the concepts that represent some of the building blocks available to you when designing your Active Directory.

Windows 2000 Domains   In many ways a domain in Windows 2000 is the same as a domain in Windows NT. A Windows 2000 domain is still a logical unit rather than a physical one, and domain objects such as servers, computers, and users can be located in different geographic areas but still be part of the same domain. The new Active Directory domain database, which replaces the SAM database, can be used to keep track of more objects than would be found in a Windows NT domain. A Windows 2000 domain can, theoretically, hold millions of objects compared to about 5,000 objects in a Windows NT domain. This capability means that large companies can include everything in a single domain, which is easier to manage than multiple domains.

A Windows 2000 domain, along with being a repository for information, is also a replication and security boundary. A user account created in a domain will be automatically replicated to all domain controllers within the domain, but will not be automatically replicated to domain controllers in a different domain. As a security boundary, Windows 2000 domains maintain the permissions and rights to their own resources.

Organizational Units   Some of the functions that were domain-wide under Windows NT have been delegated to a new Windows 2000 object called an **organizational unit (OU)**. An OU is a way to logically subdivide a domain. One of the problems with Windows NT 4 domains is that they could not be divided into pieces. Once a user was given a right to do something they had that right in the entire domain.

For example, a company creates a multiserver manufacturing domain with Windows NT 4 that includes a server containing top-secret information. A user given the right to back up files on the domain could then do so on every server in the domain, including those on the top-secret computer. In order to separate the single computer containing sensitive files, it became necessary to create another domain just for the single computer. Giving users access to this new domain would necessitate creating additional user accounts and rights.

In Windows 2000, organizational units are used to solve this type of problem. A single domain can be subdivided into several OUs. The manufacturing domain could have a top-secret OU and a production OU. Each OU can be its own administrative unit, be given an administrator, and have its own policies. A user could be given the right to back up files in the rest of the manufacturing domain but not in the top-secret OU.

Objects   An **object** refers to an identifiable domain resource that has attributes. A user account is an object with attributes such as logon name and password. Other types of objects are files, directories, and printers. Objects reside in the Active Directory database and are usually associated with organizational units.

When diagramming a network design in Windows NT, domains were drawn as circles, while in Windows 2000, domains are notated as triangles and the organizational units are circles.

Tree   A **tree** is a group of one or more related domains. In a tree, domains must be related by sharing a contiguous DNS namespace. When domains are joined in a tree, two-way transitive trusts are formed between domains. Domain trees will be discussed in more detail in Chapter 11.

Forest   A **forest** is a group of one or more trees that have separate DNS namespaces. Forests will also be discussed in detail in Chapter 11. In this chapter you will work with a single domain model.

Site   A **site** is a group of one or more well-connected subnets. A domain can have many sites or a site can contain multiple domains. Sites help control timing of Active Directory replication.

Becoming a Domain Controller

Once you understand how DNS works and are familiar with the terminology for Active Directory, the next step is to begin work in a domain environment. You will first create a new domain by promoting a stand-alone server to a domain controller.

In order to become a domain controller a server must have access to a DNS server that is responsible for the domain records. The first server you convert to a domain controller will also become the DNS server.

> Non-Microsoft DNS servers can be used with an Active Directory domain, but they must be able to support dynamic updates and SRV records. Currently, UNIX DNS servers that use BIND version 8.1.2 or later can be used with an Active Directory network.

In the following exercises you will—

- Configure a server to be a domain controller by setting the TCP/IP options
- Run the DCPROMO program to create a domain controller
- Configure a second computer to be a DNS client of the first domain controller
- Convert the second computer to a domain controller that participates in the domain created on the first computer

It is assumed that you are working with another server in a network environment. For multiple groups of servers, make sure each pair is given a unique domain name.

Exercise 1

SETTING THE FIRST DOMAIN CONTROLLER'S TCP/IP OPTIONS

Domain controllers must have a static IP address. Windows DNS will not correctly install on a server that uses a dynamic IP address. In the following exercise you set a static IP address and then set the DNS address.

1. Log on to the server that will be the first computer in the domain. Make sure you log on as administrator.
2. Right-click the *My Network Places* icon and click Properties.
3. Right-click the *Local Area Connection* icon and click Properties.
4. Click *Internet Protocol TCP/IP* and then click the Properties button.
5. Make sure the IP address is static and you are using your assigned IP address. Make sure the subnet mask is filled in properly. Also, make sure the computer's IP address appears in the DNS address section. (You will be using the computer's own IP address for the DNS address because DNS will be installed on this computer.)
6. Close the Properties window and return to the desktop.

Exercise 2

CREATING THE FIRST DOMAIN CONTROLLER IN A DOMAIN

In this exercise you create a new domain. During the steps to create the domain you will be given the option of creating a new domain or joining an existing domain. You will also be asked whether the domain being created will belong to a forest or be part of a new forest. Because it will be a new domain, you will not join an existing domain and will not join your domain to an existing forest of domains.

1. Click Start, click Run, and then key **dcpromo**.
2. Click OK to run this program.
3. At the Welcome to Active Directory Installation Wizard click <u>N</u>ext to continue.
4. At the Domain Controller Type window click *Domain controller for a new domain* and click <u>N</u>ext (Figure 6.3).

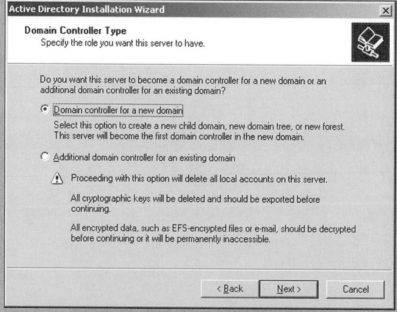

Figure 6.3

5. Click *Create a new domain tree* and click <u>N</u>ext.
6. Click *Create a new forest of domain trees* and click <u>N</u>ext.
7. Key *your domain name.local* (substituting the name you have been assigned for *your domain name*) for the full DNS domain name and click <u>N</u>ext (Figure 6.4).

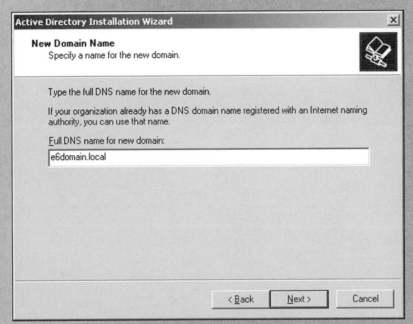

Figure 6.4

8. The NetBIOS domain name should be filled in. Click Next.
9. Accept the default database and log locations and click Next.
10. Accept the default SysVol location and click Next.
11. When you receive a message indicating that the wizard cannot contact a DNS server for your domain, click OK (Figure 6.5).

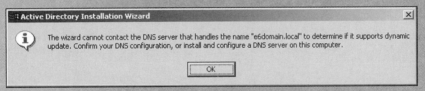

Figure 6.5

When a new domain is installed, Windows attempts to contact a DNS server. If, during the domain installation process, a DNS server cannot be found, you are presented with the option to install Windows 2000 DNS on the current computer.

12. Click Yes to install and configure DNS on this computer and click Next.
13. At the Permissions window, click *Permissions compatible with pre-Windows 2000 servers* and click Next (Figure 6.6).

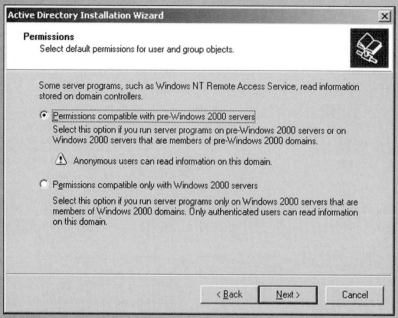

Figure 6.6

This option determines if the network can support classic Windows NT 4 RAS servers.

14. For the Directory Services Restore Mode password key **classroom.** (Remember, passwords are case sensitive! Key your password in lower case.) Press the Tab key and key **classroom** in the Confirm password box, and then click <u>N</u>ext.

15. View the summary to make sure it is correct and click <u>N</u>ext.

The process of creating a domain controller may take several minutes. The Active Directory database is being built and configured.

16. When asked, insert the Windows 2000 Install CD and click OK.

17. If you see the Files Needed window, key in the path to the *I386* directory on the Windows 2000 Install CD. (Make sure to insert the CD if you are installing from CD. If you are using a CD that autostarts you will see a Windows 2000 Server window with the options to install 2000, install components, browse the CD, or exit. Click Exit.)

During this step, the files needed for DNS are copied from the Windows 2000 Install CD and DNS is installed on the server.

18. At the Completing the Active Directory Installation Wizard screen, click Finish.

19. Click Restart.

Exercise 3

VERIFYING INSTALLATION OF ACTIVE DIRECTORY

After the first server in the domain has been converted, it will take time for the Active Directory database to be built and for the required DNS records to be inserted into the DNS namespace. Before adding a second server to the domain, you must verify that Active Directory is running and that the required records have been inserted in the DNS namespace. To check for completion of the Active Directory startup processes you can verify that the Active Directory records appear in DNS by using the DNS Manager.

1. Click Start, Programs, Administrative Tools, and then click DNS. You see the DNS Manager MMC (Figure 6.7).

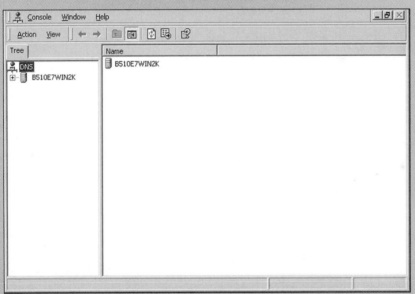

Figure 6.7

2. Click the plus sign next to your computer name to expand it.
3. Click the plus sign next to *Forward Lookup Zones* to expand it.
4. Click the plus sign next to your domain name to expand it. You see a set of folders under your domain name (Figure 6.8).

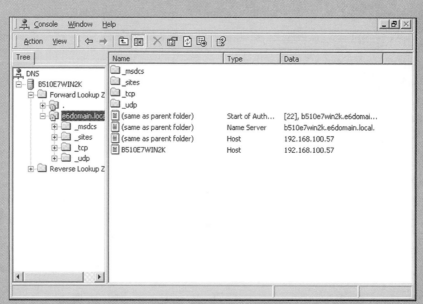

Figure 6.8

You should see four folders like those that appear in Figure 6.8. If you do not see all the folders your computer is not yet finished building the Active Directory and inserting the DNS records. You will need to wait before attempting to promote your second domain controller. The DNS manager screen does not refresh automatically, so you will need to press the F5 key to refresh it, or close it and open it again.

If all four of your folders do not build you can try starting and stopping the netlogon service. At a command prompt, key

```
net stop netlogon

net start netlogon
```

Promoting a Second Domain Controller into an Existing Domain

The first domain controller has been created and you can now proceed to add an additional domain controller to the domain. In order to promote the second computer to be a domain controller, it must be able to contact the DNS server running on the first machine. Remember, DNS was automatically installed on the first computer when it was converted to a domain controller. The following steps should be done on the second server in order to make it a DNS client of the first server.

Exercise 4

BECOMING A DNS CLIENT

In order to become a DNS client, the second computer must identify the first computer as the DNS server. This process requires setting the IP address for the DNS server on the second computer to the address of the first server.

1. Log on to the second server as the administrator.
2. Right-click the *My Network Places* icon and click Properties.
3. Right-click the *Local Area Connection* icon and click Properties.
4. Click to highlight the *Internet TCP/IP* protocol and click the Properties button.
5. Set this server with a static IP address that is different from the first server. Make sure you also set the subnet mask.
6. Click *Use the following DNS server addresses* and enter the IP address of the first server in your domain (Figure 6.9).

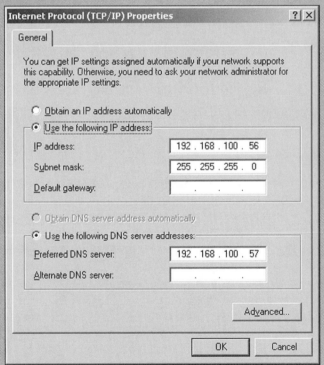

Figure 6.9

7. Click OK to close the TCP/IP Properties page.
8. Click OK to close the Local Area Connection Properties dialog box.
9. Close the Network and Dial-up Connections window.

Exercise 5

TESTING THE DNS CLIENT

The command line tool nslookup can be used to test the connection to DNS running on the first server.

1. From the second server, click Start, click Run, key **cmd**, and click OK.
2. At the command line key **nslookup** *domain name* (where *domain name* is the domain name you assigned to the first server) and press Enter.

The nslookup program will attempt to contact the DNS server address you entered in the previous steps and you may receive a message that will appear something like the following:

```
DNS Request timed out

Timeout was 2 seconds

Can't find server for address XXX.XXX.XXX.XXX

Default servers are not available

Server: Unknown

Address: XXX.XXX.XXX.XXX


Name: A1Computer.Adomain.Local

Address: XXX.XXX.XXX.XXX
```

You will see IP addresses in place of the *X*s and your computer name and domain after the Name prompt. Do not worry about the first part of the message indicating an error. As long as you receive back a result in the second portion that shows the fully qualified server name and IP address, the second server has successfully queried the DNS server.

Another step you will want to take to help ensure a smooth transition to a domain controller is to synchronize the time of the machine you are promoting with the first domain controller in the domain. As you will learn in a later chapter, Active Directory uses date and time parameters for a variety of tasks. If a server has an incorrectly set date or time, it could affect how it works with Active Directory.

A service called the Windows Time Service, or W32Time, helps keep the time setting on all the domain controllers synchronized with the first domain controller. To make sure the time is set for the machine you wish to add to an Active Directory domain, use the following command from the command line, substituting the name of the first domain controller for *servername*:

```
net time \\servername /set /y
```

Exercise 6

ADDING A SECOND DOMAIN CONTROLLER

You have set the IP address and the DNS address on the second server and you are now prepared to promote your second server to be a domain controller in the domain hosted by the first server. In the following exercise, you add the second server to the domain as another domain controller. Make sure that the first domain controller is running and is accessible to the second server over the network.

1. On the second server, click Start, click Run, key **dcpromo**, and click OK.
2. At the Welcome to Active Directory Installation Wizard, click <u>N</u>ext to continue.
3. Click *Additional domain controller for an existing domain* and click <u>N</u>ext (Figure 6.10).

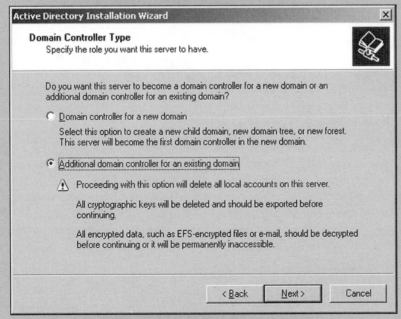

Figure 6.10

This server will be added to an existing domain and will not be host to a new domain.

4. For the username key **administrator**, for the password key **classroom**, and for the domain key the domain you want to join. (You must have access to an administrator account in order to join a server to an existing domain.) Key just the domain part of the name and not the local part. When done, click Next.

The next screen requests the full DNS name. The name you enter for the DNS domain should be the complete domain name assigned to the first server. For example, if the domain name on the first server is A10domain.local, then it is the domain name you would enter.

5. Make sure the DNS domain name is correct and click Next.
6. Accept the default paths for the database and log and click Next.
7. Accept the default paths for the SysVol and click Next.
8. For the password, key **classroom** and confirm with **classroom** and click Next.
9. To accept the summary, click Next.

At this point, Active Directory will be configured on the second server. This process involves, among other things, copying the Active Directory database to the second server. This process can take several minutes.

10. When the Completing Active Directory Installation Wizard screen appears, click Finish.
11. Click Restart Now to restart your machine.
12. After the second server has rebooted, you can check to see whether your machine is now part of the domain. Right-click the *My Computer* icon on the desktop and click the Identification tab. The domain name of the first server should be listed.

Troubleshooting the Domain Creation Process

During the domain creation or server promotion process, a set of log files are created that contain messages detailing the process of running the DCPROMO program. If problems occur during the domain creation or server promotion process, you should check the log files. These files are located in the *winnt\debug* folder and are named dcpromoui.log and dcpromo.log. Even though these files are not easy to read, you can probably decipher what went wrong if you spend time digging through the logs. Some of the most common reasons promotion to a domain controller fails are—

- DNS communication problems

- Time synchronization problems between the two machines

- Attempting to place the SysVol file on a volume that is not formatted with NTFS5

Another tool that can be used to locate problems with promoting servers to domain controllers is the event viewer. The event viewer maintains a record of software processes and is often the first place to check when troubleshooting your system. Three types of events that can appear in the event viewer are—

1. *Information:* Informs you that something has happened. This type of event does not represent an error condition.

2. *Warning:* Informs you of an event that could cause a problem depending on your situation.

3. *Error:* Indicates a failure of some event or service.

You will learn much more about the event viewer in a later chapter that deals with Windows troubleshooting.

Exercise 7

VERIFYING DOMAIN CONTROLLER PROMOTION

After promotion of a domain controller you should check both the DNS server and directory service logs to make sure no errors were recorded.

1. Click Start, Programs, Administrative Tools, and Event Viewer. You see the Event Viewer window (Figure 6.11).

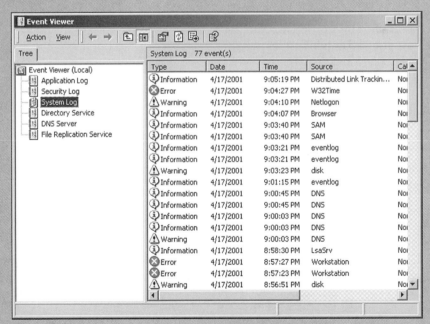

Figure 6.11

Native versus Mixed Mode Domains

By default, Windows 2000 domains operate in mixed mode. A **mixed mode** domain will support Windows NT 4 backup domain controllers (BDC) and is used when network servers on the same network are running both Windows 2000 and Windows NT. It is possible to use both network operating systems on the same network because Windows 2000 domain controllers have a special feature called a PDC emulator. The PDC emulator causes a Windows 2000 domain controller to appear as a primary domain controller (PDC) to Windows NT 4 BDCs. It allows the Windows NT 4 BDCs to function normally. Once all the network domain controllers have been switched over to Windows 2000, the network can be converted from mixed mode to **native mode**. This change can only be made if all the Windows NT 4 BDCs have been switched over because these servers cannot function in a native mode domain.

Some of the advantages of a native mode domain include the following:

- Full multimaster replication
- Floating RID pool
- Nested global groups
- Transitive trusts
- Directory enabled DNS
- Universal groups

The conversion to native mode is not reversible. To go back to a mixed mode domain requires the reinstallation of Windows 2000. The initial conversion to native mode can be done on any domain controller. However, after the network has been converted to native mode each domain controller must be rebooted. The domain controller servers do not all have to be rebooted at exactly the same time, but the new functionality provided by native mode cannot be used until all the domain controllers have been rebooted.

Use caution when converting to native mode—OK is the default! If you accidentally hit the Enter key you will convert your domain to native mode.

Exercise 8

CONVERTING TO NATIVE MODE

The first eight steps should only be done on one domain controller in the domain. Step 9 should be performed on both domain controllers in the domain.

1. Click Start, Programs, Administrative Tools, Active Directory Users and Computers.
2. Right-click your domain name.
3. Click Properties.
4. Click Change Mode.
5. Click Yes at the warning message to change your domain to native mode.
6. Click OK at the Domain Properties window. (Notice the domain operation mode is now listed as native mode.)
7. Click OK at the operation completed successfully message.
8. Close the Active Directory Users and Computers window.
9. Each domain controller in the domain must be rebooted before it will operate in native mode. Wait about 15 minutes to be sure that Active Directory has replicated to the second machine in your domain before rebooting it.

Multimaster Replication

With a Windows NT 4 domain the primary domain controller must be functioning in order to change the SAM database. A change to the SAM database is then replicated out to the backup domain controllers. With Windows 2000, the concept of a primary domain controller no longer applies. Changes are made to the Active Directory database, a copy of which is located on all domain controllers in the domain. The changes to an Active Directory database on one domain controller will be automatically replicated to other domain controllers in the same domain. This process of propagating a change in Active Directory to all domain controllers in a domain is called *convergence*. The following discussion provides an overview of this process. It will be discussed in much greater detail in the Active Directory chapter.

Each domain controller has at least two replication partners (assuming at least three domain controllers in the domain). The following example shows how convergence works in a single site domain with three domain controllers named RedDC, WhiteDC, and BlueDC (Figure 6.12).

FIGURE 6.12 *The Convergence of Domain Controllers*

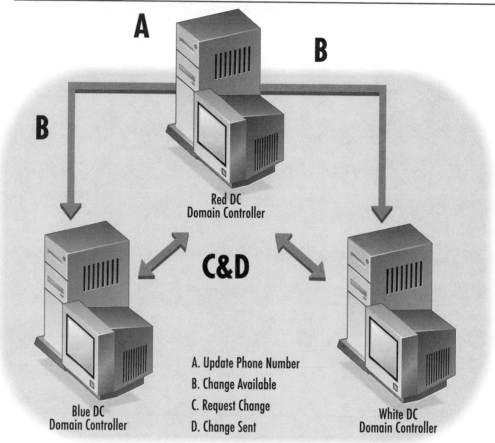

Red DC
Domain Controller

C&D

A. Update Phone Number
B. Change Available
C. Request Change
D. Change Sent

Blue DC
Domain Controller

White DC
Domain Controller

- An Active Directory user object on RedDC is updated with a user's phone number.

- Within five minutes, RedDC notifies WhiteDC and BlueDC that it has changes.

- WhiteDC and BlueDC each request a copy of the change. Because this change was made to the attribute phone number in a user object, it is only the attribute (the phone number) that will be replicated, not the entire object.

- RedDC sends the change to one of the requesting domain controllers, waits 30 seconds, and sends the change to the second requesting domain controller.

What happens if a change is made to the user's phone number on RedDC and a change is also made to the same user's phone number of BlueDC before convergence takes place? Each property in an object has a property version number

(PVN) that indicates how many times the property has been modified, and a time stamp that indicates when the property was last modified. These two values are used to determine which change will be replicated to the rest of the domain controllers. Assuming convergence was complete before the changes to the phone number in our example, the phone number on RedDC and BlueDC would have the same original PVN. We will use a PVN of 1. After the change took place on RedDC, it would increment the PVN by one and have a new PVN of 2. The same would happen at BlueDC. If two changes are received that have the same PVN number as would be the case in this example, the change with the later time stamp will be used as the final change.

When a new domain controller is brought into the system, a service called the Knowledge Consistency Checker (KCC) will introduce the domain controller into the replication ring so that it has two replication partners. If the ring becomes too large, the KCC will build additional connections across the ring so that the hop count between domain controllers is always three or less. The KCC is also responsible for building new links if a domain controller is taken out of the loop.

Starting a Microsoft Management Console

Now that your machine has become a domain controller, you will want to administer the entire domain instead of simply your own machine. The new Windows 2000 administrative tool called the Microsoft Management Console (MMC) allows each administrator to customize his or her own environment by adding whatever tools are needed. The tools that can be added are called snap-ins. The MMC also gives third-party vendors a standard to use when writing administrative tools for their products. In order to begin working within your domain, you will want to create your own MMC.

The following exercise illustrates how to create a new MMC and add the snap-in tools needed to create and manage users in your domain, which should be done on both domain controllers.

Exercise 9

CREATING AN MMC
1. Click Start and then click Run.
2. In the Open box key **mmc** and click OK.

This command creates a blank MMC that you can configure with the snap-in tools you wish to use. You should maximize this window for ease of use.

3. From the Menu bar click Console, then click Add/Remove Snap-in.
4. At the Add/Remove Snap-in dialog box click Add.

5. In the Available Stand-alone Snap-in dialog box, click *Active Directory Users and Computers* and then click Add. (It will show up in the Add/Remove Snap-in dialog box.)
6. In the Available Stand-alone Snap-in dialog box, click *Active Directory Sites and Services* and click Add. (It will show up in the Add/Remove Snap-in dialog box.) The MMC now looks like Figure 6.13.

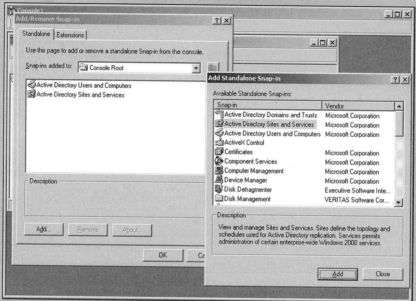

Figure 6.13

7. Click Close at the Add Stand-alone Snap-in dialog box.
8. You should now be back at the Add/Remove Snap-in dialog box and see the two snap-ins. Click OK.

You can save the console for later use with the following steps.

9. Click the Console menu item of the MMC and click Save.
10. Leave the Save In setting at the default of *Administrative Tools*.
11. In the File name box key **A1Main Console** (**A2Main Console**).
12. Accept the Default Save as type of *Microsoft Management Console (*.msc)*.
13. Click Save.

Now an option for the Main Console will appear under Start/Programs/Administrative Tools.

Exercise 10

1. Click Start, Programs, Administrative Tools, and then click the MMC you created in the previous exercise.
2. Click the plus sign next to the *Active Directory Users and Computers* icon in your open MMC. You should now see *your_domain_name.local domain*.
3. Click the plus sign next to the *your_domain_name.local domain* icon to expand it. You should see a screen like Figure 6.14.

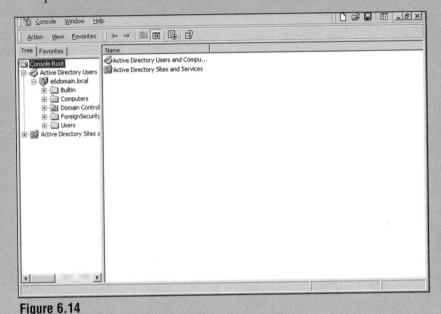

Figure 6.14

In your MMC on the left side of the screen you should see the name of your domain. When the domain is expanded you will see what appears to be five folders. These folders represent generic container units. The five folders you see are:

> *Builtin*: This folder holds the objects that represent local groups that are automatically built when the domain was created.

> *Computers*: This folder holds the objects that represent computers on the network. If you upgraded from a Windows NT 4 system any computer accounts that were transferred will be located here.

> *Domain Controllers*: This organizational unit, by default, holds the accounts for the domain controllers on the network.

> *ForeignSecurityPrincipals*: This folder holds objects from other domains.

Users: The *Builtin* user accounts and global groups are located here as well as any user accounts that were transferred from a Windows NT 4 system due to an upgrade.

 Notice that the folder that represents an organizational unit has a small icon of a book on the folder. The generic containers do not.

The following exercise illustrates creating a new organizational unit and watching it replicate to other domain controllers. More details about organizational units will be found in later chapters.

Exercise 11

CREATING AN ORGANIZATIONAL UNIT

In this exercise you will create a new organizational unit named A1Unit on the first domain controller and an organizational unit named A2Unit on the second domain controller.

1. Log on to one of the domain controllers as administrator.
2. Start the MMC you created in a previous exercise.
3. Right-click the *your_domain_name.local* icon and click New\ Organizational Unit.
4. Name your organizational unit A1Unit or A2Unit, depending on whether you are logged on to the first domain controller or the second. Click OK. Your organizational unit should now appear.
5. Wait several minutes and press the F5 key to refresh your MMC. Within a few moments you will see the organizational unit created by your partner as your domain controller replicates with the other domain controller.

If waiting for your changes to appear seems to take forever, you can manually force replication to happen. To do so, you will use the Active Directory Sites and Services snap-in that you installed into your MMC in a previous exercise.

6. From your open MMC, click the plus sign next to your *Active Directory Sites and Services* snap-in to expand it.
7. Click the plus sign next to *Sites/Default-First-Site-Name/Servers*.
8. Click the plus sign next to the computer you want to replicate.
9. In the console tree click the NTDS settings.
10. In the details pane you will see the replication path(s) that are set up for the server you selected. Right-click the connection you are interested in replicating and click Replicate now.
11. Click OK to acknowledge that replication has taken place.

CHAPTER summary

➤ Domains are the primary security and replication objects in a Windows 2000 network. Windows 2000 domains are related to, but different from, DNS domains. Within domains, organizational units are used to organize network users and resources and to provide a security and management boundary within a domain. A Windows 2000 network can consist of multiple domains, and each domain can have other subdomains. A domain controller is a computer running the Active Directory network database, which is used to identify network resources and users.

CHAPTER terms

Active Directory	A distributed database that contains information about network users, computers, and resources.
Authoritative	The ability to own and change namespace records. A DNS server is authoritative with respect to a set of DNS records if the server does not have to forward name resolution requests to another server.
DNS tree	A namespace within a DNS server.
DNS	Domain Name System: A program that contains and locates names and IP addresses for network computers and resources.
Domain controller	A computer that is running Active Directory.
Domain	A resource and security boundary in a Windows 2000 network identified by a DNS record.
Dynamic updates	A feature of Windows 2000 DNS that allows computers to automatically update DNS records.
Forest	A group of domain trees within the same Active Directory database.
FQDN	Fully qualified domain names: A domain name that includes the object and the domain. For example, a1server.a5domain.local is an FQDN.
Iterative query	A query by a DNS server that may not return the requested IP address but rather the address of another DNS server that can provide more information.
Mixed mode	A mode used by Active Directory for networks that contain Windows NT servers.
Namespace	A group of names within a bounded area that can be resolved. For example, DNS contains namespaces for domains.

Native mode	A mode used by Active Directory for networks that do not contain any Windows NT servers.
Object	An element in an Active Directory database.
OU	Organizational unit: A container object in Active Directory that can contain user, computer, and other organizational unit objects, used as a security and administrative boundary within domains.
Recursive query	A query by a DNS server that will only return the final IP address of the requested resource to the resolver.
Resolver	A client computer attempting to locate a network resource or computer by requesting the IP address from a DNS server.
Site	A group of one or more well-connected subnets.
Tree	A element in Active Directory that consists of a group of related domains that share a contiguous namespace. For example, xyz.domain.local is a top-level domain and mycompany.xyz.domain.local would be a subdomain in the same domain tree.

CONCEPTS review

Multiple Choice

1. A group of one or more well-connected subnets is called a(n):
   a. Organizational unit.
   b. Domain.
   c. Tree.
   d. Forest.
   e. Site.

2. Which of the following can be used to logically subdivide a domain?
   a. Organizational unit
   b. Domain
   c. Tree
   d. Forest
   e. Site

3. Multiple domains sharing a contiguous DNS namespace are called:
   a. Organizational units.
   b. Domains.
   c. Trees.
   d. Forests.
   e. Sites.

4. A group of one or more trees that does not share a contiguous DNS namespace but is located in a single Active Directory database is called a(n):
   a. Organizational unit.
   b. Domain.
   c. Tree.
   d. Forest.
   e. Site.

5. What command is used to promote a stand-alone server to a domain controller?
   a. Setup
   b. winnt32
   c. Converge
   d. dcpromo
   e. None of the above

6. The process of propagating a change in Active Directory to all domain controllers in a domain is called:
   a. Convergence.
   b. Promotion.
   c. Duplicating.
   d. Copying.
   e. None of the above.

7. The type of DNS query typically performed by a resolver is a(n):
   a. Root query.
   b. Recursive query.
   c. Domain query.
   d. Iterative query.
   e. None of the above.

8. The top of a DNS tree is called the:
   a. Root.
   b. Leaf.
   c. Branch.
   d. Base.
   e. None of the above.

9. The MMC:
   a. Uses snap-ins.
   b. Can be saved.
   c. Stands for Microsoft Management Console.
   d. Allows the administrator to customize his or her environment.
   e. All of the above.

10. Multimaster replication:
    a. Changes are limited to the primary domain controller.
    b. Changes can be made to any domain controller.
    c. Can be done in either native or mixed mode.
    d. Cannot involve more than five domain controllers.
    e. None of the above.

11. The service responsible for maintaining the replication ring in a domain is called the:
    a. Knowledge Consistency Checker.
    b. Netlogon.
    c. DNS.
    d. Replicator.
    e. None of the above.

12. An iterative query can return:
    a. The complete TCP/IP address being sought.
    b. A replication ring.
    c. The TCP/IP address of another DNS server.
    d. Both a and c.
    e. None of the above.

13. An example of a top-level domain in the public DNS tree is:
    a. com.
    b. edu.
    c. org.
    d. gov.
    e. All of the above.

14. The snap-in used to force replication of the Active Directory is:
    a. Active Directory Users and Computers.
    b. DNS.
    c. Active Directory Sites and Services.
    d. Knowledge Consistency Checker.
    e. None of the above.

15. Identifiable domain resources are called:
    a. Objects.
    b. Attributes.
    c. Roots.
    d. Leaves.
    e. Both a and c.

Short Answer

1. List two advantages of using the Microsoft Windows 2000 implementation of DNS.
2. List two advantages of running a Windows 2000 domain in native mode.
3. Describe the name and the location of the Active Directory database file.
4. Briefly explain the purpose of an organizational unit.
5. Give an example of a fully qualified domain name.

LAB exercises

Exercise 1 – Creating and Saving a New MMC with Snap-ins

1. Log on as an administrator.
2. Create a new MMC.
3. Add the Active Directory Users and Computers, Disk Defragmenter, Disk Management, and Group Policy snap-ins.
4. Save the MMC with your name and the word Console. For example Joe's Console.
5. Close the MMC.

Exercise 2 – Viewing the dcpromo.log File

1. Double-click the *My Computer* icon.
2. Open your system drive.
3. Open the *winnt* folder.
4. Click the Show Files button.
5. Open the *debug* folder.
6. Double-click to open the dcpromo.log file.
7. Find the line that says it is validating the path of the SysVol.
8. What are the two requirements for the path of the SysVol?
9. What is the computer's DNS computer name root set to?

Exercise 3 – Adding Properties to an OU and Replicating those Properties

1. Open your MMC.
2. Click the *Active Directory Users and Computers* snap-in to open it.
3. Right-click your OU and click Properties.
4. For a description, key **Organization Unit for the A1(A2) group** and click OK.
5. Wait several minutes and press F5 to refresh you Active Directory Users and Computers screen. (You should see the description on both your OU and your partner's OU as the domain controllers replicate.)

PROBLEM SOLVING exercises

Exercise 1

The office has one Windows 2000 domain controller, three Windows NT 4 backup domain controllers, and 200 Windows 98 machines. Tell whether the domain should be operating in native or mixed mode, and explain why.

Exercise 2

A stand-alone server fails to promote to a domain controller in a domain. The stand-alone machine communicates properly with the DNS server. What steps should be taken to troubleshoot the machine?

USERS AND GROUPS 7

Performance Objectives

After completing this chapter you will be able to:

- Discuss and identify the prebuilt accounts for administrator and guest
- Create a new user account
- Modify a user's account properties
- Rename, delete, and copy accounts
- Reset passwords
- Discuss the different types of groups

Introduction

One of the most important yet time-consuming aspects of network administration is managing user accounts. A user account is necessary for individuals and applications to access and use the resources on the server and is the first gateway into a network system. Improperly designed user accounts can result in frustrated and angry users— just what a network administrator does not want to deal with. This chapter teaches you how user accounts work, the different types of user accounts, and how to create and manage user accounts. You will also learn about Windows 2000 groups, which will be one of the important elements in a network design.

What Are Users and Groups?

A **user account** is an object used to control access to a server and a domain. A **group** is a named collection of rights and permissions that can contain, among other things, user accounts. Each user must belong to some group. When a user account is created, it is automatically assigned to default groups, but the user can join additional groups. User accounts can be created first and then assigned to groups or a group can be created before user accounts.

User Account Management Tools

With Windows 2000 Professional, or on a stand-alone Windows 2000 Server, user accounts are managed with the computer management tool and are stored in the local SAM database. However, user accounts in such an environment only apply to their own host computer and are not meaningful in the context of a domain. When a server is part of a Windows 2000 domain, user accounts reside within Active Directory and are managed with the Active Directory Users and Computers MMC, found under the Administrative Tools menu. Accounts can also be managed with the Active Directory Users and Computers snap-in with a custom MMC. This snap-in was used in Chapter 6 to create an organizational unit. In this chapter it will be used to create and manage user accounts. Although this chapter focuses on the use of domain-wide accounts, most of the topics cover stand-alone accounts as well.

Prebuilt Accounts

When Windows 2000 is first installed, two **prebuilt accounts** are automatically created: *administrator* and *guest*. These accounts cannot be deleted but they can be renamed. The administrator account is powerful and its use must be carefully guarded. Immediately after building your domain, a second administrative account should be created. This second account provides a backdoor into the system if the first account is accidentally removed or its password forgotten.

Of course, everyone who builds a Windows 2000 computer system knows that the default account is administrator. If a hacker attacks your system, it is the first account name they will look for and hit. To help guard against such attacks it is recommended that the administrator account be renamed so it appears to be a regular user account. (Don't forget to change the account comment as well!) Going one step farther, a dummy account named "Administrator" could be created and given no power over the system. This way, if a hacker was looking for a way into your system, they would most likely go after the account named "Administrator," which is powerless.

This simple level of security would not deter an experienced hacker. The security ID (SID) of an account identifies it as an administrator account, even if the account's name has been changed.

Guest is the second account automatically created during Windows 2000 installation. This account is disabled by default and, in most cases, should be left that way. In some situations, the guest account will allow anyone access to the domain, even if they do not have a valid domain account. For example, a user named Joe who does not have a valid account on the domain uses a Windows 98 workstation, but does not log on to the domain. Joe uses the local workstation and then tries to access a resource on the domain. If the guest account is enabled on the domain and Joe tries to access a domain resource without a domain account, the domain will assume Joe is a guest and use the guest account to allow access to domain resources, even though Joe does not have a network account.

One solution to this problem would be to check each folder and file on the domain to make sure the guest account does not have access, which is difficult because guest is a member of the Everyone group that has complete access to files and folders by default. The second option is to just disable the guest account. In general, enabling the guest account can open a large security hole on your system. If you need a guest account on your domain you are usually better off creating an actual user account with limited abilities.

Accounts such as administrator and guest are not the only prebuilt accounts you might see in Windows 2000. Networking resources programs such as Internet Information Services (IIS) create special user accounts.

User Account Naming Standards

New user accounts should follow some naming standard in order to make the accounts easier to manage. If no naming account standard has been established then one should be created. The purpose of a naming standard is to make creating user accounts easy, provide some level of security to the network, and make it simple for users to log on to the network by using their account name.

Typically, the account name is derived from the first and last name of the user. The format of the account name might be the first letter of the first name and the entire last name, or the entire last name and the first two letters of the first name. For example, someone named "Joan Edwards" might be given the user account "jedwards" or the account name "edwardsjo." Special purpose user accounts may be assigned names that correspond to their purpose. For example, an account used to back up a database might be named "sqlbackup." If more than one person will be using such accounts, it is best to restrict the accounts' rights.

Whatever the naming standard, it must agree with the basic Windows 2000 naming rules, which are as follows:

1. User names can be up to 20 characters long including letters, numbers, periods, spaces, and some symbols. For ease of administration, do not use spaces in user names. You may find yourself having to enclose them in quotes to use them in certain situations.

2. User names cannot contain the following characters: < > , : ; / \ ? * + = " [ ].

3. User names must be unique within the domain; they cannot be the same as another user, computer, group, or domain account name.

Each user account contains a user name and the user name consists of two parts. The first part is the user name and the second part is the name of the domain. The two parts are separated by an @ symbol. For example, a user account for Joan Edwards in the sales domain might have the user name of jedwards@sales.local (which looks like an e-mail address). Older Windows and Windows NT 4 clients can use the first part of the name to log on to the network, while Windows 2000 clients can use either the first part or the full name to log on to the network. This naming format indicates what domain the user belongs to.

Users can be directed to log on to the network by using their full user name (for example, Joan Edwards), in which case they do not have to indicate which domain they want to log on to. This format is sometimes an easier way to have users log on to the network because they don't have to remember their own domain.

How User Accounts Work

Even though a user account is associated with a user name (for example, "jedwards"), the network identifies a user with a unique 48-bit combination called the **security ID (SID)**. The SID is used by Windows 2000 to identify the user and link the user to groups. An example of an SID is shown here:

```
S-1-5-21-7-7328577-2386797909-3654163385-500
```

The SID contains information identifying the domain to which the user belongs as well as the **relative ID (RID)** of that user. The domain portion of the SID is common to all users in the domain, but the RID is a unique number assigned by the domain controller to each user. In Windows NT 4 the only machine that could create user accounts was the primary domain controller (PDC), so the PDC held the entire pool of RID numbers for the domain. This restriction is also true of a Windows 2000 domain operating in mixed mode. Because Windows NT 4 backup domain controllers (BDCs) expect one machine to have all of the RID numbers, the *first* domain controller built in a Windows 2000 mixed mode domain will be the RID master and the only domain controller capable of providing RID numbers for new users. Once a domain has been converted to native mode operation, the RID pool is distributed among all the domain controllers in the domain. A network that has distributed the RID assignment responsibilities to multiple domain controllers is said to have a floating RID pool. This pool speeds up the process of creating users because any available domain controller can be contacted for an RID, rather than a single RID master.

Once the SID has been checked, the user can log on to the network. The following steps outline the process of a user logging on to a network:

- When a user logs on to the network, a domain controller checks that user's SID and password against the Active Directory database.

- After validating the user, the domain controller checks the list of security groups in the domain to determine to which groups the user belongs.

- The user is then given logon credentials. These logon credentials are basically a set of keys. A validated user gets one key based on who the user is and a key for each group to which the user belongs. These keys will be used when the user tries to access network resources.

If a user's group memberships are changed, the changes do not take place until the user logs off and logs back on.

Exercise 1

CREATING A NEW USER ACCOUNT

The following exercise illustrates how to create a new user account. If you are working with another student on another server, one set of answers will be used on one computer and the second used on the second computer. For example, in step 4 you are prompted to fill in the first name box with Madison (Steve). One computer in the pair should use "Madison" for the first name and the second computer should use "Steve" for the first name. If no second answer is placed inside parentheses after the first answer, the same value should be used for both computers.

1. Click Start, click Programs, click Administrative Tools, and then click Active Directory Users and Computers.
2. Right-click the *Users* folder in the left window.
3. Click New and then click User. The screen looks like Figure 7.1.

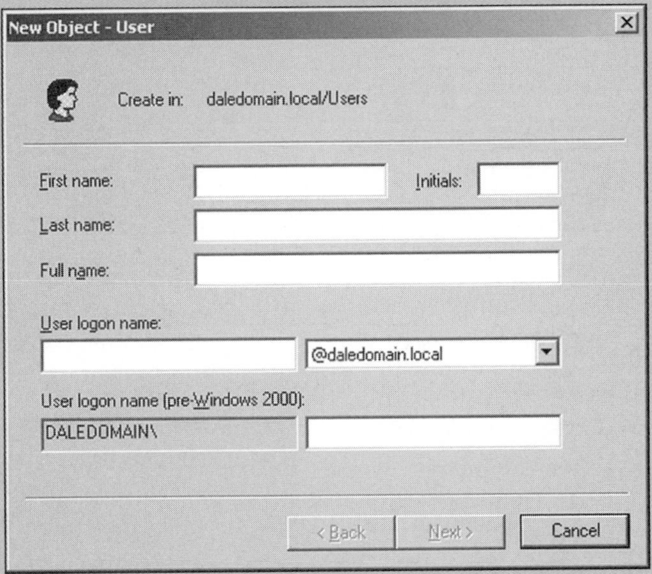

Figure 7.1

In this dialog box you enter the information for the new user. This information is as follows:

First name, Last name, Initials, and Full name: These fields are fairly self-explanatory and are used to record basic information about the user.

User logon name: The user logon name in Windows 2000 is different from Windows NT. In Windows 2000 it is called the universal principal name (UPN) and consists of the user's unique identifier and the user's domain. The first text box holds the logon name and the second drop-down list box holds the domain name. The user logon name alone can be used to log on to a server or the logon name and the domain name, in the format logonname@domain.name, can be used.

User logon name (pre-Windows 2000): This section is used to set a different logon name for users running prior versions of Windows. The first box displays the domain name in UNC format and cannot be changed. The second box holds the unique portion of the user's name. It is easiest if the second text box in this section matches the *User logon name* field for a Windows 2000 logon.

4. Click in the First name box and key **Madison (Steve)**.
5. Click in the Initials box and key **D (J)**.
6. Click in the Last name box and key **Buffett (Wallace)**.
7. Click in the User logon name and key **MBuffett (SWallace)**.
8. All boxes should be filled. Accept the information by clicking <u>N</u>ext.

You see the dialog box in Figure 7.2. This dialog box allows you to set the user's password and set password options.

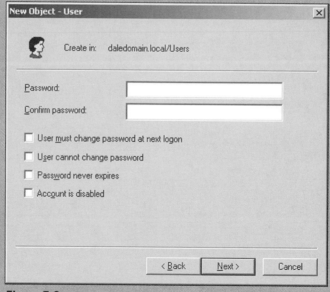

Figure 7.2

Password: This text box is used to enter the user's password. The letters are masked as they are keyed. Be careful because passwords are case sensitive.

Confirm password: This text box confirms the previously entered password. It ensures the password was correctly entered.

User must change password at next logon: This option forces the user to select a new password at next logon instead of keeping an initially assigned password. It is a good option to select because it makes users choose their own passwords, which are more secure, and users are more likely to remember their own passwords.

User cannot change password: This option prevents a user from changing his or her password. It is helpful when several people are using the same account. For example, if a timekeeper account is used by individuals on both first and second shift, this option would be used to prevent the second shift person from changing the password.

Password never expires: This option is used to override maximum password age that is set in the domain password policies. For individual accounts the password can be set to never expire. This option is sometimes necessary for accounts that are created for processes such as nightly backups. The nightly backup process is not capable of changing the password, so if the password expired the process would simply not run. Unfortunately, many administrators set this option on their own accounts, which is a bad idea because the administrator account is the most important account to guard by changing the password!

Account is disabled: This option allows the administrator to easily enable and disable an account. For example, if a worker is going on medical leave for a month, his or her account should be disabled. Remember, the guest account is disabled by default.

9. In the Password box key **code1**. (Remember, that passwords are case sensitive—key **code1** in lower case.)
10. In the Confirm password box rekey **code1**.
11. Make sure no check mark appears in the *User must change password at next logon* check box and that all other option boxes are clear.
12. Click Next to accept your entries.
13. Look over the summary screen to make sure the information is correct and click Finish.

The user account just created should appear in the Active Directory Users and Computers screen.

Exercise 2

MODIFYING A USER'S ACCOUNT PROPERTIES

In this exercise you modify the account created in the previous exercise.

1. In the Active Directory Users and Computers window, right-click the user just created and click Properties. You see the dialog box in Figure 7.3.

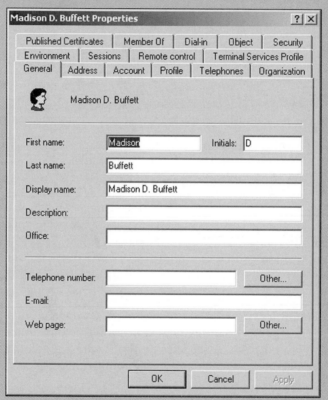

Figure 7.3

The resulting dialog box allows you to view and change almost all aspects of a user's account. The tabs displayed in this dialog box will depend on the configuration of your system.

2. Click the Account tab. You see a dialog box like Figure 7.4.

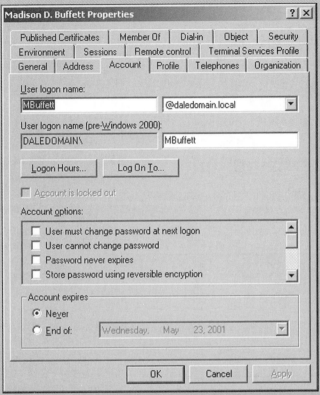

Figure 7.4

Clicking the Account tab displays the user logon name and options set during account creation. Several more options can be set in this dialog box for a user.

> **Account is locked out**: This option, located just below the Logon Hours button, is enabled if the user entered an excessive number of wrong passwords. As the administrator, you simply need to remove the check mark to reset the account.

> **Account expires**: Most of the time you will not want user accounts to expire and will accept the default value of Never. For accounts that should automatically expire on a specific date, perhaps for a consultant who will be leaving the company, click the End of: option button and enter a date. Expired accounts are not deleted, simply disabled.

> **Logon Hours**: This option is used to restrict the times users can log on to the domain.

> **Log On To**: This option is used to restrict the specific computers, by name, that the user can log on to.

Additional account option check boxes are displayed on this dialog box that were not available when the user was first created. Scroll down to see these. Some of the more important account options are:

Account is disabled: This option is used to disable an account without removing the account.

Smart Card is required for Interactive Login: This option forces the user to supply a physical device for login such as a digitally encrypted smart card or a fingerprint reader device.

Account is trusted for delegation: This option allows the account to be forwarded by the authenticating server, as valid, to another validating server. This process occurs when an application program must log on to one server and access resources on another server.

3. Click the Logon Hours button. You will see a screen like Figure 7.5.

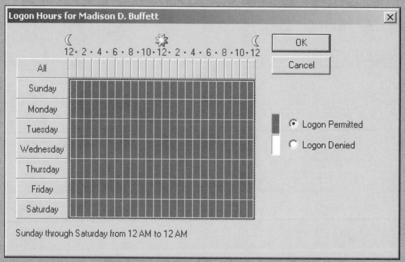

Figure 7.5

By default all accounts can log on at all times. However, at times you may not want certain accounts to be used, such as at night or over the weekend. Restricting the days and times this user can log on to the domain is done by highlighting the boxes that represent restricted times and clicking *Logon Denied*. The hours when the user is denied access are shown with white boxes.

4. Restrict this user from logging on all day Sunday and on Saturday after 12:00 noon.
5. Click OK to accept the changes.

The logon hours restrictions are not absolute. For example, if you remove the ability to log on starting at 6:00 p.m. each night for user SJones, she will not be able to log on at 6:01 p.m. However, if SJones logs on to the system at 5:59 p.m., this option will not force her to log off. An additional option must be set in a policy that forces the user to log off when the logon hours expire. This topic will be covered in the later chapter on group policies.

6. Click OK to close the user account Properties dialog box.

Four of the tabs under the Properties menu—General, Address, Telephones, and Organization—allow you to store contact information for the user. Contact information includes telephone numbers, address, organization, title, e-mail address, and so on. This information is optional but can be useful.

Renaming, Deleting, and Copying Accounts, and Resetting Passwords

When you right-click on an account, you will see other options on the drop-down menu besides Properties. The important options are as follows:

Rename: This option is used to rename an account. It is useful because a unique SID is used to identify each account to Windows 2000. The name of an account can be changed without changing the SID, so that renaming an account will not cause the loss of any account properties. For example, a user with the account named LRodriguez, your payroll clerk, is leaving the company. A new employee named KPham is replacing her. Rather than create a new account for KPham, the LRodriguez account can be renamed. In this way you ensure that KPham has all of the same rights and permissions needed to perform the payroll clerk job. Another advantage of renaming accounts rather than creating new accounts is that you do not use another CAL.

Delete: This option is used to delete a user account. Use this option carefully. Remember a unique SID identifies each account to the operating system. Once an account has been deleted it is gone for good. Even if a new account is created with the same user name it will be assigned a different SID and will therefore not have the same group memberships or permissions as the original account.

Copy: Instead of creating a new account from scratch, this option allows you to make a copy of an existing account. When an existing account is copied, certain features of new account will be the same as the original account, such as the group memberships and logon hours. Using the Copy option prevents you from having to type in all the information.

Resetting Passwords: A user's password cannot be reset in the user's account properties. You must right-click the user name and click Reset Password from the menu. You will need to enter the new password twice, just as you did when you first created the account.

Delegating Authority

In the previous chapter you learned about organizational units (OU). An OU is used to organize a domain by, among other things, serving as a container for users and computers. One of the important features of an OU is its ability to be used as a security boundary and allow local administrators assigned to the OU to manage users also assigned to the OU. For example, you may want to appoint one user from within the marketing OU to be able to reset passwords of the other users in the marketing OU. It frees up the administrator to deal with other issues. This new feature in Windows 2000 is called **delegating authority**. You can delegate authority for many different tasks using a delegation wizard.

The following exercise illustrates giving a user in an organizational unit the ability to create and manage other users within that organizational unit. On the second domain controller, use the options inside the parentheses.

Exercise 3

ASSIGNING USER RIGHTS WITHIN AN ORGANIZATIONAL UNIT

1. Start the MMC you created in the previous chapter or start the Active Directory Users and Computers tool from the Administrative Tools menu.
2. Click the plus sign next to *Active Directory Users and Computers Snap-in* to expand it, and click on the plus sign next to your domain to expand it.
3. Right-click the *A1Unit* (*A2Unit*) OU, and click Delegate Control from the shortcut menu. A wizard is used to perform the delegation.
4. Click <u>N</u>ext to start the Delegation Control Wizard. You see the Users or Groups dialog box (Figure 7.6).

Delegation of Control Wizard

Users or Groups
Select one or more users or groups to whom you want to delegate control.

Selected users and groups:

Add...   Remove

< Back   Next >   Cancel

Figure 7.6

5. Click the <u>A</u>dd button in the Users or Groups window. You see a list of users and groups.

6. Click *Madison D. Buffett* (*Steve J. Wallace*) in the list of users and click <u>A</u>dd. This user has been selected (Figure 7.7).

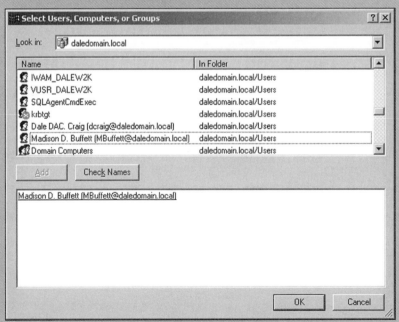

Select Users, Computers, or Groups

Look in: daledomain.local

Name	In Folder
IWAM_DALEW2K	daledomain.local/Users
VUSR_DALEW2K	daledomain.local/Users
SQLAgentCmdExec	daledomain.local/Users
krbtgt	daledomain.local/Users
Dale DAC. Craig (dcraig@daledomain.local)	daledomain.local/Users
Madison D. Buffett (MBuffett@daledomain.local)	daledomain.local/Users
Domain Computers	daledomain.local/Users

Add   Check Names

Madison D. Buffett (MBuffett@daledomain.local)

OK   Cancel

Figure 7.7

You could continue to select additional users or groups in this way.

7. Click OK to leave the Select Users, Computers or Groups window. The user has been selected (Figure 7.8).

Figure 7.8

8. Click Next at the Users or Groups window. You see a list of the common tasks to be delegated to the selected user (Figure 7.9). You could also create a custom set of tasks.

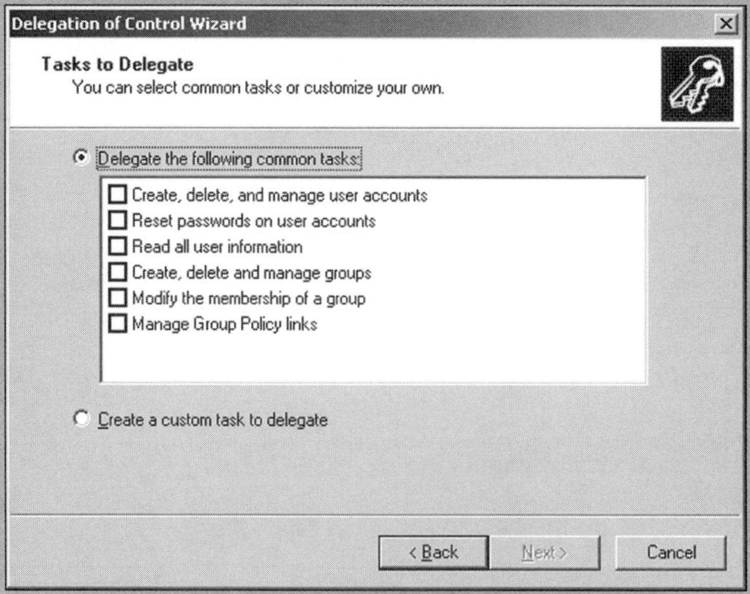

Figure 7.9

9. Click the *Create, delete, and manage user accounts* check box to choose this option, and then click <u>N</u>ext.
10. View the summary and click Finish.

Although delegating a task to a user is fairly easy, finding out what has already been delegated is not so simple. You can view what has been delegated for each individual object, but Windows 2000 does not offer a concise overview of everything. Make sure you document delegations to organizational units so you can easily look up who has permission for each organizational unit.

The following exercise illustrates how to discover what tasks have been delegated for an OU. Even though you have used the wizard to create the delegation rights, you could also use the screens you will see in these steps to add to or delete from the delegated tasks.

Exercise 4

VIEWING DELEGATED RIGHTS

1. Open the MMC previously created, or open Active Directory Users and Computers and click the plus symbol next to your domain.

In order to see some of the OU properties, you must set the Advanced Features option. This option is not set by default.

2. Click <u>V</u>iew and then click Advanced Features.
3. Right-click *A1Unit* (*A2Unit*) and click Properties. You should see a Security tab (Figure 7.10). If you don't see this Security tab, you must set the Advanced Features option from the View menu.

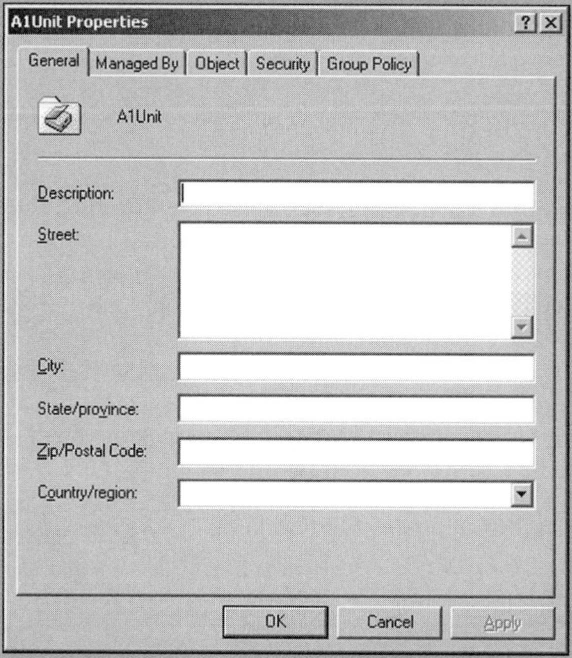

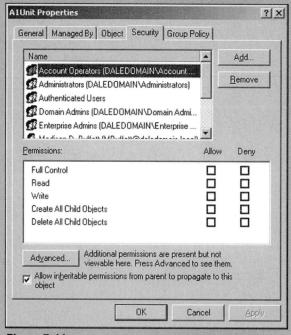

Figure 7.10

4. Click the Security tab. You see the security settings for this OU (Figure 7.11).

Figure 7.11

5. Scroll through list of names and click *Madison D. Buffett* (*Steve J. Wallace*). At this point it seems as though some of the permissions in the permissions box should be checked but they are not. You must use the Ad**v**anced button to display security details.
6. Click the Ad**v**anced button. You see the dialog box in Figure 7.12.

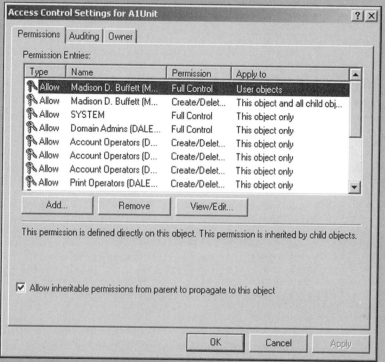

Figure 7.12

7. Highlight the line with your user's name (*Buffett* or *Wallace*) and the *Create/Delete* permission, and then click View/Edit. You will see what permissions the user has. (Figure 7.13)

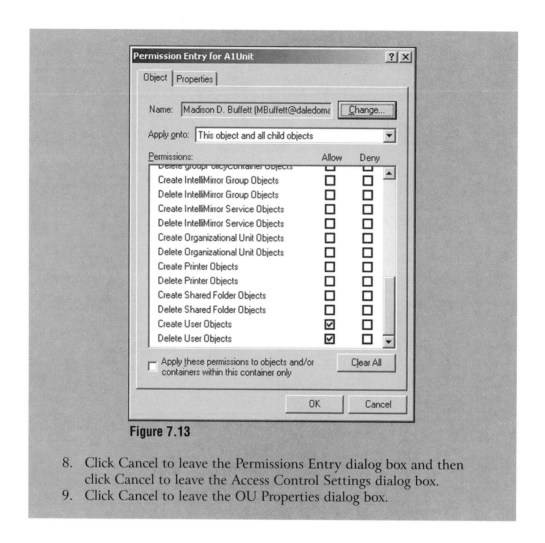

Figure 7.13

8. Click Cancel to leave the Permissions Entry dialog box and then click Cancel to leave the Access Control Settings dialog box.
9. Click Cancel to leave the OU Properties dialog box.

Testing Delegated Authority

In order to test to see whether your user truly has the ability to create new users in the OU, you will need to log on to the system with the user account. In an actual production network you would not want general users logging on directly to the server. By default, users do not have the right to log on to servers in Windows 2000, only administrators. If a general user were to sit down at the server and attempt to log on they would receive an error message. In a lab situation you will need to use your server as both a server and a workstation. In order for you to be able to create users and then log on to your servers with their IDs you will need to complete the following two exercises.

Exercise 5

TESTING THE USER LOGON WITHOUT RIGHTS TO LOG ONTO A SERVER

1. Press Ctrl+Alt+Del and click Log off the server.
2. Click Yes to confirm your logoff.
3. Press Ctrl+Alt+Del to obtain a logon screen.
4. Log on with the user name MBuffett (SWallace) and password code1 and click OK.
5. Write down the error message you receive. This error message should indicate that you do not have rights to log on locally with the user ID.
6. Click OK to accept the error message.

Exercise 6

CREATING A GROUP POLICY THAT ALLOWS USERS TO LOG ON TO A SERVER

1. Log on the system as administrator.
2. Click Start, click Programs, click Administrative Tools, and click Domain Controller Security Policy. You will see a screen that looks like Figure 7.14.

Figure 7.14

3. Click the plus sign next to *Security Settings*, and then the plus sign next to *Local Policies*, to expand the options.
4. Click the *User Rights Assignment* icon to see the policies listed in the right window.

5. If necessary, scroll down and double-click *Log on locally* on the right-hand side of your screen. You should see that this policy has been defined for the administrators and several other administrative groups and accounts (Figure 7.15).

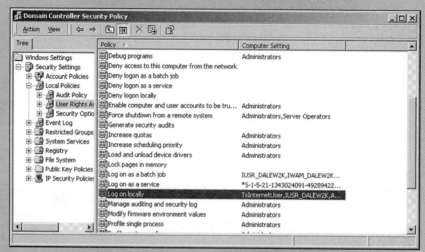

Figure 7.15

Do NOT remove these groups and accounts. If you do not see any other groups or users listed, you are probably in the Domain Security Policy and not the Domain Controllers Security Policy. In that case, close the window and start again at step 2.

6. When you double-click the *Log on locally* policy in the right side of the window, you see the Security Policy Setting dialog box in Figure 7.16.

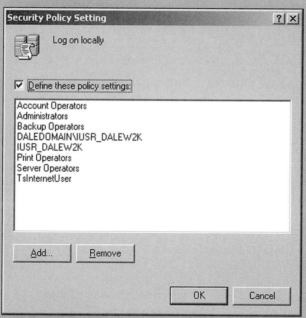

Figure 7.16

7. Click the Add button to add a new user to the local policy.
8. Click Browse in the Add user or group box.
9. After a minute a list of the users and groups of your domain should appear. Scroll down to select the *Domain Users* group and click Add. The dialog box will look like Figure 7.17.

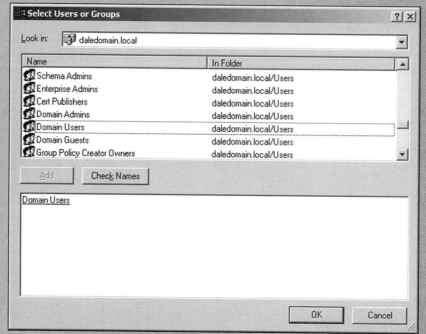

Figure 7.17

10. Click OK to leave the Select Users or Groups dialog box.
11. Click OK to leave the Add user or group dialog box.
12. Make sure that the Domain Users group is listed in the Security Policy Setting dialog box and click OK.
13. Close the Domain Controller Security Policy window.
14. Wait several minutes and try logging on with your user name again. After convergence has taken place you should be able to log on.

Now that your user can log on to the system you can test to see whether the delegation of power worked. The following exercise tests delegation in the organizational unit.

Exercise 7

TESTING DELEGATION IN THE ORGANIZATIONAL UNIT

1. Log on as MBuffett (SWallace), start an MMC, and add the Active Directory Users and Computers Snap-in.
2. Right-click the A1Unit (A2Unit) OU and click New\User from the option menu.
3. Add the following user information:

4. Right-click your partner's OU and see if you have a New option on your shortcut menu.

Introduction to Groups

In a network environment that may include hundreds of users, it quickly becomes cumbersome dealing with individual user accounts. It is much easier and less time-consuming to work with groups of users. The purpose of groups is to provide a way to organize and manage user accounts. A group defines a security boundary within which users can be placed. The group boundary constrains who can be added to the group and what the users in the group can be allowed to do. The permissions assigned to the users of a group are limited by the nature of the group itself.

Windows 2000 contains two different types of groups: distribution groups and security groups. **Distribution groups** are new to Windows 2000, but if you are familiar with e-mail programs you have probably used a distribution group. An e-mail distribution group allows you to send a message to multiple people by simply typing in the name of the group instead of having to type in every person's e-mail address. Distribution groups are used the same way in Windows 2000. In a later chapter you will learn to distribute software using group policies. Distribution lists allow you to define who will receive the software. In future versions of Windows 2000, distribution lists created in Windows 2000 will be useable in Exchange. No SID is associated with a distribution group.

Security groups are the same types of groups found in Windows NT. **Security groups** can be used to control access to resources such as printers and files because each security group has an SID. When someone attempts to access a network resource, Windows 2000 will check the group the user belongs to and, if the group has the correct rights, any user who belongs to the group can have access as long as individual rights don't override group rights. The objects to which groups are assigned access are called security objects.

Windows 2000 has four different security groups. Three of the security groups—local groups, domain local groups, and global groups—come directly from Windows NT. A fourth security group is new to Windows 2000 and is called a universal group.

Groups can have a maximum of 5,000 members.

Types of Security Groups

Local groups are typically used on Windows 2000 Professional and stand-alone servers. These groups are applicable only on the machine on which they were created and do not have meaning within the context of a domain.

Domain local groups are limited to the domain within which the group was created. Members of the domain local group have access only to resources within the domain where the group was created, but the group can include members from any domain. The purpose of the domain local group is to provide access to domain-specific resources.

For example, if a color laser printer was installed in your domain and you wanted to limit access to the printer, you could create a domain local group called ColorLaserUsers. You would then give the ColorLaserUsers group access to the printer. Inside the ColorLaserUsers group you could place individual accounts, global groups, or universal groups. Domain local groups work only within their own domain. They cannot be used in a different domain even if that domain is a trusted domain.

Global groups are the inverse of domain local groups. A global group can be assigned rights to resources in any domain on the network. However, members of this group can only come from the domain within which the group was created. User accounts should be placed in global groups, and these global groups should be added to local or domain local groups to give users access to resources.

For example, all the people in the marketing department might be placed into a global group called Marketing. You could then give the entire Marketing group permission to access folders and resources across the network instead of having to assign each individual account access to the resources, as long as you created the Marketing group in the same domain as its users. You could also place the Marketing global group into the ColorLaserUsers local group and give all of the Marketing users access to the color laser printer. Global groups can be used in the domain where they originated, or in a different domain in the same Active Directory tree, or in a trusted domain in another tree. Global groups can contain user accounts from the local domain, or, if the Windows 2000 domain is functioning in native mode, global groups can contain other global groups from the same domain.

Universal groups are the new type of security group introduced with Windows 2000 and can be used only if the Windows 2000 domain has been converted to native mode. Universal groups combine some of the best features of both domain local groups and global groups because they can contain other groups and also be used across domains. Universal groups can contain individual users, global groups, and universal groups from any domain, and can be used to control access to any resource or object in any of the domains. Universal groups appear to make everything much simpler, and you may be tempted to use them in all situations, but watch out for the catch. Universal groups are handled differently in replication and can create an abundance of network traffic in a multidomain environment. This issue will be discussed in more detail in the Active Directory chapter.

To summarize:

- Local groups apply only to a single computer and cannot be used on a domain.

- Domain local groups can apply only to resources in the domain within which they were created but can include members from any domain.

- Global groups can apply to resources in any domain but can only include members from the domain within which they were created.

- Universal groups can apply to resources in any domain and can include members from any domain, but the network must be running in native mode.

Working with Groups

With only four types of security groups, it may seem easy to use groups to manage resources and rights. In fact, things can easily become complicated. To better understand how to use groups, it is helpful to summarize groups in terms of where they can be created, what they apply to, and who can belong to each group. Table 7.1 summarizes this information.

TABLE 7.1 *Summary of Group Information*

Group Type	Where Created	Applicable To	Allowable Members
Local	Workstations and stand-alone servers	Server-local security objects such as folders and printers	Local users, local domain users, global groups from the local domain, universal groups from the local domain and any domain in the forest in native mode
Domain Local	Domain controllers	Security objects in local domain	Domain local groups (in native mode), global groups, universal groups from local and trusted domains and users and computers from any trusted domain
Global	Domain controllers	Security objects in any trusted domain	Global groups (native mode), users and computers from local domain only
Universal	Domain controllers	Any security object in any domain	User, computers, global groups, universal groups from any domain

Example of Group Planning

The following general guidelines can be used when planning an implementation of groups on your network.

A. If possible, convert the network to native mode to make universal groups available and allow more flexibility in group assignments and nesting.

B. Create global groups to hold users and try to keep common users in the same group. For example, members of the marketing department should be assigned to a marketing group. Users can be added to more than one global group. Remember, global groups can access resources in any domain but can only contain members from the domain within which the group was created.

C. Create domain local groups for access to local domain resources. A domain local group should not contain users but only set access rights on specific resources. For example, a domain local group could be created and set with access rights on a specific network printer. Remember, domain local groups can be set to access resources only in the domain within which the group was created, but they can contain members (or groups) from any domain.

D. Create universal groups for special access across domains. You should limit the number of universal groups because the information in these groups is placed in the global catalog and replicated across the network.

Consider the network outlined in Figure 7.18.

FIGURE 7.18 *Network of Domains and Shared Resources*

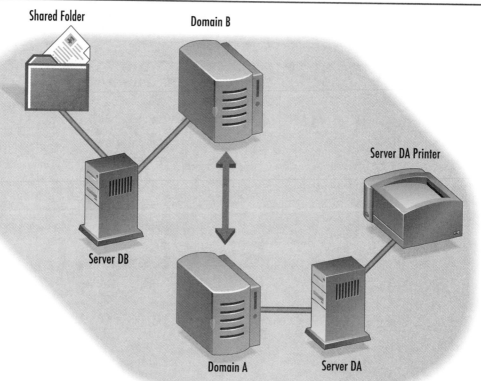

This simple network has two domains: DomainA and DomainB. Each domain has a server with a shared folder on ServerDB and a shared printer on ServerDA. Both DomainA and DomainB are in the same Active Directory tree, which means that each domain trusts the other domain.

The following resources must be shared on this network:

- ServerDA Printer must be shared by accounting users located in both DomainA and DomainB.

- ServerDB Shared Folder must be accessible by users in the marketing department. These users belong to DomainA.

- Information on ServerDA and ServerDB must be backed up by a user who belongs to DomainB.

Three resources must be shared: the printer on DomainA, the shared folder on DomainB, and the backup files on both servers. A prebuilt local group on each server is named Backup Operators. This group has rights to back up files on the server.

The following steps would be used to implement groups in the sample network:

1. Domain local groups named Accounting Data and PrinterDA are created and given access to the shared folder (*Accounting Data*) and the printer (PrinterDA).

2. Global groups named Marketing, AccountingA, and AccountingB are created.

3. Marketing users in DomainA are added to the Marketing group, accounting users in DomainA are added to AccountingA, and accounting users in DomainB are added to AccountingB.

4. The AccountingA and AccountingB groups are added to the Accounting Data group, and the Marketing group is added to the PrinterDA group.

5. The Backup user account is added to the default Builtin local group named Backup Operators located on ServerDB and on ServerDA.

Builtin and Predefined Groups

During installation of Active Directory a set of default user groups is created: builtin groups and predefined groups. The builtin groups are found in the Builtin container viewed from the Active Directory Users and Computers snap-in, and the predefined groups are found in the Users container. Some of the group names in these two containers are similar, for example, *Users* (Builtin container) versus *Domain Users* (Users container). The difference between these groups is based on the group type. The groups located in the Users container are domain groups and the groups in the Builtin container are local groups. The local groups are only recognized on a specific server and do not have rights in the domain.

For example, an easy way to give domain users the rights to back up files on a server is to add the domain users group from the Users container to the backup operators group located in the Builtin container. Once the domain users group is added to the local backup operators group, members in the domain users group can access the resources on the local server.

Table 7.2 lists some of the predefined users and groups automatically created when joining a domain.

TABLE 7.2 *Predefined Users and Groups Created When a Domain Is Joined*

Default Users

Administrator: This account is automatically created when Windows 2000 is first installed. This account cannot be deleted and is a member of the Administrators group.

Guest: This account is automatically created when Windows 2000 is first installed and is for people who don't have regular accounts. By default this account is disabled.

Default Groups

Domain Admins: This global group is used to administer the domain. It is part of the Administrators group on all computers that have joined the domain.

Domain Users: This global group includes all domain user accounts. When a new domain account is created it is automatically added to this group.

Enterprise Admins: This group is a universal group if the domain is running in native mode; otherwise it is a global group. Members in this group can make changes to Active Directory. The Administrator account on the forest root system is automatically a member of this group.

Administrators: This built-in group has unlimited rights on the local system. When the computer with this group joins a domain, the Domain Admins and Enterprise Admins groups are added to this group.

Users: This builtin group can run and install applications, use printers, and lock the computers.

Guests: This builtin group has the default member account Guest.

Power Users: This builtin group, by default, has no members. It has many of the capabilities of Administrator such as creating accounts, other groups, and shares.

Account Operators: This builtin group only exists on domain controllers and by default has no members. This group has the ability to create and manage accounts and groups, except for those in the Builtin container and domain controller's OU. Also, this group cannot modify the Administrators and Domain Admins groups.

Server Operators: This builtin group is only created on domain controllers and by default has no members. Members of this group can log on to the server, manage shares and services, back up files, and shut down the system.

Print Operators: This built-in group is only created on domain controllers. Members of this group can manage printers.

Backup Operators: This builtin group can back up and restore files and start and shut down the server.

At times you may see reference to builtin groups that are not listed anywhere under your Active Directory Users and Computers snap-in. You may see these groups when you are looking to see who is connected to a particular resource. Some examples of these groups follow:

- Anonymous Logon: a user who has logged on anonymously, such as an FTP user

- Authenticated Users: all users who have been authenticated on the system

- Creator Owner: the creator or owner of an object

- Everyone: all accounts including Guest

- Interactive: a user accessing the machine from the console

- Network: all users accessing the machine over the network

- Service: an account logged on as a service

- System: the Windows 2000 operating system

Exercise 8

VIEWING BUILTIN AND DEFAULT GROUPS

In this exercise you view the contents of the Builtin container.

1. Open the MMC you created in the previous chapter or open Active Directory Users and Computers.
2. Click the plus sign next to *Active Directory Users and Computers* snap-in.
3. Click the plus sign next to your domain name to expand it.
4. Click the *Builtin* folder icon. A list of the builtin groups appears in the right window (Figure 7.19).

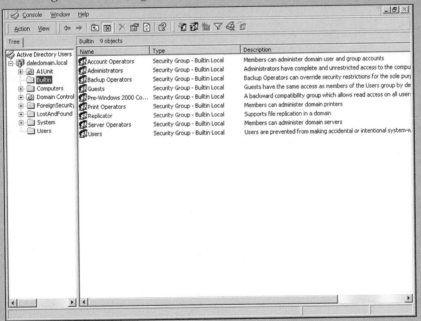

Figure 7.19

Notice that the *Type* field in the right window identifies these groups as Security Group – Builtin Local.

5. Click the *Users* folder. A list of default groups and users appears in the right window (Figure 7.20).

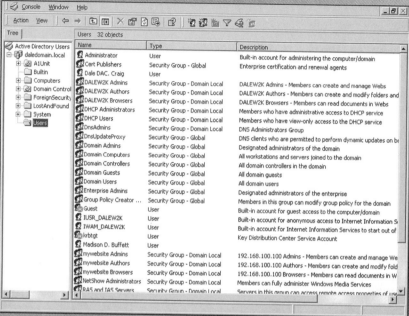

Figure 7.20

6. Close the Active Directory Users and Computers window.

Creating Groups

Groups can be created and placed in several different locations on the domain controller. Normally, groups are created and placed within organizational units because group policies can be applied to OUs.

Exercise 9

CREATING GROUPS

Note: This exercise should be done on one of the domain controllers.

1. Open the MMC you created or open Active Directory Users and Computers.
2. Click the plus sign next to *Active Directory Users and Computers* snap-in to expand it.
3. Click the plus sign next to your domain name to expand it.
4. Right-click your domain name.
5. Click New/Group from the menu. You see the New Object - Group dialog box in Figure 7.21.

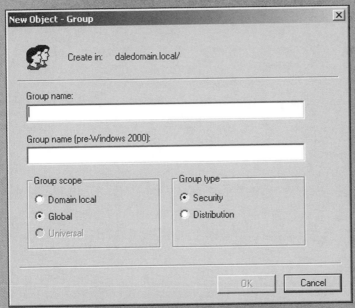

Figure 7.21

6. Key **AUsers** in the *Group name* field (substituting your assigned letter for A).
7. Make sure *Global* is selected for Group scope and *Security* selected for Group type and click OK. The group is added under the domain name.
8. Right-click the new group AUsers and click Properties.
9. Click the Members tab and click Add.
10. Scroll down and select both users *Madison Buffett* and *Steve Wallace* by holding down the Ctrl key and clicking the user name. (If you do not have these users, select two other users.)

11. Click the Add button to add these users to the group.
12. Click OK to leave the Select Users, Contacts, or Computers dialog box.
13. Click OK to leave the AUsers Properties dialog box.

Exercise 10

CREATING GROUPS IN ORGANIZATIONAL UNITS

Groups are normally created and placed in organizational units to allow group policies to be applied to the OU, which will affect all groups inside the OU. (This topic is covered in a later chapter.) Creating groups within OUs is just like creating a group under the domain.

Note: In this exercise an organizational unit will be created on the primary domain controller and on the secondary domain controller, created in the previous chapter. When the instructions indicate to perform a task on the A1Computer, use the primary domain controller, and use the secondary domain controller when prompted to use the A2Computer.

1. Right-click the A1Unit OU (A2Unit OU), click New, and then click Group.
2. Create a Global Security group named A1Users (A2Users).
3. Right-click the Organizational Unit and then right-click the newly created group.
4. Click Properties.
5. Click the Members tab.
6. Click the Add button, click *Madison D Buffett (Steve J Wallace* on the secondary domain controller), and add these users to the group.

CHAPTER summary

➤ In order to access network resources, users must have an account on the network. The user account contains information about the user and a set of restrictions about when and where the user can log on to the network. User names and passwords should follow established rules and conform to the Windows 2000 naming rules.

➤ Each user must be part of a group. A group is a container for user accounts. Users placed within a group fall under security restrictions for the group. Windows 2000 comes with a set of prebuilt groups, each with different restrictions.

CHAPTER terms

Delegating authority	Assigning the rights to control user and group accounts to users other than the administrator, normally with Organizational Units.
Distribution group	A container object used to hold name objects such as an e-mail list.
Domain local group	A security group whose members can access resources only within the domain where the group was created.
Global group	A security group whose members can come only from the domain where the group was created.
Group	A container object that holds user information.
Local group	A security group for stand-alone computers.
Prebuilt accounts	A set of user accounts automatically created with the installation of Windows 2000.
RID	Relative ID: A code identifying a user or computer to the network. The RID is a code that uniquely identifies a security object, but without the domain information.
Security group	A container object that controls access to network resources.
SID	Security ID: A code identifying a user or computer to the network. The SID includes the domain of the object.
Universal group	A security group only available in native mode.
User account	A security object in Windows 2000 used to verify access to network resources.

CONCEPTS review

Multiple Choice

1. *Objective 1:* You have a user named GDuane in the IS department who is leaving the company at 5:00 p.m. on February 2. Company policy dictates that users who leave the company should have their access to the network revoked as soon as they leave on their last day. *Objective 2:* GDuane must have access to the system until he leaves in order to finish his work. *Objective 3:* You want to go on vacation February 1–4. Which of the following will meet all three objectives?

   a. Place a time restriction on the account so that GDuane cannot log on after 5:00 p.m.
   b. Set an expiration date on the account.
   c. Set the user password to change itself back to a default password at 5:30 p.m. on February 2.
   d. Both a and b meet all three objectives.
   e. All three objectives cannot be met.

2. You are the administrator for a small company. You have one broker and are in the process of hiring a second broker who will need to perform the same tasks as your first broker. What is the best way to give broker2 access to the system and be sure that broker2 has all the of the rights he needs to do the same job as broker1?

   a. Rename the broker1 account to broker2.
   b. Create a new account for broker2 and give that account all the same rights and permissions as broker1.
   c. Copy the broker1 account to the name broker2.
   d. Copy the administrator account to the name broker2.
   e. Give broker2 the logon ID and password to the broker1 account.

3. You are the administrator for a small company. You have a broker who is leaving the company, and you are replacing her with a new broker who will have the same duties. What is the best way to give the new broker access to the system?

   a. Rename the broker1 account to broker2.
   b. Create a new account for broker2.
   c. Copy the broker1 account to the name broker2 and delete the broker2 account.
   d. Give broker2 the logon ID and password for the broker1 account.
   e. Give broker2 the logon ID and password for the guest account.

4. Which of the following is NOT true for user names in Windows 2000?
   a. They can be both upper- and lowercase.
   b. They can be up to 20 characters.
   c. They can contain spaces and periods.
   d. They must be at least 8 characters.
   e. All of the above are true.

5. Which of the following is NOT possible for users' passwords?
   a. Users can have blank passwords.
   b. Users can have their user name as part of the password.
   c. Passwords can be both upper- and lowercase.
   d. Passwords can never expire.
   e. All of the above are possible.

6. Which of the following cannot be set as a user account property?
   a. Reset a user password.
   b. A date for the user account to expire.
   c. Certain hours when a user cannot log on to the system.
   d. Certain machines that a user can log on to.
   e. All of the above can be set.

7. The basic feature(s) of the builtin groups are:
   a. They can manage any computer in the domain.
   b. They can only be used to manage domain controllers.
   c. They can only be used by Domain Admins.
   d. They are only used to manage local computer resources.
   e. None of the above.

8. What is the relationship between the SID and the RID?
   a. The SID is contained in the RID.
   b. The RID is contained in the SID.
   c. The SID is created by reversing the RID.
   d. The RID is created by reversing the SID.
   e. None of the above.

9. Delegating authority to an organizational unit means:
   a. Moving the OU to a domain controller.
   b. Placing a Domain Admin inside the OU.
   c. Allowing an OU account to manage OU users.
   d. Allowing an OU account to manage domain users.
   e. None of the above.

10. The reason that security groups can be used to control access to computer and domain resources is:
    a. Security groups are automatically created by Windows 2000 during installation.
    b. Security groups are automatically created on the domain by running dcpromo.
    c. Security groups contain the Domain Admins group.
    d. Security groups have an SID.
    e. All of the above.

11. A global group:
    a. Can be assigned rights to any resource in the domain.
    b. Can only contain members from the domain within which the group was created.
    c. Can contain other global groups from the same domain if Windows 2000 is using native mode.
    d. All of the above.
    e. None of the above.

12. A domain local group:
    a. Can only access resources within the domain in which the group was created.
    b. Can access resources in any domain.
    c. Can only contain users from within the domain in which the group was created.
    d. Can only contain members of local groups.
    e. Can only contain members of universal groups.

13. A universal group:
    a. Cannot be assigned to other groups.
    b. Can access resources anyplace in the domain.
    c. Can only include members from the domain within which the group was created.
    d. None of the above.
    e. All of the above.

14. What is the difference between the Domain Admins group and the Enteprise Admins group?
    a. Domain Admins can be added to local groups and Enterprise Admins cannot.
    b. Enterprise Admins can access resources in other Active Directory forests and Domain Admins cannot.
    c. Domain Admins is part of the domain users group and Enterprise Admins is not.
    d. Enterprise Admins can be part of the universal group and Domain Admins cannot.
    e. None of the above.

15. What is the main difference between the power users group and the account operators group?
    a. Members of the power users group can create accounts and account operators cannot.
    b. The account operators group exists only on domain controllers while the power users group can exist only on member servers.
    c. The power users group can create shares and the account operators group cannot.
    d. The account operators group by default has Guest as a member and the power users group by default has no members.
    e. None of the above.

Short Answer

1. You delete an account for a user named DJean. That user returns to the company one week later. You recreate an account with the logon DJean. Will the user have the same access as before? Why or why not?
2. What are the advantages of having an MMC?
3. What is a UPN and what are its two parts?
4. How do you start up a brand new MMC?
5. Under what conditions would you have universal groups?

LAB exercises

Each of the following labs assumes you have finished the exercises in the chapter and any previous labs. Begin each lab logged on as the administrator unless you are told differently.

Exercise 1 – Adding Contact Information for a User

1. Open the Active Directory Users and Computers MMC.
2. Locate and right-click the MBuffett account.
3. Click Properties.
4. Click the Address tab and key the following:

Street:	**3191 Weaver Ave**
City:	**Divide**
State/Province:	**CO**
Zip/Postal Code:	80224
Country/Region:	**UNITED STATES**

5. Click the General tab and key in the following:

   Telephone number: **(303) 555-1234**

6. Click OK to close the Properties dialog box.

Exercise 2 – Creating a New Account

1. Open the Active Directory Users and Computers MMC.
2. Create a new account with the following attributes in the Users container:

   First Name: **Katie**
   Middle Initial: **B**
   Last Name: **Lake**
   User logon name: **KLake**
   Password: **classroom**
   Does not need to change the password at first logon

Exercise 3 – Creating a New Account by Copying an Existing Account and Noting which Attributes Are Copied

1. Open the Active Directory Users and Computers MMC.
2. Locate and open the properties of the Administrator account and add the following contact information.

   In the General tab, under *Display Name:* **Administrator**
   In the General tab, under *Office:* **LAN Room**
   In the Organization tab, under *Department:* **IS Department**

   Note the following values:

   In the General tab – Description
   In the Account tab – whether or not the password expires
   In the Member tab – member of which groups?

3. Right-click the Administrator account and click Copy.
4. Create a new administrative account with the following attributes:

   First Name: **admin1**
   Middle Initial: (leave blank)
   Last Name: (leave blank)
   User logon name: **admin1**
   Password: **classroom**
   Does not need to change the password at first logon

5. In which container is the account created? Why?
6. Go to Properties on the new account and check the attributes listed in step 2. Which ones were copied?

Exercise 4 – Renaming an Account

1. Open the Active Directory Users and Computers MMC.
2. Locate and right-click the account for Katie B. Lake and click Rename.
3. Key **Nicholas Taylor** and press Enter.
4. Fill in the Rename user box with the following information:

First Name:	**Nicholas**
Last Name:	**Taylor**
Display Name:	**Nicholas Taylor**
Username logon name:	**NTaylor**
User logon name (pre-Windows 2000):	**NTaylor**

5. Click OK.

Exercise 5 – Deleting an Account

1. Open the MMC you created in exercise 1.
2. Right-click the account for Nicholas Taylor and click Delete.
3. Click Yes to confirm you want to delete the account.

PROBLEM SOLVING exercise

The network has three domains named DomainA, DomainB, and DomainC. The first domain in the Active Directory Forest is DomainA. The network printers are located in DomainB and the company database and database files are located in DomainC. All the default Windows 2000 groups are still in place. You must create the following accounts for the indicated tasks. For each account, indicate which groups the account will belong to.

User Account One – This account will be used by a general user located on DomainC. This user will use resources only on DomainC.

User Account Two – This account will be given out to a user in DomainA to access resources in DomainC. This user will not require any special administrative rights.

User Account Three – This account can be given out to any user in any domain and used to manage network printers and back up database files.

User Account Four – This account will be given out only to a user in DomainA and will be used to manage other user accounts only in DomainA.

User Account Five – This account will be given out to a user in any domain and will be used to manage other user accounts in any domain and manage resources in any domain.

User Account Six – This account will be given out to a user in DomainC so the user can log on to the local computer and start and stop the company database. This user should have no other rights.

PROFILES AND POLICIES

Performance Objectives

After completing this chapter you will be able to:

- Discuss the purpose of profiles
- Create a user profile
- Create a roaming profile
- Discuss the purpose of policies
- Create a domain-wide policy
- Create an organizational unit policy
- Create organizational unit policies that override domain policies
- Create domain policies that cannot be blocked
- Automatically install software through a policy
- Create a user logon script

Introduction

The three aspects to managing network users include creating user accounts, configuring network resources to be accessible by users, and giving users rights to perform tasks. In the previous chapter you learned to create and manage user accounts. In the next chapter you will learn to configure network resources to be accessible to users. In this chapter you learn how to give users rights to perform tasks.

One of the benefits of a network is the ability to control the network user's environment. The environment will include both the network resources visible to the user as well as the local computer settings. Controlling the local environment is an important aspect to network management because local computer settings often affect how the user accesses network resources. Also, controlling the local computer environment from the network makes managing network clients easier. In this chapter you learn to use profiles and group policies to control the user environment.

Profiles

The idea of profiles is not new to Windows 2000. Profiles are available in almost all versions of Windows, both Windows NT and Windows 95/98. A **profile** is a collection of local computer settings, such as the type of wallpaper or screensaver. Once created, a profile can be saved and then automatically applied the next time a user logs on to the computer. The settings contained in the profile are applied to the computer environment and allow users to customize their environment and see those changes each time they log on to the computer.

Windows 95/98 allows users to "log on to" the system even if the computer is not connected to a network. A user account created on a stand-alone Windows 95/98 computer is primarily used to select different profiles.

The first time a user logs on to a computer, he or she gets a copy of the default user profile, which is located in the *Default User* folder (which is hidden). The *Default User* folder is found in *Documents and Settings* on the drive that holds the system files. Any changes made to the *Default User* folder will be reflected in new user profiles. When the user logs off the system, changes to the computer environment made while using the system are saved back into the *Documents and Settings* folder inside a folder named after the user and will include changes made to the system colors, wallpaper, and so on. The next time the user logs back on to that computer, Windows 2000 will, based on the logon name, locate the user's profile folder and load the profile settings. It is called a local profile and is held locally by the computer. It will only apply when the user logs on to that particular machine.

Another folder under the *Documents and Settings* folder is called *All Users*. Any changes made to that folder will be reflected in the profiles of all users the next time they log on.

The default folders containing profile information include the following:

- *Application Data* holds information required by installed application programs. When an application program is installed on a domain controller, the installer program normally asks if this program should be installed for all users or just for the logged on user. This folder is hidden by default.

- *Desktop* contains the shortcuts and files that will appear on the desktop of the user.

- *Cookies* contains cookie files created during Internet sessions.

- *Favorites* contains favorite links to Web sites as found in Internet Explorer.

- *Local Settings* contains computer specific application data and temporary files. This folder is hidden by default.

- *My Documents* stores user documents.

- *Nethood* holds shortcuts to network resources as specified in My Network Places. This folder is hidden by default.

- *Printhood* provides shortcuts to printers. This folder is hidden by default.

- *Recent* contains shortcuts to the most recently accessed files and folders. By default this folder is hidden.

- *Send To* contains items that appear on the Send To menu. (Right-click a file and click Send To.) By default this folder is hidden.

- *Start Menu* provides user-specific shortcuts to start menu items. Not all start menu items will be found in this folder because some items are required for all users.

- *Templates* holds various application templates, such as templates for Excel, Word, and Powerpoint. By default, this folder is hidden.

- **Ntuser.dat** contains registry settings that will be applied to the local computer when the user logs on. By default this file is hidden.

Exercise 1

CREATING A LOCAL PROFILE ON A COMPUTER

In this exercise you create a new profile by creating a new user and logging on to the system. You also change the screen background image and view the results by logging back on as the same user.

1. Log on to your computer with the administrator account.
2. Open My Computer or Explorer, open the drive where your system files are located, and open the *Documents and Settings* folder. Note the folders displayed. These folders contain profile settings.

You will next create a new user. In the previous chapter you used the graphical user interface tools. Here you will use a command line tool.

3. Click Start, click Run, key **CMD**, and press Enter.
4. In the command window, enter the following command and press Enter. Make sure you key exactly what is displayed and leave a single space between each word.

```
net user dorothy password /ADD
```

You should see the message *The command completed successfully*. You must make sure this user can log on to the local server. One way to make sure is by adding the user account to the Builtin Server Operators group. This task also can be done from the command line.

5. From the command line, key the following command. Make sure you put a single space between each word:

```
net localgroup "server operators" dorothy /ADD
```

You should see the message *The command completed successfully*. You will next ensure that a user was created.

6. In the command line, enter the following command and press Enter.

```
net user dorothy
```

You should see information about the user just created.

7. Click Start, click Shut Down, click *Log off Administrator*, and click OK.
8. Log back on to the system with the user ID **dorothy** and the password **password**.
9. Open My Computer or Explorer and open the folder named *Documents and Settings*. You should see a profile folder named *dorothy*.
10. Double-click this folder to open it.
11. Click the Tools menu and then click Folder Options.
12. Click the View tab in the Folder Options dialog box and click *Show hidden files and folders*.
13. Click the OK button to close the Folder Options dialog box. You should now see the hidden folders in the *Profile* folder (hidden folders are displayed slightly gray).
14. Close this folder.
15. Right-click on the desktop and click Properties.
16. Click the Background tab, select the Blue Lace background, choose the Tile option, and click OK
17. Log off the system and log back on with the new account just created (dorothy). The profile setting for the desktop background should have been saved and you will see a new background.
18. Log off the system and log back on with the administrator account. The background setting that was added to Dorothy's user profile is not used for the administrator's account.

Roaming Profiles

In the previous exercise, a local profile was created and stored on the local computer. This profile works only on the local computer. If you want users to keep their settings no matter what computer on the network they log on to, they must have **roaming profiles**, which are stored on a server rather than on individual computers. When users log on to a workstation, a replica of the server-based profile is copied down to the *Documents and Settings* folder on the local workstation and the settings are then applied. Any changes users make during their session on the workstation will be automatically copied back up to the server when users log off.

Exercise 2

CREATING A SERVER-BASED ROAMING PROFILE

Note: In this exercise you must be using two networked computers in the same domain.

In this exercise you create a new user, create a roaming profiles shared folder, set the user profile settings, and log on to the other system with the user.

1. Log on as administrator to machine A1Computer (A2Computer). (Substitute your own letter for the *A*.)
2. Click Start, Run, key **CMD**, and press Enter to open a command window.
3. Enter the following command to create a user on the domain controller (select A1User for the A1computer and A2User for the A2computer).

    ```
    net user A1User password /add
    ```

4. Key **exit** and press Enter to close the command window.

You will next create a roaming profiles folder.

5. Double-click the *My Computer* icon to open it.
6. Double-click the drive where your system files are located.
7. Right-click on a white space in the drive and then click <u>N</u>ew and Folder.
8. Name the folder *roamingProfiles*.
9. Right-click the folder and click Sharing. You see the dialog box in Figure 8.1.

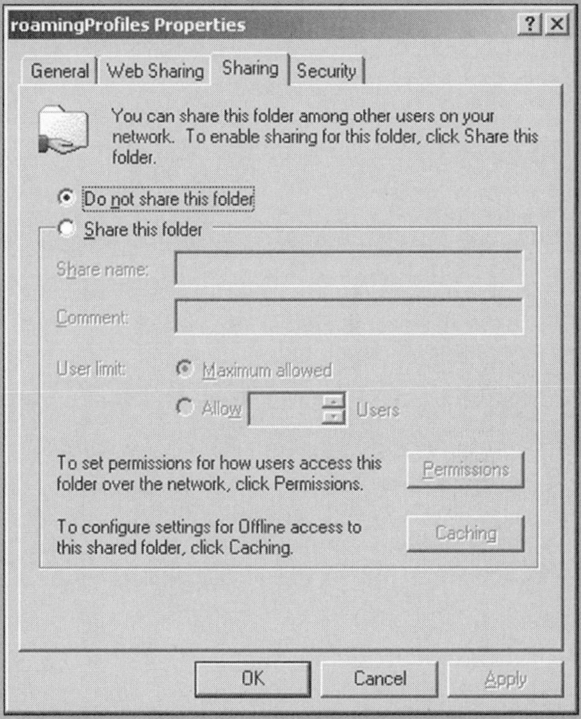

Figure 8.1

10. Click *Share this folder*. A share name will be automatically created as in Figure 8.2.

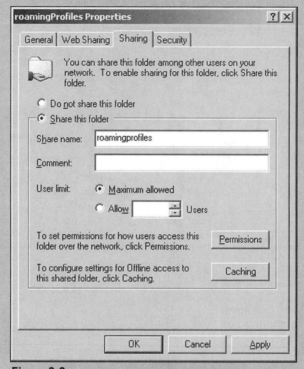

Figure 8.2

(Sharing makes a resource available on the network. It will be discussed in more detail in the next chapter.)

11. Accept all the defaults and click OK. A hand should appear under the folder to indicate it is shared.

You will next set the profile properties for the newly created user.

12. Close My Computer and start your MMC, or start Active Directory Users and Computers.
13. Locate the A1User (A2User) user and double-click the user name to display the properties.
14. Click the Profile tab. You see the dialog box in Figure 8.3.

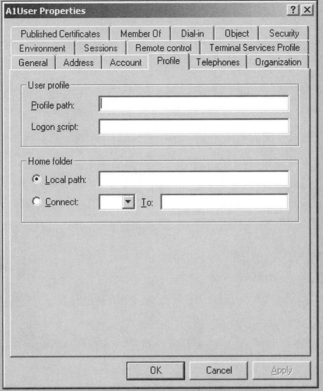

Figure 8.3

15. In the Profile path box key **\\A1Computer\roamingprofiles\ %username%** (**A2Computer\roamingprofiles\%username%**).

This command sets the location of the profile folders to be used when this user logs on to a computer. The *%username%* is a placeholder that is automatically replaced by the account name of the current user. Rather than specify an exact profile path name, using this placeholder name means that all profiles can include the same profile path string.

16. Click OK to close the Properties dialog box.

Exercise 3

TESTING THE ROAMING PROFILE

In this exercise you log on to the computer with this user account, change the wallpaper, copy a file into the *My Documents* folder, and then log off. You will then log on to the second domain controller with this user account and view the settings.

1. Click Start, click Shut Down, and click *Logoff Administrator*.
2. Log on to the A1Computer (A2Computer) with A1User (A2User) with **password** as the password.
3. Right-click on the desktop, click Properties, click the Coffee Bean background (A1User) or Blue Lace 16 (A2User), click Tile, and click OK.
4. Double-click the *My Documents* icon on the desktop to open the folder.
5. Right-click inside the folder, click New, and then click Text Document.
6. Press Enter to accept the default text document name and then double-click the new document to edit it.
7. Key the name of the user (A1User or A2User) in Notepad, click File, and click Save.
8. Close Notepad.

You will now log off the system as A1User (A2User) to save the profile settings into the indicated profile folders.

9. Click Start, click Shut Down, and click *Logoff A1User (A2User)*.
10. Log on as administrator.

Your administrator profile should not display the user settings.

11. Log off as administrator and log on with the user created on the other domain controller. On A1Computer, log on as A2User and on A2Computer log on as A1User.

You should see the appropriate background and find the text file saved in My Documents.

Roaming profiles can also be set as mandatory so that any changes the user makes to the profile will be discarded. Each time the user logs off and back on they will receive the original mandatory profile without any changes. Reverting back to the original profile is helpful if several people share an account or profile. Exercise 6 at the end of the chapter shows you how to make a profile mandatory.

Introduction to Group Policies

Profiles have been used on Windows operating systems for many years. Recently, a more powerful tool called Policies has been introduced. Group policies are perhaps one of the most powerful aspects of the Windows 2000 operating system. If not handled correctly they can also be the most troublesome. **Group policies** allow the network administrator to install software, redirect folders, and put restrictions on the system that determine what users can and cannot do. For example, an administrator can create a group policy object (GPO) that will prevent users in the domain from changing the wallpaper on their desktop. Despite what the name suggests, group policies are not applied directly to groups. They can only be applied to sites, domains, or organizational units. The process of applying a GPO is called linking. A single GPO can be linked multiple times so, for example, multiple OUs could all use the same GPO. Also, a single OU can have multiple GPOs linked to it.

Differences between System Policies and Group Policies

In previous versions of Windows, administrators created their system policies using a tool called the system policy editor and stored all policies in a single file. With Windows 2000, the administrator can create policies by using a snap-in to an MMC. The policies are not stored in a single file but rather in something called a group policy object (GPO). One group policy object can hold multiple different policy settings, or you can create multiple GPOs so that each GPO holds a single setting. The GPO is made up of two pieces, a group policy container (GPC) and a group policy template (GPT). The GPC is stored in the Active Directory and the GPT is stored in the *SysVol* folder. Both of these pieces must be replicated to all domain controllers. By default, group policies replicate between domain controllers every five minutes.

Several other differences can be noted between the old system policies and Windows 2000 group policies. System policies were often written directly into the registry. When the policy file was deleted the entries still remained in the registry. Windows 2000 group policies will eliminate their own entries from the registry when they are removed. Also, system policies were applied only when logging on

Group policies apply only to Windows 2000 machines. On networks with down-level clients, such as Windows 98 machines, the system policy editor meant for that operating system must still be used.

and logging off. Group policies are applied to clients when they log on or log off and every 90 minutes by default.

Several policies are built by default when Windows 2000 Server is installed, including the default domain policy and the default domain controllers policy. In Chapter 7 you modified the default domain controllers policy to allow users to log on to the local domain controller. You accessed the default domain controller policy by picking the Domain Controller Security Policy from the Administrative Tools menu. In the next section you will change the default domain policy by using the Active Directory Users and Computers snap-in.

Creating Domain-Wide Account Policies Using the Group Policy Editor

Most policies are applied to sites, domains, or OUs, but several policies, once they are set, apply to the entire domain. These domain-wide policies cannot be overwritten by different policies set at sites or OUs. These domain-wide policies are the account policies. They include password policies, account lockout, and Kerberos policy. The password and account lockout policies will be discussed here and Kerberos will be dealt with in Chapter 12.

In Chapter 7 you learned to create users but you did not have any account policies in place. Account policies dictate such things as how long a user can keep his or her password. In a production network it is best to create account policies before creating users, because then all the user accounts will be held to the domain-wide standards. Users who exist in the domain prior to the implementation of account policies will be forced to comply with the new policies the next time they log on or when they next change their password, depending on which policies are set. The default account policies in Windows 2000 tend to leave things open with few restrictions. As the administrator, you will want to define policies to help secure your system.

Exercise 4

SETTING PASSWORD POLICIES

In this exercise you set domain-wide password policies.

1. Start the Active Directory Users and Computers program and expand the options under Active Directory Users and Computers.
2. Right-click your domain name and click Properties from the drop-down menu.
3. Click the Group Policy tab. You see the Group Policy dialog box as shown in Figure 8.4.

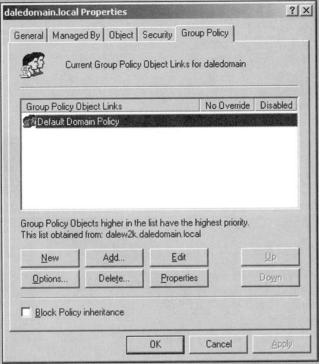

Figure 8.4

4. Click *Default Domain Policy* and click <u>E</u>dit. You see the Group Policy MMC in Figure 8.5.

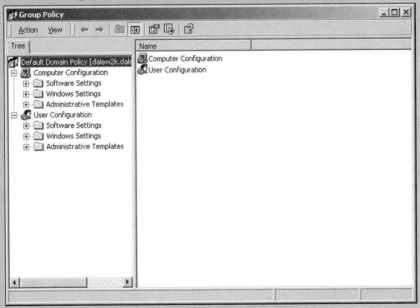

Figure 8.5

Group policies are divided into two main categories: computer policies (under the *Computer Configuration* icon) and user policies (under the *User Configuration* icon). User policies tend to apply to user settings such as desktop configurations. Computer policies apply to items that are machine specific, such as software and printer configurations. You will, however, find many areas of overlap between the two categories. To avoid confusion, your best strategy is to take some time and become familiar with where different policies can be set.

5. Click the plus sign next to each of the following icons under Computer Configuration to expand them:

    Windows Settings
    Security Settings
    Account Policies

    The result looks like Figure 8.6.

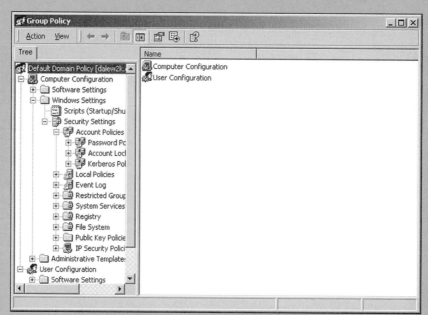

Figure 8.6

6. Click the *Password Policy* icon. The policies for passwords are displayed in the right screen as in Figure 8.7.

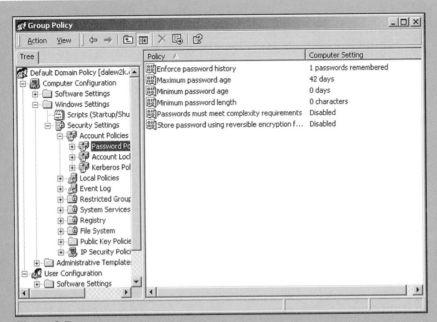

Figure 8.7

One of the options on the right half of the screen is *Maximum password age*. This policy is used to set the maximum time a user can keep a password before being forced to change it. Evaluate your own environment before setting this policy. If users on your network access a mainframe system where they must change their password every 42 days, set the maximum password age at 42 days. That way the users can keep their passwords synchronized. Also, it is better to not set 30 days as the maximum password age. Your users will tend to use January, February, and so on as their passwords because they are easy to remember!

7. Double-click *Maximum password age*. You see the password age policy setting in Figure 8.8.

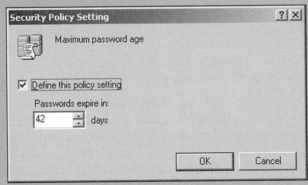

Figure 8.8

8. Click *Define this policy setting* and set the Passwords expire in option to 21 days.
9. Click OK to accept the settings.

The other options you see under the password policy are:

Minimum password length: This policy requires user passwords to be at least a certain number of characters long. If you set this policy to require six character passwords, a user could not enter the word *boat* as their password. Passwords can be up to 56 characters long; however, most users would never remember or be able to type something that long on a consistent basis. Be reasonable when you select a minimum password length. Due to the way some of the password cracking engines work, the best passwords are either seven characters or a multiple of seven. User accounts that are created before a minimum password length policy is put into effect will not be in compliance with the policy. These users will be forced to comply the next time they change their password.

Passwords must meet complexity requirements: This policy goes beyond requiring a password to be a certain length. If you enable this policy, passwords need to match a builtin password filter. The filter has the following requirements:

- The password must be at least six characters long.

- The password cannot contain the user name.

- The password must contain characters that include at least three of the following: uppercase letters, lowercase letters, numeric characters, or special symbols.

Enforce password history: This policy prevents a user from switching back and forth between two passwords all the time. If this policy is set to 4, the user must go through four different passwords before using the original password again.

Minimum password age: This policy determines how long a user must keep a password before changing it. This policy becomes important when using the password history option. If the password history is set to three, but a minimum password age is not set, users could immediately change their password three times, allowing them to return to their original password.

Store passwords using reversible encryption for all users in the domain: This policy would be selected if the network had Macintosh clients. These clients (as well as some other non-Windows clients) cannot log on using the native Windows 2000 password security and so must use their own encryption methods. This option can also be set at the level of individual accounts and does not need to be set for the entire domain.

Exercise 5

SETTING ACCOUNT LOCKOUT POLICIES

Another important account policy is the account lockout policy. In the following exercise you set an account lockout threshold.

1. If not already open, run the Active Directory, Users, and Computers program, and click Computer Configurations, Windows Settings, and Security Settings.
2. Click the *Account Lockout Policy* icon on the left side of the screen. You see the set of account lockout policies as shown in Figure 8.9.

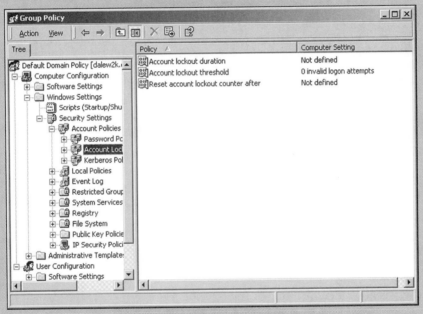

Figure 8.9

One of the policies on the right side of the screen is the Account lockout threshold, which determines how many times a user can enter the wrong password before they are locked out of their account.

3. Double-click *Account lockout threshold* to display the Security Policy Setting dialog box (Figure 8.10).

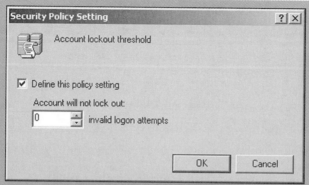

Figure 8.10

If this policy is set to lock out *after* three invalid logon attempts, the user can try four times to log on. The key word here is *after*. If the user enters the wrong password the first three times, he or she will have one more chance to log on. If the fourth attempt results in the correct password, the user gets into the system. However, if on the fourth attempt another incorrect password is entered, the user will be locked out of the network. As a network administrator, you need to evaluate your own environment before setting this option. Users who are unfamiliar with computers, or who work on many different computer systems, may require this number to be set higher. The maximum number of attempts is 999 and the minimum is zero. If you set the value to zero, the account will never lock out a user. This option can create a significant security risk because password-cracking programs can try to determine the password indefinitely without consequence.

4. In the Account lockout threshold setting box click *Define this policy setting* and set the invalid logon attempts to *3*.
5. Click OK to accept the settings.

Other account lockout policies include the following:

Account lockout duration: This policy determines how long an account will be locked out after the lockout threshold has been reached. That is, how long must the user wait after entering too many invalid passwords before the user can attempt to log on to the system again? The maximum is 99999 minutes and the minimum is zero. If you set the value to zero, the account remains locked after a failed logon attempt until an administrator unlocks it.

As the administrator, you may wish to select this option so you can keep abreast of what is happening on your system. If you have a user who calls you every morning because his or her account is locked out, you may suspect someone has been tampering with the account overnight. You may never become aware of the problem if the account unlocked itself after 4 hours.

Reset account lockout counter after: This policy determines how long the system keeps track of bad password attempts before locking the user out of the network. The minimum is one minute and the maximum is 99999 minutes. For example, assume the account lockout threshold is set at 3 and the reset account lockout is set at 360 minutes. A user logs on to the network in the morning after two bad password attempts and then logs off for lunch. After lunch the user attempts to log on and types in the wrong password two more times. Because the system remembers the two bad attempts from the morning, the user will be locked out.

Most of the password settings also apply to administrators. Administrators will be forced to meet the complexity, history, and minimum password length policies. They will not be held to the maximum password age settings if you set their password to never expire. However, choosing that option for an administrator poses a large security risk for your system. Administrator passwords are also not subject to account lockout.

Application of Multiple Policies at Different Levels of the Organization

The password and account policies you previously set are not the only ones that can be set for an entire domain, but they are the only ones that must be applied across the entire domain. Other domain-wide policies can be blocked locally at the site or OU level. Still other policies can be set in multiple locations, and the rules of inheritance must be taken into account to determine how the policies are applied. An organizational unit will be a parent or child with respect to another OU, with a child placed inside a parent. When policies are attached to a parent, they are by default applied to the child. This process is called policy inheritance. A child policy can override a parent policy unless the parent policy is set so it cannot be overridden.

The order in which all policies are applied is first Windows NT system policies, then local policies, site group policies, domain group policies, OU group policies, and child OU policies. Child OUs will, by default, inherit policies from their parent. Another factor is the three possible ways to set a policy. Policies can be not configured, enabled, and disabled. A child OU will not inherit settings that are marked Not configured in the parent policy, but children do inherit both enabled and disabled settings from their parent.

In the next set of exercises you will create a policy at the domain level and then test to see that the policy has been inherited by the OUs. Although a default domain policy already exists and can be edited, it is preferable to create new group policy objects (GPOs). The advantage of creating new GPOs for each setting or small number of settings is that it makes troubleshooting group policies much easier. If you have a GPO for each setting you can give the GPO an appropriate name and easily identify what that GPO does. You can also delete a GPO for a particular setting without deleting any other settings. The disadvantage of creating multiple GPOs is that GPOs are loaded one by one at logon time, increasing the logon time for users. If your group policy structure is fairly simple, you may consider putting all of your settings in a single GPO. Being able to troubleshoot group policies in an organization is probably more critical than the slight delay multiple GPOs create when a user logs on.

Group policies can easily become the most confusing and frustrating part of Windows 2000. It is important to carefully document your group policy settings. Use the following diagram to help keep track of your policies.

For each level fill in the policy name (underlined) and whether the policy will be mandatory (no override) or block inheritance. Indented containers will inherit policies from higher level containers.

Company Domain → <u>Domain Policy</u> (no override)

    Organizational Unit for Departments → <u>All Department Level Policy</u> (no override)

        Organizational Unit for Sales → <u>Sales Department Policy</u>
        Organizational Unit for Accounting → <u>Accounting Department Policy</u>
            Organizational Unit for Secure Accounting → <u>Secure Accounting Policy</u>
        Organizational Unit for Marketing → <u>Marketing Department Policy</u>

    Organizational Unit for Information Systems (IS) → <u>All IS Policy</u> (no override)

        Organizational Unit for Development → <u>Development Policy</u>
        Organizational Unit for Maintenance → <u>Maintenance Policy</u>

In previous chapters you created accounts for MBuffett and SWallace. The MBuffett account is located in the A1Unit OU and the SWallace account is in the A2Unit OU. The Administrator is not a member of any OU in particular but simply an account within the domain. For all of the exercises in this chapter you will create or change a policy and then test the policy on the same machine it was created. Although this format causes numerous logon and logoff procedures, it helps eliminate the time it takes for a policy to replicate between domain controllers.

Exercise 6

SETTING A GROUP POLICY FOR THE DOMAIN

1. Log on to A1Computer as the administrator, open your MMC (or run Active Directory Computers and Users), and click the plus sign next to *Active Directory Users and Computers* to expand it.
2. Right-click your domain name and click Properties.

3. Click the Group Policy tab. You see a listing for the Default Domain Policy.
4. Click the New button to create a new policy.
5. Key the name **Hide IE and My Network Places** for your new policy and press Enter.
6. With the *Hide IE and My Network Places* policy highlighted, click the Edit button. You see the Group Policy edit window in Figure 8.11.

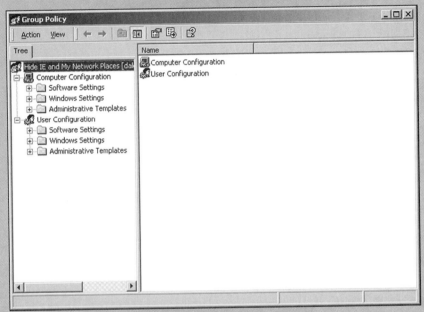

Figure 8.11

7. Under User Configuration click *Administrative Templates* to expand the options.
8. Click on the *Desktop* folder to display the policies in the right window (Figure 8.12).

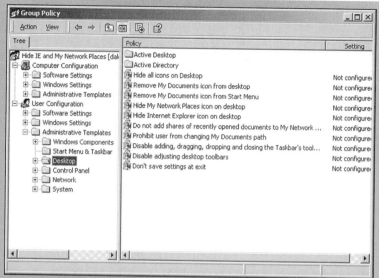

Figure 8.12

You will set the policies to hide the *Internet Explorer* and *My Network Places* icons on the desktop.

   9. Double-click the *Hide Internet Explorer icon on desktop* policy. You see the policy dialog box in Figure 8.13.

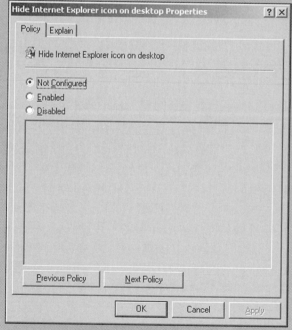

Figure 8.13

10. Click *Enabled* and click OK. The policy option in the Group Policy window should now show the message *Enabled*.

11. Double-click *Hide My Network Places icon on desktop*, click *Enabled*, and click OK. The message for this option should now show *Enabled*. The policies should look like Figure 8.14.

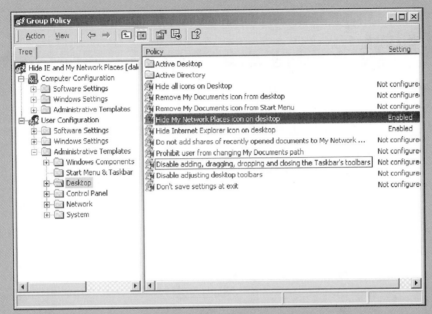

Figure 8.14

12. Close the Group Policy window and close Active Directory Users and Computers.

13. If necessary, log off the computer and log on to A1Computer as MBuffett. The *Internet Explorer* and *My Network Places* icons should not be displayed on the desktop.

14. Log off as MBuffett and log back on to the computer as administrator. Are the icons still in place?

This exercise shows that the policy to remove icons from the desktop, applied at the domain level, is automatically inherited by the child A1Unit organizational unit. Because the MBuffett account is contained in the A1Unit OU, the policy was applied to the account.

At certain times, you may not want a particular OU to inherit settings from the domain policy. Inheritance can be blocked in two ways;

- Explicitly apply a policy setting to a child unit that contradicts the policy setting coming from the parent
- Use the Block Inheritance option within the child OU

In the next exercise you will create a policy for A1Unit that disables the Hide IE from Desktop policy setting.

Exercise 7

SETTING A CONTRADICTORY POLICY FOR AN OU

1. Log on to A1Computer as administrator, open your MMC (or run Active Directory Users and Computers), and expand the options under your domain name.
2. Right-click the A1Unit organizational unit and click Properties.
3. Click the Group Policy tab.
4. Click the New button, name your new policy **Do Not allow removal of IE**, and press Enter.
5. With the *Do Not allow removal of IE* policy highlighted, click the Edit button.
6. Under the User Configuration section, expand *Administrative Templates*.
7. Click the *Desktop* folder to display the policies in the right window (Figure 8.15).

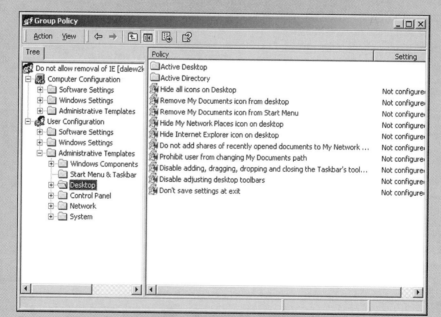

Figure 8.15

8. Double-click the *Hide Internet Explorer icon on desktop* policy to display the policy dialog box.
9. Click the <u>D</u>isabled button and click OK. The option for this policy should now say *Disabled*.

When setting policies, the options not configured, enabled, and disabled can lead to confusion. Some of the policies are positive (allow something) while other policies, like Hide Internet Explorer icon on desktop, are negative. When this type of policy is enabled, the action described in the policy will take place. When this type of policy is disabled, the action described in the policy will not take place.

10. Close the Group Policy window.
11. Click Close to close the A1Unit Properties window.

To review, you have created a domain-wide policy to hide the *Internet Explorer* desktop icon. This policy will be inherited by all organizational units in the domain. You have created another policy local to the A1Unit OU that disables this policy. That is, the policy will not be in effect for the A1Unit organizational unit.

Exercise 8

TESTING THE CONTRADICTORY OU POLICY

In this exercise you test the OU policy created in the A1Unit OU.

1. Log on to A1Computer as MBuffett.
2. Look for the *Internet Explorer* icon on the desktop. It should be present, because the A1Unit OU policy was applied after the domain policy, and the OU policy contained a setting that contradicted the domain policy.
3. Look for the *My Network Places* icon on the desktop. It should not be present because the domain-level policy was inherited by the A1Unit OU and was not contradicted by a policy set for the OU.
4. Repeat steps 1 through 3 and log on as SWallace and administrator. Do the icons for *Internet Explorer* and *My Network Places* appear?

By creating a contradictory policy for the child OU, you can override a particular setting or settings inherited from the parent. This capability was demonstrated in the previous exercise when you set a policy for the A1Unit that contradicted the domain policy. The A1Unit policy caused Internet Explorer to be seen from the desktop, MBuffett who belongs to the A1Unit OU sees Internet Explorer on the desktop.

However, the policy set at the OU level did not contradict the setting of Hide My Network Places set in the domain policy. Users in the A1Unit OU still do not see the *My Network Places* icon on their desktop.

Blocking Inheritance

If you do not want any policies or settings from the parent to be inherited by the child, you can use a feature called block inheritance. Setting **block inheritance** keeps all parental policies and settings from applying to the child. This option eliminates the need to create a contradictory policy for each setting to be overridden. Remember that if a child does not inherit a policy, it will not be passed down to any grandchildren OUs. For example, in a three-tiered setup with a grandparent, parent, and child OU, where block inheritance is set at the parent OU, the child OU would inherit policies from the parent OU but not from the grandparent OU. In the next exercise you will set block inheritance for the A2Unit OU.

Exercise 9

BLOCKING INHERITANCE OF A GROUP POLICY

In this exercise you block inheritance of the group policy to the A2Unit OU.

1. Log on to A2Computer as the administrator and open your MMC (or run Active Directory Users and Computer).
2. Click the plus sign next to *Active Directory Users and Computers* to expand it.
3. Click the plus sign next to your domain name to expand it.
4. Right-click *A2Unit* and click Properties from the drop-down menu.
5. Click the Group Policy tab.
6. Click *Block Policy inheritance* and click OK (Figure 8.16).

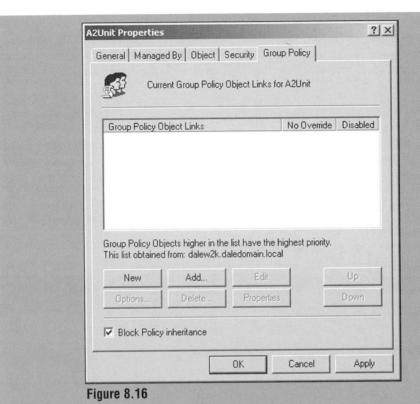

Figure 8.16

The domain policy should be blocked from applying to this organizational unit. All users within this OU will not be subject to the domain policy.

Exercise 10

TESTING THE BLOCK INHERITANCE

1. Log on to A2Computer as SWallace.
2. Does the *Internet Explorer* icon show up on the desktop? Why or why not?
3. Does the *My Network Places* icon show up on the desktop? Why or Why not?
4. Repeat steps 1 through 3 logged on as MBuffett and as administrator.

No Override Policies

Being able to block inheritance or overwrite a setting from a parent policy is useful because it allows individual OUs to have different policies based on their needs. However, you may decide that the parent policy should be applied regardless of the wishes of the child units. In this case a **No override** option can be set on the parent policy. If both a No override exists on the parent policy and a block inheritance exists on the child policy, the parent policy will win the battle. A no override option set at the parent level will also cause a contradictory policy at the child level to be ineffective.

For example, suppose the network administrator does not wish users to browse the network and sets a policy to remove the *My Network Places* icon from the desktop. A user with administrator rights over an OU could create a **contradictory policy** that placed this icon back on the desktop, or simply select the Block Inheritance option. To maintain control over a set of core domain-wide policies, the network administrator could mark the policy with a No override setting.

In the next few exercises you will set the No override option at the domain level and watch the results at the OUs.

Exercise 11

SETTING NO OVERRIDE ON A GROUP POLICY

Note: This exercise should be done on one domain controller only. The domain-wide policy will be replicated to the other domain controllers in the domain.

1. Log on to A1Computer or the A2Computer as the administrator.
2. Open your MMC or run Active Directory Users and Computers.
3. Click the plus sign next to *Active Directory Sites and Services* to expand it.
4. Right-click your domain and click Properties from the menu.
5. Click the Group Policy tab.
6. Click the *Hide IE and My Network Places* policy and click the Options button. You see the Options dialog box in Figure 8.17.

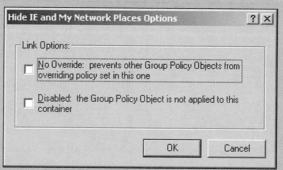

Figure 8.17

The options are *No Override* and *Disabled*. The first option prevents child OUs from blocking inheritance or creating contradictory policies. The second option disables the policy so that it cannot be set. This option will also be inherited by child OUs.

7. Click *No Override* and click OK. You see a check mark in the dialog box indicating that the selected policy is set to No Override (Figure 8.18).

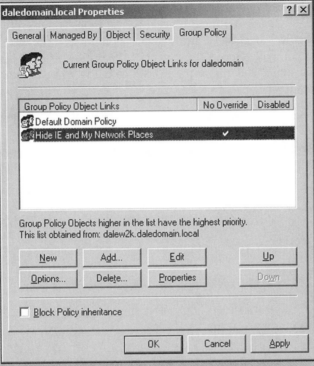

Figure 8.18

8. Click OK to close the domain Properties dialog box.

Exercise 12

TESTING THE NO OVERRIDE OPTION

1. Log on to A2Computer as MBuffett.
2. Does the *Internet Explorer* icon show up on the desktop? Why or why not?
3. Does the *My Network Places* icon show up on the desktop? Why or Why not?
4. Repeat steps 1 through 3 logged on as SWallace and administrator.

Linking Policies

Once a policy has been created you can apply it as a **linking policy** to other containers. This ability prevents the administrator from having to recreate policies multiple times to be used in several places. In the following exercise you will use the Do Not Allow Removal of IE group policy you created for A1Unit and link it to A2Unit. First you will remove the No override option from the Hide IE and My Network Places GPO at the domain level to allow you to see the results of linking the policy to the A2Unit.

Exercise 13

REMOVING THE NO OVERRIDE OPTION

Note: This exercise should be done on only one of the domain controllers in the domain.

1. Log on to A1Computer as the administrator.
2. Open your MMC or run Active Directory Users and Computers.
3. Click the plus sign next to *Active Directory Users and Computers* to expand it.
4. Right-click your domain name and click Properties from the menu.
5. Click the Group Policy tab.
6. Click the *Hide IE and My Network Places* policy and click the Options button.
7. Remove the check mark from *No Override* and click OK.
8. Click OK to close the domain Properties dialog box.

Exercise 14

LINKING THE OVERRIDE IE REMOVAL GROUP POLICY TO THE A2UNIT

In this exercise you link a group policy object to the A2Unit OU that was created in another OU.

1. With your MMC or the Active Directory Users and Computers program still running, click the plus sign next to *Active Directory Users and Computers* to expand it.
2. Click the plus sign next to your domain name to expand it.
3. Right-click *A2Unit* and click Properties from the drop-down menu.
4. Click the Group Policy tab. No group policy objects should display for this OU.

5. Click the Add button. You see the Add a Group Policy dialog box (Figure 8.19).

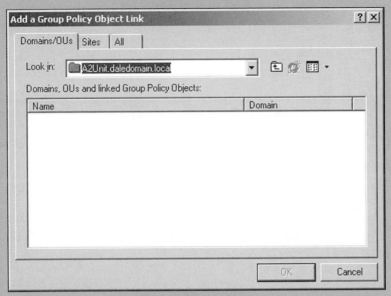

Figure 8.19

6. Click the All tab. You should see the *Do not allow removal of IE* policy listed (Figure 8.20).

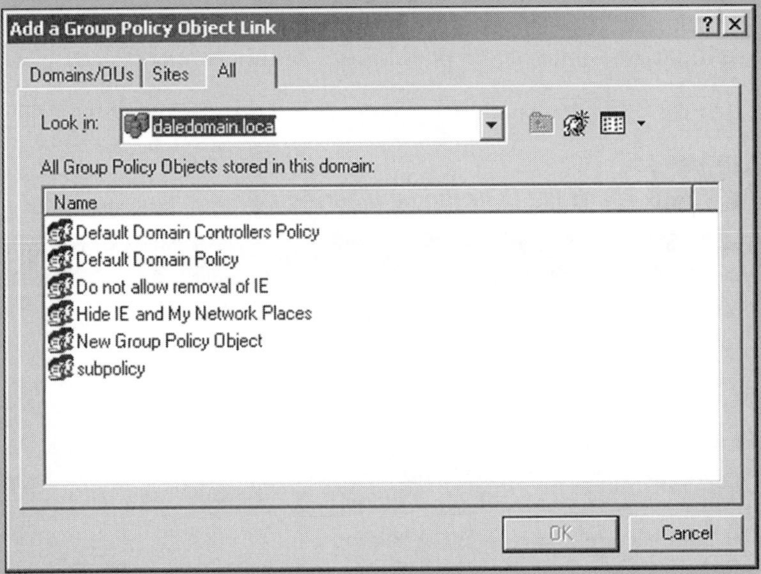

Figure 8.20

Exercise 15

TESTING THE LINKING OF A POLICY

In this exercise you test the policy linked in the previous exercise.

1. Log on to A1Computer as SWallace.
2. Does the *Internet Explorer* icon show up on the desktop? Why or why not?
3. Does the *My Network Places* icon show up on the desktop? Why or Why not?
4. Repeat steps 1 through 3 logged on as MBuffett. Are the results the same?

Obviously, limiting both the number of policies in your organization and the levels at which they are applied has certain advantages. Inheritance and the options to block it or contradict it can make troubleshooting your group policies difficult. Table 8.1 summarizes some of the possibilities of inheritance.

TABLE 8.1 *The Results of Policy Inheritance*

Parent Action	Child Action	Resulting Child Policy
Set Policy A	Nothing	Policy A
Set Policy A	Create Contradictory Policy A2	Policy A2
Set Policy A	Set Block Inheritance	No Policy A
Set Policy A (No Override)	Nothing	Policy A
Set Policy A (No Override)	Create Contradictory Policy A2	Policy A
Set Policy A (No Override)	Set Block Inheritance	Policy A

In Chapter 7 you could set a time restriction on a user account that would not allow a user to log on after a certain time. For example a 5:00 p.m. time restriction would mean the user could not log on at 5:01 p.m. That restriction did not, however, force a user off the system who was already logged on. If the user logged on at 4:59 p.m., that user would not be forced off the system at 5:00 p.m. In order to force a user off at the restricted time, you need to set a group policy. Select where you want the policy to apply (either the domain level or at some lower OU) and display the policies under Computer Configuration/ Windows Settings/Local Policies/Security Options. Select and enable the *Automatically log off users when logon time expires* policy.

Controlling Policies

As you have learned, policies can be set to almost completely control a user's environment. Other policies that control how the policies themselves are applied are found in the section Computer Configurations/Administrative Templates/System/ Group Policy and in User Configuration/Administrative Templates/System/Group Policy. For example, a policy named *Group Policy slow link detection* allows you to determine the rate at which policies are transferred from the domain controllers to the other computers. The default transfer rate of a policy is 500 KB per second. If a domain controller within a domain is on the other end of a slow link, the transfer rate of policies may overrun the link. By setting this policy, the transfer rate can be changed. Another powerful policy management feature is the ability to change how often policies are refreshed on the user's computers. This option is set by changing the *Group Policy refresh interval for computers*. The default update interval is every 90 minutes.

The policy update interval can be set as short as just a few seconds or up to 45 days. Very short intervals should be avoided because they cause excessive network traffic and can interfere with the user's work. When a policy is updated, the desktop is refreshed and open menu items will be closed.

Group policies are much more powerful than the old system policies found in previous versions of Windows. Many more features are provided than were covered in this chapter. Three new features, however, deserve some explanation because they are especially helpful to administrators. These features are folder redirection, software installation, and logon/logoff scripts.

Folder Redirection

One of the new capabilities provided by the Windows 2000 group policy feature is the ability to redirect folders. Many network administrators can attest to the frustration felt when a computer's hard drive crashes with all of the user's work saved on the local computer in the *My Documents* folder, which the user never backed up. In the past, users were often encouraged to place data files on a home drive located on the network server to avoid this type of problem. Implementing this safety precaution was another matter. By default, most Windows application programs default to the *My Documents* folder, located on the local computer. Users often forget to change the destination of their saved files to the network folder. The folder redirection feature solves this problem.

Folder redirection allows the network administrator to create a policy that will redirect the user's *My Documents* folder to the server. When users save their work they can continue to use the *My Documents* folder, but the information will be stored on a network server. Other folders that can be redirected are the *Application Data*, *Desktop,* and *Start Menu* folders. In the following exercise you will redirect the *My Documents* folders for users in your A1Unit and A2Unit OUs. By default the *My Documents* folder is stored in the *Users Profile* folder under the *Documents and Settings* folder on the system drive of the local machine.

Exercise 16

REDIRECTING MY DOCUMENTS WITH A POLICY

In this exercise you will create a policy that redirects the *My Documents* folder to a folder located on a server.

1. Open My Computer and on the system drive of the A1Computer to create a new folder called *userdata* at the system root drive (for example, drive D). This folder must be shared in order to have the *My Documents* folder information automatically stored.
2. Right-click the *userdata* folder and click the Sharing Menu option.
3. Click the Share this Folder option.
4. Accept all the defaults and click OK. A hand should appear under the folder to indicate it is shared.

You will next set a policy for the organizational unit.

5. Open your MMC Active Directory Users and Computers snap-in or run the Active Directory Users and Computers program.
6. Right-click *A1Unit (A2Unit)* and click Properties from the menu.
7. Click the Group Policy tab and click New.
8. Name the new policy **Redirect My Documents** and press Enter.

9. With the *Redirect My Documents* policy highlighted, click Edit.
10. Display the policies for *User Configuration/Windows Settings/Folder Redirection* (Figure 8.21).

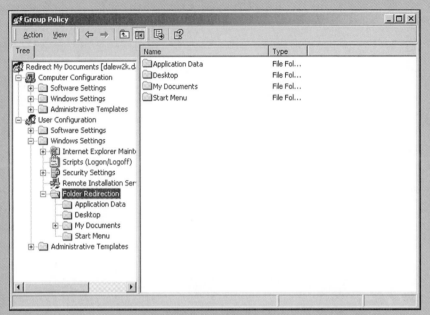

Figure 8.21

11. In the right side of the window, right-click the *My Documents* folder and click Properties. You see the My Documents Properties dialog box.
12. On the Target tab, click the Setting drop-down list box and click *Basic – Redirect everyone's folder to the same location*. A Target folder location text box is displayed.
13. In the Target folder location text box key

    \\A1computer\userdata\%username%

    The dialog box should look like Figure 8.22.

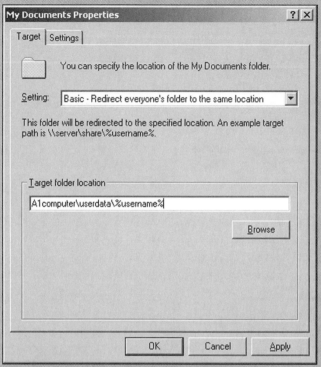

Figure 8.22

14. Click the Settings tab.
15. Under the Policy Removal area, click *Redirect the folder back to the local userprofile when the policy is removed*. The dialog box should look like Figure 8.23.

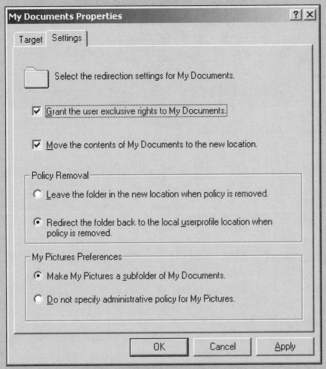

Figure 8.23

16. Accept all other defaults and click OK.

Note: The %username% variable will pull the user's logon name and create a folder named for the user. In this way each user will have his or her own individual folder.

17. Click the Close button to exit the Policy Editing dialog box.

Exercise 17

TESTING THE FOLDER REDIRECTION POLICY

In this exercise you will test the redirected *My Documents* folder.

1. Log on to A2Computer as Mbuffett. This user is in the A1Unit OU and this OU has a policy to redirect the *My Documents* folder to the A1Computer server.
2. Open the *My Documents* folder.
3. Right-click within the folder window and click New Text Document.

Software Installation

Another new feature of group policies is the ability to automatically perform software installations. One of the most time-consuming activities of a network administrator is the installation of a new software package on the network workstations. Many times the administrator is forced to sit down at each workstation that needs the new software and install it manually. For several years, Microsoft has offered an application called Systems Management Server (SMS) that allows the administrator to install software on remote computers without ever touching the actual machine. Unfortunately, SMS was not included with the NT operating system and had to be purchased separately. (SMS has many other functions in addition to installing software, such as inventory and remote control functions.) With Windows 2000, Microsoft has included the software installation capability from SMS through the use of group policies.

In order for software to be installed by way of group policies, it must be created as a Microsoft Installer package file. These files have the extension **msi**. Currently, not many software vendors use msi packages for their software, but this situation will quickly change. If you are feeling ambitious you can create your own msi packages using tools such as Visual Studio. In Chapter 3 you learned how msi files are installed and how if a program component is missing it will be automatically reinstalled.

Windows 2000 includes an msi file named adminpak.msi in the *winnt**system32* folder that allows you to install the administrative tools on machines of your choice. This package allows you to easily create administrative workstations.

Some third-party vendors make installation software that creates these msi files. The best known is InstallShield.

The two ways to distribute msi based applications are through publishing the software package or by assigning the software package. Software can be published to a user, but not actually installed automatically. Instead, it is made available in the *Add/Remove Programs* icon and can be installed at the user's discretion. Assigning software is slightly different. Software can be assigned to either a user or a computer. If software is assigned, when the computer boots up or the user logs on, the software will be automatically installed. Actually at this point the install process is not complete but will finish the first time the user clicks on the program. If part of the program gets deleted, it will be reinstalled the next time the user logs on.

If you are only interested in publishing a package you can use a shortcut. Create a text file with the extension .zap. The file will have the following format. You can then publish the .zap file exactly as you would an msi package. It will not work to assign a package.

Contents of the .zap file.

```
[application]
FriendlyName  =  name that will appear in Add/Remove Programs
SetupCommand  =  path to the executable that does the install (often called
                 setup.exe)
DisplayVersion  =  version of the software being installed
[ext]
```

associated file extension, followed by the equal sign. For example, bmp =

A sample file would be saved with the file name newdatabase.zap:

```
[application]
FriendlyName = New Database Program
SetupCommand = \\A1computer\programs\setup.exe
DisplayVersion = 1.5
[ext]
xdb = ]
```

Exercise 18

INSTALLING SOFTWARE WITH A GROUP POLICY

In the following exercise you install a program using a group policy.

1. On the A1Computer create a folder called *SWInstall*.
2. Right-click this folder and click Sharing.
3. Using the displayed dialog box, set the following options for this folder:

Share name:	**SWInstall**
Comment:	**Software Install Folder**
User limit:	**Maximum Allowed**
Permissions:	**Accept default**

4. Copy the file called winmemory.msi from the CD that comes with your textbook to the *SWInstall* folder.

You will set the group policy for just the users in the A1Unit OU.

5. Open Active Directory Users and Computers, right-click *A1Unit*, and click Properties.
6. Click the Group Policy tab and click New.
7. Name your new group policy **Software Install** and press Enter.
8. Make sure your Software Install policy is selected and click the <u>E</u>dit button.
9. On the Group Policy window, select the options under *User Configuration/Software Settings*.
10. Right-click the *Software Install* icon, click <u>N</u>ew, and then click Package.
11. In the Filename box, key the full path to the application. In this case it will be **\\A1computer\swinstall\winmemory.msi**. Click Open. You see the Software Deployment dialog box in Figure 8.24.

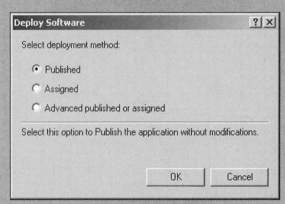

Figure 8.24

The third option, *Advanced published or assigned*, allows you to set specific options rather than accept the default options for the first two selections.

12. Click *Assigned* and click OK.
13. Close the Group Policy window.

Next you will restrict the policy to only users of the A1Unit OU.

14. In the A1Unit OU Properties dialog box, click the *Software Install* policy and click the Properties button.
15. In the Software Install Properties dialog box, click the Security tab.
16. Click the A<u>d</u>d button to add a user.

17. Scroll through the list of users, click *MBuffett*, and click A<u>d</u>d.
18. Click the OK button to close the Select Users, Computers, and Groups dialog box.
19. Select the user just added (*MBuffett*) in the upper list and check the Apply Group Policy Allow check box in the lower list (Figure 8.25).

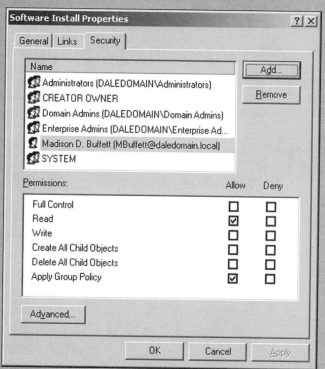

Figure 8.25

20. Click *Authenticated Users* and click <u>R</u>emove.
21. Click OK to leave the Software Install Properties dialog box.
22. Click Close to close the A1Unit Properties dialog box.
23. Close Active Directory Users and Computers.

The user in A1Unit OU now has a policy to automatically install software.

Exercise 19

TESTING THE SOFTWARE INSTALLATION POLICY

When a user with the Software Installation policy logs on to a computer, a shortcut to the software is placed on the Start menu. Clicking the shortcut either runs the program or, if the software is not yet installed, causes the package to be installed. If a user without this profile logs on to the computer, the shortcut is not displayed on the Start menu.

1. Log on A1Computer (A2Computer) as MBuffett.
2. Click the Start button and select the WinMemory program; it should now install and run. (Check how much memory Windows 2000 leaves free on your computer!)
3. Click the Exit button to exit the program.
4. Log off A1Computer (A2Computer) and log back on as SWallace. Do you see the WinMemory program? Why or Why not?

Logon and Logoff Scripts

In previous versions of Windows, scripts have been used to perform functions for the user automatically. Anything that could be done using a DOS batch file could be done using a script. For example, a logon script could connect a user to a shared folder whenever that user logs on. With Windows 2000 most functions, such as connecting a user to a resource, can be set up in the user profiles. Therefore, scripts are not used as much for user configuration, but you will probably still find them handy at times.

Scripts in Windows 2000 run using group policies. Unlike older versions of scripts, which ran in a command window that popped up at logon time, Windows 2000 scripts run in the background so they will be invisible to the user. Windows 2000 scripts are also more flexible than their predecessors and can be run both when a user logs on and logs off. Such scripts can be written as command line batch files, using a scripting language such as VBScript or JavaScript, or as executables. Batch files are easy to use in that that they can be created and edited with Notepad because they are simply ASCII text files.

Table 8.2 lists some common network command line instructions used in logon batch files.

Down-level clients such as Windows 95/98 or NT cannot use group policies. The network administrator must set command line scripts for these clients in the User Property dialog box, under the Profile tab in the Logon Script text box. The script file itself must be located on the domain controller in the *winnt\SYSVOL\sysvol\domainname\scripts* folder. This command corresponds to the netlogon share needed by down-level clients.

T A B L E 8.2 *Batch Commands*

Batch Command	Purpose	Example
Net use *driveletter:* \\server\share	Assigns a drive letter to a network folder	net use x: \\server\folder
Net use *driveletter:* /d	Removes a shared drive letter	net use x: /d
Net time *servername* /set /y	Synchronizes the time on the local computer with the time on a domain controller	net time \\server /set /y
Net user *username password* /add [/domain]	Creates a user on the local system or on the domain controller (with the /domain option)	net user MBuffett password /add
Net user *username* /delete	Removes a user	net user SWallace /delete
Net group *groupname username* /add [/domain]	Adds a user to a group	net group "Server operators" MBuffett /add
Net group *groupname username* /delete	Removes a user from a group	net group Administrators SWallace /delete
Net share *sharename = path* [/delete]	Adds or removes a share	net share userprofiles = "c:\userdata" net share userprofiles /delete
Net view [*target*]	Displays computers or shared resources (target can be a domain or computer)	net view \\A1computer new view /domain:A1domain

Exercise 20

CREATE LOGON SCRIPT

In the following exercise you will create logon scripts that will make a connection to the netlogon share each time your user logs on to the system.

1. On A1Computer (A2Computer) log on as administrator, and open Active Directory Users and Computers.
2. Display the Group Policy window for the A1Unit OU (A2Unit OU).
3. Create a new group policy called A1Logon Script (A2Logon Script).
4. Edit the Logon Script Group Policy and display the options in the User Configuration/Windows Settings/Scripts window.
5. Double-click the *Logon Script* icon in the right window. You see the Logon Properties dialog box in Figure 8.26.

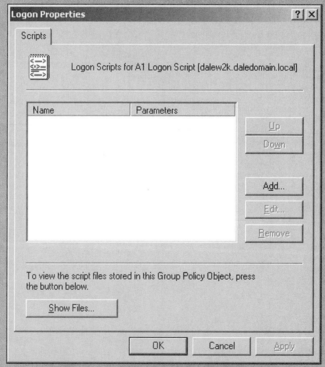

Figure 8.26

6. Click Add to add a new script.
7. In the Script Name text box key **A1logon.bat (A2logon.bat)** and click OK.

8. Click the Show Files button. (It will allow you to create the logon batch file and store it in the group policy.) An empty folder is displayed.
9. Right-click the *Logon* folder, click New, and then click Text Document from the menu.
10. Rename the document to **A1logon.bat** (**A2logon.bat**) and click Yes on the warning about changing the extension.
11. Right-click the A1logon.bat (A2logon.bat) file and select Edit.

You will now create the batch file instructions.

12. If you are creating the A1logon.bat file key:

```
net use q: \\a1computer\netlogon
```

If you are creating the A2logon.bat file key:

```
net use q: \\a2computer\netlogon
```

13. In the Notepad window, click File, click Save, and then click File and click Exit.
14. Click OK to close the Logon Properties dialog box.
15. Close the Group Policy window.
16. Click Close on the A1Unit (A2Unit) Properties window and exit Active Directory Users and Computers.
17. Log off your computer.

This script is physically stored under the *Group Policy* folders for the OU. Users within the OU will automatically run this script when they log on to the system.

Exercise 21

TESTING LOGON SCRIPTS

1. Log on to A1Computer (A2Computer) as MBuffett (SWallace).
2. Open the *My Computer* icon. You should see a disk drive connection (q:) to the Netlogon share on your computer.

CHAPTER summary

➤ Profiles and policies are used to control the user's environment. Profiles consist of a set of folders stored under the user's logon name and containing various types of information, including desktop settings, favorites, and files. These profile folders are automatically created on the local computer when the user logs on to a system. A user profile can be made roaming by creating a shared folder on the server to hold the profile information and modifying the user account so the profile information is saved to the shared folder.

➤ Policies are sets of rights assigned to an Active Directory object and called group policy objects (GPOs). A GPO can be applied to domains and organizational units. Users assigned to these domains and OUs will fall under the policy. If an OU is contained inside a domain or another OU, the policies applied to the parent container are by default applied to the child container. The policies can be blocked from applying by creating a contradictory policy at the child level that overrides the parent policy, or the block inheritance policy can be selected at the child level. At the parent level policies can be identified as having no override property, and they cannot be blocked at the child level. Policies can be used to enforce security (password) and environment (software settings), and to automatically install software.

➤ Network users can be assigned logon or logoff scripts. These scripts can be batch files and are assigned to user accounts through a policy.

CHAPTER terms

Block inheritance	An option used in a child OU that prevents nonmandatory policies from being inherited from the parent.
Contradictory policy	A policy created in a child OU that is the same as an inherited policy but with different application options. A contradictory policy will override an inherited policy.
Folder redirection	Using a group policy to automatically redirect common folders (such as *My Documents*) to a network share.
Group policies	A set of rights and settings assigned to domains or organizational units and applied to users or computers.
Linking policy	Using the same policy in different OUs and domains.
msi	Microsoft Installer package file used with the group policies for software installation.

No override policies	An option for policies set at the parent level that forces children to accept the policy. These policies cannot be overridden at the child level.
ntuser.dat	The file in the user profile that contains registry settings.
Profile	A set of information and preferences assigned to a user and saved when the user logs off the network.
Roaming profile	A profile that is stored on a domain controller and automatically used on each client when a user with the profile logs on.

CONCEPTS review

Multiple Choice

1. Which of the following account policies will apply to users in the entire domain?
   a. Account lockout
   b. Password policies
   c. Kerberos policy
   d. Both a and b
   e. A, b, and c

2. Your *Account lockout threshold* is 4, the *Account lockout duration* is set to 0 and your *Reset account lockout after* is set to 5 hours. You have a user who attempts to log on to the system at 8:00 a.m. and keys his password incorrectly three times before finally getting into the system. The user logs off at 11:30 a.m. and goes to lunch. The user returns at 12:00 p.m. How many more times can the user key an incorrect password before his account is locked out?
   a. He is already locked out.
   b. 4
   c. 1
   d. 0
   e. He will never be locked out.

3. If the following policies are set for the accounts in the domain, which policy allows an exception for an individual user?
   a. Enforce password history of 3 passwords remembered.
   b. Maximum password age of 37 days.
   c. Minimum password age of 1 day.
   d. Minimum password length of 7 characters.
   e. Passwords must meet complexity requirements.

4. What type of file is used for software installation?
   a. msi
   b. exe
   c. com
   d. dat
   e. None of the above

5. Which of the following has the proper syntax for connecting a share called Finance on a server called Savannah in a domain called Georgia?
   a. Net share T: \\Georgia\finance
   b. Net share T: \\Savannah\finance
   c. Net use T: \\Georgia\finance
   d. Net use T: \\Savannah\finance
   e. None of the above

6. You want a software package to be installed on a particular computer. You want to make sure the software appears in the Start menu and is always available to the users of that machine. You would:
   a. Publish the package to the computer.
   b. Publish the package to the user.
   c. Assign the package to the computer.
   d. Assign the package to the user.
   e. Both a and c.

7. In order to make a profile mandatory you must:
   a. Set the attribute on the ntuser.dat file to be read only.
   b. Rename the ntuser.dat file ntuser.man.
   c. Delete the ntuser.dat file.
   d. Rename the ntuser.dat file mandatory.dat.
   e. Set the attribute on the ntuser.dat file to be hidden.

8. As the top-level OU you want to set policies that must be followed by your child OUs. You need to:
   a. Set the policy to be read only.
   b. Make the policy mandatory by renaming it policy.man.
   c. Set the block inheritance option on the policy.
   d. Set the No override option on the policy.
   e. Both a and d.

9. By default, group policies are applied:
   a. Only when a user logs on.
   b. Only when a user logs off.
   c. Every hour.
   d. Every 90 minutes.
   e. Only at logon and logoff time.

10. Group policies can be applied to:
    a. Groups.
    b. Sites.
    c. OUs.
    d. Both b and c.
    e. a, b, and c.

11. A software program has been assigned to a computer. A user deletes a dll needed for the software program to run. To fix this you must:
    a. Manually copy the dll back to the machine.
    b. Create a new group policy to assign the software program again.
    c. Create a new group policy to publish the software program.
    d. Nothing; it will fix itself the next time the computer boots.
    e. Remove the software program using the *Add/Remove Programs* icon, and then add it back in using *Add/Remove Programs* icon a second time.

12. Which of the following is true about profiles for Windows 2000 machines?
    a. A profile is automatically created when a user logs on to a machine.
    b. By default profiles are roaming.
    c. By default profiles are kept on the local hard drive.
    d. By default profiles are mandatory.
    e. Both a and c.

13. An advantage of creating multiple group policies instead of a single group policy with multiple settings is:
    a. Shorter logon times.
    b. Single group policies can be applied to down-level clients.
    c. Single group policies cannot be overwritten.
    d. Ease of troubleshooting.
    e. None of the above.

14. You want a Notepad document to appear on the desktop of all new users but not on the desktop of existing users. You would:
    a. Place the Notepad document in the desktop folder of the *Default User Profile*.
    b. Place the Notepad document in the desktop folder of the *All Users Profile*.
    c. Create an msi file and use group policies to publish the Notepad document.
    d. Manually add the Notepad document to the new users' desktop.
    e. Add the Notepad document using Add/Remove Programs.

15. Which of the following can be done with group policies?
    a. Folder redirection
    b. Software installation
    c. Logon scripts
    d. Forced logoff at a certain time
    e. All of the above

Short Answer

1. If the *Password must meet complexity requirements* policy is set, which of the following passwords are valid for a user with the logon name DWu? Explain your answers.

   DWUdwu
   4EverWIN2K
   I8FOOD
   lone*state
   123456
   AaAaAa1
   Win2K

2. Write a logon script that will do the following:

   - Set the time of the workstation to be the same as a server called Widget1.

   - Disconnect a connection to an R drive.

   - Connect the user's T drive to a share called Finance on a computer called Widget2.

3. You have a top-level OU called Western, a child OU called Colorado, and a grandchild OU called Divide. You want the *Internet Explorer* icon to appear on the desktop of users in Colorado but not appear on the desktop for users in Western or Divide. What would be the best way to configure this requirement using the fewest policies?

4. What is the path to local profiles?

5. Your users store their files in the *My Documents* folder but they do not back them up. How can you provide protection for your users without changing their work habits.

LAB exercises

Each of the following exercises assumes you have finished the steps in the chapter and any previous exercises. Begin each exercise logged on as the administrator unless you are told differently.

Exercise 1 – Removing a Group Policy

1. On A1Computer open the Active Directory Users and Computers snap-in in your MMC.
2. Open the Group Policy for your domain and delete the Hide Internet Explorer and My Network Places policy.
3. Click *Remove the Link* and delete the group policy object permanently.
4. Confirm that you want to permanently delete the GPO and close your Group Policy dialog box.
5. Log on to A1Computer As MBuffet. Do you see both the *Internet Explorer* icon and *My Network Places*? Why or Why not?
6. Repeat step 5 for both the administrator and SWallace. What are the results?

Exercise 2 – Creating a Minimum Password Length Policy

1. Open Active Directory Users and Computers.
2. Move through the Default Domain Policies/Computer Configuration/Windows Settings/Security Settings/Account Policies directories.
3. Double-click *Password Policies*.
4. Double-click *Minimum password length*.
5. Check the *Define this Policy Setting*.
6. Set *Password must be at least* to be 4 characters.
7. Click OK.
8. Close the MMC and save the settings.

Exercise 3 – Creating a User and Testing the Minimum Password Length Policy

1. Open the MMC you created in Exercise 1.
2. Under the Users container in the Active Directory Users and Computers snap-in create an account with the following attributes:

User Name:	**JCristan**
First Name:	**Janet**
Middle Initial:	**M**
Last Name:	**Cristan**
Password:	**one**

   Does not need to change the password at first logon

3. Write down the error message you receive. Write down the minimum number of characters a password must contain.
4. Click OK to accept the error message.
5. Click Back to return to the previous screen.
6. Fix the problem by entering the password **code1** and clicking *Finish the user account*.

Exercise 4 – Setting and Testing the Enforce Password History Policy

1. Open Active Directory Users and Computers.
2. Set a password history policy to 3.
3. Close the MMC and save the settings.
4. Press Ctrl+Alt+Del and log off.
5. Confirm you want to log off by clicking Yes.
6. Press Ctrl+Alt+Del and log back on as JCristan with the password of **code1**.
7. Press Ctrl+Alt+Del to obtain a logon screen.
8. Click *Change Password* and change the password to **code2**.
9. Click OK on the window verifying that the password has been changed.
10. Click *Change Password* and change the password to **code1**. Write down the error message you receive. Click OK to accept the error message.
11. Continue to change the password by incrementing the number at the end until you can change back to the initial password of code1. Write down the last password you used before being able to change back to the initial password.

Exercise 5 – Adding to the All Users Profile

1. Log on as administrator and open the *My Computer* icon.
2. Move through the Documents and Settings directory and open the *All Users* folder.
3. Double-click to open the *Desktop* folder.
4. Right-click inside the *Desktop* folder, click New and click Text Document.
5. Name the text document Profile Test.
6. Close the open windows and log off the system.
7. Log back on as JCristan. Do you see the text document on the desktop?
8. Log on as SWallace. Do you see the text document on the desktop? Will you see it if you log on as administrator?

Exercise 6 – Making a Profile Mandatory

(Remember that A1User's roaming profile is stored in the roamingprofiles share on the A1Computer and A2User's roaming profile is stored in the roamingprofiles share on the A2Computer. You will change the roaming profile that is located on your own machine and log on as the user whose profile is located on your machine.)

1. Log on to A1Computer (A2Computer) as administrator and open the *My Computer* icon.
2. Double-click the *roamingprofiles* directory to open it.
3. Double-click the *A1User (A2User)* directory to open it.
4. To view the hidden files click <u>T</u>ools from the menu bar and click Folder Options.
5. Click the View tab and click *Show hidden files and folders*.
6. Click to remove the check mark from *Hide file extensions for known file types* and then click OK.
7. Right-click *ntuser.dat* (do not pick the ntuser.dat.log file) and click Rename.
8. Rename the ntuser.dat file to ntuser.man.
9. Close the open windows and log off the machine.
10. Log back on to the machine as A1User (A2User).
11. Right-click on the desktop and click Properties.
12. Click the Background tab, pick the coffee bean background, and click OK.
13. Note the look of the desktop and log off the system.
14. Log back on the system as A2User (A1User). Were the changes saved?

PROBLEM SOLVING exercises

Exercise 1

Answer the following questions based on Figure 8.27 and the scenario given.

FIGURE 8.27

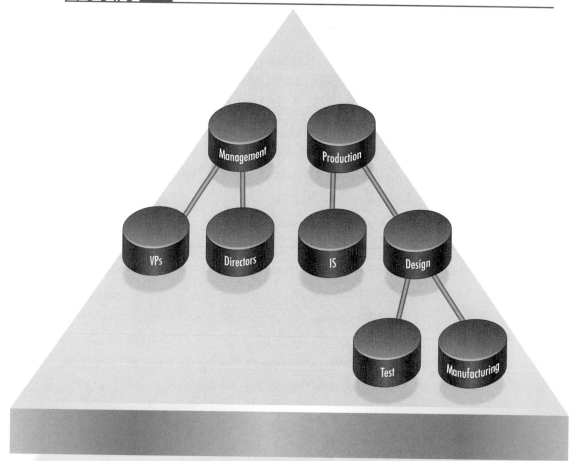

You have a single domain with two top-level OUs. One called Management and one called Production. Underneath the Management OU you have two sublevel OUs called VPs and Directors. Under the Production OU you have two sublevel OUs called IS and Design. Under the Design OU you have two sublevel OUs called Test and Manufacturing.

At the domain level is a policy that sets the maximum password age to be 36 days and sets the Hide the Internet Explorer icon on the desktop set as enabled.

At the Management level OU is a policy that sets Hide the Internet Explorer icon on the desktop as disabled.

At the VP level OU is a policy that sets the maximum password age to be 45 days and blocks inheritance.

At the Production level OU is a policy that sets the *Disable changing wallpaper* to be enabled.

At the Design level OU is a policy that sets the Disable Add/Remove Programs to enabled, blocks inheritance, and sets the No override option.

At the Test level OU is a policy set that blocks inheritance.

a. How long can a VP keep a password before it expires?
b. Will Directors see IE on their desktop?
c. Will users in the Test OU be able to add and remove programs?
d. Will users in the Manufacturing OU have IE on their desktops?
e. Will users in the IS OU have IE on their desktops?
f. Will users in the Manufacturing OU be able to add and remove programs?
g. Will users in the Manufacturing OU be able to change their wallpaper?

Exercise 2

Answer the following questions based on Figure 8.28 and the scenario given.

The following policies have been put in place:

HQ has one policy that has the following settings:
    Hide IE on desktop enabled
    Remove run command enabled

Management has one policy that has the following settings:
    Disable changing wallpaper enabled
    Remove run command disabled
    No override

VP has one policy that has the following settings:
    Block inheritance

Directors has one policy that has the following settings:
    Disable changing wallpaper disabled

HR has one policy that has the following settings:
    Block inheritance

FIGURE 8.28

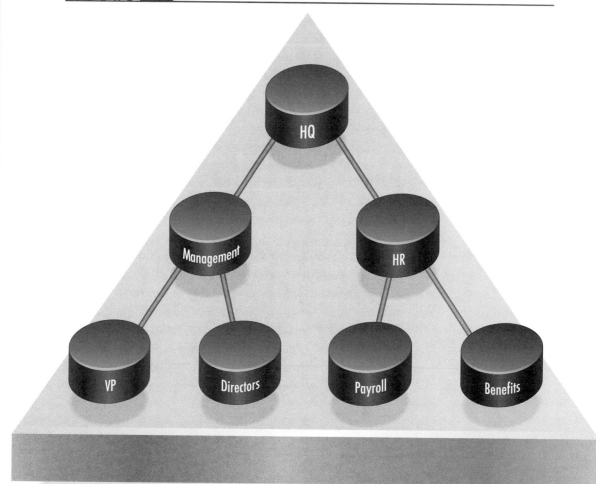

a. Which OUs will see IE on their desktop?
b. Which OUs will have the run command available to them?
c. Which OUs will be able to change their wallpaper?

SHARING, PERMISSIONS, AND THE DISTRIBUTED FILE SYSTEM 9

Performance Objectives

After completing this chapter you will be able to:

- Create a share
- Link to a share
- Use the command line to access a share
- Set permissions on a share
- View permissions on a share
- Discuss the difference between share permissions and file/folder permissions
- Set file/folder permissions
- View file/folder level permissions
- Prevent permission inheritance
- Create a distributed file system (Dfs) share root
- Share multiple folders under a Dfs share
- Create a Dfs replication share

Introduction

One of the main reasons that personal computer networks were developed was the high cost of peripheral devices. In the past, most companies could not afford to purchase a laser printer for every employee's computer. When employees needed a laser printout they often had to stand in line for their turn at the computer that did have an attached laser printer. This necessity was not only inconvenient, but also a waste of the employee's time. With a network, devices such as laser printers could be attached to the network and shared among employees, without the employees having to leave their desk to print.

This chapter teaches you how to define and manage shared resources on a network. It includes setting permissions on the resources to control which users have access and how the resources can be used. You also learn how to use the distributed file system (Dfs), which is new to Windows 2000.

Shared Network Resources

The idea of creating a shared resource that can be used throughout the network is a well-established concept. Many resources can be shared, such as folders, drives, and ports. In order to share a file you must put the file in a folder and share the entire folder. A file cannot be shared on its own. A shared resource is also called a **share**.

By default, some of the resources on a Windows 2000 server are automatically shared. They include Netlogon, SYSVOL, Admin$, IPC$, and a share for the root of each drive, such as C$. These shares are mostly administrative and are used by the administrator or the system itself.

You can view all the shares on a domain controller from a command prompt with the command:

net share

This command will display both visible and hidden shares.

As the network administrator you will need to decide which resources are required by your users and create shares for those resources. A simple way to share a folder is to locate that folder in either My Computer or Windows Explorer, right-click the folder icon, and click the sharing option. You will see a window like Figure 9.1. It includes the following options.

FIGURE *Folder Sharing Options*

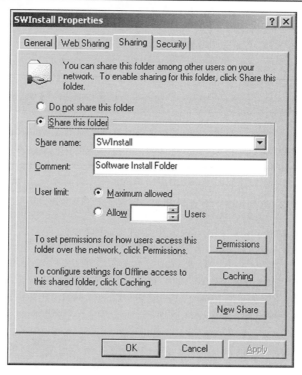

- Share name is the name given to the share. It can be different from the resource name, but must follow specific rules.

- Comment lists information about the share.

- User limit indicates the number of users that can access the share at the same time.

- Permissions set the groups and users allowed to access the share and their level of access.

- Caching is used to access the share offline.

- New Share creates additional shares on the same resource.

By clicking *Share this folder*, you begin the process of sharing a resource. Windows 2000 will select a default share name that is the same as the name of the resource. In most cases it is best to accept the default so you can easily track what resource is tied to what share name. If you choose to change the share name you must follow these rules:

- The length of a share name depends on what type of client is being used to access the share. DOS and Windows 3.1 clients will only be able to connect to a share if the share name is 8 characters or less. Share names for Windows 95/98 clients can be up to 15 characters, and Windows NT and Windows 2000 clients can access share names that are as long as 255 characters.

- Share names can contain alpha or numeric characters.

- Share names can contain spaces.

- Share names cannot contain any of the following special characters:

  | / ? \ * +] = [: ; " < >

- Share names can be upper or lowercase. They are not case-sensitive, but they are case compliant, which means that the case of the share name will be kept. If you key the share name in as Policies, it will maintain the *P* as a capital letter. If you try to connect to the share from a command line and key **policies** instead of **Policies**, you will still be connected, but the share name will always appear in My Network Places or My Computer as Policies.

- If a share name is followed by a $, such as policies$, the share is called a hidden share. It will be hidden from the browser, which is a system that maintains a list of all shared resources and displays the list when you press the Browse button. Even though it is hidden, the shared resource is still available and can be connected to if you know its location and share name. Administrators often use hidden shares. Because the hidden share does not appear in the browsing system, users are less likely to know the share exists and therefore are less likely to try to connect to the share.

One exception to the rules for share names: in order for a Windows 95 machine to see a printer share, the share name must be 12 characters or less.

Even though spaces can be included in a share name, they are not recommended because share names with spaces need to be enclosed in quotation marks in some situations, such as when you are trying to attach to the share from a command line. Also, long share names can be burdensome to key. Try to create share names descriptive enough to be meaningful without making them too lengthy. The easiest way is to use letters and numbers, not special symbols. Following these guidelines helps to keep things simple.

Creating Comments

After naming the share, the next field on the Sharing tab is the *Comment* field. You should key something in this field that accurately describes the share. Because you want to limit the length of the share name, this field is a good place to be more descriptive.

Setting the User Limit

By default, Windows 2000 does not define a limit to the number of people who can connect to a share concurrently. The Underline limit box appears on the Sharing tab with the Maximum allowed radio button selected. In many cases this default is perfectly acceptable. You probably don't care how many people are using a public data share at any one point in time. However, situations may arise where you would want to control the number of users who can connect to a share at the same time. For example you may share an application for which you have a limited number of licenses. You would not want to allow an unlimited number of people to have access to that application at the same time.

The second radio button under the User limit box on the Sharing tab allows you to set a limit. If you set the limit to 3, only three users can connect to the share at one time. The fourth person who tries to connect will see an error message. When one of the three users already connected to the share disconnects, the fourth user will be able to access the share.

> The actual text of the error message will vary depending on the type of workstation. Windows NT and 2000 machines will be the most understandable. They will display the message "No more connections can be made to the remote computer at this time because there are already as many connections as the computer can accept." Windows 95 machines will display, "This request is not accepted by the network." Unfortunately error messages are often vague and not terribly useful in determining the real problem.

An important point to remember about limiting the number of share users: the limit set is on the number of *connections* to the share. Users accessing other data inside the share, but not using the application, still account for one connection. For this reason, you may want to put each application inside its own share with no other data. In this manner, users will only attach to the share and take up a connection if they want to use the specific application.

Exercise 1

CREATING A SHARE

In this exercise you create a share, which should be done on both domain controllers. The instructions for the first domain controller are outside the parentheses, and the instructions for the second domain controller are inside the parentheses.

1. Double-click to open the *My Computer* icon.
2. Double-click to open the drive that contains your system files.
3. Click File from the menu bar and click New and then Folder from the drop-down menu.
4. Name the new folder *Wordprocessing (Spreadsheets)*.
5. Right-click the folder and click Sharing from the drop-down menu. You see the Properties dialog box in Figure 9.2.

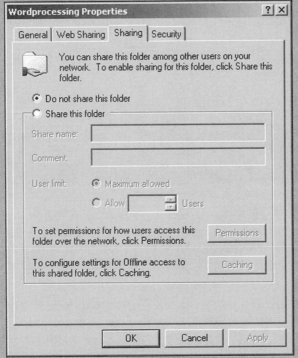

Figure 9.2

6. Click *Share this folder* and accept the default share name.
7. In the Comment box key **Wordprocessing Files** (**Spreadsheet Files**).
8. Set the User limit to 1 user.
9. Click OK again to close the Wordprocessing (Spreadsheets) properties dialog box.

Once a folder is shared, a small hand will appear under the folder to indicate that it is shared (Figure 9.3).

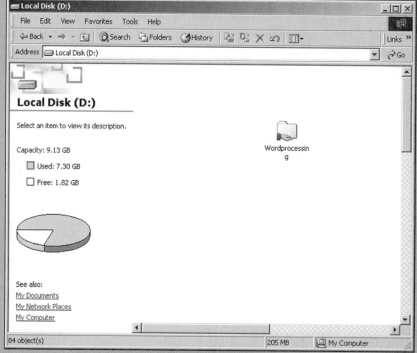

Figure 9.3

The hand will only be visible if you are logged on as the administrator.

Defining Share-Level Permissions

One of the buttons on the Sharing tab of the properties window was the Permissions button. The Permissions button is used to set which users have access to the share and what type of access they have. The three levels of share permissions are as follows:

- **Read:** A user or group given read access to a share will be able to see objects inside a share. Folders or documents inside a share can be opened, and applications in the share can be executed.

- **Change:** A user or group given change access can run programs; add, delete, change, or rename objects; and see objects, such as folders or documents, inside a share.

- **Full Control:** A user or group given full control can (a) do everything included in the change permission, (b) take ownership of objects in the share, and (c) give permissions to other users for objects contained in the share.

An Allow setting for any one of these options allows the user or group to perform the functions stated. A Deny setting will refuse to allow the user or group to perform the functions.

> The No Access share permission from Windows NT days no longer exists. You can now use the Deny option to deny access to a particular function—read, change, or full control—instead of having to deny access to the entire resource.

Shares can be created on both FAT and NTFS partitions. Recall from Chapter 4 that NTFS partitions have additional security options not found on FAT partitions. NTFS partitions track the ownership of objects, but FAT partitions do not. Ownership is the key difference between full control and change access. Because FAT partitions do not track ownership, change and full control access are the same on a FAT partition. Full control of a share on a FAT partition does not give the user any additional privileges over the share than if they had change access. If the share is created on an NTFS partition, someone with full control not only has the ability to manipulate objects in the share but also can give other users permission to do the same thing.

Setting Share Permissions

When a share is created, the default permissions on that share give the Everyone group full control of the share. As explained in Chapter 7, the group Everyone includes all users, guests, and administrators on the system. If you do not want Everyone to have full control of the share, you can change the **share-level permissions**. Remember that you cannot share individual files, only folders. Shares are created at the folder level. When you put permissions on a share, those permissions also apply to everything inside the share. If a user has read access to a share called Policies, that user would also have read access to files inside the share. You could not give a user read access to the share and change access to the files inside the share.

Another important fact about share-level permissions is they only apply when a user is connected to the share. They *do not apply* if a user attempts to access the resources on the local machine without being connected to the share. For example, assume the *Policies* folder resides on the D drive of machine A1Computer. If a user sits down at the console of A1Computer and opens the *Policies* folder directly by using My Computer, the share-level permissions would not apply.

Working with Interactions between User Permissions, Group Permissions, and Multiple Group Permissions

Because you can give both users and groups different permissions to the same share, it is important to understand what happens when individual permissions and group permissions are combined. If a user is a member of a group that has permissions to a share and the user also has individual permissions to the share, the user's effective permissions are the combination of the two. For example, if a user has read access to a share and a group to which that user belongs has change access, the user's effective permission would be change plus read. The same holds true for multiple groups. If the previous user also belonged to another group that had full control of a share, the user's effective permissions would be read + change + full control. Technically, full control has read and change rights already included so it is safe to say the user would end up with full control. This concept is illustrated in Figure 9.4.

FIGURE 9.4 *Interaction of Permissions among Users and Groups*

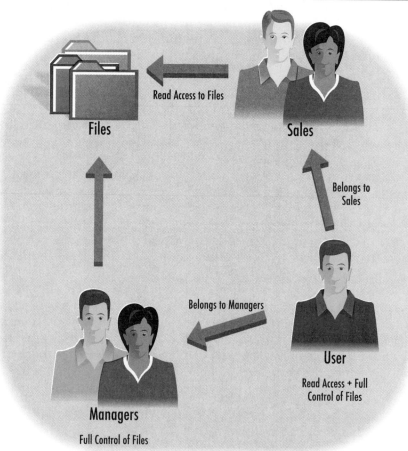

Read Access to Files

Files

Sales

Belongs to Sales

Belongs to Managers

User

Read Access + Full Control of Files

Managers

Full Control of Files

The option to deny access is a somewhat special case. If a user is allowed read access to a share but a group to which that user belongs has change access denied, the user would not be able to read the share. Table 9.1, in which Dorothy belongs to the Services group, demonstrates the concept of effective permissions.

T A B L E 9.1 *Example of Interactions among Access Permissions*

Dorothy's Permission	Services Group's Permissions	Effective Permission for Dorothy
Read	Change	Change
Change	Read	Change
Change	Change Denied	Changed Denied
Change Denied	Change	Changed Denied

When a share is newly created the default permissions give the group Everyone full control. If you do not want Everyone to have full control, it may be tempting to first deny full control access to the Everyone group. Do not use this approach. The Everyone group includes all users, guests, and administrators. If you deny full control to Everyone, you also deny full control to all included groups, along with the Administrator group. This command effectively denies the administrator's access to that share. Your best approach to locking down permissions is to first add all users and groups that you want to have access, and then simply remove the Everyone group from the list. In the following exercise you change the permission of the share created in the previous exercise.

Exercise 2

ADDING PERMISSIONS TO A SHARE

1. With the *My Computer* icon still open, right-click the *Wordprocessing (Spreadsheets)* share and click Sharing from the shortcut menu.
2. Click the Permissions button. You see the Permissions dialog box in Figure 9.5.

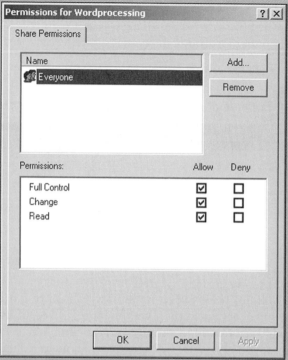

Figure 9.5

The upper portion of the dialog box lists the groups and users, and the lower part displays the permissions for the selected group or user.

3. In the Permissions for WordProcessing (Spreadsheets) dialog box click the Add button. You see a list of users and groups (Figure 9.6).

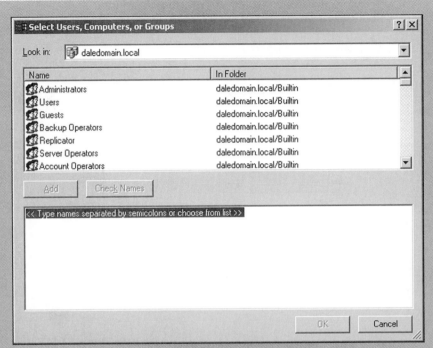

Figure 9.6

4. Scroll down through the names in the name box, click *Domain Admins*, and click the **A**dd button to add this group to the lower window.

5. Click the OK button to return to the Permissions for Wordprocessing (Spreadsheets) dialog box.

The Domain Admins group is added in the Permissions dialog box (Figure 9.7).

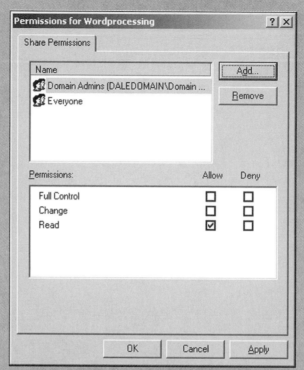

Figure 9.7

Notice that by default the Domain Admins group has only read access.

6. Click *Domain Admins*, and then click the Allow check box for Full Control. Now, all three check boxes should be checked. You can now remove permissions from the Everyone group.
7. Click *Everyone* in the upper window.
8. Unselect the Full Control and Change check boxes. Only Read should now be checked, as it is in Figure 9.8.

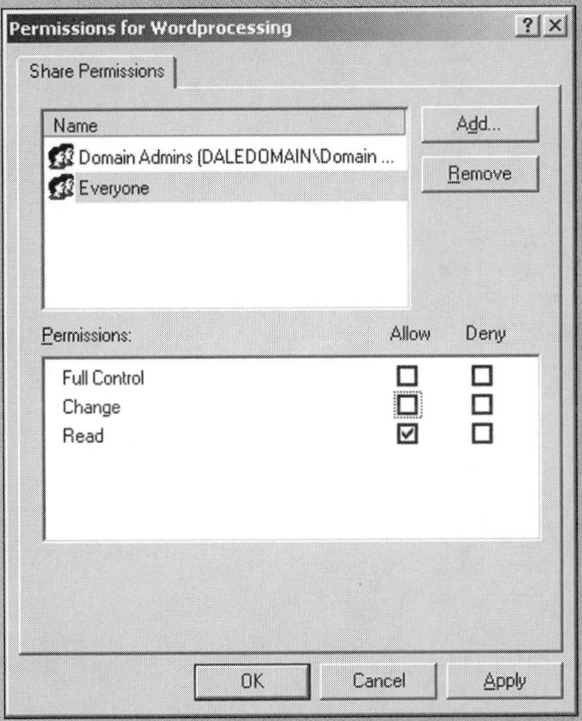

Figure 9.8

9. Click OK to close the Permissions dialog box.
10. Click OK again to close the WordProcessing (Spreadsheets) Properties dialog box.

Using Shares

Now that the share has been created and permissions applied, users will want to access the share. Shared resources, except hidden shares, will be picked up by the browsing system and displayed under the *My Network Places* icon. Users can attach to or map shared resources by using My Network Places, My Computer, Windows Explorer, or by keying commands at a command prompt. In the following exercise you connect to a share using My Computer.

Exercise 3

CONNECTING TO A SHARE

1. From the desktop, right-click the *My Computer* icon.
2. Click the Map Network Drive option. You see the Map Network Drive dialog box in Figure 9.9.

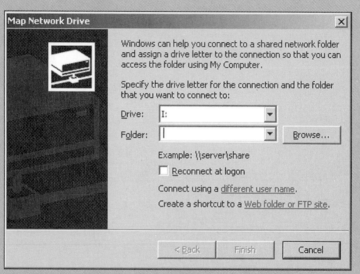

Figure 9.9

This dialog box allows you to map a shared resource to a logical drive letter. A drive letter is displayed in the Drive text box. This logical drive letter will be the first drive letter that you are not currently using on your machine. For example, it will never be C because you have a C drive local to your machine.

3. Accept the default drive letter and click the Browse button next to the Folder text box. Rather than key the name of a share, you will select it from a dialog box. You may have to wait a few minutes for the Browse dialog box to be displayed (Figure 9.10).

Figure 9.10

4. If necessary, click the plus sign next to *Entire Network* to expand it and click the plus sign next to the *Microsoft Windows Network* icon to expand it.
5. Click the plus sign next to your domain name to expand it.
6. You should now see the name of your partner's computer. Click the plus sign next to your partner's computer to show the shares (Figure 9.11).

Figure 9.11

7. Click the share on your partner's computer (*Spreadsheets* if you are using the A1Computer and *Wordprocessing* if you are using the A2Computer). Click OK to close the Browse dialog box. The shared folder name should appear in the Folder text box (Figure 9.12).

Figure 9.12

8. If necessary, take the check mark out of the *Reconnect at logon* box to prevent the system from automatically reconnecting to this share each time you log on.
9. Click Finish. A window opens that is a connection to the share on your partner's machine. Close this share window.

Once you are finished using a share you can disconnect it and free the logical drive letter to be used again.

Exercise 4

DISCONNECTING A SHARE

1. Double-click to open the *My Computer* icon. You will see a connection to the share (a disk drive icon with a network connection and the name of the share).
2. Right-click the connection to the share and click Disconnect from the shortcut menu.

Using the Command Line

The preceding steps show how to browse for a shared resource in case you do not remember the location and name of the share. If you know both the share name and server where the share is located, you do not need to use the browse button. In the Folder text box simply key the universal naming convention (also called the uniform naming convention) or UNC of the shared resource. A UNC is written in the following format, \\servername\sharename. The UNC for the Wordprocessing share on A1Computer would be \\a1computer\wordprocessing. Keying the UNC saves the time of browsing through domains and servers to find a share.

Another reason for using the UNC is that the results you see from the browsing system are not always timely. Computers that are up may not appear in the browser immediately and computers that have been shut down may still appear in the browser. As the administrator you need to know how to connect to a share without relying on the browser system. You should be able to connect to a share from the command prompt or map a share by keying the UNC instead of locating it through the browser. This method will also allow you to connect to hidden shares. In the next exercise you will connect to the share using the command prompt and test the permissions you set on the share.

Exercise 5

CONNECTING TO A SHARE USING THE COMMAND PROMPT AND TESTING PERMISSIONS

1. Log on as the administrator.
2. Click Start, click Run, key **CMD** in the Open box and click OK. A command window is displayed.
3. In the command window, key

        net use t: \\a2computer\spreadsheets

    on A1Computer, and key

        (net use t: \\a1computer\wordprocessing)

    on the A2Computer.

This command maps the disk drive letter *t* to the share on the other computer.

4. In the command window change to the t drive by keying **t:** and pressing Enter. You will next test the share permissions.
5. From the Command prompt key the command **copy X:\winnt\win.ini** and press Enter (where *X* is the letter of the drive containing your system files).
6. Key **DIR** from the command prompt to display a directory listing of drive t.
7. Change to the C drive by keying **c:** and pressing Enter.

8. Disconnect the share by keying **net use t: /d.**
9. Exit from the Command window and log off from your computer.
10. Log back on to your computer as MBuffett (SWallace).
11. Repeat steps 2 through 8, but on step 5 substitute the file named system.ini located in the *winnt* folder.
12. Log off as the user and log back on to your computer as administrator.

Introduction to File and Folder Permissions

Shares and share-level permissions have been a part of Microsoft PC networks since their origin. As networks have grown, so has need to provide security. Share-level security is somewhat primitive, and with today's more complicated networks, more security is needed. With the introduction of Windows NT and the NTFS file system, a new type of security was introduced called file and folder permissions. File and folder permissions are much more powerful than share-level permissions, and they differ from share-level permissions in several ways:

- File and folder permissions can be applied directly to both folders and files.
- File and folder permissions can be more specific.
- File and folder permissions can only be used on an NTFS partition.
- File and folder permissions protect files and folders from someone logging on to the console of the machine where they are kept.

Remember that share-level permissions can only be applied to a share, they cannot be applied directly to a file or a folder.

Defining File and Folder Permissions

The only option you have with share-level permissions is the ability to grant or deny read, change, or full control access to a share. You could not give a user the right to delete files but not read them. **File/folder permissions** allow you to assign permissions individually. For example, you could give a user the right to delete a file without being able to read the file. You can set 13 different permissions:

- *Traverse Folder/Execute File:* The ability to open subfolders within a folder and execute files
- *List Folder/Read Data:* The ability to view files and subfolders within a folder and view the contents of a file
- *Read Attributes:* The ability to read attributes such as hidden or system on a file

- *Read Extended Attributes:* Allows you to view additional attributes that some programs place on a file such as who authored the file
- *Create Files/Write Data:* The ability to change data in a preexisting file or create a new file in a folder
- *Create Folders/Append Data:* Ability to add data to a preexisting file (not change the data already in the file) and create new subfolders in a folder
- *Write Attributes:* Ability to add or change attributes such a hidden or read only
- *Write Extended Attributes:* Ability to add or change extended attributes
- *Delete Subfolders and Files:* Ability to delete subfolders and files within a folder (not the ability to delete the folder itself)
- *Delete:* Ability to delete an object (Remember, you cannot delete a folder until it is empty, so you must have the ability to delete subfolders and files within the folder first.)
- *Read Permissions:* Ability to view the NTFS permissions associated with a file or folder
- *Change Permissions:* Ability to change the NTFS permissions associated with a file or folder
- *Take Ownership:* Ability to become the owner of the object, thereby giving yourself the ability to set permissions on the object

For the convenience of the administrator, these permissions can be, but do not have to be, assigned individually. They are grouped into bundles of permissions that will meet most needs. These bundles are listed here along with the individual permissions that each bundle includes.

- *Full Control:* Includes all 13 individual permissions
- *Modify:* Includes all individual permissions except Delete Subfolders and Files, Change Permissions, and Take Ownership
- *Read & Execute:* Includes Traverse Folder/Execute File, List Folder/Read Data, Read Attributes, Read Extended Attributes, and Read Permissions
- *Read:* Includes List Folder/Read Data, Read Attributes, Read Extended Attributes, and Read Permissions
- *Write:* Includes Create Files/Write Data, Create Folders/Append Data, Write Attributes, Write Extended Attributes, and Read Permissions

In the following exercise you create a new file and folder and view the default file and folder permissions.

Exercise 6

CREATING A FOLDER AND FILE

1. Log on to A1Computer (A2Computer) as the administrator.
2. Double-click to open the *My Computer* icon.
3. Double-click to open the drive that contains your system files.

4. Click File from the menu and click New and Folder from the drop-down menus.
5. Name the new folder *Marketing (Publications)*.
6. Double-click to open your newly created folder.
7. In the folder window, click File from the menu bar and click New and then Text Document from the drop-down menu.
8. Name your new text document ReadOnly.txt.
9. Close the *Marketing (Publications)* folder.

Exercise 7

VIEWING THE DEFAULT FILE AND FOLDER PERMISSIONS

1. Log on to A1Computer (A2Computer) as the administrator.
2. Double-click to open the *My Computer* icon.
3. Double-click to open the drive that contains your system files.
4. Right-click *Marketing (Publications)* and click Properties from the drop-down menu.
5. Click the Security tab. You see the Security dialog box (Figure 9.13).

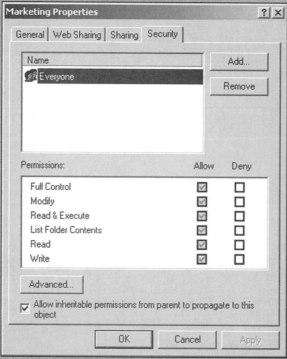

Figure 9.13

This dialog box lists the users and groups and the bundles of file and folder permissions assigned. Each bundle name consists of a set of individual permissions. Notice that the check boxes are checked but are gray to indicate that the permission is inherited from a parent. (Inheritance of permissions will be explained later in the chapter.)

6. Click the Advanced button to display the Access Control Settings dialog box in Figure 9.14.

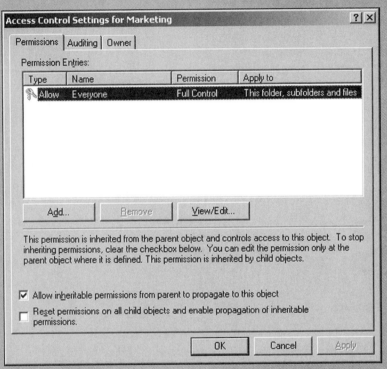

Figure 9.14

7. Highlight the Everyone group and click the View/Edit button. You see the Permission Entry dialog box in Figure 9.15.

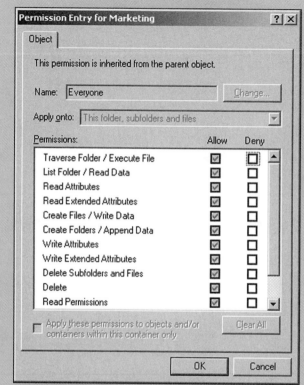

Figure 9.15

What permissions are checked? Can you uncheck a permission? Notice that the check boxes are grayed out.

8. Click OK to close the Permissions Entry for Marketing (Publications) dialog box.
9. Exit the Permissions dialog box.

A feature that was badly needed in Windows NT was inheritability of permissions. This concept has been included with Windows 2000. By default, a folder or file will inherit the permissions of its parent. However, you can also choose to set explicit permissions for an object and override the inherited permissions. The Access Control Settings window displayed in Figure 9.14 contains two check boxes at the bottom of the window. The first box is labeled *Allow inheritable permissions from parent to propagate to this object.* The reason the check boxes are grayed out and you could not uncheck permissions in step 7 of the previous exercise is because the permissions for the Everyone group are inherited from the parent drive and cannot be changed. If you want to set explicit permissions for a group that are different from the inherited permissions, you must prevent inheritance from taking place. If you de-select the Allows inheritable permissions from the parent to propagate to the object check box, you will be presented with the option to copy the permissions from the parent or remove them. If you choose to copy the permissions the Everyone group will still have permissions to the object but you will be able to change those permissions. If you choose to remove the permissions, the Everyone group will no longer appear in the permissions list. In the following exercise you will remove inheritability and set explicit permissions on a folder.

When a file is copied, the new copy of the file will inherit the permissions of its container. If a file is moved, it will maintain its own permissions.

A command line utility called Cacls.exe can be used to set file/folder-level permissions. In order to view the parameters available with this command, key **cacls /?** at a command line prompt.

Exercise 8

SETTING PERMISSIONS ON A FOLDER

1. Log on to A1Computer (A2Computer) as the administrator.
2. Double-click to open the *My Computer* icon.
3. Double-click to open the drive that contains your system files.
4. Double-click the *Marketing (Publications)* folder, and click *readonly.txt*.
5. Press Ctrl-C and Ctrl-V to copy the file, then rename the file deleteonly.txt.
6. Right-click the new file deleteonly.txt and click Properties from the drop-down menu.
7. Click the Security tab.
8. Click Add, scroll down and click *Domain Admins*, and click Add.
9. Scroll down and click *MBuffett (SWallace)*, and then click Add. Both users should be added to the window (Figure 9.16).

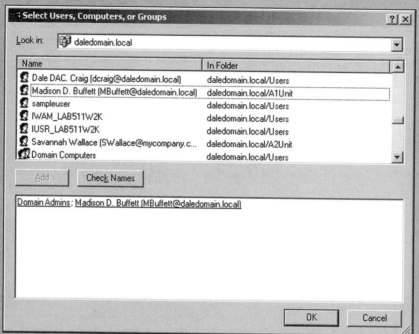

Figure 9.16

10. Click OK to leave the Select Users, Computers, or Groups dialog box.
11. In the deleteonly.txt Properties dialog box click *Domain Admins* and then click to put a check mark at *Allow Full Control*. Notice what other boxes are checked automatically.
12. In the deleteonly.txt Properties dialog box click *MBuffett (SWallace)* and then click the Advanced button.
13. In the Access Control Settings for deleteonly.txt dialog box click *MBuffett (SWallace)* and then click the View/Edit button.
14. Remove all the existing check marks from the Allow boxes by clicking the Clear All button.
15. Click to put a check mark in the *Allow* box for Delete (Figure 9.17).

Figure 9.17

16. Click OK to leave the Permission Entry for deleteonly.txt dialog box.
17. Click OK to leave the Access Control Settings for deleteonly.txt dialog box.
18. Click to remove the check mark from *Allow inheritable permissions from parent to propagate to this object*. You see a dialog box asking you how to handle the inheritable permissions (Figure 9.18).

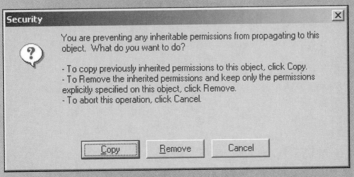

Figure 9.18

19. At the security warning, click <u>R</u>emove to prevent parental permissions from being copied to this folder. Note what group is removed from the permission box.
20. Click OK to close the deleteonly.txt Properties dialog box.

Interaction between Share and File/Folder Permissions

Two different types of permissions have been discussed so far in this chapter; share-level permissions and file/folder permissions. Each type of permission has been discussed individually but they can also be used together. In the case where both types of permissions are employed, the user will effectively have the least of the two types of permissions. For example if a user has full control as a file/folder permission to a folder but has read as a share-level permission, that user will only have read access when connecting to the folder using the share. It also works the opposite way. If a user has read as a file/folder permission and full control as a share-level permission, the user's effective permission will still be read. Keep in mind that share-level permissions are only effective when the user connects to an object using the share. If the user were to sit down at the console of the computer containing a folder and access that folder directly through the file system, the share permissions for that folder would not be in effect. The following exercise illustrates the interaction between these two types of permissions. To refresh your memory on how the share permissions work, take a look at the results you got in the exercise of connecting to a share using the command prompt and testing permissions.

Exercise 9

SETTING FILE/FOLDER PERMISSIONS ON A LOCAL COMPUTER

1. Log back on to your computer as the administrator.
2. Right-click the shared folder created in the Create Share exercise (either *Wordprocessing* or *Spreadsheet*).
3. Click Properties from the drop-down menu. You see the Properties dialog box.
4. Click the Security tab.
5. Click the A<u>d</u>d button.
6. Scroll down and click *Domain Admins* and then click the A<u>d</u>d button.
7. Click *MBuffet (SWallace)* and click the A<u>d</u>d button.
8. Click OK to close the Select Users, Computers, or Groups dialog box.
9. In the Properties dialog box, click the *Domain Admins* group and click *Allow Full Control*.
10. Click *MBuffett (SWallace)* and click *Allow Full Control*.

11. Click to remove the check mark from the *Allow inheritable permissions from parent* check box. You will see a warning message.
12. Click the <u>R</u>emove button in the warning message window.
13. Click OK to close the Properties dialog box.

Exercise 10

TESTING THE COMBINATION OF SHARE AND FILE/FOLDER PERMISSIONS

1. Log on to your computer as MBuffett (SWallace).
2. Click Start, then Run, and then key **CMD** in the Open box and click OK.
3. Key

       net use t: \\a2computer\spreadsheets
       (net use t: \\a1computer\wordprocessing)

4. Change to the t drive by keying **t:** and pressing Enter.
5. From the <u>C</u>ommand prompt key the command **copy l:\winnt\system.ini** and press Enter (where *l* is the system drive).
6. Key **DIR** from the command prompt to display a directory listing of drive t.
7. Even though you now have full control to the folder, were you able to copy the file? Why or why not?

Exercise 11

TESTING FILE/FOLDER PERMISSIONS ON A LOCAL COMPUTER

1. If necessary, log on as MBuffett (SWallace).
2. Open My Computer, open your system drive, and open the *Winnt* folder.
3. Click *Show Files Link* to display the files in this folder.
4. Scroll down to find the file named system. (By default, file name extensions are not displayed. This file is actually named system.ini.)
5. Right-click this file and click Copy.
6. Click the *Up Folder* icon to show the root files on your drive.
7. Open the *WordProcessing (Spreadsheet)* folder.
8. Right-click an empty area of the window and click Paste. Were you able to paste the file into this folder? Why could you perform this task here when it could not be done when you were connected to the share?

You have now seen both types of permissions that can be used in Windows 2000: share-level permissions, which are older and less capable, and file/folder permissions. Because the file/folder permissions can do all of the functions that share permissions can do and more, it is easiest to leave the share-level permissions at their default values and use the file/folder permissions to secure an object. In any case it is important to document all permission settings.

Distributed File System

The **distributed file system (Dfs)** is a new feature in Windows 2000. This section discusses the domain-based Dfs, which makes use of Active Directory. Dfs can also be done in a stand-alone environment but does not have as many capabilities as the domain-based model. Domain Dfs can be used in two ways: it can provide users with a single point of access to resources that are actually stored in multiple places on the network, and it replaces the directory replication service found in Windows NT by allowing you to create a file on one server and have that file automatically copied to other servers.

Whichever way you use Dfs, you must first create a root. The root is the shared folder to which the users will attach in order to gain access to the files. You can only have one Dfs root per server. When using Dfs as a single point of reference for resources located in multiple places, you would create links to the root after creating the Dfs root. For example, your company has applications spread out among three different servers. You do not want your users to have to remember that server2 has the spreadsheet application and server3 has the database. Using Dfs you can create a root share called *applications* on server1 and then create links to the different servers that contain the spreadsheet and database. When the user connects to the root share, *applications*, it would appear to that user that the spreadsheet and database applications are subfolders of the applications folder, when in reality they are located on server2 and server3. In the following exercise you create a Dfs root and create links to other servers.

Exercise 12

CREATING A NEW DFS ROOT

This exercise should be done on the A1Computer in the domain.

1. Click Start, then Programs, then Administrative Tools, and then Distributed File System.
2. Right-click *Distributed File System* in the tree on the left side of the screen and click New Dfs Root from the drop-down menu.
3. At the wizard click <u>N</u>ext to continue. You see the New Dfs Root Wizard dialog box in Figure 9.19.

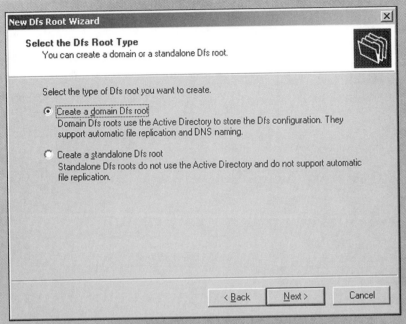

Figure 9.19

4. Accept the default of *Create a domain Dfs root* and click Next.
5. The Domain name box should display the name of your domain (Figure 9.20). In the case of multiple domains, make sure your domain is selected and click Next to continue.

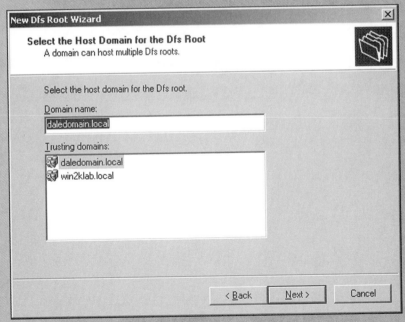

Figure 9.20

6. The server name box should display the name of your server. Click Next to continue. You see a dialog box to define the share (Figure 9.21).

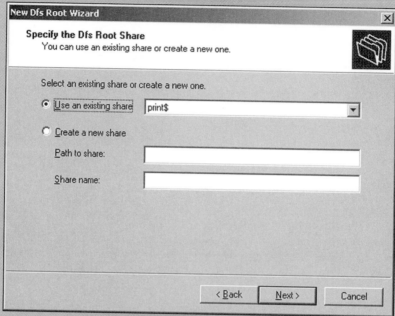

Figure 9.21

7. Click *Create a new share*.
8. In the Path to share text box key **X:\UserApps** and press the Tab key (where *X* is the drive letter containing your system files).
9. In the Share name text box key **UserApps**. The dialog box should now look like Figure 9.22.

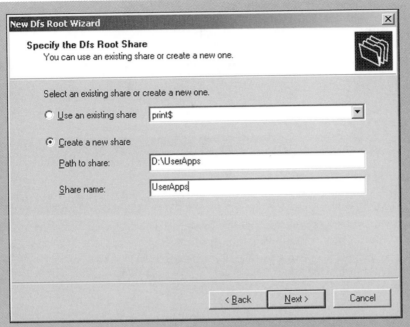

Figure 9.22

10. Click <u>N</u>ext to continue.
11. You should receive a message informing you that the folder does not exist. Click Yes to create the folder. You see the Name the Dfs Root dialog box (Figure 9.23).

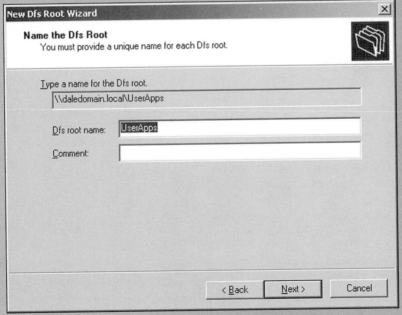

Figure 9.23

12. Accept the default Dfs root name and key **ADomain User Applications** in the Comment text box, and then click Next to continue.

13. Review the settings you have selected and click Finish. You should now see your root in the distributed file system tree.

Exercise 13

CREATING A NEW LINK TO THE DFS ROOT

This exercise should be done from the A1Computer in the domain.

1. With the Dfs window open, right-click the Dfs root you just created that is listed on the left side of your screen.

2. Pick New Dfs Link from the drop-down menu. You see the Create a New Dfs Link dialog box in Figure 9.24.

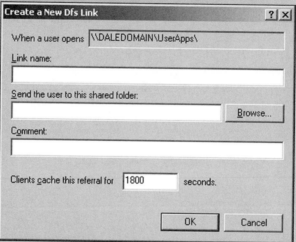

Figure 9.24

3. For the Link name key **Spreadsheets** and press the Tab key.

4. In the Send the user to this shared folder text box key the UNC share name for the Spreadsheets share on the A2Computer in the domain. It will appear this way:

   `\\A2Computer\spreadsheets`

5. Press the Tab key twice.

6. In the Comment text box key **Spreadsheet Application Programs**. The dialog box will now look something like Figure 9.25.

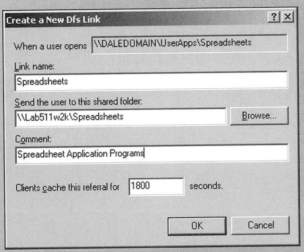

Figure 9.25

7. Accept the default at the Clients cache this referral for text box and click OK to continue.

> The Clients cache this referral for text box refers to how long a client will store information about the location of a Dfs shared folder before asking the server again for its location. If the location of a Dfs shared folder is going to change, you may want to make this number lower so the clients will have to check at the server more frequently for the location.

You have now created a link to the share on the second domain computer. You will now add a second link to a share on the A1Computer.

Exercise 14

ADDING AN ADDITIONAL DFS LINK

Do this exercise from A1Computer only.

1. Repeat the steps from exercise 13 to add a link to the WordProcessing share located on A1Computer. Use the link name wordprocessing and the path of \\A1computer\wordprocessing. In the Comment text box key **Wordprocessing Application Programs**. You should now see two links to your root (Figure 9.26).

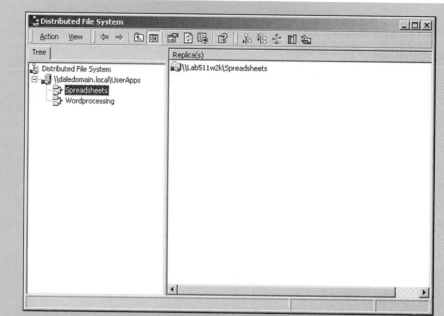

Figure 9.26

Exercise 15

TESTING THE DFS LINKS

Do this exercise from A2Computer only.

1. Right-click your *My Computer* icon and click Map Network Drive.
2. Accept the default for the drive letter and in the Folder text box key
   \\A1computer\Userapps.
3. Take the check mark out of *Reconnect at logon* and click Finish.
4. Double-click the *My Computer* icon to open it. You should see a
   connection to *\\A1computer\Userapps.*
5. Double-click the *\\A1computer\Userapps* connection to open it. You
   should see both the *Spreadsheets* and the *Wordprocessing* folders even
   though they are located on two different machines.

Copying Files with Dfs

The second function of Dfs is to provide a way to copy files automatically to multiple servers. Replication is important because you may want multiple machines to have identical copies of files, for example, logon scripts. With logon scripts you want whichever domain controller validates a user to provide the user's logon script, but you do not want the network administrator to have to manually copy the logon scripts to each domain controller. The ability to replicate files also provides fault tolerance and load balancing. If one replica is down or busy, the user can access files from a different replica. Replication is handled by a service called file replication service (FRS).

Because Dfs relies on the file replication service, it is important to make sure that the file replication service is running. To check the status of a service, click Start, Programs, Administrative Tools. Click the Computer Management menu item. Double-click the *Services and Applications* icon. Then on the right-hand side of the screen double-click the *Services* icon. You will see a list of the services. Make sure the file replication service is started and set with the Startup Type on automatic. This setting will assure that FRS starts each time the server is rebooted.

To set up replication you must designate one server to be the master. The master is the server where the files are originally placed. You can then set up other servers to replicate those files. A replica set may have as many as 128 members. When you set up Dfs you will also have the choice of automatic or manual replication. Automatic replication can be done only on NTFS partitions. The default synchronization interval for automatic synchronization is 15 minutes. If you want to use replication on a FAT partition, you must select to replicate manually. In the following exercise you set up a Dfs root and create shares to be replication partners.

Exercise 16

CREATING AN ADDITIONAL DFS ROOT ON A SECOND SERVER

Do this exercise from the A2Computer.

1. Click Start, then Programs, then Administrative Tools, and then Distributed File System.
2. Right-click *Distributed File System* in the tree on the left-hand side of the screen and click New Dfs Root from the drop-down menu.
3. At the wizard click <u>N</u>ext to continue.
4. Accept the default of *Create a <u>d</u>omain Dfs root* and click <u>N</u>ext.

5. The Domain name text box should display the name of your domain. Click Next to continue.
6. The server name text box should display the name of your server. Click Next to continue.
7. Click *Create a new share*.
8. For the path key **X:\CompanyPolicy** and press the Tab key (where X is the drive containing your system files).
9. In the Share name text box, key **CompanyPolicy** and click Next.
10. You should receive a message informing you that the folder does not exist. Click Yes to create the folder.
11. Accept the default Dfs root name and key **ADomain Company Policy** in the Comment text box.
12. Click Next to continue.
13. Review the settings you have selected and click Finish.

 Dfs uses the file replication service. You may have to shut down and restart the second domain controller to make sure the FRS is running.

Exercise 17

CREATING A POLICIES SHARE

Do this exercise on both domain controllers.

1. Create a folder on the X drive named *Policies* (where X is the drive containing your system files).
2. Share this folder using the default share name and the default permissions.

Now that you have a Dfs root on A2Computer and policy shares, you can link the policy share on A1Computer to the Dfs root.

Exercise 18

CREATING A NEW LINK TO THE DFS ROOT

Do this exercise from the A2Computer.

1. Open the Distributed File System program and right-click the Dfs root listed on the left-hand side of your screen.
2. Pick New Dfs Link from the drop-down menu.
3. For the Link name, key **Policies** and press the Tab key.
4. In the Send the user to this shared folder text box key **\\A1computer\policies** (the share on the A1Computer) and press the Tab key twice.
5. In the Comment text box key **A1computer Policy link**. The dialog box looks like Figure 9.27.

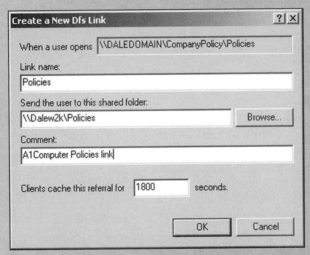

Figure 9.27

6. Accept the default for the Clients cache this referral for text box and click OK to continue. You should now see the *Policies* link shown in Figure 9.28.

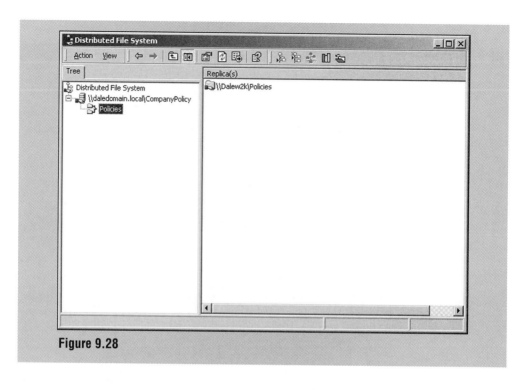

Figure 9.28

You now have a link to your Dfs root so that when a user attaches to the root on A2Computer they will see the *Policies* folder that is actually located on A1Computer. Next you will set up the Policies share on the A1Computer to replicate with the Policies share on the A2Computer.

Exercise 19

ADDING A REPLICA SET TO A DFS ROOT

Do this exercise from A2Computer only.

1. Open the Distributed File System program, right-click the *Policies* Dfs link on the left-hand side of your screen and click New Replica from the drop-down menu.
2. In the Send the user to this shared folder text box, key **\\A2Computer\Policies** (or the name of the second domain controller).
3. Click *Automatic replication*. The dialog box should now look like Figure 9.29.

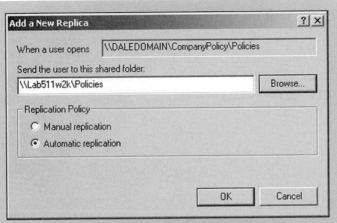

Figure 9.29

4. Click OK.
5. When the Replication Policy dialog box comes up you will see both replicas. They should have a value of No in the *Replication* field (Figure 9.30).

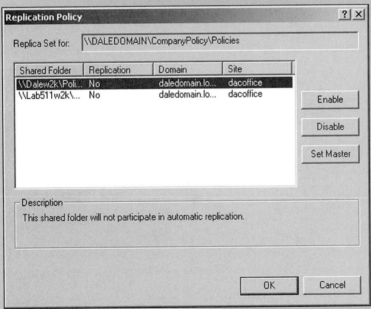

Figure 9.30

6. Click the A2Computer entry and click the Set Master button.
7. Click the A1Computer entry and then click the Enable button. Both machines should now say Yes in the *Replication* field (Figure 9.31).

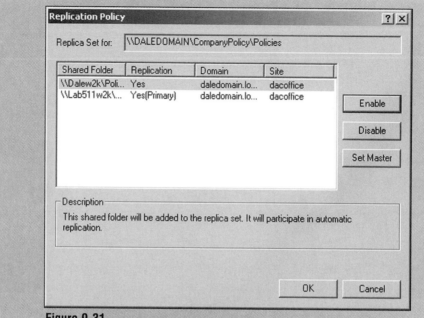

Figure 9.31

8. Click OK to leave the Replication Policy dialog box.

Exercise 20

TEST THE REPLICATION CONNECTIONS

Do this exercise from A2Computer only.

Right-click the *Policies Dfs* replica on the left-hand side of your screen and click Check Status from the drop-down menu. If all the connections are proper, you will see a green check mark next to each replica (Figure 9.32).

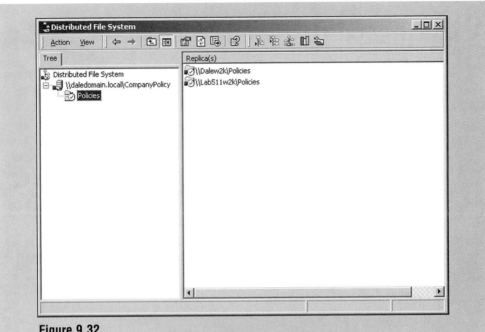

Figure 9.32

Exercise 21

WATCHING FILES REPLICATE

Do this exercise from A2Computer only.

1. Double-click the *My Computer* icon on your computer.
2. Double-click the drive where the *Policies* folder is located and double-click the *Policies* folder to open it.
3. Create a new text document in the folder called test.
4. Wait approximately 15 minutes and open the policies share on the A1Computer. You should see a copy of the text document.

CHAPTER summary

➤ Sharing resources is one of the main purposes of a network. In order to share resources, computers must create a share on a folder or printer. The share can be given a name different from the folder and has share-level permissions. These permissions define which users and groups can access the share and how they can use the share. A number of default shares are created when Windows 2000 is installed, primarily administrative shares. Share-level permissions only apply to folders. All files in the shared folder inherit the folder permissions. Windows 2000 includes the ability to define file/folder permissions, which allow the administrator to set a high level of security.

➤ The distributed file system is new to Windows 2000 and is used to define network-level shares that can include folders distributed across several servers. A Dfs root must be created on a domain controller and then Dfs shares created under the root. A single Dfs share can contain folders linked to different shares on different domain controllers. Another feature of Dfs is the ability to replicate data between Dfs links. A Dfs replica is a set of shared folders such that when files are placed in the master folder it is automatically replicated to the linked folders.

CHAPTER terms

DFS	Distributed file system: A system on Windows 2000 that allows multiple shares across the network to be linked and allows file replication between shares.
File/folder permissions	Access permissions set on individual files (requires NTFS).
Share	A resource shared on the network.
Share-level permissions	Access permissions set on the share and automatically applied to all files and folders within the share.

CONCEPTS review

Multiple Choice

1. How many Dfs roots can you have on a server?
   a. 1
   b. 2
   c. 255
   d. It depends on what type of client is trying to connect to the Dfs root.
   e. Infinite

2. What is the maximum length for a share name if you are trying to connect to it from a Windows 2000 Professional machine?
   a. 8 characters
   b. 12 characters
   c. 15 characters
   d. 255 characters
   e. None of the above

3. What service needs to be running in order for Dfs to function?
   a. Directory replication service
   b. File replication service
   c. Duplicator service
   d. Both a and b
   e. None of the above

4. Which of the following is the proper command to connect to a share named Publications on a server named Illinois in a domain called Midwest?
   a. Net share r: \\Midwest\Publications
   b. Net share r: \\Illinois\Publications
   c. Net use r: //Illinois/Publications
   d. Net use r: \\Midwest\Publications
   e. None of the above

5. Which of the following names would cause a share name to be hidden?
   a. Finance /hidden
   b. Finance$
   c. $finance
   d. Finance(hide)
   e. None of the above

6. Phil belongs to a group called Fishing. If Phil has read permissions granted to a share called Canneries and the Fishing group has change permissions granted to the Canneries share, what are Phil's effective permissions to the share?
   a. Read
   b. Change
   c. Full control
   d. No access
   e. None of the above

7. The default permissions on a share are:
   a. Administrators: Full control, Users: Read.
   b. Everyone: Read.
   c. Everyone: Full control.
   d. Everyone: Change.
   e. Administrators: Full control.

8. By default the number of users who can connect to a share is:
   a. 1.
   b. 10.
   c. 255.
   d. Unlimited.
   e. None of the above.

9. Which of the following is not true about file/folder permissions?
   a. They can be used to protect files on the local machine.
   b. You can assign delete permission to a file without assigning read permission.
   c. You can assign permissions to both files and folders.
   d. By default they are inherited.
   e. They can be used on FAT32 partitions.

10. Gil belongs to the Accounting group and the Finance group. If Gil has read permissions granted to a file called budget, the Finance group has full control access denied to the file called budget, and the Accounting group has change access granted to the budget file. What are Gil's effective permissions to the budget file?
    a. Read
    b. Change
    c. Full control
    d. No access
    e. None of the above

11. The concept of ownership:
    a. Is only meaningful on an NTFS partition.
    b. Can only be applied to folders, not files.
    c. Is what distinguishes between full control and change.
    d. All of the above.
    e. Both a and c.

12. Which of the following cannot be used in a share name?
    a. Space
    b. Numbers
    c. Dollar sign
    d. Underscore
    e. None of the above

13. The budget file has permissions set for Everyone of read access. The file is moved to a folder where the Everyone group has change access. The permission on the budget file once it has been moved will be:
    a. Everyone: Read.
    b. Everyone: Change.
    c. Everyone: Full control.
    d. The file will not have any permissions on it.
    e. None of the above.

14. Dfs can have how many members in a replica set?
    a. 1
    b. 2
    c. 128
    d. 255
    e. None of the above

15. Which of the following is the proper syntax for a UNC pointing to a share named Denver on a server named West?
    a. \\West\Denver
    b. \\Denver\West
    c. //West/Denver
    d. \Denver\West
    e. /Denver/West

Short Answer

1. Explain the difference between using Dfs links and using links as members in a replica set.
2. You have a share with the default permission of Everyone: Full control. Only administrators should have access to the share. You first grant administrators full control access and then change the permissions on the Everyone group to full control denied. What is the problem with this solution?
3. Write the command that would connect a share named Oaklawn on a server named Maine.
4. Explain why you might want to hide a share name.
5. Give two examples of shares that are created automatically when a Windows 2000 server is built.

LAB exercises

Exercise 1 – Creating a Folder and Sharing It from the Command Line

1. Log on as the administrator, click the Start button, and click <u>R</u>un.
2. Key **cmd** in the Open box and click OK to start a command line prompt.
3. The prompt you see indicates the default drive, which is where your system files are located. Write down the drive letter to use in the next step. _____
4. To create a folder, key

        md\newfolder

5. To share the folder, key

        Net share newshare=driveletter:\newfolder

   (You should receive a message telling you the folder was shared successfully.)

6. Key **Exit** to close the command line window.
7. Open My Computer and view the folder you created. Is it shared? (You may have to press F5 to refresh the screen before you see the hand under the folder.)
8. What are the permissions on the share?

Exercise 2 – Setting Permissions on a Folder Using the Cacls Command

1. Log on as the administrator and pull up a command line prompt.
2. Change into the *winnt\ssytem32* folder by keying

        cd\winnt\system32

3. To give MBuffett change access to the new folder from the command line key

        Cacls driveletter:\newfolder /G Mbuffett:c

4. Answer the question *Are you sure?* by keying the letter **Y**.
5. Close the command line window.
6. Through My Computer view the file/folder permissions on the folder. Were permissions inherited from its parent?
7. Add the administrators group and give them full control of the folder.

Exercise 3 – Copying a File and Viewing File/Folder Permissions

1. Create a new text document called DJW inside the new folder. Write down the file/folder permissions on the file.
2. Copy the DJW file to the *Policies* folder you created earlier. Check the permissions on the DJW file in the *Policies* folder. What are the permissions? Are they the same as the permissions on the DJW file in the new folder? Why or why not?

Exercise 4 – Moving a File and Viewing File/Folder Permissions

1. Rename the DJW document in the *Policies* folder to be BFP.
2. Right-click the BFP document and click Cut.
3. Open the new folder window.
4. Right-click somewhere in the new folder window and click Paste.
5. Both DJW and BFP should now be in the new folder window. Check the permissions on BFP. Are they the same as the permissions on DJW? Why or why not?

Exercise 5 – Deleting a File from a Dfs Replica

1. Log on to A1Computer and delete the text file from the policies share.
2. Wait approximately 15 minutes and look in the policies share on A2Computer. Does the text file appear?

PROBLEM SOLVING exercise

Consider the following situation and answer the questions.

All permission inheritance is left at the defaults. Sam is a member of the Clerks group.

The *Top* folder is shared with the share name Topshare, and the Everyone group has read share permissions. There are no other share-level permissions on the share.

The *Middle* folder is shared with the share name Middleshare, and the Everyone group has full control share permissions. There are no other share-level permissions on the share.

The file/folder permissions on the *Top* folder are full control for Administrators and change for Managers.

Inside the *Middle* folder is a document named Document2.

Inside the *Top* folder is a file called Document1. The specific file/folder permissions set on Document1 are Clerks Read Denied and Sam Read.

In the *Single* folder the Clerks have change access.

There are no other specific file/folder permissions assigned on any file or folder.

1. If Document1 was moved to the *Single* folder, what would the file/folder permissions be on Document1?

2. In order to give Managers full control of the *Bottom* folder, what must be done?

3. What are Managers file/folder permissions on Document1?

4. Could an administrator connected to the Topshare rename Document2?

5. Could an administrator connected to the Middleshare delete Document2?

6. What file/folder permissions does the Clerks group have to Document2?

7. What would Sam's effective permission be to Document2 if he was connected to the Middleshare?

8. Could a manager connected to the Topshare create a new file in the *Top* folder?

9. What are Sam's effective file/folder permissions to Document1?

10. A copy of Document1 is made and placed in the *Single* folder. What would the file/folder permission be on the copy of Document1?

MICROSOFT NETWORK INFRASTRUCTURE 10

Performance Objectives

After completing this chapter you will be able to:

- Discuss TCP/IP addressing
- Discuss and perform TCP/IP subnetting
- Use various TCP/IP utilities
- Discuss the Dynamic Host Configuration Protocol (DHCP) process
- Install and configure a DHCP server
- Discuss concepts with IP addressing
- View and discuss DNS host records
- Create Active Directory Integrated Lookup Zone
- Create a reverse lookup zone
- Transfer DNS zone data from primary to secondary DNS servers
- Discuss the purpose of the Windows Internet Naming Service

Introduction

The ability to install and manage a Windows 2000 network will require knowledge of the network infrastructure. The network infrastructure includes the protocols used to transfer information and the operation of network services that allow domain controllers and clients to communicate. In this chapter you learn more about the TCP/IP protocol, how to configure parts of the network with this protocol, and how to use some of the important network infrastructure services.

Network Infrastructure

The network infrastructure is like a highway in that it includes the protocols and services necessary for computers on a network to communicate. The basic elements of the network infrastructure include the following:

- TCP/IP
- Dynamic Host Configuration Protocol (DHCP)
- Domain Name System (DNS)
- Windows Internet Naming Service (WINS)

TCP/IP is the common language used by the network systems to communicate with each other. Understanding this language is critical to understanding how the other infrastructure elements work. The DHCP service is used to provide IP addresses to network devices and to manage ranges of addresses. The DNS infrastructure component provides a way to locate computers and services on the network based on their host name. The WINS infrastructure component works like DNS, but works with **NetBIOS** names (that use the NetBEUI protocol—see below) rather than host names.

TCP/IP Addressing

One of the main changes from Windows NT that makes Windows 2000 more suitable for enterprise networks is the adoption of TCP/IP as the core protocol. Windows NT used **NetBEUI**, which was a proprietary Microsoft protocol. The problem with NetBEUI was that it was not routable and so did not allow for much interaction with other systems. TCP/IP is the standard protocol used on the Internet and on many large networks.

In order for a computer or network device to communicate on a TCP/IP network, it must have, at a minimum, two things: a unique TCP/IP address and a **subnet mask**. (The address will be considered here and the subnet mask will be explained in a later section.) For example, consider how addressing works on the Internet. Because each machine that is going to communicate on a public network like the Internet needs a unique IP address, a multinational committee called **InterNIC** was assigned the task of handing out addresses. InterNIC prevents the duplication of IP addresses.

Octets and the Binary Numbering System

Each one or zero is called a **bit** and each group of eight bits is called an **octet** (also called a **byte**). An IP address consists of four octets and if written in binary format would appear as—

```
11100001.1000001.10100000.00000011
```

In order to understand how IP addresses work you must understand the binary numbering system. Binary works just like our decimal numbering system, except it is a base 2 system instead of a base 10 system. To understand a different base numbering system, it is helpful to review how the decimal system works.

Because people have 10 fingers it is natural that the human race uses a decimal counting system. The decimal system has 10 digits: 0, 1, 2, 3, 4, 5, 6, 7, 8, 9. The base of the system is 10, and the value of a number depends on its position. For example, which would you rather have, 4 or 40 dollars? Forty of course! Even though zero does not have any value in itself, it holds a place and moves the 4 over from the one's spot to the ten's spot making the 4 more valuable. To the left of the ten's place is the hundred's, thousand's, ten thousand's, and so on. If you convert those numbers to scientific notation you will see that each position is 10 raised to some power. The one's position is 10 raised to the power of zero, the ten's position is 10 raised to the first power, the hundred's is equal to 10 times 10, or 10 raised to the second power. This concept is illustrated in Figure 10.1.

FIGURE 10.1 *Illustration of a Number in Base 10*

$$423 \quad = \quad 4 \times 10^2 + 2 \times 10^1 + 3 \times 10^0$$

In Figure 10.1, the number 423 is created by using the base number 10, raising it to the appropriate power (2, 1, or 0), and multiplying it by the number of elements. In other words, 423 is made up of four 100 elements plus two 10 elements plus three 1 elements.

The binary system works in the same way as the decimal system, except binary uses only two digits, 0 and 1, and its base number is 2. Figure 10.2 shows the positions in the binary numbering system and their equivalent values in the decimal system.

FIGURE 10.2 *Position Values of Numbers in Base 2*

2^7	2^6	2^5	2^4	2^3	2^2	2^1	2^0
128	64	32	16	8	4	2	1

Because our numbering system is decimal, working with binary numbers can be difficult. Rather than work with a binary value like—

11100001.1000001.10100000.00000011

Most people find it more convenient to use the equivalent decimal number—

225.129.160.3

Using the chart in Figure 10.2, a binary number can be converted to a decimal value. Each octet can range in value from 0, if all eight bits are zero, to 255 if all eight bits are ones. For example, using the base number and the position, the octet can be written as—

$$
\begin{aligned}
00000011 = \quad & 0 \times 2^7 + \\
& 0 \times 2^6 + \\
& 0 \times 2^5 + \\
& 0 \times 2^4 + \\
& 0 \times 2^3 + \\
& 0 \times 2^2 + \\
& 1 \times 2^1 + \\
& 1 \times 2^0
\end{aligned}
$$

Calculating the number (where zero times anything returns zero) gives—

$$0 + 0 + 0 + 0 + 0 + 0 + 1 \times 2^1 + 1 \times 2^0$$

and using the chart in Figure 10.2 to convert binary values to decimal gives—

$$0 + 0 + 0 + 0 + 0 + 0 + 2 + 1$$

Adding these numbers finally gives the decimal value 3.

Using this technique allows you to convert an octet to a decimal value—

```
11100001.1000001.10100000.00000011
225     .129     .160       .3
```

Although you will likely never deal with octets, understanding how binary values work will be important later in the chapter when you work with IP addresses.

IP Address Classes

IP addresses can be assigned to computer and network devices and can also be assigned to entire networks or network segments. The IP address attached to message packets will consist of the specific device IP address along with the network IP address. Because a single IP address had to contain both the network and device addresses, parts of the IP address were assigned to identify the network (the network portion) and parts to identify the device (the host portion). The network portion of the address is similar to the street name portion of your home address, and the host portion of the address compares to the number portion of your home address. All the houses on your street will have the same street name but each house will have a unique number. Groups of IP addresses were classified based on how much of the IP address was used to identify the network and how much was used to identify the device. These classes were A, B, C, D, and E.

The first three classes—A, B, and C—are identified by the first three bits of an IP address. Class A addresses use the first octet for the network address and must start with 0. Class B addresses use the first two octets for the network address and must start with 10. Class C addresses use the first three octets for the network address and must start with 110. For example, the network portion of a binary IP address for these classes of addresses are as follows:

```
01011001                  – Network part of a class A address
1011011001100100          – Network part of a class B address
110100111110101111001110  – Network part of a class C address
```

All IP addresses where the first octet contained a value from 0 to 127 were called class A addresses, which meant that the first octet is the network portion of the address and the last three octets are the host portion of the address. If a company was given a class A network address, all the computers would have the same numbers in the first octet but have different numbers in the remaining octets for each individual machine on the network. For example, a company with a class A address could assign the following IP address to their network computers and devices:

```
102.001.125.99
102.234.007.135
102.199.244.24
```

In this case, the first octet contains the number 102. All these machines would be considered to be on the same network and would know how to communicate between themselves, just like you could probably find another house located on your street without too much effort.

Class A addresses are designed for the biggest networks. Because all of the octets except the first can be used as host addresses, more than 16 million (256 × 256 × 256) host addresses are possible per class A network. However, a limited number of class A addresses are available, and all of them are currently taken.

For example, IBM has been assigned the class A address 9.0.0.0, Hewlett-Packard 15.0.0.0, and AT&T 12.0.0.0.

In a class B network the first two octets are used as the network portion of the address and the last two octets used as the host portion. Therefore, a class B network could have more than 65,000 (256 × 256) possible different hosts. If a company had a class B network, it may have addresses that look like the following:

```
135.101.10.22
135.101.10.200
131.101.211.56
131.101.221.199
```

The first two octets, which identify the network, are constant for all the addresses (135.101), and the last two octets vary. Notice that the first octet must start with an address greater than or equal to 128, but less than 192.

In a class C network the first three octets would be used to identify the network and the last octet would vary. Each class C network has only 256 possible addresses. This small number may seem limiting, but many more class C network addresses are available.

The class D addresses are never used to identify a single machine. Instead, they address a group of machines. Just like you sometimes receive mail at your home addressed to *postal customer* or *occupant*, many other people received the same piece of mail with the same name. This name *postal customer* identifies a group of people who will all receive the same message. In the same way, multiple network devices with IP addresses receive messages sent to a class D address. For example, all routers running a protocol called **Open Shortest Path First (OSPF)** would receive a message addressed to the class D address 224.0.0.5.

Class E addresses were set aside for future use; however, in all likelihood they will not ever be used because TCP/IP version 6 will be implemented before the class E addresses are needed.

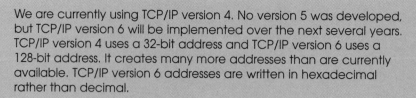

We are currently using TCP/IP version 4. No version 5 was developed, but TCP/IP version 6 will be implemented over the next several years. TCP/IP version 4 uses a 32-bit address and TCP/IP version 6 uses a 128-bit address. It creates many more addresses than are currently available. TCP/IP version 6 addresses are written in hexadecimal rather than decimal.

Table 10.1 summarizes the IP address class information and indicates which addresses are available, which are reserved, and which are nonroutable.

T A B L E 10.1 *IP Address Class Information*

Class	Address Range	Status
A	0.0.0.0	Reserved
	1.0.0.0 to 126.0.0.0	Available
	10.0.0.0 to 10.255.255.255	Nonroutable
	127.0.0.0	Loopback address used for testing
B	128.0.0.0 to 191.254.0.0	Available
	172.16.0.0 to 172.31.255.255	Nonroutable
	191.255.0.0	Reserved
C	192.0.0.0	Reserved
	192.0.1.0 to 223.255.254.0	Available
	192.168.0.0 to 192.168.255.255	Nonroutable
	223.255.255.0	Reserved
D	224.0.0.0 to 239.255.255.255	Multicast group address
E	240.0.0.0 to 255.255.255.254	Reserved
	255.255.255.255	Broadcast

Subnet Mask

The second piece of information needed to make a device communicate on a TCP/IP network is the subnet mask. The subnet mask is used to determine which portion of the IP address identifies the host portion and which part identifies the network portion. For example, you write a letter to a friend and address the envelope:

123 1st Street

You can tell by the space between the 3 and the 1 which portion is the house address and which portion is the street address. If that space was not there and the address was written as:

1231st Street

the post office would not know whether to send the letter to 1 231st Street, 12 31st Street, or 123 1st Street. The space inserted between the numbers gives meaning to the address and ensures correct delivery.

The subnet mask has the same function for a TCP/IP address as the space has in a home address. The subnet mask separates the network portion of the IP address from the host portion. Any bit that is masked (contains a 1 value) indicates the network portion of the address. Unmasked bits (contain a 0 value) indicate the host portion. Subnet masks for original class-based A, B, and C networks are shown here—

Class A = 11111111.00000000.00000000.00000000 or 255.0.0.0
Class B = 11111111.11111111.00000000.00000000 or 255.255.0.0
Class C = 11111111.11111111.11111111.00000000 or 255.255.255.0

Subnetting Class Addresses

The original class system worked fine for many years before the explosion of the Internet. If you had 50 computers in your company that needed to talk on the Internet, you called up the InterNIC and they assigned you a class C address. It meant you actually had more addresses than you needed, but no one cared because plenty of addresses were available. Things have changed because of the current shortage of IP addresses. If you only need 50 addresses, you will not be given a complete class C address. The class C address will be divided and you will be given a portion of the address.

This division is done by combining the IP address with a mask value that borrows bits from the host address and uses them as part of the network address. The mask value is constructed by using the following two rules:

Rule 1: 2 to the power of masked bits minus 2 is equal to the number of subnets.

Rule 2: 2 to the power of unmasked bits minus 2 is equal to the number of hosts in each subnet.

For example, you have a class C network that needs to be divided into six subnets. 2 raised to the 3rd power is 8. Subtract 2 from 8 and you are left with 6, which is the number of subnets you need (Rule 1). Therefore, your mask (which starts as a default class C mask) must borrow three bits from the host ID part of the mask and make those three bits part of the network portion. When borrowing bits you always borrow from the high end. The subnet mask would look like the following:

11111111.11111111.11111111.11100000

Because the three bits borrowed from the host portion of the mask network are in the high-order positions, their values, converted to decimal, are 128, 64, and 32. Added together they make 224. This value is used in the last octet of the mask. In dotted decimal format the resulting subnet mask would be—

```
255.255.255.224
```

So, a class C address with the subnet mask of 255.255.255.224 would have five bits making up the host portion of the address (11100000). 2 raised to the 5th power minus 2 is 30, so there can be 30 hosts on each of the six subnets (Rule 2).

Microsoft follows older rules for subnetting that state neither the host nor network portion of the address can be all ones or all zeros. For that reason, you must subtract 2 from the number of hosts or subnets. Most new routers can handle all zeros and all ones, so you may not need to loose those hosts or subnets.

Sometimes subnet masks are indicated with something called **classless interdomain routing (CIDR)** notation. With CIDR notation, the IP address would be followed by a slash and number, indicating how many binary digits in the address are used to represent the network portion. For example, the network mask 255.255.0.0 would be represented by /16 (the number of bits in the first two octets). A class B address with subnet mask could be written as 132.122.45.33 /16 and a class C address could be written as—

```
221.218.156.23 /24
```

This format may seem like a shorthand way of writing subnet masks, but using this information to build routing tables allows much more flexibility in assigning small groups of host addresses. For example, consider the following address written in CIDR format:

```
205.167.122.48 /30
```

Masking the first 30 bits of the address leaves the last two bits available for host addresses. For this subnet, then, the only host addresses that can be used are—

```
205.167.122.48
205.167.122.49
205.167.122.50
205.167.122.51
```

CIDR recognizes that the class-based method of grouping IP addresses is limited.

Setting IP Addresses and Subnet Masks

You set a TCP/IP address and subnet mask on your machine during installation. You do not want to change them; however, you can view them.

Exercise 1

VIEWING IP AND SUBNET MASK INFORMATION
1. Right-click the *My Network Places* icon and click Properties from the drop-down menu.
2. Right-click the *Local Area Connections* icon and click Properties from the drop-down menu.
3. Click to highlight *Internet Protocol (TCP/IP)* and click Properties.
4. Write down the settings for address and subnet mask:
   _____, _____
5. You should also have settings for the DNS server. Note the DNS address here: _____
6. Click the Cancel button to leave the Internet Protocol and Local Area Connections Properties dialog boxes.
7. Close the Network and Dialup Connections window.

You may have noticed a place for a default gateway address. A default gateway is not necessary if the computer is only going to communicate with other machines on its own network. If the computer needs to communicate with equipment outside its network, such as a Web server on the Internet, the computer will need the address of a default gateway. The default gateway helps to direct messages from one network to another.

Microsoft uses the term *default gateway*, but typically the hardware used to help direct messages from one network to another is a router.

TCP/IP Utilities
Several utilities available with TCP/IP are used to view and test the configuration of the TCP/IP protocol. In the previous exercise you viewed your TCP/IP address by right clicking the *My Network Places* icon. You can also use a command line tool named ipconfig.

Exercise 2a

USING IPCONFIG

1. Click Start and then Run.
2. Key **cmd** in the Open text box to start a command line window and press Enter.
3. At the command prompt key **ipconfig** and press Enter. You should see your IP address and subnet mask (Figure 10.3).

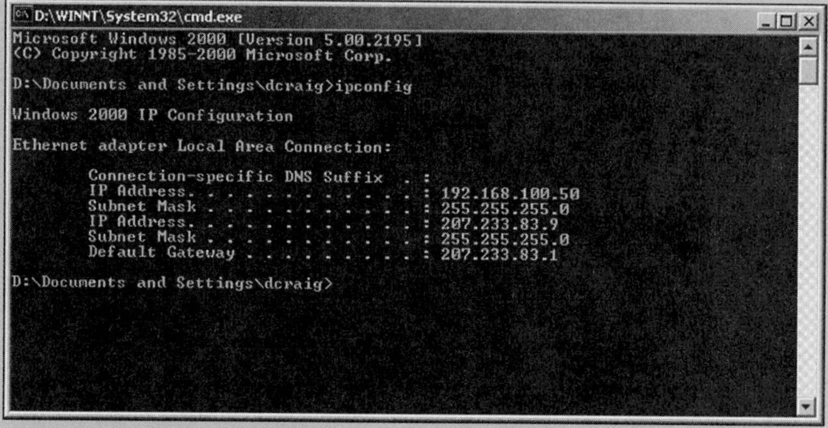

```
D:\WINNT\System32\cmd.exe                                      _ □ X
Microsoft Windows 2000 [Version 5.00.2195]
(C) Copyright 1985-2000 Microsoft Corp.

D:\Documents and Settings\dcraig>ipconfig

Windows 2000 IP Configuration

Ethernet adapter Local Area Connection:

        Connection-specific DNS Suffix  . :
        IP Address. . . . . . . . . . . . : 192.168.100.50
        Subnet Mask . . . . . . . . . . . : 255.255.255.0
        IP Address. . . . . . . . . . . . : 207.233.83.9
        Subnet Mask . . . . . . . . . . . : 255.255.255.0
        Default Gateway . . . . . . . . . : 207.233.83.1

D:\Documents and Settings\dcraig>
```

Figure 10.3

4. Leave the command window open for the next exercise.

Another commonly used utility is the **Packet Internet Grouper** (**PING**) command. Using this command you can attempt to contact another machine running TCP/IP. If the machine answers, you know the machine is running with the TCP/IP protocol loaded and properly configured and that a pathway is established between you and that machine.

Exercise 2b

USING PING

At the command prompt in the open command window key **ping** and your partner's address. For example—

    ping 192.168.100.17

You should receive a reply from your partner's machine that looks like the following:

    Pinging 192.168.100.17 with 32 bytes of data:

```
Reply from 192.168.100.17: bytes=32 time <10ms TTL=128
Reply from 192.168.100.17: bytes=32 time <10ms TTL=128
Reply from 192.168.100.17: bytes=32 time <10ms TTL=128
Reply from 192.168.100.17: bytes=32 time <10ms TTL=128
Ping statistics for 192.168.100.17:
      Packets: Sent = 4, Received = 4, Lost = 0
      (0% Loss),
Approximate round trip times in milli-seconds:
      Minimum = 0ms, Maximum = 0ms, Average = 0ms
```

Dynamic Host Configuration Protocol

As you have seen, management of IP addresses on a TCP/IP-based network is critical. Every device connected to the network must have a valid and unique IP address and subnet mask in order to send and receive network messages. Without an IP address network clients (and servers) cannot connect to the network. When setting up a server or client, the network administrator has the choice of manually entering an IP address or configuring the client to get its own IP address. When an IP address is manually assigned to a particular computer and is not expected to change, it is called a **static IP** address. An IP address selected from a range of addresses and automatically assigned as the client boots is called a **dynamic IP** address. IP addresses are automatically assigned to network clients by use of the **Dynamic Host Configuration Protocol (DHCP)**.

Using dynamic IP addresses by way of DHCP rather than assigning static IP addresses during client installation is preferred for two reasons:

1. Dynamically allocating addresses often requires fewer IP addresses to service the same number of hosts than if static IP addresses are used.

2. During the process of assigning an IP address to a client, other network information can also be assigned, such as the subnet mask, IP addresses of DNS servers, and gateway addresses. This capability makes it easier to update the IP information used by multiple clients.

A DHCP server supplies the IP address in response to a client request. The DHCP server works like a library. If the library has six copies of a book, the first six people who request the book may check it out. The seventh person who comes in must wait for one of the books to be returned before he or she can check out the book. The DHCP server has a list of valid addresses it can give out to requesting clients. However, once those addresses are used the next requesting client must wait for an address to be returned. The network administrator is responsible for setting the ranges of IP addresses and configuring other values on the DHCP server.

DHCP is based on an older protocol called a BootP protocol.

Because DHCP is a standard protocol, non-Microsoft servers can be used as DHCP servers. Many companies use UNIX machines to perform DHCP and DNS tasks. However, on a Windows 2000 network it is preferable to use a Microsoft DHCP server because a Microsoft DHCP server works both with dynamic DNS to automatically update DNS records and with Active Directory.

The DHCP Process

An apparent paradox exists with a TCP/IP network that uses dynamic IP addresses. If the network client must have an IP address in order to use the network and if it must receive an IP address from the network when it boots, how can it both use and not use the network? This problem is resolved by use of the DHCP protocol. Network clients send a general broadcast message requesting an IP address. The general broadcast contains the client's network MAC address. (This unique hardware address identifies the network interface card.) When a DHCP server hears this broadcast it responds by sending a message back to the referenced MAC address. The return message contains an IP address and other information.

The process of retrieving an IP address from a DHCP server follows:

1. A network client boots and sends a **DHCPDISCOVER** broadcast over the network. The broadcast is a request by the client for any DHCP server that is listening to supply an address. The client will wait a random number of seconds between 1 and 10 before sending this broadcast message to ensure that a group of clients doesn't attempt to send multiple requests to a DHCP server at the same time and overwhelm the server.

2. After sending the DHCPDISCOVER broadcast, the client goes into a wait state and listens for a return broadcast.

3. A DHCP server on the local network, listening for DHCPDISCOVER broadcasts, will respond to the client by sending a **DHCPOFFER** message. This message contains a suggested IP address for the client to use and the address of the server sending the offer.

If the DHCP server is not on the local network and is behind a router, you must either have DHCP relay enabled to forward the broadcast message to the DHCP server, or the router must be RFC 1542 compliant. Although routers typically do not pass along broadcasts, 1542 compliant routers are programmed to pass DHCP broadcasts along to the next network segment.

4. When the network client receives the DHCPOFFER message it responds directly to the DHCP server (using the DHCP server's address, not a broadcast) with a **DHCPREQUEST** message. The DHCPREQUEST is the client accepting the address offered. If more than one DHCP server responds with an offer, the client will typically request to accept the first offer it receives.

5. Once the DHCP server receives a DHCPREQUEST message from the client, it responds with a **DHCP acknowledgment** (**DHCPACK**) message that contains an IP address and other information. By sending a DHCPACK the server is acknowledging that the client is taking the offered address and will mark that address as taken in its database.

This process is illustrated in Figure 10.4.

FIGURE 10.4 *DHCP Process*

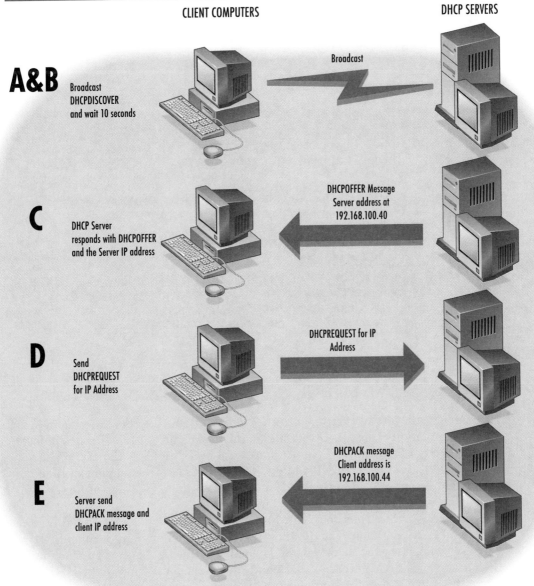

CLIENT COMPUTERS

DHCP SERVERS

A&B Broadcast
DHCPDISCOVER
and wait 10 seconds

Broadcast

C DHCP Server
responds with DHCPOFFER
and the Server IP address

DHCPOFFER Message
Server address at
192.168.100.40

D Send
DHCPREQUEST
for IP Address

DHCPREQUEST for IP
Address

E Server send
DHCPACK message and
client IP address

DHCPACK message
Client address is
192.168.100.44

Windows 2000 clients and DHCP servers can perform additional steps to ensure the validity of the IP address. A Windows 2000 client, once it is given an IP address in the DHCPOFFER broadcast message, can be configured to send an Address Resolution Protocol (ARP) message out to the network with the IP address it has just been offered by the DHCP server. A response from the ARP message lets the client know that a duplicate IP address is being offered. The client will then send a DHCPDECLINE message back to the DHCP server. Likewise, the DHCP server can be configured to send a PING message out to the network for the IP address it is about to allocate. If the server receives a response from the PING message, it knows that someone on the network has already been allocated the IP address. The DHCP server will then mark the address as bad and send another address.

A Windows 2000 client will attempt to use an IP address even without a DHCP server. If a Windows 2000 client boots and does not have a static IP address assigned and cannot contact a DHCP server for a dynamic IP address, then one of the following scenarios will occur:

- The client attempts to contact the last DHCP server it used for an IP address. It will also ping the last gateway for which it had an IP address in an attempt to ascertain whether it is still on the same network. If the client has an unexpired lease on an IP address, it will keep using the lease.

- If the client still cannot contact a DHCP server, after its lease has expired it will randomly select an IP address from the range 10.0.0.0 (nonroutable IP addresses). The client will ping the network after selecting an address. If another client is already using the IP address, it will select another address.

IP Address Leasing

The DHCPACK message returned to the client contains the IP address along with other information. This other information might include the IP addresses of local DNS servers, a local gateway, subnet mask, and WINS information. It will also include the lease time of the IP address. The lease time is the amount of time the client can use the IP address before it must contact the DHCP server for a new IP address or renew its lease on the existing address.

Three time values are associated with **IP address leasing**: duration time, renewal time, and rebinding time. The duration time is the total amount of time the IP address will be assigned to the client. The renewal time is the time at which the IP address must be renewed. At that point, the client must contact the DHCP server from which it initially received its IP address and request to renew the lease on its IP address. The rebinding time is when the client starts requesting an IP address from *any* DHCP server, not just the one from which it initially received its IP address. If the first DHCP server is down or not accessible, this process allows the client to start requesting an IP address from any available DHCP server using the DHCPREQUEST message.

For example, a DHCP server might have the following values set:

> Duration time = 1 hour
> Renewal time = 30 minutes
> Rebinding time = 50 minutes

The client would use these values in the following way:

1. When an IP address is first received from the DHCP server, the timer values are set on the client.

2. After 30 minutes of the IP lease time of one hour are used up, the client requests to renew the IP address from the DHCP server it initially contacted. If the server does not respond, the client keeps sending requests.

3. When 50 minutes of the one-hour lease time are up, and if the client was unsuccessful in contacting the original DHCP server, the client sends a general DHCPREQUEST broadcast to any other DHCP server.

4. When the full hour lease time is up and if the client has not contacted a DHCP server to get a new IP address, it stops using its IP address and network processing ends.

Choosing a short lease time can affect the network. If you set a lease time of 10 minutes, then every 5 minutes the network clients will start requesting new IP addresses, leading to excessive network traffic as multiple clients send DHCPREQUEST messages. You would probably want to choose a short lease time if your network information such as the default gateway was going to change. By making leases short, the clients receive updated information more often. The other reason to make a lease short is because you are short on IP addresses. By making a lease short, addresses will not be assigned to computers that are not being used. So if an employee goes on vacation and does not turn on his machine for three days, a short lease would ensure that the IP address leased to that machine would be released for someone else to use. If your network information does not change often and you have enough addresses, long lease times are much more efficient and cause less network traffic.

Installing DHCP

Configuring a client to use DHCP is an easy task. You simply need to click *Obtain an IP address automatically* on the Internet Protocol Properties dialog box (Figure 10.5).

FIGURE 10.5 **Enabling DHCP for Clients**

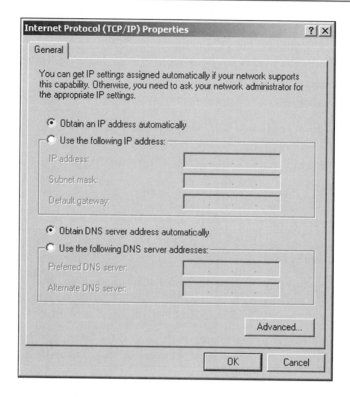

This option should only be used for clients and stand-alone servers. Domain controllers do not function properly with a dynamically assigned address, so you do not want to select this option on your machine.

Setting up a DHCP server is a bit more complicated than making a machine a DHCP client. A Windows 2000 server can be used as a DHCP server by installing the DHCP networking component. This installation must be done carefully in a lab situation because your network may already have a DHCP server. Installing a "rogue" DHCP server that responds to DHCPREQUEST messages with invalid IP addresses could cause major problems on a network. It is best if you can isolate your test computers from the rest of the network. Microsoft has a feature in Windows 2000 DHCP that only allows authorized DHCP servers to operate on a Windows 2000 network, but this safeguard may not prevent all problems with rogue DHCP servers.

DHCP servers must have static addresses. A machine cannot be both a DHCP server and a DHCP client.

Exercise 3

Configuring DHCP

After the DHCP server is installed it must be configured. Configuring a DHCP server involves the following:

- Setting a scope, which is the range of IP addresses the DHCP server will give out to clients

- Setting the IP release duration

- Setting the DHCP options for items like the addresses of the gateway and the DNS servers

- Authorizing the DHCP server to issue IP addresses

The last step, authorizing the DHCP server in the domain, helps prevent someone from installing a DHCP server on their own computer and handing out invalid network addresses. Under Windows 2000, only servers within the domain can be authorized by an administrator to hand out IP addresses. However, this restriction does not prevent non-Windows 2000 DHCP servers from issuing IP addresses.

Exercise 4

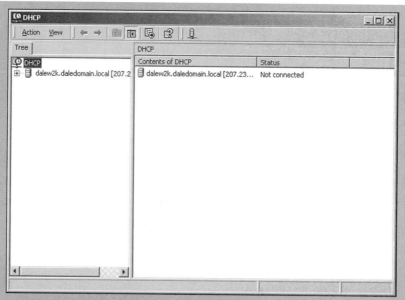

Figure 10.6

Before using this server you need to create a scope. A scope is a range of IP addresses the DHCP server will allocate to clients.

2. Right-click the server and click New Scope.
3. Click <u>N</u>ext to start the New Scope Wizard. You see a dialog box requesting a name and description for the scope (Figure 10.7).

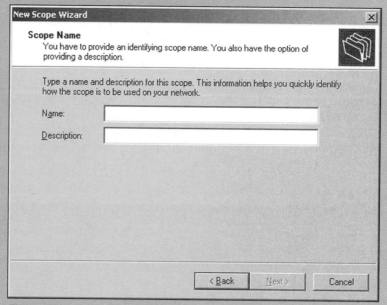

Figure 10.7

This information identifies what part of the network the DHCP IP addresses are designated for.

4. Key **Accounting** in the Name text box and click Next.

You see a dialog used to set the IP address ranges (Figure 10.8). Normally you are given a block of IP addresses that the DHCP server will send to the clients. In the next exercise your instructor will provide you with a range of class C addresses to use. You will enter the starting and ending ranges of these addresses.

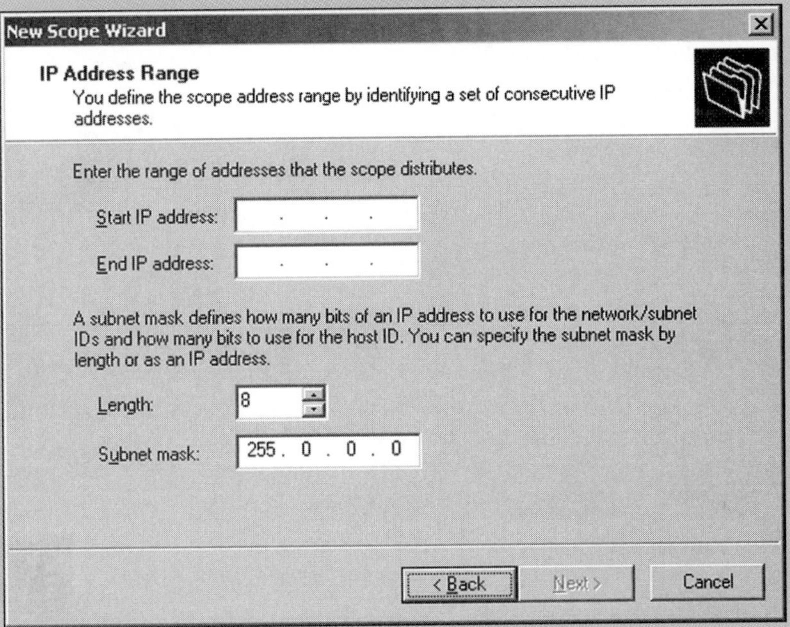

Figure 10.8

5. For the Start IP address, enter the first IP address of your range, such as **192.168.100.10**.
6. For the End IP address, enter the last IP address in your range, such as **192.168.100.70**.
7. Set the length to *24* to indicate that 24 bits are masked and correspond to a subnet mask of 255.255.255.0. The completed dialog box will look like Figure 10.9.

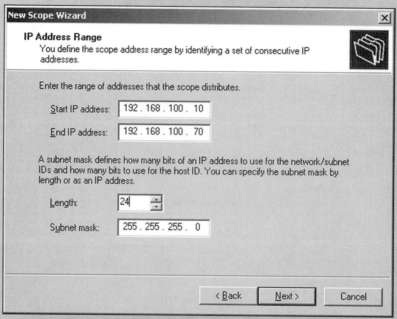

Figure 10.9

8. Click the Next button to continue. You see the Add Exclusions dialog box in Figure 10.10.

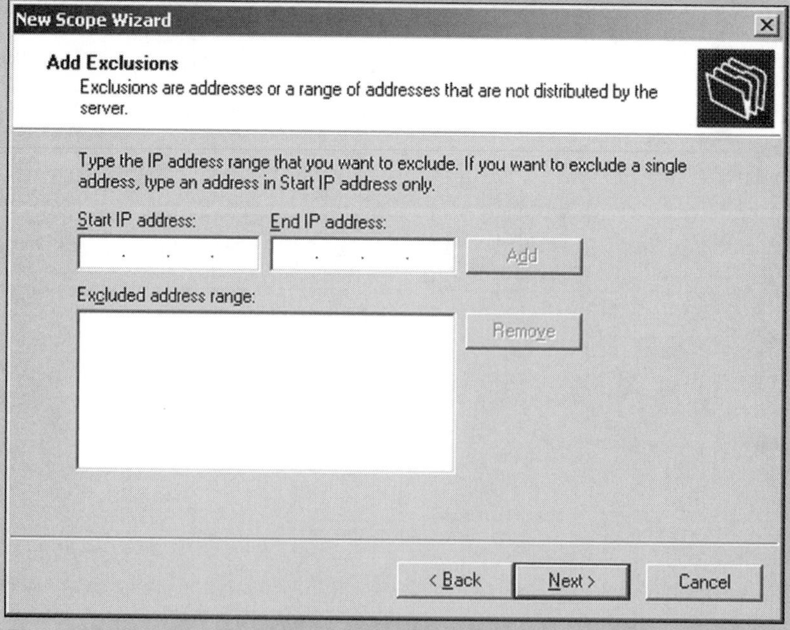

Figure 10.10

In this dialog box you could enter IP addresses within the scope range that you do not want to be given out when the DHCP server issues addresses. These addresses are likely static addresses assigned to domain controllers or printers. Actually, it is usually better to leave static addresses out of the scope altogether rather than exclude them. In other words, if you have 30 addresses available and need 2 static addresses, simply do not include the first two addresses in the scope.

9. Click the Next button to display the Lease Duration dialog box (Figure 10.11). It allows you to set the amount of time a client can hold an IP address.

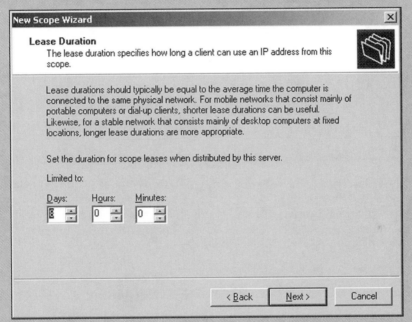

Figure 10.11

10. Set the lease to 8 days, 0 hours, and 0 minutes (which should be the default) and click the Next button. You will be asked if you want to configure the DHCP options.
11. Leave the Yes option selected and click Next to view the router IP address page. Here is where you would add the address of the router you use to access other networks. If you do not have a router you will leave this box blank.
12. Click Next to view the Domain Name and DNS Servers dialog box (Figure 10.12).

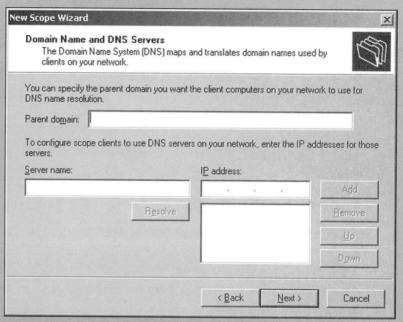

Figure 10.12

At this dialog box you would enter the name of the domain and the server names and IP addresses of the DNS servers in the domain. This information will be provided to the client so it has the address of an available DNS server. Because your machine is a DNS server, you will fill in your machine's information.

13. Key the name of your domain name in the Parent domain text box. For example, **a1domain.local.**
14. In the Server name text box key the name of your computer. For example, **a1computer.**
15. In the IP address text box key your IP address and click Add. The completed dialog box will look like Figure 10.13.

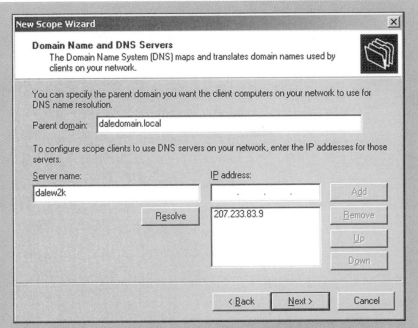

Figure 10.13

16. Click <u>N</u>ext to view the WINS Servers dialog box. At this dialog box you would enter the server names and IP addresses of the WINS servers. WINS will be discussed in more detail later in the chapter.

17. Click <u>N</u>ext to view the Active Scope dialog box, click <u>N</u>ext to activate the scope, and then click Finish.

The DHCP server is now running and has addresses to allocate but it is not authorized to do so. The following steps show you how to authorize a server to hand out addresses. This exercise should only be done if your classroom network is separated somehow from any production networks so you do not end up handing out incorrect DHCP addresses to production clients.

Exercise 5

AUTHORIZING A DHCP SERVER

As the administrator in the DHCP management utility window, notice that the DHCP server you created has a small red down arrow. This symbol indicates the server is not authorized to hand out addresses. The status section on the right-hand side of the window should also indicate the server is not authorized.

1. Right-click the *Server* icon and click Authorize.

2. Wait a few minutes and press the refresh function key (F5). When the *Server* icon displays a small green arrow, it is active and handing out IP addresses (Figure 10.14).

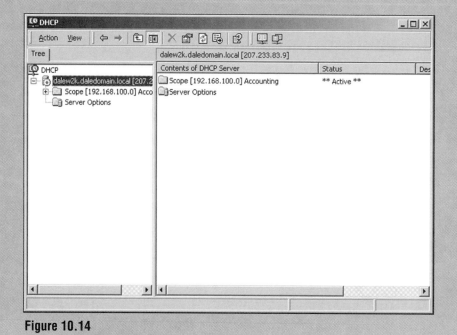

Figure 10.14

DNS

You first encountered DNS in Chapter 6, which explained the structure of the DNS **namespace** and the types of queries that are performed to resolve a name to a TCP/IP address. This chapter examines in greater detail the role of the DNS server, which is the computer actually responsible for doing the name resolution. Because the DNS namespace is not owned or controlled by a single organization, many different groups may use their own DNS server to maintain their part of the namespace tree. For example the DNS server for the company emcp.com would be concerned with maintaining information about computers in emcp.com. The portion of the namespace described and controlled by a DNS server is called a zone.

A DNS server can maintain two different kinds of zones: a forward lookup zone and a reverse lookup zone. The **forward lookup zone** resolves names to IP addresses by use of **host records** (also called **A records**). A host record contains the name and corresponding IP address of a host. When you installed Active Directory on the first computer in your domain it also became a DNS server. A forward lookup zone for the domain was created. In the following exercise you view the host records and forward lookup zone on your DNS server.

Exercise 6

VIEWING HOST RECORDS

1. Log on to the A1Computer as administrator, click Start, click Programs, click Administrative Tools, and click DNS. You see the DNS management program (Figure 10.15).

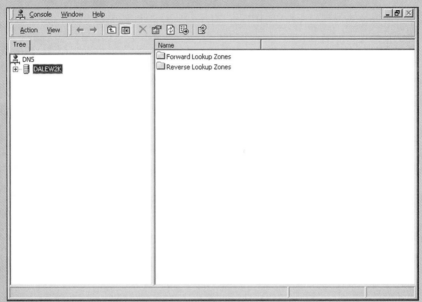

Figure 10.15

2. On the right side of the screen double-click the folder named *Forward Lookup Zones*.
3. On the right side of the screen double-click the folder named for your domain. You see a set of host records and a set of folders (Figure 10.16).

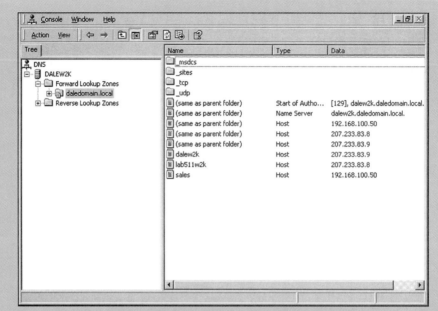

Figure 10.16

The host records have the word "Host" in their *Type* field. You should see at least one host record for your computer and one for your partner's computer. These host records should list the computer name and IP address. These records were created dynamically when your machines booted up.

Dynamic DNS

In traditional DNS systems, which are often run on UNIX-based computers, the host records have to be entered manually by an administrator. The result is that each time a computer is added or deleted, changes its name, or changes its IP address, the administrator must manually update the record on the DNS server. As more network information is added to the DNS namespace tables, manually updating the DNS server became a significant task. To solve this growing problem, a new version of DNS was proposed through the request for comments process.

Because the Internet and Internet-related protocols and software are public in nature, defining standards must be done in a cooperative manner. The **Request for Comments** (**RFC**) system is just such a process. Proposals for new protocols or standards, or proposed changes to existing standards, are submitted as requests for comments and managed by the **Internet Engineering Task Force** (**IETF**). The IETF Web page (www.ietf.org) maintains a list of all RFCs. Each RFC is numbered based on when it was submitted.

Windows 2000 takes advantage of a relatively new feature of DNS defined in April 1997 by RFC 2136. This RFC allows on-the-fly or dynamic changes to DNS records and is called **Dynamic DNS**. This dynamic update feature on DNS servers allows a Windows 2000 domain controller to register itself with the Windows 2000 DNS server when the domain controller first boots up. Dynamic updates remove much of the burden of maintaining a DNS server, but they can also pose a security risk. If the administrator must manually enter all host records, it is harder for a hacker to introduce an unauthorized DNS entry and allow messages to be sent to a rogue computer.

The netlogon service is responsible for dynamically registering a domain controller with a DNS server. If, for some reason, a domain controller fails to register itself, you can open a command window and stop and then restart the netlogon service by entering the following two commands from a command window:

```
net stop netlogon
net start netlogon
```

Windows 2000 clients and servers are able to dynamically update their own records in DNS, but down-level clients, such as Windows NT or Windows 95/98 computers, do not have this capability. A setting in DHCP allows the DHCP server to automatically register the records of down-level clients with DNS. Review Exercise 5 at the end of this chapter illustrates this process.

Another new feature of Windows 2000 DNS is something called an **Active Directory-integrated DNS zone**. Active Directory-integrated zone files are replicated along with the other information in the Active Directory database to provides a measure of fault tolerance, because any domain controller running DNS will, through Active Directory, have all the information contained in any Active Directory zone files. In the next exercise you will install DNS on the second domain controller in your domain. After DNS is installed you should see the same Active Directory-integrated zones that appear on the first controller.

Exercise 7

INSTALLING THE DNS SOFTWARE ON A SECONDARY DNS MACHINE

1. On the second domain controller, click Start, then Settings, and then Control Panel.
2. From the Control Panel double-click Add/Remove Programs.
3. Click the Add/Remove Windows Components button and wait for the wizard.
4. Click *Networking Services*.
5. Click the Details button.
6. Click the check box next to *Domain Name System* and then click the OK button.
7. Click the Next button at the wizard. DNS will be installed on the computer.
8. When prompted for the Windows 2000 Install CD, click OK.
9. Key the path for the installation files on your Windows Install CD. For example, key **e:\I386** and click OK to start copying files. The install process may take several minutes.
10. Click Finish to complete the installation of DNS.
11. Click Close on the Add/Remove Programs window and close the Control Panel. You now have DNS installed on the second domain controller.
12. Click Start, then Programs, then Administrative Tools, and then DNS.
13. On the right side of the screen open the folder named *Forward Lookup Zones* by double-clicking it and then double-click the folder named for your domain. Do you see the same information on both DNS servers? Leave this window open for the next exercise.

Start of Authority Records

Besides host records you see two other kinds of records listed in the DNS window: Start of Authority and Name Server. The name server record (see p. 407) indicates which servers contain DNS namespaces and can answer DNS queries. The **start of authority record** (**SOA**) defines which DNS server is the primary DNS server for a domain. Traditionally the primary DNS server has the only changeable or master copy of the zone file. Notice that each of your domain controllers claims to be the SOA for your domain's zone because the zone is Active Directory-integrated, so all copies of the zone file are changeable. This integration provides fault tolerance and eliminates having only a single master copy. Changes to the zone can be made from any DNS server. Traditional DNS systems have no built-in fault tolerance. Changes to the zone file must take place on the primary DNS server. Those changes can then be transferred to secondary DNS servers if any have been created. Secondary DNS servers can help answer inquiries, but changes to the zone cannot be made on a secondary DNS. If the primary DNS server goes down no changes can be made. The secondary DNS machines will not promote themselves to be a primary. In the following exercise you will view the type of zone file on your DNS servers.

Exercise 8

VIEWING THE DNS ZONE FILES

1. On the first domain controller, click Start, then Programs, then Administrative Tools, and then DNS.
2. Click the plus sign next to your computer name to expand it and click the plus sign next to *Forward Lookup Zones* to expand it.
3. Right-click your domain name in the left-hand portion of the screen and click Properties. You see the Properties dialog box in Figure 10.17.

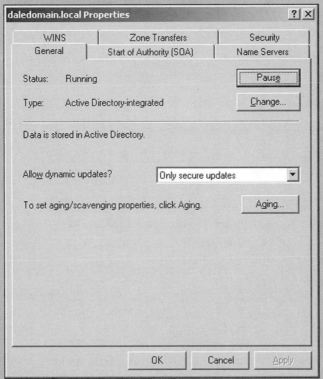

Figure 10.17

Make sure the General tab is selected. What type of zone is it? Notice also an option to turn off dynamic updates if you choose and a button to pause or start this zone on the DNS server.

4. Click the Start of Authority (SOA) tab. You see the dialog box in Figure 10.18.

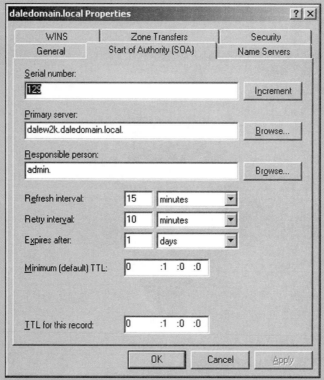

Figure 10.18

In addition to defining the primary DNS server for the domain, the SOA records provide information for transferring the zone file between primary and the secondary DNS servers when the zone file is not Active Directory-integrated. These settings are defined as follows:

- A Serial number indicates the version of the zone file. Each time the zone file is changed the serial number is incremented. If the serial number of the zone file on the primary server is higher than that on the secondary server, the secondary server knows no changes need to be copied.

- The Refresh interval indicates to the secondary servers how often to contact the primary server to check for changes. If your zone file does not change often, you may want to extend your refresh interval in order to reduce network traffic between the primary and secondary DNS servers.

- The Retry interval indicates to the secondary servers how long to wait before they try to contact the primary DNS server again if their previous attempt at contact failed.

- The Expires after interval indicates how long the secondary servers can keep the zone file if they cannot contact the primary DNS server for a **zone transfer**. For example, if the primary DNS server is down and the expires after interval is set for 2 days, a secondary server will continue to answer name resolution requests for 2 days. After that time period, the secondary DNS server will assume its information is out of date and will not resolve any more inquiries until it gets a zone transfer from the primary. If you intend to make major changes to your DNS server and want them to be propagated quickly to the secondary DNS servers, this interval should be set to a low value.

- The Minimum (default) TTL indicates to the secondary server how long it can cache the information from the primary. All DNS servers cache information they receive from other DNS servers. In this way, if a resolver (a client requesting an IP address) asks for an address that has recently been located for another resolver, the DNS server will have that address in cache and will not have to go through the process of finding it again. This feature greatly speeds up the resolution process. You would not, however, want information to be cached indefinitely in case something changes. If your zone file changes often, you will want to set this value low so the secondary DNS servers are handing out up-to-date information. If your zone does not change often, you can set this number high to reduce traffic.

5. Click OK to close the dialog box, but leave the DNS program open.

Name Server Records

In addition to the host records and the SOA record you see name server records. A **name server record** identifies a server that is capable of answering queries about a zone. All servers with an Active Directory-integrated zone will be name servers because they all have a copy of the zone file and can all answer questions about the zone. Computers with traditional primary and secondary zones will also be identified as name servers.

Exercise 9

VIEWING THE NAME SERVER RECORDS

1. With the DNS program open, click the plus sign next to your computer name to expand it.
2. Click the plus sign next to *Forward Lookup Zones* to expand it.
3. Click the plus sign next to your domain name to expand it. Do you see a name server record for both computers?
4. Close the Domain Properties window and exit the DNS program.

Reverse Lookup Zones

Up to this point we have discussed the records contained in a forward lookup zone. The forward lookup zone resolves names to addresses. That is, when given a valid name it returns the associated IP address. The second type of zone is called a **reverse lookup zone**. This type of zone allows a DNS server to resolve an IP address back to a name. Some applications use reverse lookups as a security measure to verify that a name and computer IP address are legitimate.

Reverse lookup zones follow a particular naming convention. The name is composed of the range of IP addresses in the zone, which are reversed and appended with "in-addr.arpa." For example the zone name for IP addresses in the range designated by 164.109.0.0/16 (using the CIDR addressing technique) would be 109.164.in-addr.arpa.

In the next several exercises you will create a reverse lookup zone that is not Active Directory-integrated.

Exercise 10

CREATING A PRIMARY REVERSE LOOKUP ZONE

1. On the first domain controller, click Start, then Programs, then Administrative Tools, and then DNS.
2. Click the plus sign next to your computer name to expand it.
3. Click the *Reverse Lookup Zones* folder. On the right-hand side of the screen you should see a message about how to add a new zone.
4. Right-click the *Reverse Lookup Zone* folder and click New Zone. You see the New Zone Wizard.
5. Click <u>N</u>ext at the wizard. You see the Zone Type dialog box in Figure 10.19.

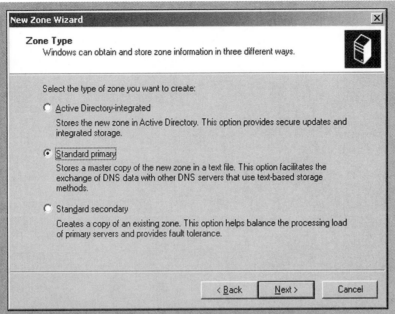

Figure 10.19

This dialog box allows you to set the type of zone. The zone can be Active Directory-integrated, Primary, or Secondary.

6. Make sure *Standard Primary* is selected and click <u>N</u>ext. You see the Reverse Lookup Zone dialog box in Figure 10.20.

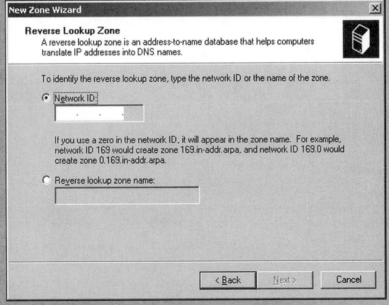

Figure 10.20

This dialog box helps you identify your zone.

7. In the Network ID text box key the first three octets of the IP address of your computer. For example, if your computer has the IP address 192.168.100.50 you would enter **192.168.100**. You will see the reverse lookup zone name automatically created (Figure10.21).

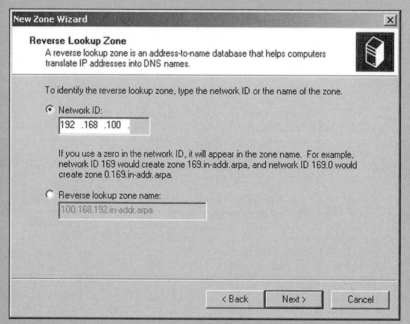

Figure 10.21

8. Click <u>N</u>ext to continue. You see a dialog box confirming that you want to create a new file with the zone name. Because this zone is not Active Directory-integrated, it will be saved as a file on the DNS server.
9. Click <u>N</u>ext to accept the default file name.
10. Click Finish to exit the wizard.

You should see the reverse lookup zone record in the right side of the DNS screen. In the next exercise you create a secondary reverse lookup zone on the second DNS server in your domain.

CREATING A SECONDARY REVERSE LOOKUP ZONE

This exercise should be done on the second domain controller in your domain.

1. On the second domain controller click Start, then Programs, then Administrative Tools, and then DNS.
2. In the DNS window, click the plus sign next to your computer name to expand it.
3. Click the plus sign next to *Reverse Lookup Zones*. On the right-hand side of the screen you should see a message about how to add a new zone.
4. Right-click the *Reverse Lookup Zones* folder and click New Zone.
5. Click Next at the wizard.
6. Click *Standard Secondary* and then click Next.
7. Make sure the Network ID text box is selected, key in the first three octets of your IP address, and then click Next. You will be asked to enter the IP address of the primary DNS server.
8. Key the IP address of the first domain controller in the domain (the server with the primary DNS zone) and click the Add button (Figure 10.22).

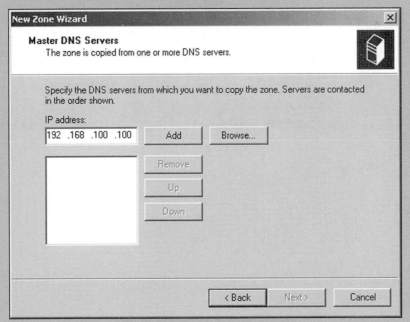

Figure 10.22

Forward lookup zones contain host records. Host records allow a resolver to request an IP address based on a name. Reverse lookup zones contain records called **pointer (PTR) records**. These records are similar to the host records found in the forward lookup zones in that they correlate a name and an address, but they allow a resolver to request a name based on having an address. In other words, the resolver may ask for the IP address of the domain *server1.emcp.net* and the DNS server, using the reverse lookup zone PTR record, would supply the address. In the next exercise you will create a PTR record for your machine.

Exercise 12

CREATE A NEW PTR RECORD IN THE PRIMARY REVERSE LOOKUP ZONE

1. On the computer that has the primary reverse lookup zone, click Start, Programs, Administrative Tools, and DNS.
2. Click the plus sign next to your computer name to expand it.
3. Click the plus sign next to *Reverse Lookup Zones* to expand it.
4. Click the plus sign next to your reverse lookup zone (located under the *Reverse Lookup Zones* folder) to expand it.
5. Right-click your reverse lookup zone and click New Pointer. You see the New Resource Record dialog box in Figure 10.23.

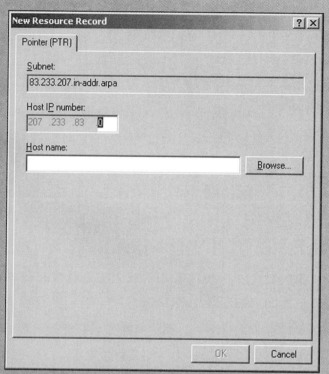

Figure 10.23

This dialog box allows you to specify the IP address and the associated host name.

6. For the Host IP number, fill in the last octet of your computer number. For example, if your computer has the IP address of 192.168.100.50 you would enter **50**.
7. Key your machine's fully qualified computer name in the Host name text box (for example **a1computer.adomain.local**) and click OK.
8. Click your reverse lookup zone. In the right-hand side of the screen you should see your pointer record (Figure 10.24).

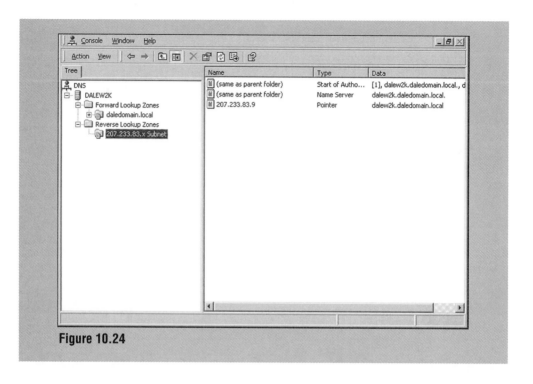

Figure 10.24

Transfer Reverse Lookup Zone from Primary to Secondary DNS Server

Now that you have configured both a standard primary and secondary zone, you can initiate a transfer of the zone file from the primary to the secondary. After the zone transfer, the secondary zone on the second domain controller will have a copy of the pointer record you created on the primary server. Remember, these zones are not Active Directory-integrated, so zone transfers do not happen automatically. Instead they must be configured. In the following exercise you will first look at the secondary reverse lookup zone to see that the pointer record created in the previous exercise does not exist.

Exercise 13

VIEWING SECONDARY DNS SERVER REVERSE LOOKUP ZONE

1. On the computer that has the secondary reverse lookup zone, click Start, Programs, Administrative Tools, and DNS.
2. Click the plus sign next to your computer name to expand it.
3. Click the plus sign next to *Reverse Lookup Zones* to expand it.
4. Double-click the reverse lookup zone to open it.
5. Look at the right-hand side of the screen. You should not see any pointer records.

In the next exercise you set up a zone transfer. First you must tell the primary server that the secondary server is going to be a name server, responsible for the zone, and then configure settings for the actual transfer process.

Exercise 14

CONFIGURING THE ZONE TRANSFER

1. If necessary, start the DNS program on the computer with the primary DNS zone.
2. Right-click your reverse lookup zone and click Properties.
3. Click the Name Servers tab. You see the Name Servers dialog box (Figure 10.25).

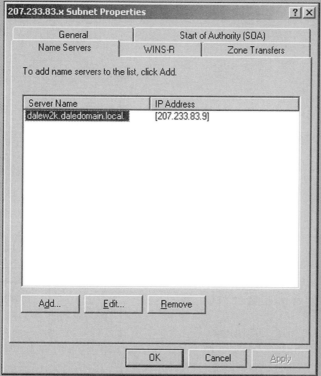

Figure 10.25

You should see only the first domain controllers name and IP address.

4. Click the Add button. You see the New Resource dialog box.

5. Key in the second domain controller's fully qualified computer name (the domain controller with the secondary DNS zone). For example, **a2computer.adomain.local**.
6. Click in the I<u>P</u> Address text box, key the IP address of the secondary DNS server, and click the A<u>d</u>d button.
7. Click the OK button. You should see both primary and secondary DNS servers listed.
8. Click the Zone Transfers tab. You see the Zone Transfers dialog box in Figure 10.26.

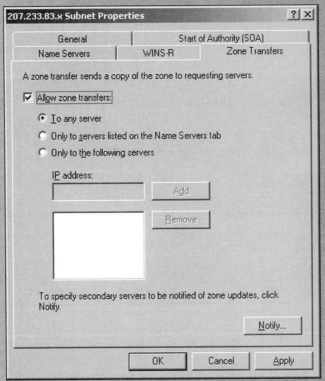

Figure 10.26

9. Click *Only to servers listed on the Name Servers tab* and click OK. This command will send zone updates only to the selected computers.
10. On the secondary DNS server, open the DNS program and view the *Reverse Lookup Zone* folder. You should see the PTR record.

Windows Internet Naming Service

Windows Internet Naming Service (**WINS**) is a legacy service from the Windows NT days. WINS is similar to DNS in that it does name resolution, but instead of resolving host names to IP addresses it resolves NetBIOS names to IP addresses. Microsoft networking products started out based on a protocol called NetBIOS. Instead of an IP address, each computer running this protocol had to have a unique NetBIOS name that it used to communicate over the network. The NetBIOS namespace is flat, so, unlike the DNS namespace, it has no branches. Therefore, prior to Windows 2000, computers had a NetBIOS name such as A2computer instead of a fully qualified domain name such as A2computer.A2domain.local. DNS resolves the fully qualified domain names of Windows 2000 computers, but legacy clients and servers may still only have a NetBIOS name. WINS is the service used to resolve NetBIOS names to TCP/IP addresses. If all of your machines are Windows 2000 systems using fully qualified domain names, you will not need to use WINS because name resolution can be done with DNS.

In order for WINS name resolution to occur, WINS must be installed on a server and the client computers must be WINS clients. The name resolution sequence is as follows:

1. On bootup, WINS client A1Computer sends a message to the WINS server that contains its name and IP address. The message from the client is a request to register its name and address with the WINS server.

2. The WINS server looks in its database to make sure that no other computer is using the name A1Computer. If no other computer is using the name, the WINS server will then store A1Computer's name and address in its database. If another machine is using the name, the WINS server will reject the request of the computer to use the name and the computer will need to be configured with a different name in order to talk on the network.

> Actually the WINS server registers services running on the client machine and not individual computers. For example, if the client computer is running both the workstation service and the browser service, the WINS database for that computer would have two entries.

3. In order for A2Computer to communicate with A1Computer, the first computer needs the IP address for A1Computer. A2Computer contacts the WINS server to find the IP address for A1Computer.

4. The WINS server looks in its database and finds the IP address for A1Computer, which it provides to A2Computer.

5. When A1Computer shuts down, it sends a message to the WINS server indicating that it will not be using the IP address or the name *A1Computer* assigned to it in the WINS database.

6. The WINS server marks the entry for A1Computer in its database as released. If another computer now tries to boot up with the name A1Computer, it will be allowed to use the name.

In order to have a WINS server on your network, you must load the WINS service. Windows 2000 Server does not have WINS loaded by default. After installation, very little maintenance of the service is required because client computers update the WINS database automatically. In order to make a client a WINS client, you simply have to provide the machine with a WINS server address, which can be done manually or through a DHCP server that provides the address of a WINS server to the client computer.

Even though WINS may no longer be necessary on networks comprised of only Windows 2000 computers, it can still be important when down-level clients are involved. It not only cuts down on network traffic, but in situations where your network is spread out over several subnets, some processes may not function without a WINS server.

CHAPTER summary

➤ TCP/IP is the new default protocol used in Windows 2000. It is a powerful protocol that allows your Windows 2000 machines to communicate with many other systems. However, it requires more configuration than past versions of Windows that ran NetBEUI. The key pieces of information that are required for a machine to communicate on a TCP/IP network are the IP address and subnet mask. Addresses are based on the binary numbering system but are written in dotted decimal format to make them easier to deal with. Subnet masks are needed to define which part of the address is the network portion and which portion is the unique host portion. The subnet mask is also used to divide class-based networks into smaller pieces. Several utilities such as PING and ipconfig help in viewing and testing your TCP/IP configuration.

➤ Dynamic addressing cuts down on the administrative work required to maintain a TCP/IP network. It allows IP addresses and other necessary information to be assigned automatically to clients as they boot up. It also allows a network to function with fewer IP addresses because machines that are not being used will not be assigned addresses. DHCP is the protocol that handles dynamic addressing on a Windows 2000 network.

➤ DNS is the service that does host name resolution on a Windows 2000 network. The DNS server holds zone files that contain the names and addresses of computers within that zone. Active Directory-integrated zones are automatically replicated to all domain controllers in the domain, while standard zones exist only on the server where they were created. A standard secondary zone can receive a zone transfer from a standard primary zone and act as its backup. Several types of records are maintained, including host, start of authority (SOA), name server, and pointer (PTR) records. Windows 2000 networks take advantage of a new feature called Dynamic DNS that allows machines to register themselves with the DNS server instead of having to be entered manually by an administrator.

➤ Where DNS does name resolution for host type names, WINS does name resolution for NetBIOS names. WINS is a proprietary Microsoft protocol and is being phased out in favor of the industry standard DNS. WINS is not installed by default on a Windows 2000 server because it is not necessary if no down-level clients are involved.

CHAPTER terms

A record	A DNS record that include the host name and the associated IP address; Also called host records.
Active Directory-integrated DNS zone	The inclusion of DNS records of a DNS server in Active Directory. DNS records are automatically replicated to other domain controllers, which provides a measure of security to DNS.
Bit	A single binary digit, either zero or one.
Byte	A group of eight bits; also called an octet.
CIDR	Classless interdomain routing: A method of referring to subnet masks by appending a slash and a number indicating the number of bits designated for the network to an IP address.
DHCP	Dynamic Host Configuration Protocol: A protocol used to automatically supply IP addresses to network clients.
DHCPACK	An acknowledgment sent from a DHCP server to a client indicating that its request for an IP address has been granted.
DHCPDISCOVER	A broadcast message sent by a client to any DHCP server to request an IP address.
DHCPOFFER	A message sent from a DHCP server to a client requesting an IP address.
DHCPREQUEST	A request for an IP address sent from a client to a specific DHCP server.
Dynamic DNS	A method whereby domain controllers can register their IP addresses in DNS and not require the administrator to perform this task.
Dynamic IP	An IP address automatically assigned to a device by a DHCP server.
Forward lookup zone	A DNS namespace used to resolve IP addresses from domain names.
Host record	A DNS record that includes the host name and the associated IP address; also called an A record.
IETF	Internet Engineering Task Force: The multinational organization that maintains RFCs and decides on the Internet standards and protocols.
InterNIC	A multinational committee organized to issue IP addresses.
IP address leasing	The process whereby a client reserves an IP address for a specified amount of time.

Name server record	A DNS record that indicates which servers contain DNS namespaces and can answer DNS queries.
Namespace	A set of related DNS records within a DNS server.
NetBEUI	Proprietary Microsoft networking protocol used in early versions of Windows.
NetBIOS	A method of identifying computers on a network with the NetBEUI protocol.
Octet	A group of eight bits; also called a byte.
OSPF	A common routing protocol.
PING	Packet Internet Grouper: A TCP/IP utility that sends a message to a device with an IP address and waits for a reply.
PTR record	Pointer record: A DNS record used to find a computer name when given an IP address.
Reverse lookup zone	A DNS namespace used to resolve domain names to IP addresses.
RFC	Request for comments: A method of creating and making changes to Internet standards.
SOA record	Start of Authority record: A DNS record that defines which DNS server is the primary DNS server for a domain.
Static IP	An IP address manually assigned to a device.
Subnet mask	A number that, when combined with an IP address, returns part of the address not masked.
WINS	Windows Internet Naming Service: A program that, when given a NetBIOS computer name, returns an IP address; only used when using NetBIOS.
Zone transfer	Moving a set of DNS records from one DNS server to another, which is not necessary when the DNS servers are Active Directory-integrated because Active Directory automatically reproduces DNS information.

CONCEPTS review

Multiple Choice

1. The type of record that resolves IP addresses to names is a:
   a. Name server record.
   b. Host record.
   c. Pointer record.
   d. Start of authority record.
   e. None of the above.

2. An address in the format of 192.168.100.10 is in:
   a. Hexadecimal notation.
   b. Dotted decimal notation.
   c. Binary notation.
   d. Quad notation.
   e. None of the above.

3. What piece(s) of information are necessary for a machine to communicate on a local TCP/IP network?
   a. TCP/IP address
   b. Gateway address
   c. Subnet mask
   d. Both a and c
   e. a, b, and c

4. The type of record that does a reverse lookup is a:
   a. Name server record.
   b. Host record.
   c. Pointer record.
   d. Start of authority record.
   e. None of the above.

5. A group of addresses that can be given out by a DHCP server is called a:
   a. Scope.
   b. Zone.
   c. Subnet.
   d. Domain.
   e. None of the above.

6. The name emcp.net would most likely be resolved to an address by a:
   a. DHCP server.
   b. WINS server.
   c. Domain controller.
   d. DNS server.
   e. None of the above.

7. Which of the following is the proper order for the DHCP process?
   a. DHCPDISCOVER, DHCPOFFER, DHCPREQUEST, DHCPACK
   b. DHCPREQUEST, DHCPDISCOVER, DHCPOFFER, DHCPACK
   c. DHCPDISCOVER, DHCPREQUEST, DHCPOFFER, DHCPACK
   d. DHCPREQUEST, DHCPACK, DHCPOFFER, DHCPDISCOVER
   e. None of the above

8. Which of the following can be assigned by a DHCP server?
   a. TCP/IP address
   b. WINS server address
   c. DNS server address
   d. Both a and c
   e. All of the above

9. The total amount of time an address will be assigned to a client in DHCP is called the:
   a. Duration time.
   b. Rebinding time.
   c. Capture time.
   d. Renewal time.
   e. None of the above.

10. A TCP/IP address on a client that does not change and is manually keyed in is called a:
    a. Fixed address.
    b. Dynamic address.
    c. Permanent address.
    d. Stationary address.
    e. None of the above.

11. Which of the following would be the proper name of a reverse lookup zone for a class C network 192.168.100.XXX?
    a. 100.168.192.in.addr.arpa
    b. 192.168.100.in.addr.arpa
    c. 100.168.192.in-addr.arpa
    d. 192.168.100.in-addr.arpa
    e. None of the above

12. Which of the following zone type(s) is authoritative for the zone?
    a. Standard primary forward lookup
    b. Standard primary reverse lookup
    c. Active Directory-integrated
    d. Both a and c
    e. a, b, and Cc

13. The process of moving records from a primary standard zone to a secondary standard zone is called:
    a. Zone synchronization.
    b. Zone replication.
    c. Zone splitting.
    d. Zone lookup.
    e. None of the above.

14. A network address with the subnet mask of 255.255.0.0 would be a:
    a. Class A.
    b. Class B.
    c. Class C.
    d. Class D.
    e. Class E.

15. Which of the following clients are capable of dynamically registering themselves with the DNS server?
    a. Windows 2000 Professional machines
    b. Windows NT 4.0 workstations
    c. Windows 98 machines
    d. Windows NT 4.0 servers
    e. All of the above

Short Answer

1. A multicast address is which class of addresses?
2. What would the subnet mask look like in dotted decimal notation for an address of 192.168.100.50/16?
3. You have two DNS servers built on domain controllers that both claim to be the SOA for a zone. What type of zone is it?
4. What features must a DHCP server have to be authorized in Windows 2000?

LAB exercises

Exercise 1 – Installing a WINS Server

In this exercise you will install the WINS server process on your A2Computer.

1. Log on to A2Computer as administrator.
2. Click Start, Settings, Control Panel.
3. Double-click Add/Remove Programs.
4. Click the Add/Remove Windows Components button.
5. When the Windows Components Wizard appears, click to highlight the words *Networking Services* (do not click the check box) and click Details.
6. Click to place a check mark in front of *Windows Internet Naming Service* and click OK.
7. Click <u>N</u>ext at the Windows Components Wizard.
8. When you are requested to insert the CD, click OK.
9. Key in the path of your source files and click OK.
10. Click Finish to complete the installation.
11. Close the Add/Remove Program window and the Control Panel.

Exercise 2 – Creating a WINS Client

In this exercise you will set up your A1Computer to be a WINS client of your A2Computer.

1. Log on to A1Computer as administrator.
2. Right-click *My Network Places* and click Properties.
3. Right-click *Local Area Connection* and click Properties.
4. Click the words *Internet Protocol* to highlight. (Do not click the check box.)
5. Click the Properties button and click Advanced.
6. Click the WINS tab and click the A<u>d</u>d button.
7. Key in the address of your A2Computer that hosts the WINS server and then click A<u>d</u>d.
8. Click OK to leave the Advanced TCP/IP Settings dialog box.
9. Click OK to leave Internet Protocol (TCP/IP) Properties dialog box.
10. Click OK to leave the Local Area Connection Properties dialog box.
11. Close the Network and Dial-up Connections window.
12. Reboot your machine.

Exercise 3 – Viewing the Installed WINS Server

In this exercise you will open up the WINS database on your server and view the records of the machines that have registered with your server.

1. Log on as administrator and click Start, Administrative Tools, and WINS.
2. Double-click the name of your server to open it.
3. Click the *Active Registrations* folder to open it.
4. Click View on the menu bar and then click Find by Owner Results.
5. Make sure *This owner* is selected and your server name is highlighted.
6. Click Find Now. You should see records that identify services offered by A1Computer and its associated IP address.

Exercise 4 – Using Parameters on ipconfig

1. Start a command line window.
2. Key **ipconfig**.
3. Write down the information supplied.
4. In the command window key **ipconfig /all**. What additional information do you see?

Exercise 5 – Setting DHCP to Register Down-Level Clients with DNS

1. Log on to your machine as administrator and click Start, Programs, Administrative Tools, and DHCP.
2. Right-click the name of your server and click Properties.
3. Click the DNS tab.
4. Click *Enable Updates for DNS clients that do not support Dynamic updates* and click OK.

PROBLEM SOLVING exercises

1. You have a class C network of 200.200.200.XXX. You want to divide the network into 14 subnets. What would be the subnet mask?
2. Convert the number 124 to binary.
3. You are using DHCP to assign TCP/IP information to your clients. You have installed a new DNS server and you want all the clients to be using the new DNS server within three days so you can take the old DNS server offline. What should you do to facilitate this process?
4. You build a Windows 2000 DHCP server in your domain and create a scope, but your clients are not receiving addresses. What must be done?
5. What command can you use to ensure a connection between two computers running TCP/IP?

ACTIVE DIRECTORY 11

Performance Objectives

After completing this chapter you will be able to:

- Discuss the purpose of Active Directory
- Discuss the operation of Active Directory and identify the various parts of an Active Directory database
- Discuss the relationship between DNS and Active Directory
- Identify and relate DNS records to an Active Directory network
- Outline and configure Active Directory replication
- Discuss the roles of flexible single master operations (FSMO)
- Move FSMO roles between domain controllers
- Move Active Directory files
- Configure domain site replication
- Discuss network design and Active Directory

Introduction

Active Directory is the central piece to a Windows 2000 network and one of Microsoft's most complex and potentially far-reaching pieces of technology. Active Directory is new to Windows 2000 and is not found in previous versions of Windows NT Server. The purpose of Active Directory is to provide a framework for accessing and using network resources. Network information is stored in the Active Directory database and automatically replicated across the network. Windows 2000 uses this database to locate resources and validate users. Because Active Directory is so central to a Windows 2000 network, its capabilities and limitations must be considered as part of the initial network design.

This chapter introduces the basic concepts behind Active Directory, illustrates how Active Directory is used in the network design phase, outlines the Active Directory database replication process, and teaches you how to configure and manage Active Directory.

Perspectives on Active Directory

The three ways to approach Active Directory are from a network design perspective, from a distributed database perspective, and from an operational perspective.

Network Design Perspective

The nature of Active Directory will affect how a network is logically and physically designed. Because Active Directory is used to find network resources and validate network users, the number of domains, their relationship with each other, and the number and location of domain controllers will be dictated by how Active Directory works. Before designing a network, understanding Active Directory is imperative.

Distributed Database Perspective

Active Directory is a database that can hold information about objects and is automatically replicated between domain controllers and network sites. The objects contained in Active Directory are used by various services in Windows 2000. Although software developers are the only ones likely to modify the structure of the Active Directory database, it is important to understand what elements make up an Active Directory database.

Operational Perspective

Active Directory is a network service that must be installed on every domain controller. Running and managing Active Directory includes understanding how Active Directory information is replicated across the network, how information within the Active Directory database is located, and how to troubleshoot problems.

Because Active Directory is such a large topic, this chapter will focus primarily on the third perspective: installing, configuring, and managing Active Directory on a network.

Directories and Directory Services

Even though Active Directory is referred to as a database, it is more accurately described as a directory. A **directory** is a structured collection of information stored in a hierarchical format. The Windows file system is an example of a directory because it stores information using folders and files where a folder can contain other folders and files. For example, many people design their own Windows filing system in a hierarchical format by creating folders named *Home* and *Work* and, under each folder, creating subfolders named *Personal*, *Family*, and *Letters* (under *Home*), and *Projects*, *Saved E-mail*, and *Memos* (under *Work*). In a hierarchical system, information is organized by placing one object inside another object (Figure 11.1).

FIGURE **11.1** *Folder Structure*

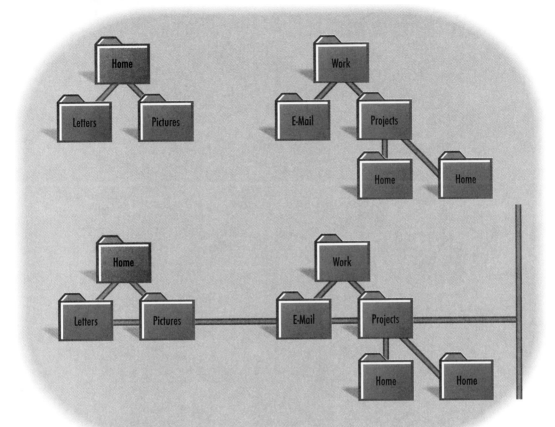

If a directory is a hierarchical set of data, a **directory service** is a way to locate and retrieve the data. In the case of Windows, a program called Explorer presents the hierarchical data as a set of folder icons. Information is located by clicking icons to display the contents of folders (Figure 11.2).

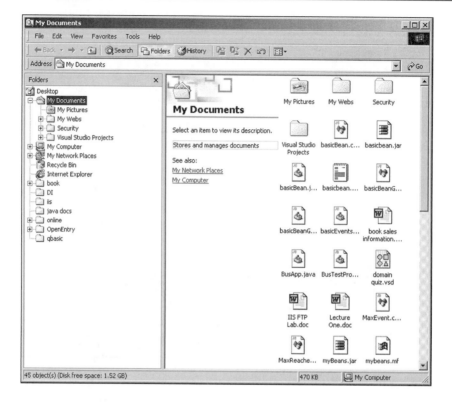

The term *directory service* is often used to refer to both the data and the services to access the data. Many different directory services are available, most of which are found on the Internet. An example would be one of the people-finder directories located on many Internet search sites. Other directory services, such as Novell NDS and Microsoft Active Directory, are integrated with a network operating system.

Active Directory Structure and Design

Active Directory is a directory service that contains **objects**. These objects include items such as organizational units, printers, users, and domain controllers. Each object has a unique identity and is assigned a set of attributes. Object attributes (also called properties) consist of an attribute type and an attribute value. For example, with a user object, an attribute type would be "e-mail" and the attribute value would be somename@emcp.com. These attributes are attached to the object and stored in Active Directory.

Namespace

The two general types of objects found in Active Directory include basic objects, like user accounts, and computer and container objects. Container objects have attributes, just like any other object, but are used to hold objects and do not represent anything on the network. These container objects can hold noncontainer objects like user accounts (called leaf objects) as well as other containers.

Active Directory organizes objects into namespaces. A **namespace** is a structure within which information can be resolved. For example, a telephone book can be considered a namespace because it contains information (last names and telephone numbers) structured in a way that allows one piece of data to be used to locate another piece of data (finding a name in an alphabetized list and then finding the associated telephone number). If you have the last name you can search the namespace to find a telephone number. This process is called resolving. (We don't say we are "resolving a telephone number," but it means the same as "looking up a telephone number.")

The namespace used by Active Directory consists of domains, trees, and forests.

Domain   A **domain** is a security, replication, and resource boundary identified by a domain name. Each computer on a network will act as part of the domain, either as a domain controller, a member server participating in the domain, or a client connecting to the domain. Domains can be confined to a single server or can span multiple servers. A **domain controller** is a computer hosting a domain and running Active Directory. A domain controller can belong to only one domain.

Tree   A **tree** is a set of domains in a hierarchical relationship. They share a contiguous DNS namespace. One domain is identified as the root and other domains extend from the root. For example, a domain named accounting.emcp.com might be derived from the root domain named emcp.com. Another domain named eastcoast.accounting.emcp.com would be further down the tree.

Forest   A **forest** is a collection of trees that share a common Active Directory. Although most companies only have a single domain tree in their Active Directory forest, additional trees can be added. Different trees can have a completely different DNS namespace and domain names (such as emcp.com and emcp.local) but are still considered to be in the same forest.

Trusts

One of the major differences in Windows 2000 from Windows NT is how trusts are treated. (A **trust** is a relationship between domains whereby users authenticated in one domain are granted login rights in the second domain.) Take a situation that has two domains: DomainA and DomainB. Because a domain is a replication boundary, a user account created in DomainA will be replicated to all domain controllers in DomainA, thus allowing the user to sit down at a client machine and log on to DomainA. However, because DomainB is its own replication boundary, the user account created in DomainA would not replicate to domain controllers in DomainB. With Windows NT, by default a user from DomainA could not sit down on a client machine in DomainB and log on because no trust relationship has been established between the two domains. The administrator could build relationships, but the trusts were one way. Therefore, if you wanted a user from DomainA to be able to log on to DomainB you would build one trust, and if you wanted a user from DomainB to be able to log on to DomainA you would have to build a second trust. Trusts in Windows NT were also not transitive. If three domains were configured so that DomainA trusted DomainB and DomainB trusted DomainC, DomainA would not trust DomainC by default. A separate trust would have to be built directly between DomainA and DomainC as illustrated in Figure 11.3.

FIGURE **11.3** *How Trusts Look with Three Domains in Windows NT 4*

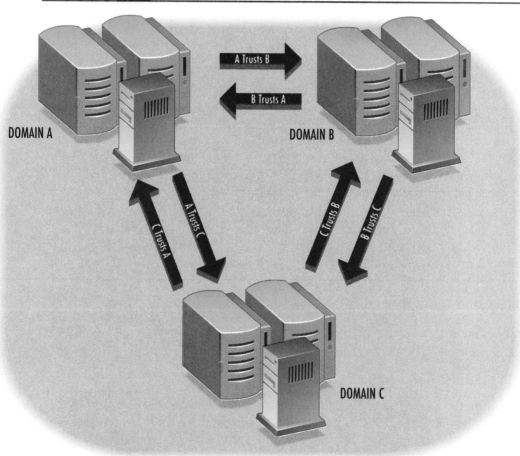

As you can see from Figure 11.3, trusts could quickly become complicated as the number of domains grew when every domain had to have a direct trust to every other domain. Windows 2000 changed this arrangement by automatically creating two-way transitive trusts between domains within a forest. Transitive means that if A trusts B and B trusts C, then A will trust C. For example, you have three domains arranged as parent, child, and grandchild. Even though a user created in the parent domain would only exist on the domain controllers in the parent domain, the user could go to a machine in the grandchild domain and log on because the grandchild domain would trust the parent domain to validate the user's login and password. This arrangement has greatly reduced the administrative overhead involved in creating and maintaining trusts (Figure 11.4).

F I G U R E **11.4** *How Trusts Look with Windows 2000 Trees and Forest*

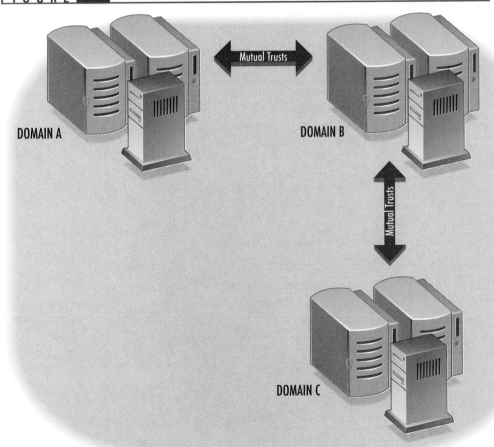

DOMAIN A

Mutual Trusts

DOMAIN B

Mutual Trusts

DOMAIN C

Trust relationships are not necessary within a domain, only between domains.

The tool used to view and manage trusts is called Active Directory Domains and Trusts. In the following exercises you will explore Active Directory Domains and Trusts.

Exercise 1

ACTIVE DIRECTORY DOMAINS AND TRUSTS

1. Click Start, Programs, Administrative Tools, and Active Directory Domains and Trusts. You see the window shown in Figure 11.5.

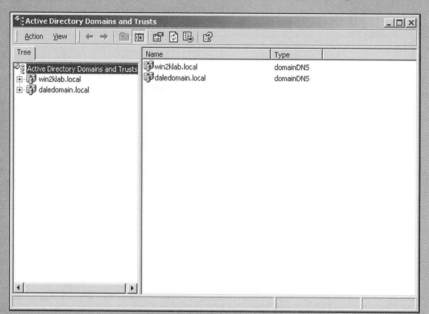

Figure 11.5

The domains within the current Active Directory forest are listed. Separate domain trees are listed individually. Clicking a domain tree displays any subdomains under the tree.

2. Right-click your current domain and click Properties. You see the domain Properties dialog box in Figure 11.6.

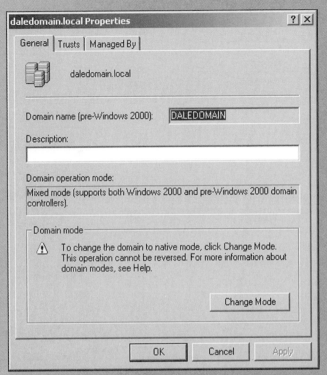

Figure 11.6

This dialog box has three tabs, General, Trusts, and Managed By. The General tab contains options to change the domain mode from mixed to native. If the network only has Windows 2000 domain controllers you should change the mode to native.

3. Click the Trusts tab. You see the Trusts dialog box in Figure 11.7.

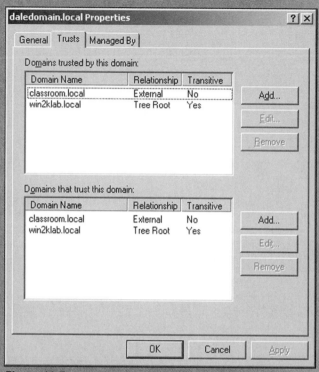

Figure 11.7

This dialog box displays the trust relationships between the current domain and other domains. If other domains have been created within your forest, they will be displayed. Windows 2000 automatically creates two-way transitive trust relationships between domains in the same tree.

4. Click the Managed By tab. It displays information about the user who is responsible for the domain. This information is saved in Active Directory and associated with the particular domain. By default this tab is blank.
5. Click the Change button, click the administrator account, and then click OK. (You could have also entered a specific user account name.)
6. Click OK to accept the changes.

Server Roles

Within a domain, servers are divided into two major groups: member servers and domain controllers. A **member server** is a computer that joins a domain but does not contain a copy of the Active Directory database. Therefore, it does not play a part in many activities, such as validating users or replicating group policies. Typically you would make a server such as a mail server or SQL server a member server. By being a member server, the server would not have to deal with the overhead of Active Directory and the server resources could be concentrated on handling mail or SQL queries.

Domain Controllers   A domain controller is a server hosting Active Directory and a domain. A single domain controller can only host one domain. Even though all domain controllers in a domain are alike in that they all hold a complete and changeable copy of Active Directory, some of the domain controllers will also hold specialized roles, such as being a **global catalog server** or an operations master.

Global Catalog Servers   This domain controller holds the **global catalog** (**GC**). By default the GC will be held by the first domain controller in the forest. A GC is maintained to speed up cross-domain searching. In a forest with a single domain, the GC is underutilized because in order to find an object in its domain a client simply needs to query a domain controller in its domain. Because all domain controllers within a domain know about all objects in the domain, the domain controller is able to answer the client's question. The GC becomes much more meaningful in a forest containing several domains, because the GC contains the names and a limited set of attributes for all objects in the forest. If a client in DomainA wants information about an object in DomainB, the domain controllers in DomainA will not know about the object. Therefore, the query is sent to the global catalog server instead. The global catalog server knows enough about each domain in the forest to tell the client where the object can be located.

By default each domain has only one global catalog server in a domain. However, additional GCs can be built. It is a good idea to have a backup GC in the domain. It may also be advantageous to have a GC located in remote sites so that clients do not have to traverse slow network links to do a global catalog lookup. Keep in mind however, that GCs replicate with other global catalog servers in the forest, so creating additional global catalog servers will increase network traffic.

Global catalog servers know about every global group in every domain in the forest, but they do not keep track of the membership of those global groups. Global catalog servers also know about every universal group in every domain in the forest. The difference is that with universal groups, the GCs also keep track of every *member* in the universal group. If you place users directly in universal groups, every time a user is added, deleted, or changed, all the global catalog servers will need to replicate, causing network traffic. A better strategy is to place global groups inside the universal groups. In that way the global catalog servers will not have to replicate every time a user changes, but instead only when a global group is added or deleted.

The following exercise illustrates how to view the GC in your domain and create a backup GC on another server. You will use a tool called Active Directory Sites and Services for this task.

Exercise 2

VIEWING AND BACKING UP THE GLOBAL CATALOG

1. On both domain controllers, click Start, Programs, Administrative Tools, and Active Directory Sites and Services. This program displays information about the sites maintained by Active Directory.
2. Click the plus sign next to the *Sites* folder to expand it.
3. Click the plus sign next to *Default-First-Site-Name* to expand it. You see a folder named *Servers*.
4. Double-click the *Servers* folder to display the servers in the default site (Figure 11.8).

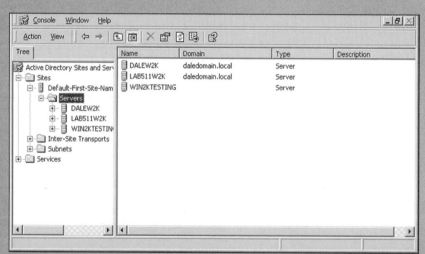

Figure 11.8

5. Click the plus sign next to your computer name to expand it. You see an object named *NTDS Settings*.
6. Right-click *NTDS Settings* and click Properties. You see the dialog box in Figure 11.9.

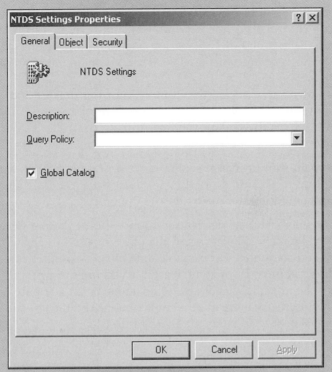

Figure 11.9

A checkbox indicates whether the selected computer has a global catalog. Which domain controller is currently the global catalog server?

7. On the computer that is not currently acting as a global catalog server, put a check mark in the <u>G</u>lobal Catalog box and click OK. This command replicates the global catalog to the selected computer.

Flexible Single Master Operations

Besides maintaining the global catalog, several other special roles are held by specific domain controllers in the forest. These roles are called **flexible single master operations** (**FSMOs**), or operations masters.

Operations master servers are domain controllers that play special roles on the network. Although the Active Directory database is automatically replicated to network domain controllers, some network tasks must reside on specific servers. These tasks, also called roles or FSMOs, are hosted by operations master servers. Of these five roles, three are associated with each domain, and two are associated with the entire forest.

The forest FSMO services are the **domain naming master** and the **schema master**. No matter how many trees or domains a forest contains, it will have only one of each of the roles. By default the first domain controller in the forest will host these roles.

- The domain naming master service controls adding and removing domains from a forest. Because every domain must have a unique identity, the domain-naming master must add the domain.

- The schema master service is used to modify the **Active Directory schema**. The schema consists of the patterns used to create network objects and attributes. For example, one of the attributes of users is their Web page address. If for some reason it was important to keep track of a user's shoe size, it would have to be added as an attribute of the object Users. Only the schema master could change the forest-wide schema allowing shoe size to be an attribute of users.

The three FSMO roles necessary for the operation of a domain are the PDC emulator, the relative ID master (RID), and the infrastructure master. Each of these roles is held by one computer within a domain.

- The **PDC emulator** role is assigned to the first domain controller in a domain. In a mixed mode this role is extremely important because Windows NT 4 backup domain controllers need a primary domain controller in order to function. They look to the PDC emulator to receive updates to their SAM databases that contain information about users and groups within the domain. Once a domain is changed to native mode, the PDC emulator is no longer needed to update NT 4 BDCs, but it still plays an important role. Once a domain is converted to native mode, multimaster replication allows changes to be made on any domain controller in the domain. The problem with this arrangement is if a user changes his or her password on one domain controller and attempts to log on to a second domain controller before the password has been replicated to that second domain controller, the user is rejected. In order to avoid this problem the PDC emulator is notified immediately if a password has been changed on any domain controller. Therefore, in the preceding example the second domain controller may not have the updated password for the user, but it could query the PDC emulator to retrieve the new user password.

- The **RID master** assigns information used to create the security ID (SID) that is assigned to security objects such as users and computers. The SID of an object is created by combining the SID of the domain within which the object is created and a relative ID number. The resulting SID uniquely identifies the object. In order to avoid duplicate SIDs, a designated domain controller is contacted by other domain controllers to get a set of RID values. By default the RID master is located on the first domain controller in the domain so it will be on the same machine as the PDC emulator. In mixed mode it is important to keep these two roles on the same machine.

- The **infrastructure master** role coordinates and replicates group membership changes. This task is assigned to a single domain controller to speed up changes to group membership and assignment of rights to network resources.

These five FSMO roles must be assigned to a specific domain controller. By default, the first server promoted to a domain controller within a forest is assigned all five roles (in a mixed mode network). In subsequent domains that are part of the forest, the first domain controller promoted within the domain is assigned the three domain roles.

FSMO roles are important because they will have an impact on the survival of a network. For example, if the forest-level server that holds the domain naming master role and the schema master role stops working, the rest of the network will continue to function, except you will not be able to change the Active Directory schema and will not be able to add new domains to the network. If the domain-level FSMO RID master stops working, other domain controllers in the domain can continue to assign SIDs to new users and computers, but when the local pool of RID values runs out, the domain controller cannot get a new set from the RID master. For these reasons it is a good idea to know which server is holding one of these FSMO roles and be able to transfer the role to another server.

Exercise 3

VIEWING AND CHANGING DOMAIN FSMO ROLES

In this exercise you will move the RID master role from the first domain controller to the second domain controller. First you will need to make a connection to your domain controller to allow the transfer.

1. On A2Computer (the second computer in your domain) open the Active Directory Users and Computers MMC.
2. Right-click the top icon in the left window that says *Active Directory Users and Computers* and click Operations Masters.
3. Click the RID tab. You see the dialog box in Figure 11.10.

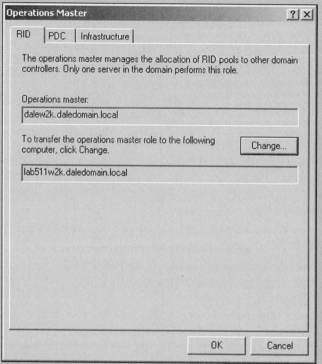

The operations master manages the allocation of RID pools to other domain controllers. Only one server in the domain performs this role.

Operations master:

dalew2k.daledomain.local

To transfer the operations master role to the following computer, click Change.

Change...

lab511w2k.daledomain.local

OK   Cancel

Figure 11.10

4. Make sure the RID tab is chosen and that the first domain controller is listed as the current RID master and the second domain controller is listed as the receiving RID master. Click the Change button to move the RID master role.

5. Click Yes when you are asked to verify that you want to move the role.

6. Click OK at the successful completion message box. You have now successfully transferred the role.

7. Click the PDC and Infrastructure tabs to view the operations master for each of those roles. Do not move these roles. When done, click OK to close this dialog box.

In the preceding exercises you use the GUI tools to transfer FSMO roles. This process works when both the receiving and transferring domain controllers cooperate. However, what about a domain controller that has crashed and is no longer working? A CMD utility can be used to seize an FSMO. The term *seizing* is a bit misleading. The new domain controller cannot actually take anything from the domain controller that has crashed. It simply means the new domain controller will perform the role. Any information gathered by the former role holder will be available to the new role holder through Active Directory.

The CMD utility to seize a role is called NDTSUTIL. Once an FSMO role is seized, the original owner of the role should never be brought back to life as an operations master because duplicate operations masters create problems on the network. In the next exercise you look at the NDTSUTIL tool, but you will not use it because it would cause duplicate RID masters on the network.

Exercise 4

USING NTDSUTIL

1. Click Start, click Run, key **CMD**, and press Enter.
2. At the command prompt enter the command **ntdsutil** and press Enter. You see the ntdsutil prompt, which looks like—

   ```
   ntdsutil:
   ```

3. Key a question mark (**?**) and press Enter to display the help information.
4. Key **roles** and press Enter to change to the FSMO roles part of the program. You see the prompt—

   ```
   fsmo maintenance:
   ```

5. Key a question mark (**?**) and press Enter to display the FSMO role help information.

Several of the commands allow you to seize roles. For example, to seize the role of RID master for the current domain controller, you would enter **Seize RID master**.

6. Key **quit** and press Enter to leave the Roles area.
7. Key **quit** and press Enter to leave the main program area.
8. Close the command window.

Accessing Information in Active Directory

Since a major reason for using a directory is to aid in the location of resources, it is important that this information be easily accessible. Microsoft provides several ways to access information within Active Directory. Each Active Directory object is stored with several different types of names, including security IDs, GUIDs, LDAP names, and user principle names (UPNs).

Security IDs (SIDs)

Domain-relative **security IDs** (**SIDs**) are created automatically by Windows 2000 for objects that will need permission to access other objects, such as user and group accounts. The names assigned to these objects must also be unique within a domain, but can be found in other domains. This system is similar to how Windows NT 4 identified such objects.

GUIDs

Each object in the Active Directory database has a **globally unique ID (GUID)**, which is stored as an attribute of that object. The GUID for an object cannot be deleted or modified. Even if objects are moved within the Active Directory database they can always be uniquely identified by their GUID because it will not change.

LDAP Names

X.500, also called Directory Access Protocol or DAP, is an industry standard protocol for performing queries against directories. Because it is an extremely large and complicated protocol that is not needed in its entirety by most organizations, a smaller version of the protocol was created called **Lightweight Directory Access Protocol (LDAP)** that can be used to locate objects. LDAP also has become an industry standard protocol for resolving directory information that allows for specifying an object's name and attributes. In LDAP, each object has a distinguished name (DN) that includes the "path" to the particular object. For example, a user named "SarahSmith" in the organization unit named "Marketing" located in the domain emcp.com could be specified with the LDAP command:

```
cn=SarahSmith, ou="Marketing", dc=emcp, dc=com
```

The letters *cn* specify a common name, which is the name given to the leaf object. The letters *ou* specify an organizational unit, and the letters *dc* specify a domain component.

This command, when sent to an LDAP name resolution program, would return information about the object. Notice that this LDAP command is like following a path through the domain (emcp.com), through the organizational unit (Marketing), and ending with the object (SarahSmith). The object name itself, in this case SarahSmith, is called the relative distinguished name (RDN) because the name SarahSmith is an attribute of the object being searched for.

Windows 2000 provides a way to access information using LDAP through Internet Information Services (IIS) 5.0. A browser can be pointed to a server hosting IIS, and an LDAP query can be executed such as—

LDAP://cn=SarahSmith,ou=Marketing,dc=emcp,dc=com

Active Directory can also be accessed with LDAP by using the Active Directory Services Interface (ADSI), which is a set of application programming interfaces (APIs) that can be used with scripting languages, Visual Basic, or Visual C++.

UPNs

A **user principle name** (**UPN**) is used to identify a user account and allow a user to log on to a domain. The format of a UPN is a user logon name, an @ symbol, and a "domain" name. A UPN looks much like an e-mail address. For example—

    SarahSmith@emcp.com

By default, a UPN includes the domain name where the user account was created. However, if, in large networks, domains become nested, the UPN may become unwieldy. (Something like "SarahSmith@marketing.eastcoast.emcp.com.") To save users from having to key this sort of UPN, the administrator can create an alternate UPN, also called an alias.

In the following exercise you create an alias for the UPN.

Exercise 5

CREATING A UPN ALIAS

1. Open the Active Directory Domains and Trusts window.
2. Right-click the top icon in the left window (*Active Directory Domains and Trusts*) and click Properties. You see the dialog box in Figure 11.11.

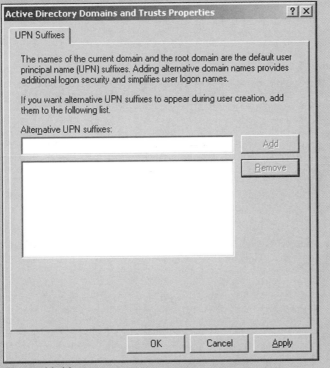

Figure 11.11

From this dialog box you can change the UPN suffixes. This change is normally made to simplify the user logon.

3. In the Alternative UPN suffixes text box key **emcp.com** and click the Add button.
4. Click the OK button to leave the dialog box and close the Active Directory Domains and Trusts MMC.

When a user in this domain logs on to the system, they can use a UPN of the form

xxxx@emcp.com

rather than the domain name.

Finding Objects in Active Directory

Objects in Active Directory are located by submitting an LDAP query to a domain controller. The LDAP query returns information about the object in Active Directory that matches the query criteria. This function is useful when searching for network resources and devices.

In the following exercise you will add a printer to your computer, share the printer, and enter information about the printer location. You will then search for this printer from within Active Directory.

Exercise 6

SHARING, ADDING, AND SEARCHING FOR A PRINTER

1. Click Start, Settings, and Printers.
2. Right-click on a shared printer (indicated by the icon of a small hand holding a printer). If you do not have a shared printer, right-click a local printer.
3. In the Printer Properties dialog box click the Sharing tab. If the printer is shared, a share name will appear in the Share As text box. If the printer is not shared, then click *Share As* and enter a share name.
4. Make sure the List in Directory box is checked. This command causes the printer information to be published in Active Directory.
5. Click the General tab and in the Location text box key:

```
Business Office Room 317
```

6. Click OK to save the changes.

The printer is now part of Active Directory and can be located using the Search tool.

7. Click Start, Search, and For Printers. You see the Find Printers dialog box in Figure 11.12.

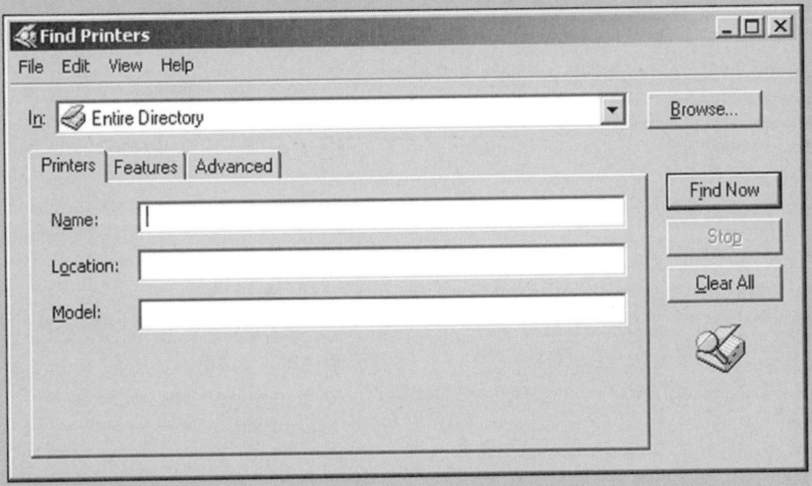

Figure 11.12

8. Click in the Location text box and key the search criteria as:

    317

This command searches for all printers in Active Directory that contain the string "317" somewhere in the location field. The * symbols are used in wild card searches and indicate an arbitrary number of characters. Thus, the criteria *317* will match "Room 317" and "Building A, 317, floor 12."

9. Click the Find Now button. You see the results of the search in a small window (Figure 11.13).

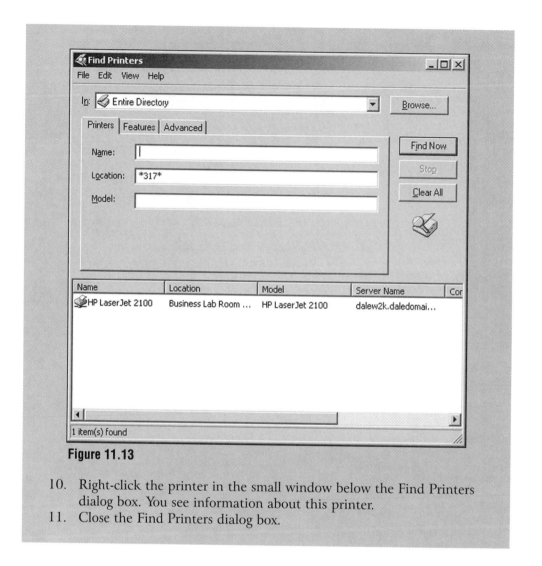

Figure 11.13

10. Right-click the printer in the small window below the Find Printers dialog box. You see information about this printer.
11. Close the Find Printers dialog box.

You can also locate users in Active Directory by using the Search dialog box and specifying a person's name. Because LDAP is a standard protocol, Internet-based servers that use this protocol can also be searched.

In the following exercise you will search for a user on both domain controllers.

Exercise 7

SEARCHING FOR USER INFORMATION

1. Click Start, Search, and For People. You see the Find People dialog box. You can use a name or e-mail address to locate a person from this part of the dialog box, but you must use the Advanced options to search if you know only part of a name.

2. Make sure the Look In list box displays *Active Directory* and then click the Advanced tab. You see the dialog box in Figure 11.14.

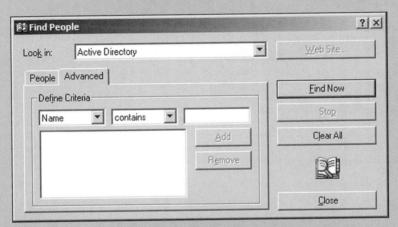

Figure 11.14

3. In the empty text box key the letter **E** and click the Add button. This command sets the criteria for the search.

4. Click the Find Now button to perform a search in Active Directory for all user names that contain the letter E. You see a list of users that match this criteria displayed as shown in Figure 11.15.

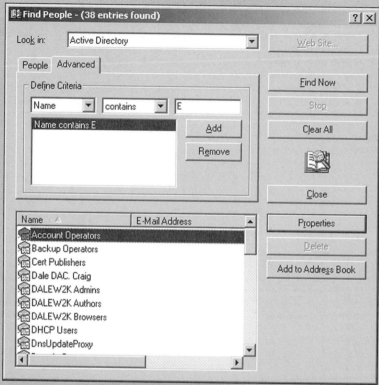

Figure 11.15

LDAP is a standard protocol, so other Internet-based services can be searched in the same way. This capability is demonstrated in the next few steps, if your computer is connected to the Internet.

5. Click the People tab and enter your name in the Name text box.
6. Click the Look in drop-down list box and click another search location such as *Yahoo!* or *Bigfoot*.
7. Click the Find Now button. An LDAP query is submitted to this site.

DNS and Active Directory

As we have learned, Active Directory is a distributed directory database that contains information about network resources and is used to validate network security. Services and users rely on DNS to locate Active Directory resources because DNS contains records that identify domain controllers and services. In Chapter 6 you explored DNS host records (records that correlate a computer name with an IP address), but a second type of DNS record is needed for Active Directory to function. That record is called a **service (SRV) record**. An SRV record contains a service name and the associated domain controller that hosts the service.

The Active Directory services identified by SRV records in DNS are LDAP, GC, and Kerberos. The SRV record will indicate which domain controllers are running each of these services. Active Directory uses these services in the following ways:

LDAP: This service is used to query a domain namespace. An LDAP query uses TCP port 389.

GC: This service is used to query a global catalog. A GC query, which is just an LDAP query directed at a different port, uses TCP port 3268.

Kerberos: This service is used to assign security rights to users and processes. The Kerberos service uses TCP port 88 for authentication and port 464 for the password service. (You will learn more about Kerberos in a later chapter.)

When a client wants to locate information in Active Directory it must first find a domain controller that is running the desired service. For example, a global catalog query can only be directed at domain controllers that have a global catalog. Because DNS holds records that reflect the kinds of services available on domain controllers, it is easy for applications to query DNS in order to locate the server hosting the desired service.

For example, assume we have a domain named emcp.com with various user accounts and resources. The two domain controllers in this domain are named DC1 and DC2. A user wishes to access a shared file on DC2. In order to access the file, the share and the security policy objects must be located in Active Directory. The client needs to use an LDAP query so it contacts the DNS server and attempts to resolve the LDAP service it needs. The DNS server looks for an SRV record that matches the requested service, locates the domain controller that hosts this service, and sends the IP address back to the client. The client then sends an LDAP request to the domain controller.

In order for this process to work, both host records and SRV records must be placed in the DNS server. With traditional DNS, records must be entered manually, but Windows 2000 domain controllers can register themselves and the services they offer. Therefore, the DNS server must be capable of accepting dynamic updates. Domain controllers automatically send updated information to their DNS server when the netlogon service is started at bootup. If multiple DNS servers exist, the information must be replicated to the other DNS servers. To accomplish this task, Microsoft DNS can be integrated with Active Directory. Each DNS server stores its records in an Active Directory database, which gets replicated across the domain. Other DNS servers can use this replicated DNS information. In order to integrate DNS with Active Directory, DNS must be hosted on a domain controller that has Active Directory.

In the following exercise you view the records in DNS that are used to locate Active Directory domain controllers and services. When a server is promoted to a domain controller, it registers a number of records with its designated DNS server.

It is helpful to understand how to read these records and how, if necessary, to modify some of the record information. The following exercise can be done on both computers.

Exercise 8

VIEWING ACTIVE DIRECTORY RECORDS IN DNS

1. Click Start, Programs, Administrative Tools, and DNS.
2. Double-click the *Forward Lookup Zone* folder in the right window and then double-click the domain name in the right window. You see the DNS records for the selected domain (Figure 11.16).

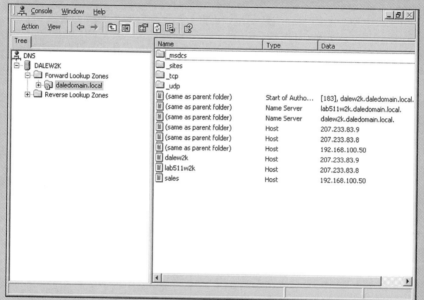

Figure 11.16

The DNS records are organized several different ways to make it easier to locate hosts and services. The four folder icons in the right window are *_msdcs*, *_sites*, *_tcp*, and *_udp*. The folder *_msdcs* holds SRV records based on their functionality. Under this folder are subfolders for *dc* (domain controllers), *domains*, *gc* (global catalog services), and *pdc* (primary domain controller services in mixed mode).

3. Double-click the *_msdcs* folder in the right window. You see a set of four subfolders as shown in Figure 11.17.

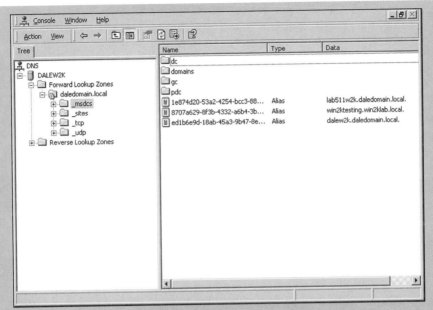

Figure 11.17

4. Double-click the *dc* folder in the right window. You see two subfolders labeled *_sites* and *_tcp*. The *_sites* folder organizes domain controllers by sites, and the *_tcp* folder lists the SRV records for all known domain controllers.

5. Double-click the *_tcp* folder. You see the SRV records in Figure 11.18.

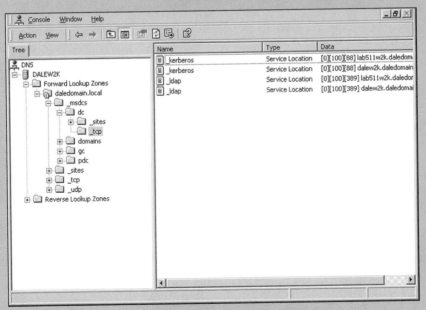

Figure 11.18

Two services are indicated by these records: LDAP and Kerberos. Each SRV record contains several pieces of information. A typical set of SRV records looks like the following:

```
_ldap        Service Location    [0][100][389] serverA.domainA.local
_ldap        Service Location    [0][100][389] serverB.domainA.local
_kerberos    Service Location    [0][100][88] serverA.domainA.local
_kerberos    Service Location    [0][100][88] serverB.domainA.local
```

The first part indicates the type of service (LDAP or Kerberos). This column is followed by the description of the record ("Service Location"). The three numbers following the description are the priority, weight, and TCP port for the service. The last part of the SRV records note the server and the domain name of the domain controller hosting the service.

When a request for SRV information is made to a DNS server, the DNS resolver picks from the records it has stored. The priority number is used when choosing the SRV records; smaller numbers have higher priority. By default the priority for all records is set to zero. If you want to force the selection of an SRV record for a particular domain controller, you can change the priority number. The weight is used as a secondary selection field when SRV records have the same priority; a record with a higher weight value will be chosen before a record with a lower weight value. Clients looking for a domain controller to perform a particular function will attempt to contact the domain controller with the lowest priority number. So if you wanted a particular domain controller to receive the majority of the LDAP calls, you would change its priority to a number lower than the rest of the domain controllers.

6. Double-click the _ldap SRV record for the second domain controller in your in the right window. (The computer name is listed under the Data heading.) You see the Properties dialog box for this record in Figure 11.19.

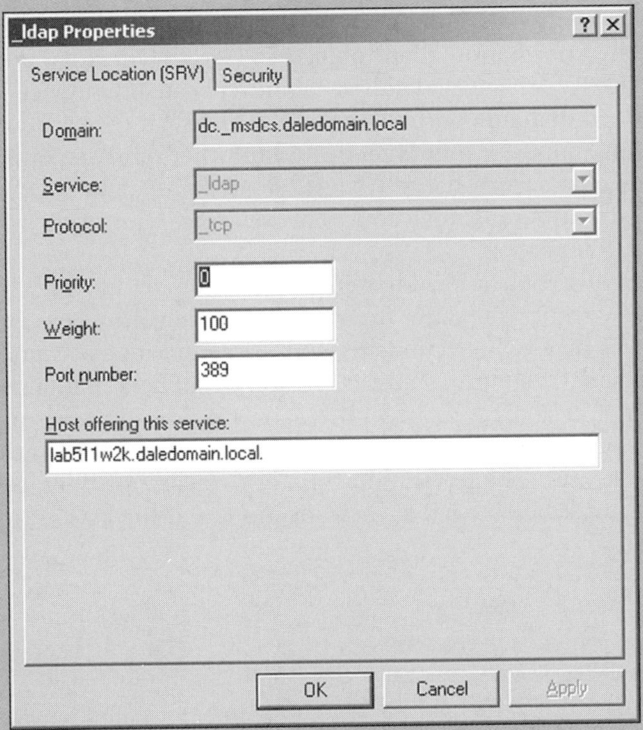

Figure 11.19

7. Reset the Priority text box to *10* and click OK to close the Properties dialog box. The first computer in the domain has a higher priority than the second, and so it will receive the majority of the ldap requests.
8. Close the DNS window.

Active Directory Replication

Because Windows 2000 has no single master domain controller that validates security rights and performs other network tasks, the Active Directory database must be available to all domain controllers. Multimaster replication was introduced in Chapter 6, but because it is important for network administrators to understand and be able to configure the replication process, it will be discussed in further detail here.

The information contained in Active Directory is used throughout the domain and the forest. Domain controllers each contain a copy of the Active Directory database, which is saved in a file named ntds.dit, which is stored in \winnt\ntds. The database consists of several parts, which are called naming contexts: the schema, the configuration, and the domain-naming context. The schema consists of the

Active Directory pattern, which is used to create new objects and assign attributes. The configuration context contains the replication topology. The domain-naming context holds the information about objects in Active Directory.

The entire Active Directory database is not replicated. Only new information is replicated between domain controllers. For example, if a user is added on ServerA, only information about the user is replicated to other domain controllers. If an existing user has a password change (that is, an attribute of an object has changed), just the changed attribute is replicated. This selective replication results in an efficient replication process.

Active Directory replication is based on a pull model in which a domain controller actively requests updates from other domain controllers. Active Directory replication can be divided into intrasite replication and intersite replication. As you will remember from Chapter 6, a **site** is a group of subnets that are well connected, such as those in a local area network. **Intrasite replication** takes place between domain controllers contained within a single site. **Intersite replication** takes place between network sites. The replication topology consists of the number of domain controllers that must be contacted, their location, and the connection speed to these controllers.

It is important that replication act on a pull instead of a push basis. To understand why, consider having two domain controllers, A and B. B is down and a change is made to A. If A pushed the change, B would miss the change because it was down. If B came up before the second change was made, B would receive the second change but not the first. In a pull situation A would notify B when the first change was made. B would not respond because it was down. If B came back up before the second change was made, B would hear A's announcement that it had a change. B would then go to A and look for any differences in its Active Directory database. It would see the first and second changes and replicate both of them.

Replication Topology and Processes

The two main aspects to Active Directory replication are the replication process itself and the replication topology. The replication process is done through a directory service remote procedure call (RPC) or by way of the Simple Mail Transfer Protocol (SMTP). Intrasite replication (replication done within a group of well-connected computers) is done by RPC. The replication process starts when a domain controller announces that it has new information. After six hours with no changes the replication process is started anyway.

Of more importance to the network administrator is the second aspect of replication, which is the replication topology. It is the "map" of domain controllers and sites that participate in the replication process. When domain controllers are added or removed, this replication map must be updated. In Windows 2000 an application known as the **Knowledge Consistency Checker** (**KCC**) is responsible for maintaining the replication topology.

Because the replication topology of a network changes, the KCC must update its replication map on a regular basis. The KCC process runs every 15 minutes and updates the topology map. KCC uses some general rules when building the replication topology map:

- Each domain controller will have two replication partners (on systems with at least three domain controllers).

- Only one link connects replication partners.

- Every domain controller must be within three "hops" of any other domain controller.

- The maximum time it takes to perform replication between any two domain controllers is 5 minutes.

- The maximum time it takes to replicate across all domain controllers is 15 minutes.

Using these rules, the KCC creates a series of replication links between each domain controller within a site.

When an Active Directory database changes on a domain controller, an update notification is sent to other controllers. The other controllers will then initiate the replication. Domain controllers also perform a regular replication once each hour. The purpose of this replication is to check the status of other replication partners. In the following exercise you view the settings for this fixed replication schedule.

Exercise 9

VIEWING THE FIXED REPLICATION INFORMATION

1. Click Start, Programs, Administrative Tools, and Active Directory Sites and Services.
2. Double-click the *Sites* folder and double-click *Default-First-Name-Site* to expand it.
3. Click the *Servers* folder in the left window, double-click the name of your server, and double-click the *NTDS Settings* icon. The window should look something like Figure 11.20.

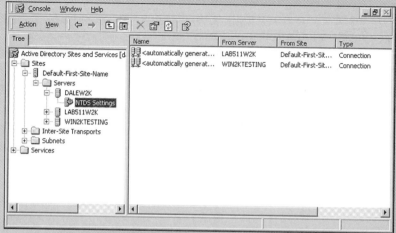

Figure 11.20

The right window displays a connection object that was created for the selected server. The connection objects are from the indicated servers. If you are logged on to the first domain controller, the connection object is from the second domain controller.

4. Double-click the connection object in the right window for the other domain controller. You see the dialog box in Figure 11.21.

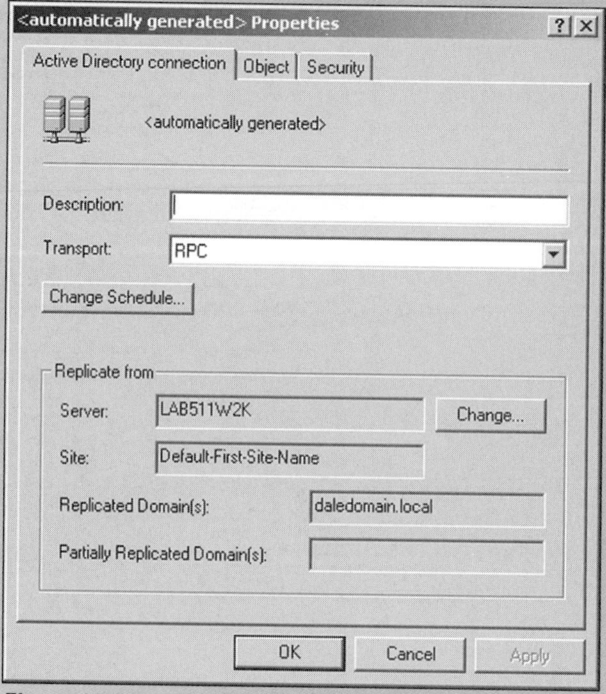

Figure 11.21

This dialog box displays information about the designated replication partner for your domain controller. This information was set by the KCC. You can manually select a replication partner, but it is a good idea to leave the selection up to the KCC.

5. Click the Change button. You see the dialog box in Figure 11.22, which allows you to manually select a replication partner.

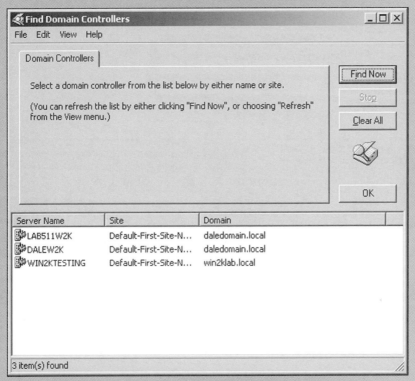

Figure 11.22

6. Click the OK button to close the Find Domain Controllers dialog box.
7. Click the Change Schedule button. You see the fixed replication schedule dialog box in Figure 11.23.

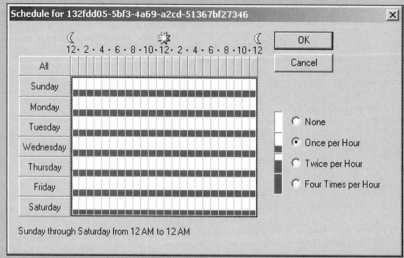

Figure 11.23

This schedule causes replication to take place every hour on a regular basis.

8. Click the Cancel button to close the scheduling dialog box and click the Cancel button to close the Connection object properties dialog box. (If you click the OK button you may be asked to designate the connection as not automatically generated. If it happens, click No and then click Cancel.)

You can manually force replication by selecting the connection object.

9. Right-click the Connection object and click Replicate Now.
10. Close the Active Directory Sites and Services MMC.

Active Directory Sites

Many networks include both high- and low-speed connections between network segments. A branch office may have a server, but may only be connected to the main company network by a 56K connection. This arrangement becomes a problem with Active Directory replication if the branch office computer system is configured as a domain controller and made part of the home company-wide domain. Remember that domains are replication boundaries, and all domain controllers must replicate the entire Active Directory regardless of how slow their connection is to the rest of the network.

To handle network segments with slower connections, Windows 2000 includes the ability to partition networks into sites. A site is a collection of computers within a well-connected subnet. By default, Active Directory creates a single site named Default-First-Site-Name. The purpose of creating sites is to better control replication between parts of a network.

The KCC automatically creates an intrasite replication topology between domain controllers inside a site. When a second site is added and domain controllers installed, the KCC on the second site also creates an intrasite replication topology. However, the administrator must manually establish the connection between the sites.

It is important to realize that sites are not necessarily different domains. A company might have a remote office connected by a slow 128K ISDN line but include the domain controller at the office in the company-wide domain. The domain controller at the remote site would still participate in the regular company network, allowing user accounts and resource allocation to be managed from the home office. The remote domain controller would still perform replication with the home office site systems (but with some significant restrictions on replication).

Active Directory provides a tool called Active Directory Sites and Services that allows you to create and manage sites. You can add this tool as a snap-in to your MMC. The following exercise will help you become familiar with Active Directory Sites and Services.

Exercise 10

USING ACTIVE DIRECTORY SITES AND SERVICES

1. Click Start, Programs, Administrative Tools, and Active Directory Sites and Services.
2. Click the *Sites* folder in the left window and then double-click the *Default-First-Site-Name* icon in the right window.

By default, Active Directory creates a single site and places the entire forest in the site. If you have multiple sites on your network, you should rename the default site so it has some meaning.

3. Right-click the *Default-First-Site-Name* icon and click Rename.
4. Enter a new name for the site (your instructor may give you a name to use) and press Enter.
5. Double-click the *Servers* folder in the right window. You should see the domain controllers in the forest.
6. Close the Active Directory Sites and Services utility.

In the following exercise you create a new site, define a subnet, and create a site link object. It should only be done from the first domain controller in the domain.

Exercise 11

CREATING AN ACTIVE DIRECTORY SITE

1. Click Start, Programs, Administrative Tools, and Active Directory Sites and Services.
2. Right-click the *Sites* folder and click New Site. You see the New Object – Site dialog box in Figure 11.24.

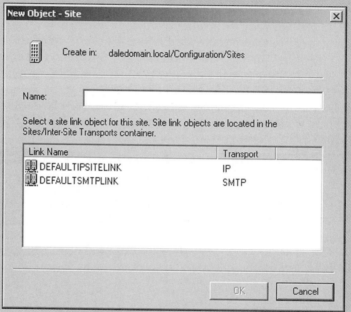

Figure 11.24

3. Enter a site name for the new site (your instructor may give you a name to use) and click the Link Name object *DEFAULTIPSITELINK*.
4. Click OK to create the site. You see a message box indicating what you have to do. Click OK to close the message box.

You must next create a subnet for the site. A subnet is a group of computers with IP addresses in a specific range.

5. Right-click the *Subnets* folder and click New subnets. You see a dialog box that is used to define the subnet IP addresses (Figure 11.25).

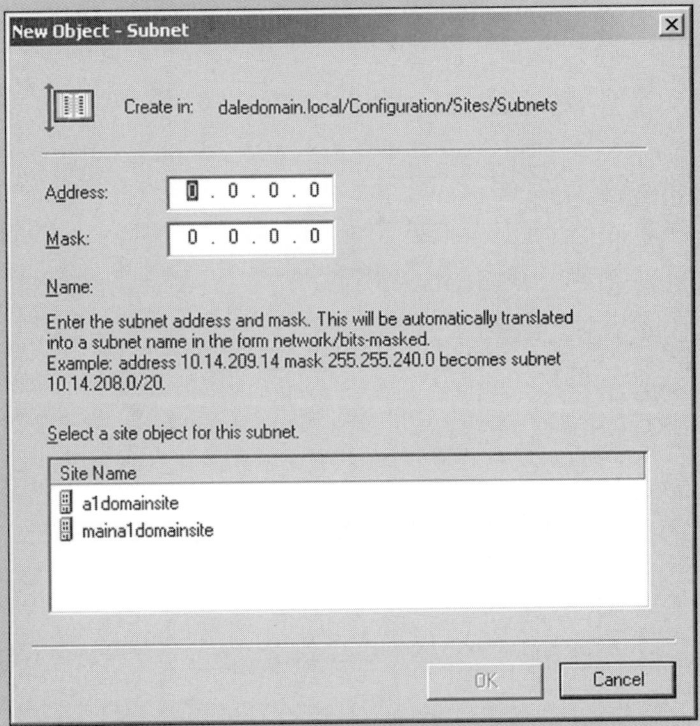

Figure 11.25

The Address text box is used to enter the IP address pattern and the Mask text box is used to enter the subnet mask.

6. In the Address text box, enter the subnet IP address for the new site. In the Mask text box, enter the subnet mask for the new site. (Your instructor will give you these addresses.)

7. After entering these numbers, select the newly created site from the list of sites at the bottom of the dialog box and click OK. (Your dialog box may look something like Figure 11.26.)

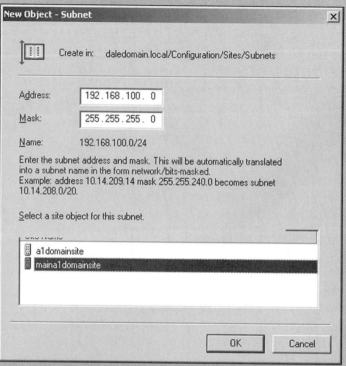

Figure 11.26

Once a new site has been created, the intersite replication protocol and schedule must be set. The replication protocol is the method the sites use to communicate. The two options for remote sites are IP and SMTP. An IP connection is suitable for a constant connection. SMTP is suitable for nonconstant batch connections.

8. Double-click *Intersites Transport Protocol*, right-click the *SMTP* folder, and click New Site Link. You see the Site Link dialog box in Figure 11.27.

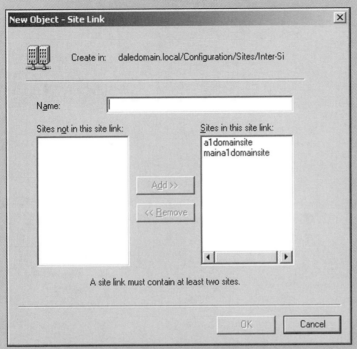

Figure 11.27

The sites to be included in the link are displayed in the right column.

9. Key **DEFAULTSMTPLINK** in the link Name text box and click OK.
10. Click the *SMTP* folder and double-click the icon of the newly created SMTP link object in the right window. (Do not click on the name.) You see the dialog box in Figure 11.28.

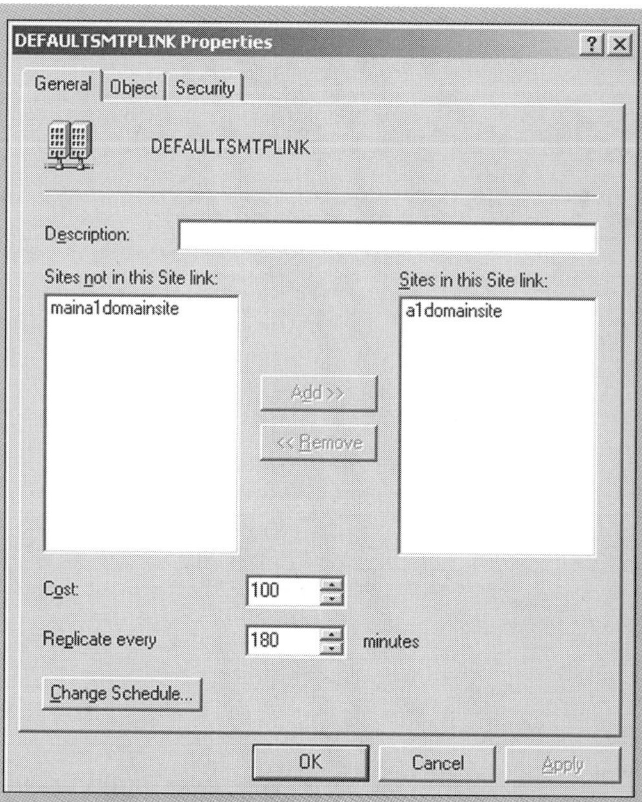

Figure 11.28

This dialog box contains a description field for the site replication object, and fields for the replication cost and the replication time. The replication cost is a number used by the KCC to configure the replication topology. A lower number indicates a faster connection between sites. Sites with slower connections should be assigned a higher number. By default, a site is given a cost of 100.

The Replicate every option sets the amount of time between replications. For slow sites this number might be increased.

11. Click the Change Schedule button to display the replication schedule. For remote sites that may not be constantly connected you might want to restrict the replication days and times.

12. Perhaps your network is especially busy on Tuesdays so you do not want replication to happen on Tuesday. Click the word *Tuesday* to highlight the entire day and then click *None*. Now replication will not happen on Tuesday. Click OK.

The last step is to move the servers into the site by selecting the server and using the move command.

13. Open the *Servers* folder from the existing site.
14. Right-click the *Server* icon for the second domain controller on the network and click Move. You see a dialog box listing the sites.
15. Select the newly created site and click OK.
16. Close the Sites and Services window.

Network Design and Active Directory

One of the important aspects of Active Directory is the effect it has on network design. Network design consists of planning the number and structure of domains, sites, and organizational units. The impact of Active Directory on this design process is based on the fact that domains cannot be easily restructured and that information must be replicated between domain controllers.

Several general guidelines need to be followed when designing a network.

- Minimize the number of domains. Unless you can give a good reason, a network should only have a single domain.

- Use organizational units as the primary structuring method within the network. Group policies can be used to control users and computers in the various OUs.

- Try to minimize the number of sites. Because site replication must be manually configured, excessive numbers of sites can become difficult to administer.

An example of how a network might be designed could be an international company with branches in different countries. With earlier versions of Windows, each physical site might have been designated as a separate domain because each site would have its own primary domain controller. Using Windows 2000, the design might be based on a corporate structure rather than a physical structure. The Accounting group would be collected under an organizational unit even though members of this group might reside in different countries.

CHAPTER summary

➤ Active Directory is used by Windows 2000 to store information about network resources and network users. This multimaster distributed database is installed on domain controllers.

➤ Active Directory is accessed by way of the Lightweight Directory Access Protocol. Clients and other domain controllers locate Active Directory services through DNS.

➤ The Active Directory database is automatically replicated between domain controllers. The replication topology is maintained by the Knowledge Consistency Checker. Active Directory domains can be divided into sites. Replication between sites must be manually established.

CHAPTER terms

Active Directory schema	The patterns used to create network objects and attributes.
Directory	A structured collection of information stored in a hierarchical format.
Directory service	A method to access information stored in a directory.
Domain	A security, replication, and resource boundary identified by a domain name.
Domain controller	A computer hosting Active Directory.
Domain naming master	An FSMO forest-level service that controls adding and removing domains from a forest.
FSMO	Flexible single master operations: A set of services that must be done on only one domain controller per domain or per forest.
Forest	A collection of trees that share a common Active Directory.
GC	Global catalog: Part of Active Directory that contains information about each Active Directory object.
Global catalog server	A domain controller that holds a global catalog.
GUID	Globally unique ID: A unique identification assigned to Active Directory objects when the objects are created.
Infrastructure master	A FSMO domain-level service that coordinates and replicates group membership changes.
Intersite replication	Replication that takes place within a site.

Intrasite replication	Replication that takes place between sites.
KCC	Knowledge Consistency Checker: An Active Directory process that builds and maintains the replication topology.
LDAP	Lightweight Directory Access Protocol: A method of performing queries in a directory.
Member server	A computer that joins a domain but does not host Active Directory.
Namespace	A structure within which information can be resolved.
Object	An identifiable item that contains a collection of properties.
PDC emulator	An FSMO domain-level service used to send updates to Windows NT 4 computers in a mixed mode Active Directory network.
RID master	An FSMO domain-level service used to create security IDs that are assigned to users and computers.
Schema master	An FSMO forest-level service used to modify the Active Directory schema.
SID	Security IDs: A domain-relative identification used to identify users, groups, and computers.
Service or SRV record	A DNS record that identifies a service on a particular domain controller.
Site	A group of well-connected subnets.
Tree	A set of domains in a hierarchical relationship.
Trusts	A relationship between domains whereby users authenticated in one domain are granted login rights in the second domain.
UPN	User principle name: A method of identifying users that includes the domain name and the user name in the format: domain@user.

CONCEPTS review

Multiple Choice

1. Intrasite replication is handled by which protocol?
   a. IP
   b. SMTP
   c. RPC
   d. TCP
   e. None of the above

2. Which of the following are ways that objects are identified in Active Directory?
   a. SID
   b. GUID
   c. LDAP name
   d. All of the above
   e. Both a and c

3. Which of the following statements does not accurately describe trusts that are automatically created in Windows 2000?
   a. They are two-way.
   b. They are transitive.
   c. They are created between domains in a tree.
   d. They are created between trees in a forest.
   e. None of the above.

4. Which of the following can only be on one domain controller in the forest?
   a. Schema master
   b. RID master
   c. PDC master
   d. Infrastructure master
   e. None of the above

5. The type of record that DNS would use to locate a domain controller running the global catalog would be a:
   a. ptr.
   b. host.
   c. srv.
   d. soa.
   e. None of the above.

6. If you have a tree with four domains, which of the following could be found in multiple places within the tree?
   a. RID master
   b. Global catalog
   c. Infrastructure master
   d. PDC emulator
   e. All of the above

7. cn=Adeline, ou="Marketing", dc=emcp, dc=com is an example of what type of name?
   a. GUID
   b. SID
   c. UPN
   d. LDAP name
   e. None of the above

8. The KCC will configure the replication topology to ensure that:
   a. The maximum time to replicate across all domain controllers is 12 minutes.
   b. The maximum time to replicate between replication partners is 5 minutes.
   c. The maximum number of hops between domain controllers is five.
   d. Each domain controller will have two connections to its replication partner to ensure fault tolerance.
   e. All of the above.

9. An object that has an SID that does not represent anything on the network but instead only holds other objects is called a:
   a. Container.
   b. Holder.
   c. Folder.
   d. Attribute.
   e. None of the above.

10. For which type of group does the global catalog track membership?
    a. Local
    b. Domain local
    c. Global
    d. Universal
    e. None of the above

11. Which protocol should you choose for replication connections to a remote site via a dial-up line?
    a. RPC
    b. IP
    c. SMTP
    d. BootP
    e. None of the above

12. SRV records in DNS for five servers appear as follows:

   (A)_ldap   Service Location   [10][10][389] serverA.domainA.local
   (B)_ldap   Service Location   [10][100][389] serverB.domainA.local
   (C)_ldap   Service Location   [10][50][389] serverC.domainA.local
   (D)_ldap   Service Location   [20][50][389] serverD.domainA.local
   (E)_ldap   Service Location   [20][100][389] serverE.domainA.local

   Which of the machines would be chosen first to process an LDAP query?
   a. A
   b. B
   c. C
   d. D
   e. E

13. Which tool do you use to create a global catalog server?
   a. Active Directory Sites and Services
   b. Active Directory Users and Computers
   c. Active Directory Domains and Trusts
   d. DNS
   e. Both a and c

14. Which of the following would not change if an object were moved?
   a. UPN
   b. LDAP name
   c. GUID
   d. All of the above
   e. Both a and c

15. A forest made up of two trees each with three domain controllers would be located in how many sites by default?
   a. 1
   b. 2
   c. 3
   d. 6
   e. None of the above

Short Answer

1. What does KCC stand for? What does it do?
2. What is LDAP?
3. In a forest with three domains, how many total FSMOs will you have?
4. Which FSMO deals with the replication topology?
5. Which type of replication is automatic, intrasite or intersite?

LAB exercises

Up to this point in the book you have been working with two domain controllers within the same domain. The following exercises will work only if you have set up one domain controller as the parent and the second domain controller as the child. In order to do this, your second domain controller must be reloaded to be a child of the first domain controller.

Exercise 1 – Reloading the Machine

Although Active Directory can be removed from a machine by running dcpromo a second time and selecting to remove Active Directory, it is much cleaner to reload the operating system because some pieces such as DNS will not be removed and have to be removed separately. Follow the steps in Chapter 2 to reload Windows 2000. Make sure when the system asks if you want to do an upgrade or new installation that you pick new installation.

Exercise 2 – Preparing the Server to Be a Domain Controller in the Child Domain

After the machine is reloaded, the TCP/IP address and options must be set before it can be promoted.

1. Log on to the server that will be the domain controller for the child domain. Make sure you log on as administrator.
2. Right-click the *My Network Places* icon and click Properties from the drop-down menu.
3. Right-click the *Local Area Connection* icon and click Properties from the drop-down menu.
4. Click *Internet Protocol TCP/IP* and click the Properties button.
5. Make sure the IP address is static and you are using your assigned IP address. Make sure the Subnet Mask is filled in properly. Also, make sure the IP address of the first domain controller appears in the DNS address section. (You will be using the DNS server on the parent domain.)
6. Close the Properties dialog box and return to the desktop.

Exercise 3 – Creating the Child Domain

In this exercise you create a child domain in the same tree and forest as your first domain.

1. Click Start, click Run, and key **dcpromo.**
2. Click OK to run this program.
3. At the Welcome to Active Directory Installation Wizard click <u>N</u>ext to continue.
4. At the Domain Controller Type window click <u>D</u>omain controller for a new domain and then click <u>N</u>ext (Figure 11.29).

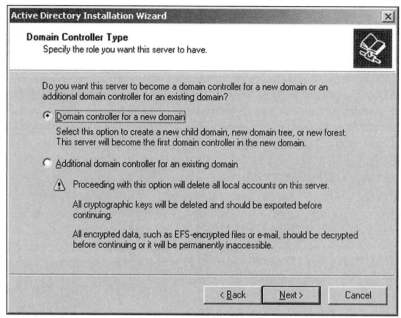

Figure 11.29

5. Click *Create a new child domain in an existing domain tree* and click <u>N</u>ext.
6. Key **administrator** for the User Name, **classroom** as the password, and key the fully qualified domain name of the parent domain, for example, **Adomain.local.**
7. Click <u>N</u>ext.
8. For the parent domain, key in the fully qualified domain name of the parent domain, for example, **Adomain.local**. For the child domain, key **Achild** (substituting your letter for A). The complete DNS name for the new domain should appear. Click <u>N</u>ext.
9. Accept the NetBIOS name by clicking <u>N</u>ext.
10. Accept the default Database and Log locations and click <u>N</u>ext.
11. Accept the default SysVol location and click <u>N</u>ext (Figure 11.30).

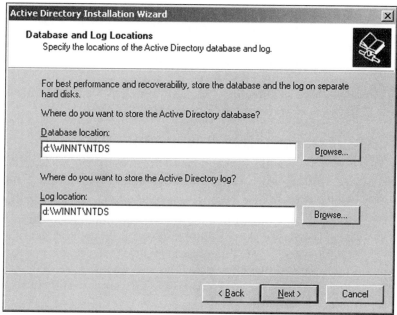

Figure 11.30

12. At the Permissions window, click *Permissions compatible with pre-Windows 2000 servers* and click Next.
13. For the Directory Services Restore Mode password, key **classroom**. (Remember passwords are case sensitive! Key your password in lowercase.) Press the Tab key and key **classroom** in the Confirm password box and click Next.
14. View the summary to make sure it is correct and click Next.
15. At the Completing the Active Directory Installation Wizard screen click Finish.
16. Restart your machine.

Exercise 4 – Seizing an FSMO

Because the RID master was transferred to the second domain controller in the parent domain and that domain controller has since been rebuilt as a child domain controller, the FSMO role of RID master no longer exists on the parent domain. To seize this role, log on to the remaining domain controller in the parent domain.

1. Pull up a command window and key **ntdsutil**.
2. At the ntdsutil prompt key **roles**.
3. At the fsmo Maintenance prompt key **connections**.
4. At the Server Connections box, key **connect to domain Adomain** (substituting your domain name for Adomain).
5. You will receive verification that you have been connected to the domain. Key **quit** to leave the Server Connections prompt.

6. At the fsmo Maintenance prompt, key **seize rid master**.
7. At the Role Seizure confirmation box click Yes.
8. You may receive several warnings. Click Yes to proceed at each one.
9. After the role is transferred, key **quit** to leave each prompt and **exit** to close the command window.
10. Open Active Directory Domains and Trusts and view the operations masters to verify the role has been transferred.

Exercise 5 – Viewing and Changing Forest FSMO Roles

In this exercise you will use the Active Directory MMC tools to locate the FSMO role owners. In the next exercise you will transfer some of these roles to another domain controller.

1. Because the domain naming FSMO can only be transferred to a global catalog server, make the child domain controller be a global catalog server.
2. On the parent domain controller, click Start, Programs, Administrative Tools, and Active Directory Domains and Trusts.
3. Right-click on the first icon in the left window and click *Connect to domain controller.*
4. In the domain name box, key the fully qualified domain name of your child domain. For example, **Achild.Adomain.local**, and click OK.
5. Right-click the first icon in the left window and click Operations Master. You will see that the domain naming master is currently the domain controller in the parent domain. The child domain controller name should be listed in the Change to box.
6. Click Change to transfer the role to the child domain controller.
7. Click Yes to confirm you want to transfer the role.
8. Click OK on the message confirming the successful transfer.
9. Close the Change operations master dialog box. Leave Active Directory Domains and Trusts open for the next exercise.

Exercise 6 – Viewing Automatically Created Trusts

This exercise can be done from both domain controllers.

1. In Active Directory Domains and Trusts, right-click the parent domain name and click Properties.
2. Click the Trusts tab. You should see that the child domain is both trusted and trusting and that the trust is transitive.
3. Close the Parent Domain Properties window.
4. Click on the plus sign next to the parent domain to expand it.
5. View the Trusts tab for the child domain. Who are its trusted and trusting domains?

PROBLEM SOLVING exercises

Exercise 1

You have a domain with four domain controllers working in native mode. One of the domain controllers crashes and you send it off to be repaired. In the meantime you continue to use the network and you create five new user accounts each week. After several weeks you attempt to create a new user in the domain and find you can no longer do so. What is wrong, and what must you do to solve this problem?

Exercise 2

Create a network design using domains, sites, and organizational units based on the following company description:

> The Super Tires Company has a main office in New York and branch offices in California, Texas, and Ohio. This company has the following corporate divisions: Sales, Accounting, Executive Board, Research and Development, and Operations. The New York main office and the Texas branch office have people in each division. The Ohio office has Sales, Accounting, and Operations. The California office has Sales, Accounting, and Research and Development.

Performance Objectives

After completing this chapter you will be able to:

- Describe the Windows security model
- Explain how the Kerberos security system operates
- Describe the public/private key security system
- Install and configure Internet Protocol Security
- Encrypt files
- Recover encrypted files
- Use security auditing
- Use security templates
- Create a network security plan

Introduction

The integrity of a Windows 2000 network is fundamental to the operation of the network. Users must be authenticated and given rights to resources, and nonauthorized users should be prevented from accessing the network. Large networks with thousands of users and multiple domains require that a detailed security policy be created. In this chapter you learn how security under Windows 2000 works, the various ways users are authenticated, how to protect files from unauthorized access, how to secure IP traffic to and from a server, and how to audit users and processes. You will also learn how to create a security policy that can be used to implement security standards and processes on your network.

Windows 2000 Security Model Overview

A Windows 2000 security model describes a Windows 2000 network in terms of user authentication and access. This model is useful to gain an overview of how Windows 2000 handles security. The primary elements in this security model are the **Security Principles**, which are groups, user accounts, and computer accounts. Each of these Security Principles is unique within a domain, but may not be unique across all domains in a forest.

The primary security functions in Windows 2000 are authentication, access control, and data protection. **Authentication** involves verifying the identity of a user or process. Before a user can connect to the network, the user must be authenticated. This process normally involves the user entering a password and having the password checked by the security systems. However, Windows 2000 also includes the ability to use digital cards or even **biometric authorization** through biometric input (such as a fingerprint or retinal scan) to verify users.

Domains are the primary security boundary. User accounts are created within particular domains and replicated to other domain controllers through Active Directory. When a user logs on to a domain, their account and password are checked against the information contained in Active Directory. In a forest that contains multiple domains, each domain trusts all other domains, which means that a user authenticated by one domain is automatically trusted by all other domains.

The second security function performed by Windows is access control. Although a user has been authenticated to connect to a network, the user is not automatically given complete access to network resources. Resources, such as shared folders or printers, can be set with permissions that define the users and groups that can access the resource and the type of access granted. When a user attempts to use a network resource, the resource permissions are checked against the authenticated user.

The third security function performed by Windows 2000 is data protection. It protects static data, such as files and folders on a domain controller, and also includes protection of information such as network traffic. Although some level of data protection is afforded by authentication and access control, in some cases extra protection must be added to a sensitive file or network session.

Authentication

The first step to using a network is user authentication, in which the users identify themselves by entering their account ID and password. Users can log on to the local computer or can log on to the domain. The Winlogon.exe program, running on a Windows 2000 computer, displays the logon screen and prompts the user to enter his or her account information. Once entered, the Winlogon program calls the **Local Security Authority** (**LSA**) process, which will then call an authentication package (MSV1_0 for logging on to the local computer and Kerberos for logging on to the domain).

If the user only has a local account (an account valid only for a specific computer) and does not have a domain account, the LSA process verifies the user account and password in the local Security Accounts Manager (SAM) database, stored on the local computer. Once the authentication process has verified the user, the LSA reads the security ID (SID) information from the SAM database associated with the user and SIDs for all groups of which the user is a member. This information is used to create an access token (a data structure that contains security keys), which is returned by the LSA to Winlogon. This access token allows the user to connect to the computer when accessing local resources. This procedure is also identified as an **NT LAN Manager** (**NTLM**) **logon**. The process is illustrated in Figure 12.1.

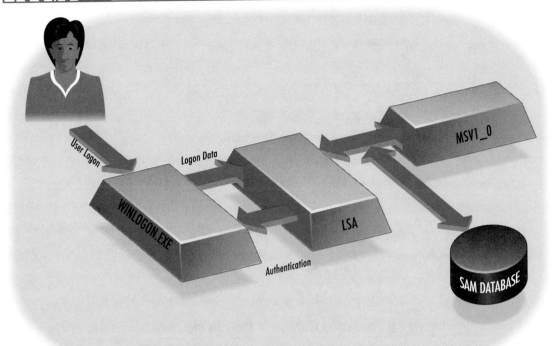

Microsoft has had challenges securely storing passwords on computers. Windows 95/98 and even Windows NT and Windows 2000 have well-known password vulnerabilities. Windows NT and Windows 2000 store some service account passwords in plain text in the registry under HKEY_LOCAL_MACHINE\SECURITY\Policy\Secrets.

Logging on to a Domain and Kerberos

Logging on to a domain is more complex than logging on to a local computer because the domain user account information is stored in Active Directory. Before domain users can connect to a local computer, they must first be authenticated within the domain. Microsoft has chosen to use the Kerberos security protocol for domain-level authentication, which is a standard protocol used by many non-Microsoft operating systems.

Kerberos is a symmetrical key ticket-based security system. Both the user and the authenticating system must know the account passwords (unlike asymmetrical systems, which will be explained later in this chapter). Tokens are used as part of the authentication process. Logging on to a domain using Kerberos involves the following steps:

1. The user enters an account and password at the Winlogon screen.

2. The Winlogon program calls the Local Security Authority (LSA), which calls a Kerberos client.

3. The Kerberos client contacts a **key distribution center** (**KDC**) and is authenticated.

4. The KDC issues a **ticket granting ticket** (**TGT**) to the client. This ticket can only be used with the **ticket granting service** (**TGS**).

5. The client attempts to use a network service or resource. The resource requests authentication from the client.

6. The client gives the ticket granting ticket to the TGS and receives a service ticket for the resource.

7. The client gives the service ticket to the network resource.

8. The network resource responds with a token that the client, using the service ticket, decrypts. If the client can decrypt the token from the resource and if the resource can decrypt the ticket from the client, the client can start using the resource.

This process is illustrated in Figure 12.2.

FIGURE 12.2 *Accessing Resources through the Ticket Granting Service*

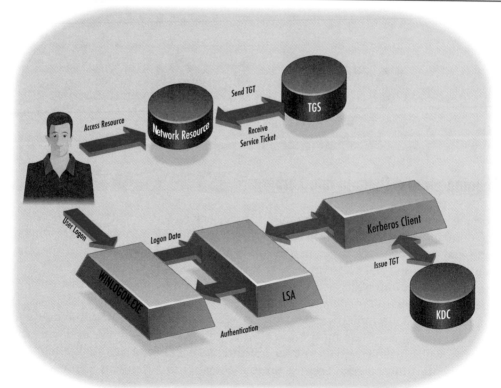

Although the Kerberos system is complex, users and resources automatically perform the procedures required for authentication. The benefit to using Kerberos is that users need only authenticate once in order to use resources across a domain. After the initial authentication, the user account uses **Kerberos tickets** rather than having to reauthenticate. These tickets are software objects that contain user security information. The second benefit to Kerberos is the mutual authentication between users and services. Rogue services cannot be introduced into the system by copying a hacked executable file because services must be able to decrypt and encrypt tickets from the user.

Exercise 1

VIEWING KERBEROS SECURITY POLICY INFORMATION

In this exercise you open the domain security program and view the Kerberos settings.

1. Click Start, Programs, Administrative Tools, and Domain Security Policy. (Be careful and do *not* click Domain Controller Security Policy.)
2. Click the *Security Settings* icon in the left window and, under the Security Settings section, click the *Account Policies* icon.
3. Click *Kerberos Policy* in the left window. You see the window in Figure 12.3.

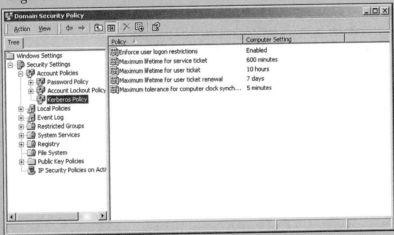

Figure 12.3

The Kerberos security policies for the domain are listed in the right window. Notice that a maximum lifetime is set for service tickets, user tickets, and ticket renewal. Another option sets maximum tolerance for clock synchronization, which time-stamps Kerberos tickets. If the ticket date and time are out of bounds, the ticket is not valid. This tolerance is set by default at 5 minutes. Changing this option can weaken security; it is best left as the default.

4. Close the Domain Security Policy window.

Public Key Infrastructures

Windows 2000 can use a variety of security protocols, depending on the service and application. Along with NTLM and Kerberos, a **public key infrastructure (PKI)** is also available. This type of security protocol is based on asymmetrical keys. Unlike Kerberos and NTLM, with PKI the password employed by the user does not have to be stored on the server. A public key system uses two keys, a public key and a private key.

A key is a piece of information used with an encryption algorithm to convert information into a format that hides the original data. Different keys, when used with the same algorithm, produce different output. Symmetric key systems, like Kerberos, use the same key, such as a password. When a user enters a password, the LSA uses a **one-way hash** algorithm on the password to create a new hashed value, such as mathematically converting the password text into a series of numbers. This hashed value is then sent to Kerberos for verification. The Kerberos KDC holds a copy of the same password entered by the user. The KDC, using the same hash algorithm and a copy of the same password, creates a hashed value and compares what it just created with what it received from the LSA. If the two match, then the passwords used to create the hashed values must also match. The problem with this type of system is that the KDC must hold a list of passwords, which might be compromised.

A public key system also uses keys and algorithms, but keys are generated in pairs. One key is kept secret by the user and is known as the private key. The second key is given to the authenticating service and is known as the public key. Data encrypted with a private key can only be decrypted with the corresponding public key. Likewise, data encrypted with a public key can only be decrypted with the corresponding private key. Therefore, once a **public/private key** pair has been generated, the network service that performs authentication only needs the public key. If an encrypted token from the user, created with the user's private key, can be decrypted by the matching public key, the user has been authenticated. Like Kerberos, a password can be used to create a hashed value, which is then encrypted by a private key and decrypted by a public key, as illustrated in Figure 12.4.

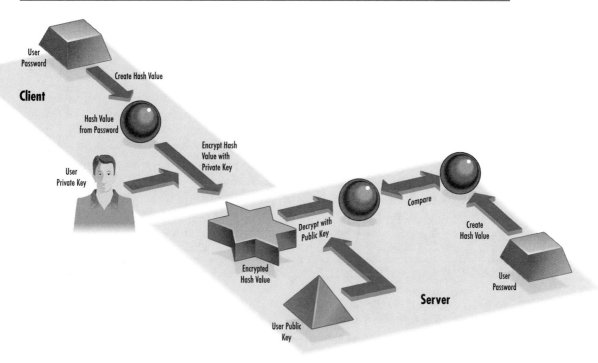

One problem with this public/private key system is impersonation. Assume that Steve wishes to receive an electronic document from Jane and ensure that the document was from her. One way to do so is by using a pair of public/private keys. Jane creates a set of public/private keys and sends the public key to Steve by way of regular unsecured e-mail. She then creates a message and encrypts the message with her private key. When Steve receives the message and is able to decrypt it with Jane's public key, he can safely assume the message is from her. Or can he? An intermediate party who intercepts the public key and sends a new key can defeat this process. This intermediary could then "impersonate" Jane by sending false messages.

This situation may seem unlikely when using an internal company network, but it is not unlikely when using a public network like the Internet. The solution to this impersonation problem is to use a trusted third party that will verify the public key. If Steve, after receiving the public key, could check the key with this trusted third party, he could verify that it was, in fact, Jane's key. This third-party checking is done by a **certificate authority** (**CA**), which maintains public keys and verifies that these keys belong to individuals through the issuance of certificates (much like the way states issue driver's licenses).

A **certificate** binds a public key with a key holder's name and key expiration date. The certificate information is then encrypted by the CA and can be decrypted with the CA's public key. Rather than give Steve her public key, Jane would instead present a certificate. Steve would use the CA's public key, decrypt the certificate, and verify that Jane's public key (contained in the certificate) is valid. This certificate process rests on the validity of the CA's public key and the ability of the CA to create certificates. Windows 2000 and Internet Explorer come with a set of CA public keys that can be used to verify certificates. Users can get a certificate from a CA that can be used in various transactions. (Some certificates are priced under $15 per year.)

Along with providing users with digital signatures, certificates are also important in network security. The **Internet Protocol Security** (**IPSec**) uses certificates to validate network traffic. An IPSec device, such as a router, can be assigned a certificate from a CA and use this certificate when communicating with other secure devices. Windows 2000 supports PKI for IPSec and file encryption. Windows also allows you to install a CA in order to create and manage certificates.

IP Security

In a networked environment, security considerations must include not only user authentication but also the IP packets as they travel between computers. Many inexpensive and easy-to-use packet "sniffing" tools allow an intruder to monitor network information. Windows 2000 includes the standards-based Internet Protocol Security (IPSec), which provides encryption for individual IP packets by configuring the IPSec policies for network computers.

IPSec works in two ways, signing the IP packets so the receiver knows from where the packets were sent (but leaving the packets unencrypted), and encrypting the packets so their contents cannot be viewed. The former uses an **authentication header** (**AH**), which is placed before the regular IP packet header and which contains the packet authentication material. The AH certifies that the packet was sent from a particular source and that it has not been tampered with. The second way IPSec protects packets is by encrypting the data part of the IP packet using the **encapsulating security payload** (**ESP**) protocol. In this method the packet is encrypted before being sent. If the receiving computer has the correct key the packet can be decrypted. IPSec will use just AH or both AH and ESP to send secure packets. Before two computers using IPSec start sending each other encrypted data, they first negotiate the session parameters, which consist of the type of encryption and whether to use AH and/or EPS.

Managing IPSec

IPSec is enabled by creating and applying policies to computers or a domain. Policies are made up of one or more rules. A rule is a collection of IPSec configuration information, including the type of authentication to use, which IP addresses to use for secure communication, and other kinds of information. Windows 2000 comes with three general policies:

Client policy: This policy causes a computer or domain controller to use IPSec when requested to do so by another system. It is commonly used with clients wishing to communicate securely with a server.

Server policy: This policy sets the server to attempt an IPSec connection with all other systems, but does not require such a connection if the other system refuses.

Secure server policy: This policy requires the server to use IPSec, even if the clients cannot handle IPSec.

Exercise 2

VIEWING AND SETTING AN IPSEC POLICY

In this exercise you view and set the IPSec policy.

1. Click Start, Programs, Administrative Tools, and Domain Security Policy.
2. If necessary, double-click the *Security Settings* icon to display the options.
3. Click the *IP Security Policies* icon. On the right side of the windows the policies are listed (Figure 12.5).

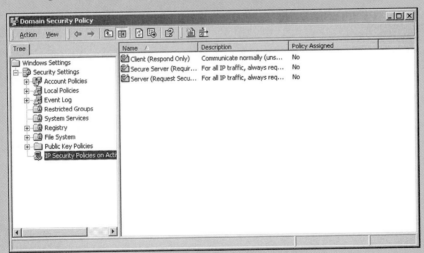

Figure 12.5

None of these policies is active (under the Policy Assigned column the value is No).

4. Right-click *Client (Respond Only)* and click Properties. You see the list of rules that can apply to this policy (Figure 12.6).

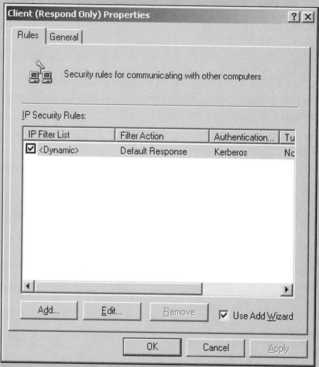

Figure 12.6

5. Make sure the Dynamic rule is checked. Click once to select this rule, and then click the Edit button. You see the Edit Rule Properties dialog box (Figure 12.7).

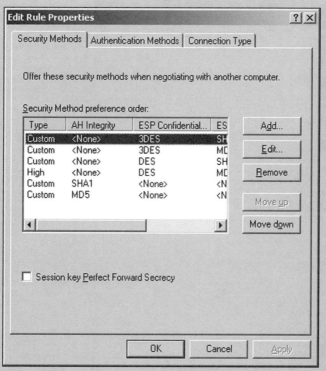

Figure 12.7

The client options are the Security Methods (which IP packets format to use in an IPSec session), Authentication Methods (the method used to make a secure connection), and the Connection Type (all network connections, remote, or LAN only).

6. Click the Authentication Methods tab. The only authentication method listed should be Kerberos.
7. Click the Add button to add a new authentication method. You see the New Authentication Method Properties dialog box in Figure 12.8.

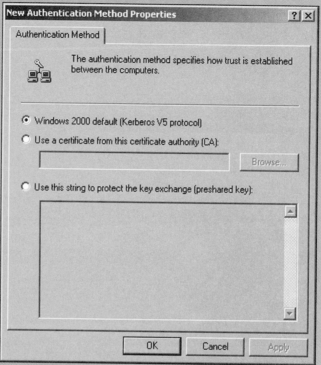

Figure 12.8

This allows you to select the type of security authentication that will be used when an IPSec session is created. The three choices are:

Kerberos: This security method is the default in Windows.

Certificate: This method requires a certificate from a CA and uses public/private key authentication.

String: This method is an agreed-upon string used by both sides in an IPSec session. Both parties hash the string and compare the results. In order to use this option, the same string must be manually entered on both computers that will participate in the IPSec session.

8. Click the last option, *Use this string to protect the key exchange*, and key the word **password** in the text box. In a real situation you would enter a longer string to make password guessing harder.
9. Click the OK button to close the New Authentication Method Properties dialog box and click OK to close the Rule Policies dialog box.
10. Click OK to close the Client Policy dialog box.

Exercise 3

CONFIGURING SERVER IPSEC POLICIES

You will next configure the Server IPSec policy.

1. Right-click *Policy Server (Request Security)* and click Properties. You see a list of rules defined for the server (Figure 12.9).

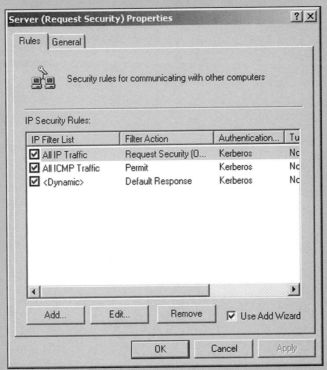

Figure 12.9

Servers have rules when sending IP packets and ICMP packets, and the rule used when acting as a client. (*ICMP* stands for Internet Control Message Protocol, which is used to send problem messages such as incomplete reception of data.)

2. Click the *All IP Traffic* rule once and click the Edit button. You see the Edit Rule dialog box in Figure 12.10.

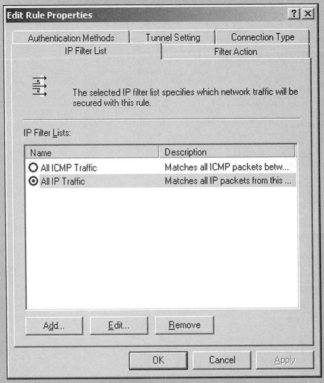

Figure 12.10

Three of the options in this dialog box are like the Client options discussed in the previous exercise. The new options are IP Filter List and Filter Action. The IP Filter List option is used to set the IP addresses that will be used with IPSec. The Filter Action option sets whether IPSec is required or whether the server should negotiate with the client. You will add a new IP Filter list.

3. On the IP Filter List tab click the Add button. You see the IP Filter List dialog box in Figure 12.11.

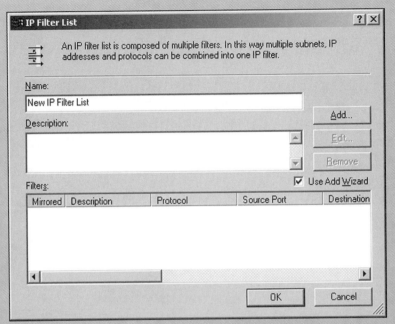

Figure 12.11

4. In the Name text box key **Accounting Database** and in the Description text box key **Secure links for the Accounting Database**.

5. Click the Add button to add a list of IP addresses to this filter. You see the IP Filter Wizard.

6. Click Next to start the wizard. You see the IP Traffic Source dialog box with an option set to My IP Address.

7. Click Next. You see the Destination address. It is the subnet you wish to secure.

8. In the drop-down list box click *A specific IP Subnet*. You see the dialog box in Figure 12.12.

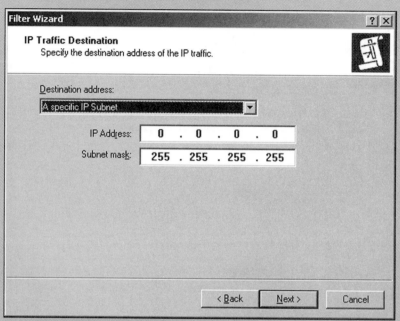

Figure 12.12

You must specify the subnet that will be the destination for the IPSec traffic.

9. Set the IP Address text box to *192.168.100.0*, set the Subnet mask to *255.255.255.0*, and click the Next button.
10. For the Protocol type, leave the option as *Any* and click Next.
11. Click the Finish button to complete the wizard and click the Close button to close the filter list. You see the new filter list in the dialog box (Figure 12.13).

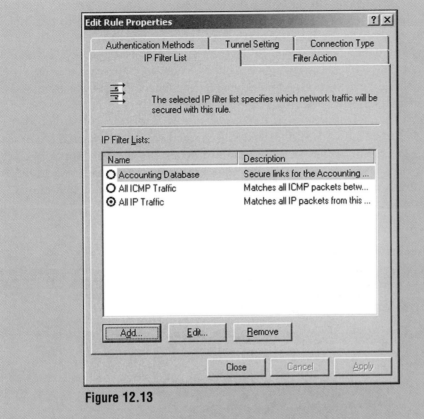

Figure 12.13

12. Click the Filter Action tab to display the options. These are Permit (allow unsecured packets under all conditions), Request Security (request clients use IPSec, but will allow unsecured connections), and Require Security (force all communications to be secure).

13. Click Close to close the Edit Rule Properties dialog box and click Close to close the Server Properties dialog box.

File Encryption

Windows 2000 can encrypt data as it passes across a network connection by using IPSec. Other types of data, such as files and folders, also need protecting, which can be done by using the **encrypting file system** (**EFS**) feature found in Windows 2000. Because Windows 2000 can be used on laptop computers, EFS is more appropriate for securing files that will be outside the protection of the company's network.

The EFS is simple to use and only requires the user to select the encrypt option for a folder or file. When a folder is encrypted, all files copied into or created within the folder are automatically encrypted. This encryption is done with a random symmetric key created by the system. This key is used to encrypt and decrypt the file or files. The key itself is then encrypted by a public key assigned to the user. When the user accesses the file, the user's private key is used to decrypt the symmetrical key, which is then used to decrypt the file. This whole process takes place automatically, and the user works with files as normal. When another user tries to open the file, they are presented with an error message. If another user attempts to copy the file to another disk, they are also presented with an error message.

EFS carries some restrictions. If the user copies an encrypted file to a diskette or hard drive formatted with FAT or FAT32, the file becomes decrypted. Another user with delete rights to the encrypted file can delete the file but cannot open it. What if the user who encrypted the files leaves? Windows 2000 automatically creates a public/private key certificate for the administrator account that allows the administrator to remove encryption on a file.

Exercise 4

USING FILE ENCRYPTION

In this exercise you will create a new user account, create an encrypted file, and log on as the new user. You will then log back on to the system as an administrator.

1. Click Start, click Run, key **CMD**, and press Enter.
2. In the command window that appears key:

   ```
   net user brendat password /ADD
   ```

   and press Enter.
3. Key **Exit** in the command window to close the window.
4. Double-click *My Computer* on the desktop.
5. Double-click the icon for the hard disk boot drive.
6. Create a folder named *secret*.
7. Right-click this folder, click Properties, and click the Advanced button on the Properties dialog box.
8. Click *Encrypt contents to secure data* and click OK. Once a folder has been encrypted, files added to the folder or created within the folder are automatically encrypted.
9. Double-click to open this new folder.
10. Right-click within the folder, click New, and click Text Document to create a new text file.
11. Double-click the text file to start Notepad, key your name, save this document with the name Secret Information, and exit from Notepad. You have now created an encrypted document from within the current account. Windows created a key and used this key to encrypt the file.

12. Log out of Windows and log back on with the new user brendat, using the password *password*.
13. Double-click *My Computer*, locate the folder named *secret*, and double-click the folder.
14. Double-click the document Secret Information. You should see an error message indicating that access to the document is not available.
15. Right-click this document, click Send To, and click *3½ Floppy A*. You should see an error message indicating that you cannot copy the file to a disk.
16. Log off the system as brendat and log back on as administrator.

When Windows automatically creates the administrator account during installation, a special set of public/private keys are created. These keys can be used by the administrator account to remove encryption from all files and folders. This capability prevents users from encrypting information and then leaving the company.

Auditing

Part of an overall security policy should include auditing, which includes monitoring access to network resources such as files and folders as well as monitoring specific actions. Auditing information is written to the security log and includes the identity of the user and the date and time of the action. For example, the following actions can be monitored through auditing:

- Logon and logoff events
- Modifying user and group account settings
- Reading and/or writing selected files and accessing selected folders

For each of these events, an audit entry for success, failure, or both will be written to the security log file.

By default, auditing is disabled. In order to use auditing, it must be turned on through a group policy setting. This setting allows the administrator to select the computers or groups that are subject to auditing and allows auditing to be enabled as group policies are dynamically updated. Once auditing has been enabled, specific events can be selected for auditing.

Enabling Auditing

Before selecting the objects to be audited, the auditing feature must be enabled by changing the group policy for the local computer or for the domain to enable the auditing of different kinds of events. The kinds of events that can be audited include the following:

Account Logon Event: This event happens when a user attempts to authenticate with the domain controller across the network.

Account Management Event: This event happens when user accounts or groups are created, modified, or deleted.

Directory Service Access Event: – This event occurs when Active Directory objects, such as OUs, are accessed.

Local Logon Event: This event happens when a user attempts to log on to the local computer.

Object Access Event: This event occurs when designated network objects such as files, folders, or printers are accessed.

Audit Change Event: This event happens when an attempt is made to change the existing audit policy.

Privilege Use Event: This event happens when a user attempt to use a privilege.

Process Tracking Event: This event occurs when various system processes are accessed.

System Events: These events happen when the security of the entire system is altered.

Each of these general events has a multitude of specific objects and settings. Once these general policies have been set, particular objects and events can be selected to be audited. It is important to set only the areas of interest and not turn on all auditing policies. As you will learn later in this chapter, the security log quickly fills with information and can become difficult to interpret.

Auditing can be applied to stand-alone computers, member servers in a domain, and domain controllers. It is best not to enable auditing for all domain controllers in a domain, but only selected systems by setting the local security settings for an individual computer or by setting the domain-level group policies.

The steps for using auditing are as follows:

- Edit the group policy on the container that holds the computers you wish to audit and enable auditing.

- Select and enable the elements to be audited.

Before specific items can be set for auditing, the general container auditing policy must be enabled. This policy is, by default, disabled. The container can be an organizational unit, a domain, a site, or a set of domain controllers.

Exercise 5

SETTING GROUP POLICY AUDITING

In this exercise you edit the group policy for domain controllers and set different types of auditing. In the next exercise you will set auditing for a particular domain controller and then select the items to be audited.

1. Click Start, Programs, Administrative Tools, and Active Directory Users and Computers.
2. Right-click the Domain Controllers container and click Properties.
3. In the Properties menu click the Group Policy tab.
4. Click *Default Domain Controllers Policy* and click the Edit button. You see the Group Policy Editor.
5. In the Group Policy Editor window, double-click *Windows Settings*, double-click *Security Settings*, double-click *Local Policies*, and then double-click *Audit Policy*. You see the Audit Policy settings (Figure 12.14).

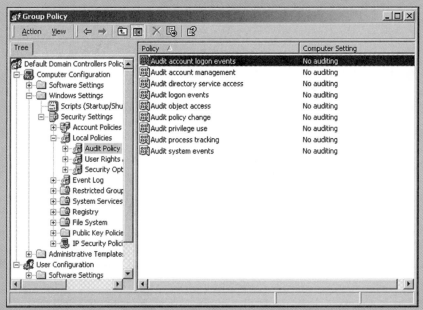

Figure 12.14

You will enable *Audit object access*, which includes files and folders, and enable *Audit account logon events*, which will track logons to the local domain controller.

6. Double-click *Audit account logon events*. You see the dialog box in Figure 12.15.

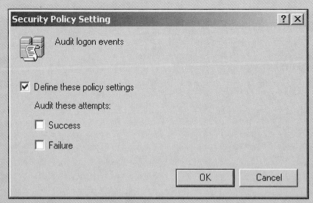

Figure 12.15

This feature allows you to audit both successful and unsuccessful logon attempts. It is useful if you want to track who logs on to the domain controller.

    7.   Click both the Success and Failure check boxes and click OK.
    8.   Double-click *Audit object access*.
    9.   Click the Success check box and click OK.

The list of audit events indicates which items have been set and what events will be tracked.

   10.   Close the Domain Controller Security Policy window.
   11.   Click OK to close the Domain Controllers dialog box and close Active Directory Users and Computers.

Setting Specific Auditing Options

Once the general auditing events have been enabled, specific objects can be identified to be audited. If the Audit object access has been enabled, selected files can be identified as being audited through the property option for files. If an entire folder is marked as being audited, every file within the folder will be audited. By default, the Everyone group is marked for auditing and all members of this group will be audited.

Exercise 6

SETTING SPECIFIC AUDITING OPTIONS

In this exercise you create a folder and file and set auditing properties on the folder.

    1.   Double-click *My Computer* from the desktop.
    2.   Double-click the drive containing the Windows 2000 system files.

3. Right-click the window, click New, and click Folder.
4. Name the folder *Secret Folder*.
5. Double-click this folder to open it, right-click in the folder window, click New, and click Text Document.
6. Name this text document Secret Files.txt.
7. Click the Folder Up button on the folder window toolbar to move up a level.
8. Right-click the folder just created and click Properties.
9. Click the Security tab and then click the Advanced button. You see the Access Control settings for the folder.
10. Click the Auditing tab to display the auditing option. In this dialog box you will set the users or groups you wish to audit.
11. Click the Add button to display a list of users and groups.
12. Scroll down and click the *Everyone* group and click OK. The list of Auditing entries is displayed (Figure 12.16).

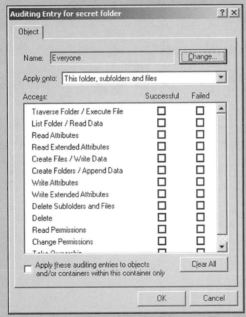

Figure 12.16

This list contains various actions that can be performed on the folder and files within the folder. Events generated by each of these actions can be selected for auditing.

13. Click the Successful option check boxes for *Traverse Folder/Execute File* and *Create Files/Write Data*, and then click the OK button.
14. Click the OK button to close the Access Control Settings dialog box and then click OK to close the Secret Folder Properties dialog box. Auditing is now enabled for this folder.

Viewing and Managing the Security Log

Once auditing has been enabled and set for a particular object or event, information is written to the security log. This log can fill quickly if a large number of security audits have been put into place. Log files have a default value that should be increased. You can also filter log files and display only selected records. You will learn more about managing log files in Chapter 13.

Exercise 7

VIEWING THE SECURITY LOG FILE

In this exercise you open the folder you just created that is being audited. You then view the security log file to locate the audit record.

1. Double-click *My Computer*, locate the new folder *Secret Folder*, and double-click this folder to open it.
2. Double-click the file contained in this folder to open it in Notepad.
3. Close the file and close the folder window.
4. Click Start, Programs, Administrative Tools, and Event Viewer. You see the Event Viewer window (Figure 12.17).

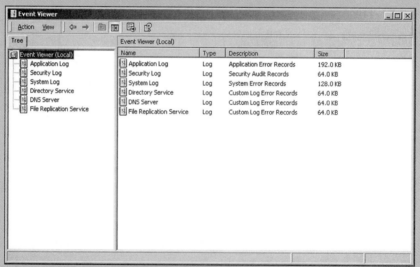

Figure 12.17

This lists the various log files maintained by Windows.

5. Click the *Security Log* icon in the left window. You should see a list of security events in the right window (Figure 12.18).

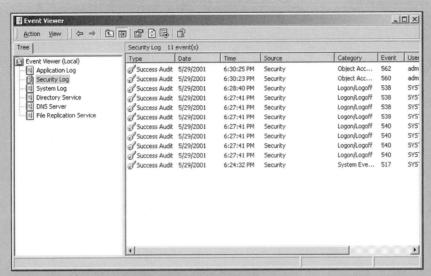

Figure 12.18

The auditing process creates these records. Notice that at lease two categories of event records will be listed, Object Access and Logon/Logoff.

6. Double-click the first Object Access event record. You see a dialog box that might look something like Figure 12.19.

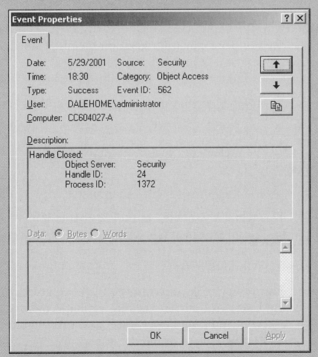

Figure 12.19

This screen lists details about the event.

7. Click the down arrow on the Event Properties dialog box to display the next event in the list. Notice that the Object Name in the list of property details should indicate your secret folder. The name of the user who accessed this folder is also listed.

8. Click the down arrow to view the remaining events in the Security Log. Notice that it contains a number of logon and logoff records. This listing results from the local computer being connected to by various services such as Kerberos.

9. Close the Event Properties dialog box by clicking OK and right-click the *Security Log* icon in the left window. You see the options for the Security Log.

10. Click *Clear All Events*, and when asked to save the log, click No.

Security Templates

Windows 2000 includes many different security settings. Because of the number and complexity of the security settings in Windows 2000, Microsoft has included a way to easily configure these settings by using security templates. A security template is a collection of security settings identified by a name. These templates are stored as text files and can be applied to a domain controller or a domain. The security templates, when applied, restructure various parts of Windows 2000. For example, a security template can enforce group membership, and if specified accounts are not to be part of a group they will be removed.

Security templates include settings in the following areas:

- Account and local policies that include password and lockout security
- Enforcement of group membership
- Access to registry keys
- Access to file system elements such as folders and files
- Access to system services

Microsoft ships several predefined security templates with Windows 2000—

Basic Security: This template is stored in the files basicwk.inf (for workstations), basicsv.inf (for member servers), and basicdc.inf (for domain controllers). These settings apply the default security settings for Windows 2000.

Compatible: This template is stored in the file compatws.inf. It configures the Users group so it can run regular Windows 2000 programs and configures the Power Users group to run older non-Windows 2000 programs that may be less secure.

Secure: This template is stored in the files securews.inf (for workstations) and securedc.inf (for domain controllers) and configures Windows for the Microsoft-recommended level of security.

Highly Secure: This template is stored in the files hisecws.inf (for workstations) and hisecdc.inf (for domain controllers) and configures computers with network traffic security. With this template, only computers running Windows 2000 and this security template can communicate with each other.

Using Security Templates

Security templates can be applied to the security policies for a system by importing the security template. Importing the template will reconfigure the existing security so it matches the template values. Another option compares a template with the existing security and notes the differences. Choosing this option is often a good idea before applying a template because it will highlight to the network administrator the impact of the security settings.

Exercise 8

APPLYING A SECURITY TEMPLATE

In this exercise you will apply a security template to a domain controller.

1. Click Start, Programs, Administrative Tools, and Domain Controller Security Policy.
2. Right-click the *Security Settings* icon in the left window and click Import Policy. You see a dialog box and a list of security template files. Check the option at the bottom of the dialog box *Clear this database before importing* to clear any existing security settings. If this option is not checked, then the security template will be merged with the existing security settings.
3. Click *DC Security.inf* and then click the Open button. The security policy has been applied to the domain controller.
4. Double-click the *Security Settings* icon, double-click *Account Policies*, and click *Password Policies*. Notice that none of the password policies are defined.
5. Right-click the *Security Settings* icon and click Import Policy.
6. Click *hisecdc.inf* and click the Open button to apply the highly secure domain controller policy.
7. Click the *Password Policies* icon and note the settings that have been applied to the domain controller passwords.
8. Right-click the *Security Settings* icon and click Import Policy.

9. Click the policy file *setup security.inf*, click the check box for the Clear this database before importing option, and click the Open button. These commands will apply the default Windows 2000 security and clear out any existing security options.
10. Check the password policy to verify that it has changed, and then close the Domain Controller Security window.

Exercise 9

TESTING A SECURITY POLICY

In this exercise you test a security policy before applying it to the system. In order to perform security configuration and analysis you must create an MMC with this snap-in.

1. Click Start, click Run, and then key **MMC** and press Enter.
2. In the blank MMC window, click the Console menu and click Add/Remove Snap-in.
3. In the Add/Remove Snap-in dialog box click the Add button.
4. In the Snap-in window scroll down, click *Security Configuration and Analysis,* and then click the Add button.
5. Click the Close button in the Add Standalone Snap-in dialog box and then click the OK button in the Add Snap-in dialog box. You see the Security Configuration and Analysis window (Figure 12.20).

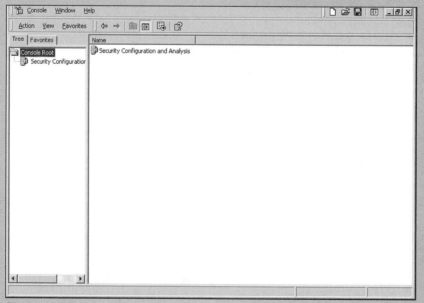

Figure 12.20

6. Right-click the *Security Configuration and Analysis* icon and click Open Database. In order to compare a template with the existing security you must create a database file.
7. For the database name key **testsecure** and click the Open button.
8. Click the highly secure domain controller security template file (*hisecdc.inf*), and click Open to import this file into the database.
9. Right-click the *Security Configuration and Analysis* icon and click Analyze Computer Now.
10. Click OK when asked for the location of the error log file. The analysis is performed and the results are displayed in the right window (Figure 12.21).

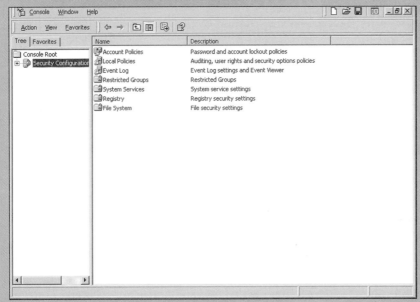

Figure 12.21

11. Double-click the *Account Policies* icon and double-click the *Password Policy* icon.

The database security settings (defined from the highly secure template) are compared to the existing security settings in effect on the domain controller. If they match, then a small green icon is displayed. If they differ, then a red icon is displayed.

12. Close the MMC console.

Creating a Network Security Plan

The security of a company network is of paramount importance; it should not be an afterthought. One of the most important elements of network security is the development of an overall network security plan. This plan will be an integral part of the network design and should direct future expansion of the network. Developing and maintaining a useful network plan can be, for large networks, a full-time job.

The steps to creating a security plan are as follows:

1. List network assets that need protection.

2. List the risks associated with each asset.

3. Identify the costs and likelihood of each risk and the cost of asset protection.

These steps are outlined in the following simple example.

Network Assets that Need Protection. The list of network assets should include domain controllers, databases, sensitive files and folders, printers, and secure connections between computers. Each item should be identified and assigned a location (if possible). Make sure that only important assets are listed rather than listing everything. For example:

Asset Name	Location	Importance
Sales Controller (salesDC)	Building 511	High
Sales Database	salesDC (s1.ndx and s2.ndx)	High
Sales Color Printer	Building 511	Medium

Risks Associated with Each Asset. A risk should be identified for each asset.

Asset Name	Risk
Sales Controller	Physical access to domain controller – damage controller
	Local logon access to user accounts – remove/change user accounts
	Local logon access to database files – delete database files
	Remote access to user accounts – remove/change user accounts
	Remote access to database files – delete database files
Sales Database	Local access to database program – change/delete records
	Remote access to database program – change/delete records
Sales Color Printer	Local printer access – print unauthorized material
	Remote printer access – print unauthorized material

Costs. The cost of each risk and the cost of asset protection should be identified. It is done here for the sales domain controller only.

Asset Name	Risk/Cost/Likelihood	Protection/Cost
Sales Controller	Physically damage controller/ High/Unlikely	Physically secure server/ Low
	Local access to user accounts/ Medium/ Unlikely	Prevent local logons to server/Low
	Local access to database files/ High / Unlikely	Prevent local logons to server/Low
	Remote access to user accounts/ Medium/ Possible	Secure administrator account/ Medium
	Remove access to database program/ High/ Possible	Restrict user access to database program/ High

The final step is to order the risks and protections several different ways, based on the risk with the most impact, on the most likely risk, and on the most expensive protection to implement. Once these ordered lists have been created, the most important risks and protections can be selected. The network administrator would then set the rules to avoid the most important risks. For example, only specific users can access the database program or files, and the sales domain controller must be backed up every night.

CHAPTER summary

➤ The main security elements in Windows 2000 are the Kerberos security system, the public/private key security system, and the Internet protocol security system. These systems are used to protect accounts, files, and data streams on a domain controller and within a domain.

➤ Kerberos is a symmetric key system where the same key is used for encryption and decryption. Public/private key certification is an asymmetrical system where one key is used for encryption and another key for decryption. Files can be encrypted using either Kerberos or public/ private key security. Auditing involves saving records of events such as file and service access and logon/logoff events.

➤ Auditing records are saved in the Security log and can be used to monitor access. Security templates consist of various security settings that can be applied to security policies.

CHAPTER terms

Authentication	Verifying the identity of a user or process.
AH	Authentication header: Part of IPSec and a protocol header added to an IP packet that is used to verify the security of the packet.
Biometric authorization	Using a physical feature such as fingerprints to authenticate a user.
Certificate	A software object issued by a certificate authority that contains a verified public key for a specified user or process.
CA	Certificate authority: A trusted entity that maintains public keys and verifies ownership of these keys.
ESP	Encapsulating security payload: Part of IPSec and the data part of the IP packet that is encrypted.
EFS	Encrypting file system: The service used to encrypt and decrypt files.
IPSec	Internet Protocol Security: An IP-level security protocol that will digitally sign and/or encrypt IP packets.
Kerberos	A symmetrical key security protocol used by Windows 2000.
Kerberos ticket	A software object that contains user security information, which is presented by a user or process to gain access to network resources.

KDC	Key distribution center: An element of Kerberos that authenticates users and distributes tickets.
LSA	Local Security Authority: A software service that is called by Winlogon.exe and used to authenticate users.
NT LAN Manager (NTLM) logon	The logon authentication process that uses the MSV1_0 authentication protocol.
One-way hash	A mathematical method of encrypting information by use of a key such that the resulting hashed information cannot be converted back to its original source.
PKI	Public key infrastructure: A set of security protocols that use public/private key services.
Public/private keys	An asymmetrical key security protocol that uses key pairs (public/private) to encrypt and decrypt information.
Security Principle	A user, group, or computer that can have security settings.
TGS	Ticket granting service: An element of Kerberos that grants tickets to authenticated users or processes.
TGT	Ticket granting ticket: A special ticket that is presented to a ticket granting service in order to get a regular Kerberos ticket.

CONCEPTS review

Multiple Choice

1. The three primary security functions in Windows 2000 are:
   a. Access, risks, and certification.
   b. Access, authentication, and data protection.
   c. Data protection, key certification, and Kerberos.
   d. Key certification, Kerberos, and authentication.

2. Windows 2000 authentication can be done by passwords and by:
   a. Digital cards.
   b. Biometric input.
   c. Fingerprint reading.
   d. All of the above.

3. The purpose of the Local Security Authority is to:
   a. Directly authenticate a user.
   b. Call an authentication service that authenticates the user.
   c. Decode user passwords.
   d. Authenticate users with the domain.

4. The default domain-level authentication protocol is:
   a. Public/private key.
   b. NTLM.
   c. SAM database authentication.
   d. Kerberos.

5. Kerberos is best described as:
   a. Asymmetrical key authentication.
   b. Symmetrical key authentication.
   c. Public/private key authentication.
   d. SAM-based authentication.

6. The primary benefit of a Kerberos-based security system is:
   a. Public key-based authentication.
   b. Single point of authentication on a network.
   c. Authentication of clients and servers.
   d. None of the above.

7. A public key infrastructure includes:
   a. Kerberos protocols.
   b. LDAP encryption.
   c. Public/private keys.
   d. Key exchanges.

8. When a public key is used to encrypt data, only the _____ key can be used to decrypt the data.
   a. Public
   b. Kerberos
   c. NTLM
   d. Private

9. A certificate authority verifies ownership of _____ keys.
   a. Private
   b. Public
   c. Kerberos
   d. NTML

10. The purpose of the authentication header in an IPSec protocol exchange is to:
    a. Certify the IP packet source and integrity.
    b. Certify the IP packet transmission history.
    c. Certify the IP packet completeness.
    d. None of the above.

11. The purpose of the encapsulating security payload (ESP) is to:
    a. Encrypt the IP packet header data.
    b. Encrypt the IP packet data.
    c. Encrypt the IP packet destination.
    d. Encrypt the IP packet source.

12. When selecting an authentication method for IPSec, you can choose Kerberos, certificate, and:
    a. Random number.
    b. String.
    c. Account name.
    d. None of the above.

13. When an encrypted file is copied to a diskette or hard drive formatted with FAT or FAT32:
    a. The file is destroyed.
    b. The file cannot be so copied.
    c. The file is reencrypted.
    d. The file is unencrypted.

14. Audit information is written to:
    a. The system audit log.
    b. The system security log.
    c. The system process log.
    d. The application log.

15. Security template files are saved with what file type?
    a. txt
    b. inf
    c. sec
    d. mdb

Short Answer

1. Outline the steps that take place when a user logs on to a computer that uses the Kerberos security system.
2. List two benefits to using the Kerberos security system.
3. Briefly explain the difference between a public key and a private key.
4. Briefly explain the purpose of a certificate authority.
5. Briefly explain the purpose of the security template files and how they are used.

LAB exercises

Exercise 1 – Creating an IPSec Policy

1. Click Start, Programs, Administrative Tools, and Domain Controller Security.
2. Double-click *Security Settings* and right-click *IP Security Policy*.
3. Click *Create IP Security Policy*.
4. Click Next to start the wizard, key **Sales Security Policy**, and click Next.
5. Make sure *Activate Default Response Rule* is selected and then click Next.
6. Click *Kerberos* and click Next.
7. Click Finish.

Exercise 2 – Edit the IPSec Policy

1. For the policy just created, in the IPSec Policy dialog box click Edit to edit the Default policy.
2. Click the Authentication Methods tab and click the Add button.
3. Click *Use this string to protect the key exchange*, key your last name, and click OK.
4. Click the Connection Type tab, click *Local area network (LAN)*, and click OK.
5. Click Close to close the dialog box and then close the domain controller security program.

Exercise 3 – Encrypting Top-Level Folder Files

1. On your system drive, create the following folder structure with the indented folder name created inside the folder above the name.

   > *Sales Information*
   > > *East*
   > > *South*

2. Right-click the *Sales Information* folder and click Properties.
3. Click the Advanced button on the General tab.
4. Click the Encrypt check box and click OK.
5. Click *Apply changes to this folder only* and click OK.

Exercise 4 – Enable Auditing for Domain

1. Click Start, Programs, Administrative Tools, and Domain Security Policy.
2. Double-click *Security Settings*, *Local Policies*, and *Audit Policies*.
3. Right-click *Audit Account Management* and click Security.
4. Click *Define these policy settings* and click Success.

5. Click OK.
6. Right-click *Audit Object Access*, click Security, click *Define these policy settings*, and then click the Success check box.
7. Click OK.
8. Close the Domain Security Policy program.
9. Click Start, Programs, Administrative Tools, and Domain Controller Security Policy.
10. Double-click *Security Settings*, *Local Policies*, and *Audit Policies*.
11. Right-click *Audit Account Management* and click Security.
12. Click the Success check box and click OK.
13. Close the Domain Controller Security Policy.

Exercise 5 – Adding a User

1. Click Start, Programs, Administrative Tools, and Event Viewer.
2. Right-click *Security Log* and click Clear All Events; if asked about saving the log file, click No.
3. Click Start, click Run, key **CMD**, and press Enter, which will take you to a command window.
4. Key **net user newuser1x /add** and press Enter. This user has been added to the default groups.
5. Click the Event Viewer window and click the *Security Log* icon. You should see some additional entries for the security log.

Exercise 6 – Creating Security Template

1. Click Start, click Run, key **MMC** and press Enter.
2. In the MMC program, click the Console menu, click Add Remove Snap-in, click the Add button, and from the snap-in list add the Security Templates snap-in.
3. Double-click the *Security Templates* icon and right-click the container under this top-level icon.
4. Click New Template.
5. Key **My Security Template** and click OK.
6. Double-click *My Security Template* to display the template properties.
7. Under Account Policies, click this new template and then double-click *Password Policies*.
8. Double-click *Minimum Password Length*, click *Define this policy*, key **5** for the password length, and click OK.
9. Right-click the *My Security Template* icon and click Save.
10. Close the MMC but do not save it.

PROBLEM SOLVING *exercises*

1. Your company has the following network security needs:

   The network has four domain controllers (DC1, DC2, DC3, DC4) and a domain named CompanyDomain.local. Three groups will be using the network: the Sales Department, the Finance Department, and the Administrative Department. The main company database is located on DC3. The DC4 server is located off-site and must communicate with the database domain controller through a secure channel. The Finance Department should be part of the Power Users group, but members of the Sales and Administrative groups should only be part of the Domain Users group. Only members of the Finance group should be able to access the database.

   Create a network security plan that outlines the risks, the network resources to be protected, and some general criteria for assessing the cost of the risks and the costs of the risk security.

2. Using the security plan developed in question 1, create a new security template that implements a security configuration dictated by the security plan.

PERFORMANCE MONITORING, BACKUPS, AND TROUBLESHOOTING 13

Performance Objectives

Upon completion of this chapter you will be able to:

- Discuss the aspects of Windows 2000 that affect performance
- Identify the various performance monitoring tools in Windows 2000
- Use Task Manager to monitor basic performance
- Identify the various elements in the performance-monitoring program
- Monitor memory, disk, and CPU performance in Windows 2000
- View and publish performance information
- Save performance information to a log file
- Use Event Viewer
- Back up a domain controller
- Discuss backing up an Active Directory database
- Create a set of emergency repair disks
- Use the recovery console
- Create a set of Windows 2000 floppy boot disks
- Review how to install a Windows 2000 Service Pack

Introduction

Installing and configuring a network is just one part of the network administrator's job. Most of the efforts involved in managing a network are the ongoing tasks of maintenance. These tasks involve creating and managing user accounts and network resources. They also include solving problems that arise in the course of network operation. These problems can be minor, such as a lost password, or they can be major, such as the loss of an entire Active Directory database. In either case, monitoring the performance of the network and network servers and troubleshooting problems are a central part of the job.

Performance Factors

One of the network components most vulnerable to failure is the domain controller. If a domain controller has hardware problems or the software installed on the domain controller is in conflict with the operating system, the impact to the network is significant. Users may have problems accessing resources located on the domain controller or may not be able to access their accounts. The most important domain controller elements, and those that should be closely monitored, are memory, the disk subsystem, and the central processing unit (CPU) performance. To better understand the monitoring information, it is necessary to understand the roles these elements play in the operation of a domain controller.

A network administrator should create a performance profile of their network servers. This set of performance statistics indicates when the server is running without problems under normal load. This baseline is important because, if later performance reports are created to identify problems, the new performance profiles can be compared to the baseline for differences.

Memory is where the operating system stores program code and data. Windows 2000 uses a virtual memory system to better use available memory. A virtual memory system makes available more apparent memory than is physically installed. It performs this trick by automatically swapping parts of physical memory to disk files. If a software application requires more memory than is physically available, the Windows 2000 virtual memory manager writes the contents of memory out to a file and clears physical memory for the new application. When the program whose memory was written to file makes a request for memory information, Windows 2000 reads the file information back into physical memory so the application will find its information where it expects it to be.

When physical memory becomes low, Windows starts swapping more and more memory data to files. This action causes the system to run slower because accessing data from disk files is many times slower than accessing information from physical memory. If the domain controller starts running slow, monitoring memory could uncover a problem.

The second critical element in domain controller performance is the disk subsystem. As you have learned, disk files are used for virtual memory, which means that the faster the disk drives the quicker virtual memory can be accessed. Monitoring the number of physical reads and writes from the hard disk system is an effective way to monitor overall performance.

The last element involved in the performance of a domain controller is the central processing unit. The CPU executes the software instructions and controls the overall speed of the system. Windows 2000 effectively uses multiple CPUs; therefore, improving CPU performance usually involves adding another CPU chip (with motherboards that support multiple CPUs). Monitoring CPU performance can also uncover misbehaving software applications that monopolize processor time.

Using the Task Manager

The **Task Manager** program is used to view and manage the software processes running within Windows. This program can also be used to view basic CPU and memory usage. As memory and CPU resources are used, the Task Manager window is updated. Using the Task Manager is not a replacement for the much more powerful Performance Monitor program, but it is useful for "quick looks" at the computer's performance.

Exercise 1

USING THE TASK MANAGER TO VIEW PERFORMANCE

In this exercise you open the Task Manager program and view the CPU and memory performance.

1. Right-click the taskbar at the bottom of the screen.
2. Click Task Manager. You see the Task Manager window displaying the currently running programs.
3. Click the Performance tab to display the performance statistics. You see a dialog box like Figure 13.1.

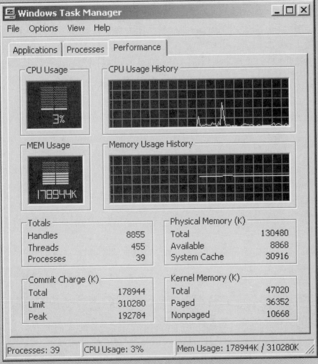

Figure 13.1

The Task Manager can be started by right-clicking the taskbar or by pressing Ctrl-Alt-Delete. By default, the Task Manager window displays on top of all other windows. When the program is minimized a small icon appears on the taskbar tray.

The Task Manager displays the following information:

- *Physical Memory:* This box indicates the amount of physical memory being used. The important item in this area is the amount of available physical memory. The numbers represent the amount of memory in thousands of bytes. Thus, if the available memory is 17455, the system has just over 17 MB free.

- *Kernel Memory:* This box shows the amount of memory dedicated to the Windows 2000 kernel. In most cases, these numbers will not change a great deal.

- *Commit Charge:* This box indicates the total amount of memory using the virtual memory manager. From Chapter 1, you learned that the virtual memory manager swaps physical memory to and from disk files. The important entry in this section is the peak number, which indicates the maximum amount of virtual memory used. If this number starts approaching the limit number (the total amount of virtual memory), the system will run slowly and could crash.

4. Write down the amount of available physical memory and the peak number in the Commit Charge area.
5. While the Task Manager is running, click Start, click Run, key **CMD**, and press Enter to open a command window. You may have to move the Task Manager window aside to see the command window.
6. In the command window locate the program named stress.exe on the CD that came with your textbook, key in the program name, and press Enter to run the program. You see a menu in the command window (Figure 13.2).

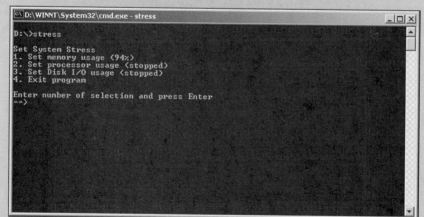

Figure 13.2

This simple program can be used to increase the memory, processor, or disk usage.

7. Key the number **1** and press Enter. You are prompted to enter the percentage of memory you want the stress program to use.
8. Key the number **95** and press Enter. The Stress program uses this amount of memory. Notice that the Task Manager window displays the increase in memory usage.
9. Key the number **2** and press Enter to set the processor usage. The stress program starts using up CPU cycles.
10. View the Task Manager dialog box and write down the amount of available physical memory and the peak number in the Commit Charge area. Compare these with the numbers entered in steps 7–9 before running the stress program.
11. In the command window key the number **4** and press Enter to exit the Stress program and close the command window.
12. Close the Task Manager dialog box.

Performance Monitor

Task Manager displays general information about CPU and memory usage, but it is inadequate for performing a detailed analysis of a system. The Performance Monitor program contains a set of powerful monitoring tools that can be used to view many different types of system performance. The Performance Monitor program also includes tools for displaying gathered information.

Microsoft allows other programs to use Performance Monitor to track performance by adding their own performance objects and counters to the Performance Monitor program. For example, when SQL Server is installed on a computer, it automatically adds a number of SQL Server performance objects to the Performance Monitor program.

An administrator monitors performance by selecting a **performance object** and displaying a counter associated with the object. Many different objects can be monitored and include things like Memory, Paging File, Physical Disk, Processor, DNS, and Thread. Each of these objects represents an element or service of Windows 2000. Each object has a set of counters used to measure a different aspect of the object. For example, the Physical Disk object has counters to measure the percent of disk read and write time, the average number of characters read from and written to the disk, and the number of disk read and write actions per second.

Given the large number of counters for all the objects, tracking performance becomes difficult not because of a lack of information but because of too much information. Table 13.1 lists some of the more important performance objects, the counters likely to be used, and the system operation the object will measure.

T A B L E 13.1 *Measurements of Selected Performance Objects*

Performance Object	Object Counters	System Operation
Cache	Copy Read Hits %	The cache is the memory used to store file system data as it is being read and written. A high number for the Read Hits counter indicates that performance is good, because data is being read from the cache and not the physical disk.
Memory	Available Mbytes and Pages /sec	The Available Mbytes counter measures the amount of physical memory available to processes. The Pages /sec counter indicates how often the memory paging file is read to or written from. A high Pages /sec counter indicates physical memory is low because the system is swapping to and from the page file.
Physical Disk	% Disk Time and Avg. Disk Queue Length	The Physical Disk object measures activities on the system hard drive. If the disk drive is performing a large number of operations, then it may not be able to keep up with the processor. If the % Disk Time counter is high and the Disk Queue Length counter (which measures the number of pending read and write operations) is high, the hard disk is not performing well.
Processor	% Privileged Time, % User Time, % Processor Time	The processor (CPU) executes instructions in either privileged mode (for operating system code) or user mode (for applications). If the percentage of time spent by the processor executing instructions becomes large, the processor is not keeping up with the operating system or applications software.

Using the Performance Monitor

The Performance Monitor program is used to set various performance monitors and collect data. A performance object is first selected, and then a counter for the object added to the monitoring window. Once added, the counter starts collecting information. Multiple counters can be added to the monitoring window. The monitoring window displays collected information several different ways. It can display information as a line graph, as a bar graph, or as a report. The information can also be saved as it is being collected for later viewing.

Exercise 2

ADDING OBJECT COUNTERS TO A MONITORING SESSION

In this exercise you add several performance object counters to a performance session and view the data several different ways.

1. Click Start, Programs, Administrative Tools, and then click Performance. If not selected, click the *System Monitor* icon in the left window. You see the Performance program in Figure 13.3.

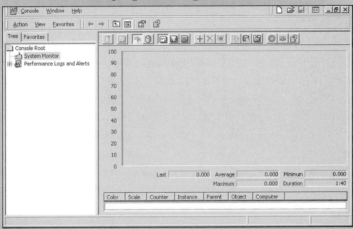

Figure 13.3

The Performance program displays a monitoring window on the right. You will add performance object counters to this right side window.

2. Click the button displaying the + sign above the monitoring window to display a dialog box that lists performance objects and counters (Figure 13.4).

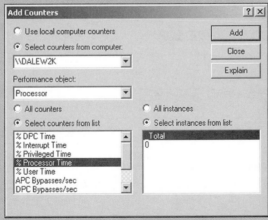

Figure 13.4

At the top of this dialog box are options used to select the computer to monitor. On a network, you can monitor other computers by selecting their names. The Performance object drop-down list box contains the performance objects that can be selected. Below this drop-down list is a list box containing the counters for the selected object. Not all objects have the same set of counters and as an object is selected the list of counters changes.

3. Click the down arrow in the Performance object list and click *Processor*.
4. Click *Select counters from list*, and then click *% User Time*, which will measure the amount of time the processor spends dealing with applications.

The list to the right of the counter list displays options for the counters. In this case, you see *Total* and *0* displayed in this second list. These two list options are used to select which CPU will be counted. If your system has multiple CPU chips, then you would see 0 and 1.

5. Click the Explain button on this dialog box. You see a text box displayed that contains a short explanation about the selected counter (Figure 13.5).

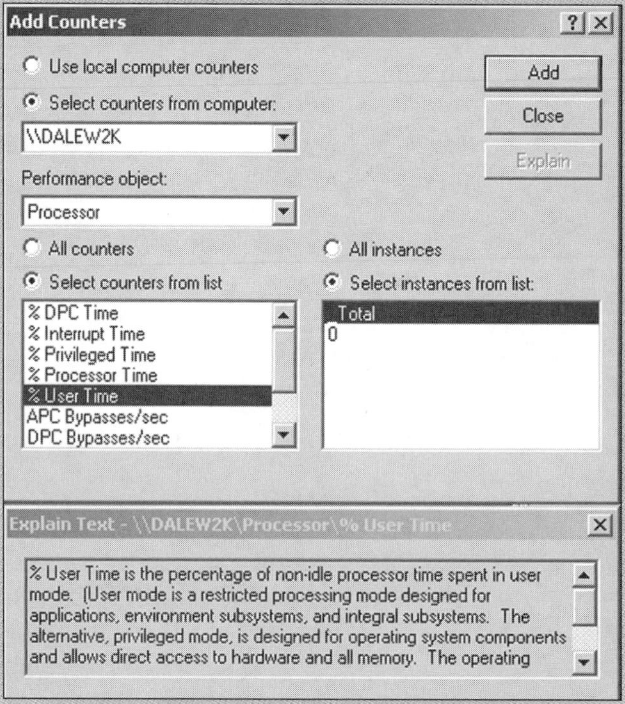

Figure 13.5

6. Click the Add button to add this counter to the Performance monitor window. The dialog box remains open so you can add additional counters.
7. In the Performance object drop-down list box click the *Memory* object and click the counter *Pages /sec*.
8. Click the Add button to add this counter.
9. Click the *Physical Disk* performance object and then click the *% Disk Time* counter. Notice that you can select the total for all disks or choose a specific disk.
10. Click the Add button to add this counter.
11. Click the Close button to close the Performance Object dialog box. You now see the Performance Monitor program displaying data from the selected counters (Figure 13.6). Each counter is assigned a different color.

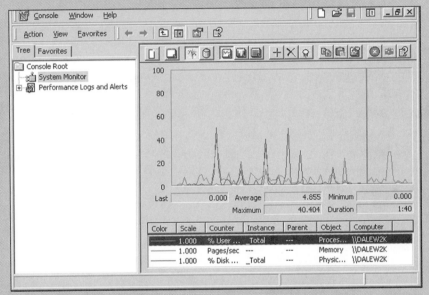

Figure 13.6

12. Click the View Histogram button in the monitoring window (located to the left of the Add button). This displays the information as a bar graph.
13. Click the View Report button to display the counter information as a set of numbers.
14. Click the View Chart button to display the information as a line chart.
15. In the View Chart window, click the object counter named *Pages/sec*. You could remove this object monitor by clicking the Delete button. You can also highlight the output from this object.

16. Click the Highlight button on the Performance dialog box. The line for the selected counter is highlighted in white.
17. Click the Highlight button again to turn off highlighting.

Saving Performance Data

Information collected by object counters can be saved in several different formats. The information from the selected objects and counters can be saved as a report and as a Web page. When the data is saved as a Web page, it allows the viewer to interact with the page. When the data is saved as a report, the default interval over which the data is measured is used and the object totals displayed.

Exercise 3

SAVING PERFORMANCE DATA

In this exercise you use the object counters selected in the previous exercise and save the data as a Web page and as a report.

1. If not already done, open the Performance Monitor program and add the following performance objects and counters:

    Processor – % User Time
    Memory – Pages /sec
    Physical Disk – % Disk Time

2. Move the mouse over the line graph display window and click the right mouse button.
3. Click Save As. You see a Save As file dialog box.
4. Key **basicdata** for the file name and set the Save as type option to *Web Page*. Save this Web page on your system drive.
5. Click the Save button to save the Web page.
6. Click the *Internet Explorer* icon on the desktop to start Internet Explorer.

7. In the Internet Explorer address box, key the location and name of the Web page just saved (for example, **D:\basicdata.htm**) and press Enter. You see an image of the line graph (Figure 13.7).

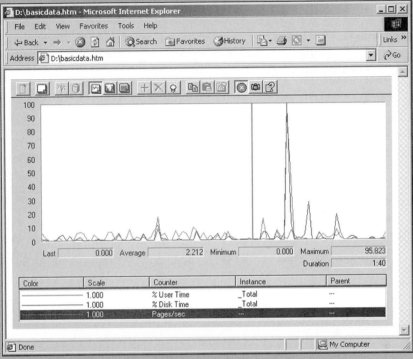

Figure 13.7

This screen appears to be a static picture of the Performance Monitor window, but it is, in fact, able to display live data.

8. In the browser, click the Freeze Data button (a button displaying a red *X*). The display will start displaying live performance data.
9. Close Internet Explorer.

Performance data can also be saved as a report by choosing a different Save as type option.

10. In the Performance Monitor window, right-click in the line graph area and then click Save As.
11. In the Save As folder dialog box key the file name **basicreport** and change the Save as type to *Report (*.tsv)*.
12. Click the Save button to save the data.

You will view this report information from WordPad.

13. Click Start, Programs, Accessories, and then click WordPad.
14. In the WordPad program click the File menu and click Open.
15. Enter the name of the report you just saved (for example D:\basicreport.tsv) and click Open. You see the performance data saved in a report format.
16. Close WordPad.

Creating and Using Performance Logs

Performance data is often collected over a period of time. The performance of a server must be tracked during its normal operating times, which may mean collecting several days' worth of data. The Performance Monitor program has the ability to automatically collect data for a specified period of time and to write this data to a log file. This log file can be formatted as a comma delimited file, a text report file, or a binary file. The benefit of a comma delimited file and a text report log file is that programs like Microsoft Excel and Word can be used to view and format the data.

Formatting performance data can sometimes be particularly important. When presenting performance data to upper management in an attempt to fund new hardware, it is helpful to display the data in an easy-to-understand format.

The Performance Logs and Alerts feature is made up of three elements—

1. **Counter Logs:** Collect data from the performance object counters.

2. **Trace Logs:** Used by programmers to collect process and thread operations.

3. **Alerts:** Used cause an event when a selected performance object counter has reached a specific value.

Exercise 4

VIEWING THE SYSTEM OVERVIEW COUNTER LOG

In this exercise you start the System Overview counter log, wait for it to collect data, and then view the results.

1. Click Start, Programs, Administrative Tools, and then click Performance.
2. Double-click the *Performance Logs and Alerts* icon to display the options.
3. Click the *Counter Logs* icon. The right window should display the default counter log *System Overview* (Figure 13.8).

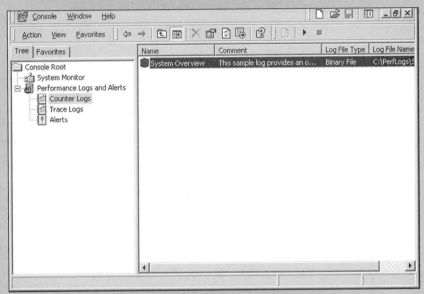

Figure 13.8

By default, the System Object log is not running and displays a red icon. When it is running the icon changes to green.

4. Right-click the *System Object* icon in the right window and click Properties. You see the Properties dialog box in Figure 13.9. The General tab displays the counters this log will use and the sampling interval.

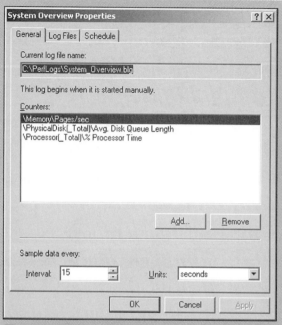

Figure 13.9

5. Click the Log Files tab. You see the dialog box in Figure 13.10. This dialog box is used to set the log file location, name, and type (text or binary) and a maximum file size.

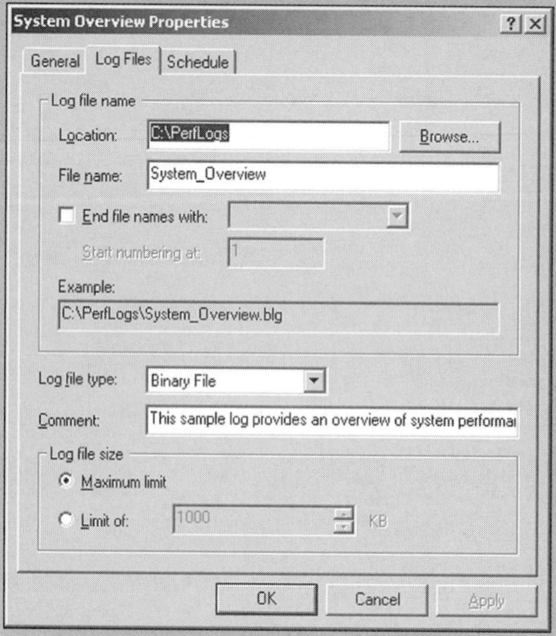

Figure 13.10

6. Click the Schedule tab. You see the dialog box in Figure 13.11.

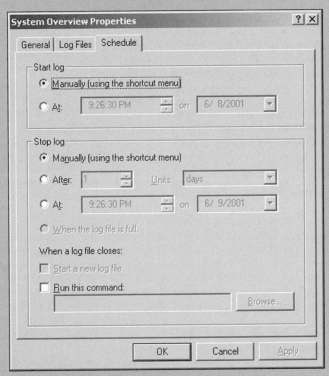

Figure 13.11

This dialog box is used to set the start and stop time for the log. When set to start and stop at a particular time, performance logs are added as a startup service to the system. You do not have to keep the Performance Monitor program running to collect log data.

7. Click the Cancel button to close this dialog box. By default, you cannot modify this System Overview log.
8. Right-click *System Overview* and click Start. The log should start running and the icon change from red to green. (If the log does not start and you see an error message, exit from the Performance Monitor program, restart the program, and try to start the log again.)
9. Wait about 10 minutes before beginning the next exercise.

Exercise 5

VIEWING LOG DATA

In this exercise you view the data collected by the log.

1. Open the Performance Monitor program.
2. Click the *System Monitor* icon to display the System Monitor window.
3. Right-click the Performance window and click Properties. You see the Sources dialog box.
4. Click the Source tab.
5. Click *Log file* and then click the Browse button to select the log file.
6. Change to the *PerfLogs* folder located on the system drive, find the file named System_overview.blg, and open this file.

The data to be displayed in the Performance window will now come from this log file and not from the operation of the system. Nothing yet displays because you must still select the counters to be displayed.

The log file may contain many weeks' worth of data and you may only wish to view part. You can select the time period by dragging the time range scroll bar and clicking the Time Range button.

7. Click the Data tab. The Data dialog box is used to set which counters found in the log file should be displayed.
8. Click the Add button to add a counter.
9. In the Performance object list box click *Memory*, click *All Counters*, and click Add.
10. Repeat this step for the other performance objects in the list. Only three objects will be displayed because the data being displayed is coming from the log file.
11. When all three counters have been added, click the Close button.
12. Click the Graph tab. It displays a dialog box used to set how the data is displayed.
13. Set the Vertical scale maximum to 40 and click the Horizontal grid check box.
14. Click OK to exit the dialog box. You see some of the system overview log data displayed.

You create custom log files by right clicking in the Counter Log window and adding a name for the log.

Exercise 6

CREATING AN ALERT

In this exercise you create an alert that will be activated when the memory counter reaches a specified point.

1. Open the Processor program.
2. Double-click *Performance Logs and Alerts* and click the *Alert* icon.
3. Right-click in the Alert window and click New Alert setting.
4. Enter the name *Memory Alert* for the alert name and click the OK button. You see the Memory Alert dialog box in Figure 13.12.

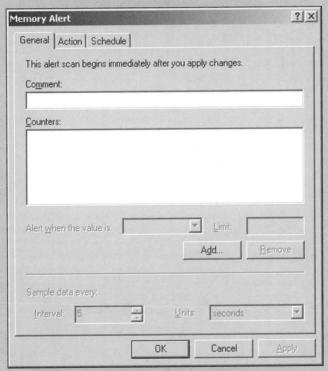

Figure 13.12

5. On the General tab, click the A_dd button to add a counter.
6. Click the memory performance object and click the *Available Mbytes* counter.
7. Click the Add button and then click the Close button. This counter is added to the dialog box.

8. In the Alert <u>w</u>hen value is section make sure *Under* is selected and key **10** in the Limit text box. This command causes the alert to be run when available memory is under 10 MB.
9. Click the Action tab. This dialog box (Figure 13.13) is used to set the actions that will be performed when the alert is run.

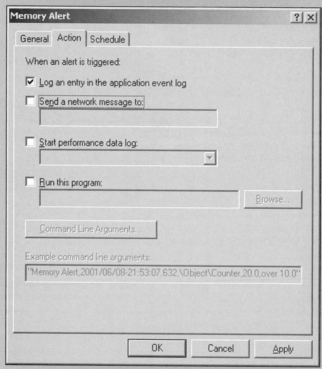

Figure 13.13

10. Click the *Send a network message to* check box and enter the name of your computer.
11. Click the Schedule tab to display the alert scheduling options. Like performance logs, an alert is automatically started when the local system boots.
12. Click *At* in the Start scan section and click *After* in the Stop scan section. Make sure 1 day is set for these options.
13. Click the OK button to start the alert. The *Alert* icon is green, indicating that it is running.

Network Monitor

The Performance Monitor program is used to monitor processes and applications on a server. However, sometimes problems must be traced out onto the network. Windows 2000 includes the **Network Monitor** program for monitoring network traffic. This program, which is not installed by default, is used to capture and display information coming to the server. The two parts to the Network Monitor program are the program itself and a network driver program. To use Network Monitor, the driver program must be installed on those computers whose network traffic will be monitored.

The Network Monitor program captures frames of data. A frame is a set of network data elements. The Network Monitor automatically captures this information. For example, when TCP/IP data is displayed, it includes the source IP address, the contents of the IP header, and the contents of the IP body. Network Monitor is useful when tracking communication problems between servers or between servers and clients. Events within Network Monitor can be created so that when a particular pattern of network packets is recognized, a program is executed or a message is sent.

Event Viewer

The Performance Monitor program is used to set object counters and display event information. Another handy tool for monitoring a server is the **Event Viewer**. This program logs events generated by different server components. An event is a collection of information generated by an application program or by system processes. When an event is created it is caught by the Event Viewer and saved in an **event log** file. The three primary logs are:

- *Application Log:* Contains events generated by the application program.
- *Security Log:* Contains security events that are generated by setting the Windows 2000 auditing service.
- *System Log:* Contains events generated by the Windows 2000 system programs.

Other common logs are:

- *Directory Service Log:* Contains events generated by Active Directory.
- *DNS Server Log:* Contains events generated by a DNS server.
- *File Replication Log:* Contains events generated by the file replication service.

The information contained in an event consists of:

- *Event Type:* Categorizes the event as a particular type.
- *Date and Time:* The date and time the event occurred.
- *Source:* The application or service that generated the event.

- *Category:* The identification of the event given to it by its originator.

- *Event Number:* A number assigned to the event.

- *User:* The user under which the event occurred.

- *Computer:* The name of the computer running the software that caused the event.

The event type is used to categorize the event. The possible event types are:

- *Information:* This event type does not indicate a problem but is used when an application or service was successful. For example, when DNS updates its records it sends an information event to the event log.

- *Warning:* This type does not necessarily indicate a problem, but may indicate a possible problem. For example, if the file replication service cannot replicate a file, it will first send a warning and retry the replication.

- *Error:* This type indicates a major problem with the service or application. For example, if the Netlogon program attempts to connect to another domain (perhaps to reestablish a share link) and fails, it generates an error event.

- *Failure Audit and Success Audit:* These events are generated by the security subsystem when auditing has been enabled and indicate either a successful or unsuccessful action.

If problems arise with a service, an application, or the system in general, the network administrator should first look at the Event Viewer. Error events are indicated by a red icon, warning events by a yellow icon, and information events by a blue icon. Red icons in an event viewer log should be investigated.

Exercise 7

USING THE EVENT VIEWER

In this exercise you open the Event Viewer, set options, and inspect several events.

1. Click Start, Programs, Administrative Tools, and then click Event Viewer. You see the Event Viewer window (Figure 13.14).

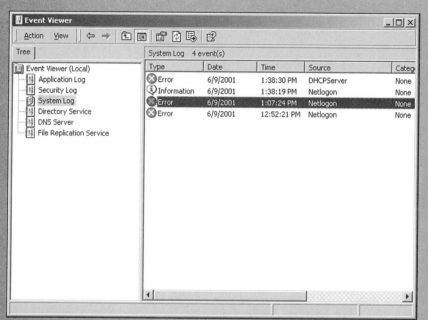

Figure 13.14

The logs are listed in the left window and the contents of the logs are listed in the right. The list of events on your system will differ from those displayed in the figures.

2. Click the *System Log* icon in the left window. The events in the system log are displayed.
3. Double-click the first event listed in the right window. You see detailed information about the event (Figure 13.15).

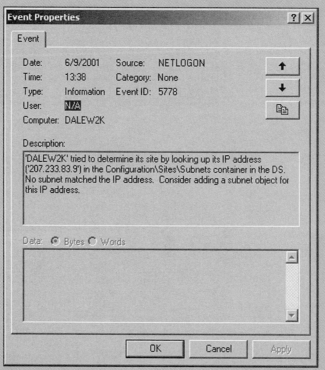

Figure 13.15

The event information in this dialog box can be copied to the clipboard and other events in the log can be viewed by clicking the up or down arrow within the dialog box.

4. Click the down arrow on the dialog box to view the next two events.
5. Click the OK button to close this dialog box.

Event logs keep saving events until the log is cleared. You might want to clear a log before installing new software or service. Events are, by default, ordered by date and time when displayed, but trying to scroll through hundreds of events can be time-consuming.

6. Right-click the *System Log* icon and click Properties. You see the Properties dialog box for the system log (Figure 13.16).

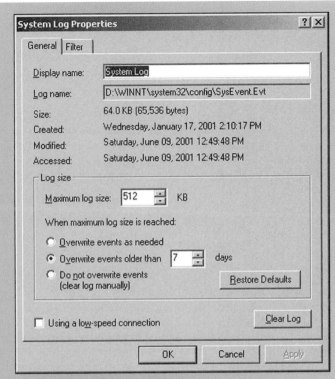

Figure 13.16

The important section of this dialog box is the Log size area. The log has a maximum size and a setting whereby logs older than seven days are overwritten. This information can be changed.

7. In the Overwrite events older than section set the number of days down to 4.
8. Click the Clear Log button to clear the contents of this system log.
9. Click No when asked if you want to save this log file.
10. Click OK to close the Properties dialog box and close the Event Viewer program.

Backing Up the Server

One of the most important tasks of the network administrator is to ensure that backups of the system are performed on a regular basis. If your system crashes and you do not have a recent backup, you had better have an updated resume! Although it is still called NTBackup, the backup program in Windows 2000 has been improved over what was found in Windows NT. It now allows you to back up to media other than tape. You are, however, still limited to backing up the local server. To back up other servers from a central location you will still need to buy a third-party product.

The backup program included with Windows 2000 is based on a product from Veritas Software called Backup Exec.

Several different types of backups can be performed. They differ based on whether the archive bit is set. The **archive bit** is a file attribute and is set whenever a file is modified in any way. The bit signals to the backup program that the file has changed and probably should be backed up. The backup will then either turn the bit off or leave it set, depending on the type of backup method selected. The different types of backup are listed here:

- *Normal:* Copies all selected files whether or not they have an archive bit set, and then resets the archive bit to off for all files backed up. This option is used to back up selected files from the server.

- *Incremental:* Copies all selected files that have the archive bit set and then resets the archive bit to off for all files backed up. This option is used to back up only those files that have been changed since the last backup (once a file has been changed, the archive bit is set on).

- *Differential:* Copies all selected files that have the archive bit set but does not reset the archive bit to off on any of the backed up files. This option is used to make a copy of all files that have changed, but does not change the archive bit so as not to interfere with regular incremental backups.

- *Copy:* Copies all selected files whether or not they have an archive bit set, but does not reset the archive bit to off on any of the backed up files. This option is used to quickly copy all files without causing their archive bit to be set and so mark them for future backups.

- *Daily:* Ignores the archive bit and copies all selected files that were modified on the day of the backup. It is used to get a "snapshot" of all files that have been modified on a particular day.

Many different backup options are available because it is not always feasible to perform a complete backup each time. On large systems, complete backups may take too long to be done overnight or may be too large to fit on a single medium. Under these conditions another type of backup must be selected. Table 13.2 lists several backup plans and the advantages and disadvantages of each.

TABLE 13.2 *Advantages and Disadvantages of Various Backup Plans*

	Advantage	Disadvantage
A. Normal complete backup every day	Makes restoring the system simple and fast because only one tape (the most recent tape) needs to be restored.	A normal complete backup could take too long to fit in an overnight window or too big to fit on your backup medium.
B. Normal complete backup on the weekend and a differential each day	When restoring, only two tapes must be restored—the complete backup and then the most recent differential— because they will have all files that have changed since the complete backup.	If many files change over the week, the differential near the end of the week may take too long to run or become too big to fit on the backup medium.
C. Normal complete backup on the weekend and an incremental each day	Backup times are kept short at night because only the files that were modified that day are backed up. Also keeps media usage to a minimum	Multiple tapes will need to be restored if the system fails because you must first restore the complete backup and then every incremental tape since the complete backup.

Some file copy utilities will modify the archive bit and throw off an incremental backup. To avoid this issue, use the daily option instead of the incremental option on the backup plan C.

Backup Plan

A server backup plan includes a schedule of when backups are done and what types of backups are performed. If a full server backup takes too long during the week, it may be necessary to back up the server over the weekend and perform incremental backups during the week. A backup plan will also include a way to identify the backup media (normally tapes) and include a set of steps for restoring the backup tapes.

For example, if a company has a server that requires 22 hours to back up, a full backup is done each weekend. Each night an incremental backup is performed and the incremental backup tape is labeled for the day of the week on which it was created (Monday, Tuesday, and so on). The incremental backup only contains files changed from the full backup. If the server crashed on Thursday, the full backup from the previous weekend would first be restored and then each incremental backup from Monday to Wednesday would be restored.

Exercise 8

BACKING UP THE SERVER

In the following exercise you will back up files from the server. You probably do not have a tape drive on your system; therefore, you will back up a file to a floppy diskette.

1. Click Start, Programs, Accessories, System Tools, and then click Backup.
2. Click the Backup tab. You see a screen that looks like Figure 13.17.

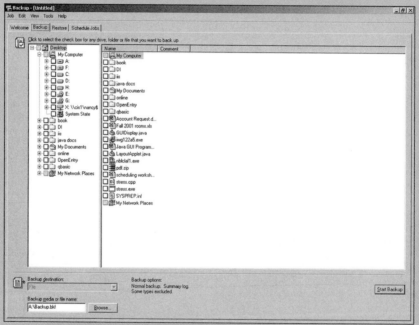

Figure 13.17

This screen allows you to select the drives, folders, and files to be backed up.

3. Double-click the C drive to expand it (or double-click the drive containing your Windows 2000 system files).
4. On the right-hand side of the screen, double-click the *WINNT* folder to expand it.
5. On the right-hand side of the screen, scroll down until you see the file named *Coffee bean.bmp* and click to put a check mark in the box next to the file.
6. Insert a disk in the A drive.

7. Make sure the Backup media or file name text box indicates *A:\backup.bfk* (this box is located at the bottom of the screen).
8. Click the Start Backup button. You should see a dialog box that looks like Figure 13.18.

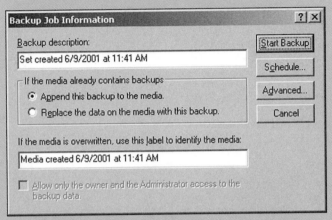

Figure 13.18

This dialog box contains the backup description, which is named for the time the backup set was created. This description can be changed if desired. We will leave it at the default.

9. Note the name of the backup set here for future use.

You also have the choice of appending the data to the media or replacing the data on the medium. If you select to append to the media, any backup files that are currently on the media will remain. If you select to replace the data, any backup files currently on the media will be erased and replaced. Other files that may be on the floppy will not be erased.

10. Click *Replace data on the media with this backup*.

You also see a check box that is labeled *Allow only the owner and the Administrator access to the backup data*. Your backup tapes hold all of the information from the system and you should guard them carefully. Tapes should be kept in a place that is accessible only to authorized people. However, if an unauthorized user does get access to a tape, selecting this check box will help prevent that person from reading the tape.

11. Put a check mark in the box that allows only the owner and administrator access to the backup data.
12. Click the Advanced button. You should see a dialog box that looks like Figure 13.19.

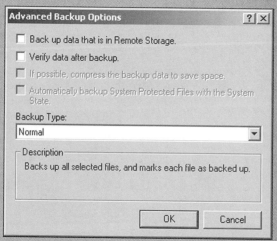

Figure 13.19

If you do not have any remote storage devices on your system, you will leave the first check box blank. Production systems may very well have remote storage devices that need to be backed up.

Verifying data after backup will take some additional time, but this option checks to be sure that the data backed up matches the original data.

13. Click to put a check mark in the Verify data after backup check box.

The third and fourth check boxes will be grayed out. Compression is only available if you are backing up to tape and backing up the system state requires more memory than is available on a floppy. Backing up the system state will be discussed in more detail in the Registry backup.

14. Leave the drop-down list box Backup Type setting as *Normal* and click OK.
15. Click Start Backup and watch the backup verify as it progresses.
16. At the Backup Progress dialog box click *Report* to view details about the backup. How long did the backup take? How long did the verification take?
17. Close the backup log window.
18. Click the Close button to close the Backup Progress dialog box.
19. Close the Backup program.

Exercise 9

RESTORING FILES

Backups do absolutely no good if they cannot be restored when they are needed. NTBackup makes it easy to restore files and folders. In this exercise you restore the file you just backed up. First you will need to rename the file that is on the hard disk so you can see that the file is actually restored from the floppy.

1. Double-click the *My Computer* icon to open it.
2. Double-click your system drive to open it.
3. Double-click the *WINNT* folder to open it.
4. If the files do not show, click the *Show files* link.
5. Scroll down to find the Coffee bean.bmp file (the extension may not show).
6. Right-click *Coffee bean.bmp* and click Rename.
7. Key **Old Coffee.bmp** and press Enter.
8. Minimize the WINNT window.

You are now ready to restore the file.

9. Double-click the *My Computer* icon to open it.
10. Double-click the A drive to open it. You should see a file named Backup.bkf.
11. Double-click the Backup.bkf file. The backup program should start up.
12. Click the Restore tab.
13. Click the plus sign next to the *File* icon to expand it, and click the plus sign next to your backup set name to expand it.
14. Put a check mark in the check box next to your system drive. The dialog box should look like Figure 13.20.

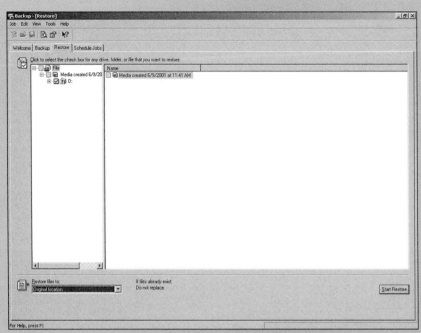

Figure 13.20

At the bottom of the dialog box is the Restore files to option. This option allows you to restore the files to their original location, an alternate location, or a single directory. Leave the selection on *Original location*.

15. Click the Start Restore button. You see a dialog box confirming the restore operation.
16. In the Confirm Restore dialog box, click the Advanced button. You see the dialog box in Figure 13.21.

Figure 13.21

17. Right-click each option and click the What's this? button for an explanation.
18. Make sure *Restore security, Restore junction points and restore file and folder data under juncture points to the original location*, and *Preserve existing volume mount points* are selected, and click OK.
19. Click OK to start the restore.
20. In the Enter Backup File Name box, make sure *Restore from backup file* indicates your backup set and click OK.
21. Click the Report button to view the summary, close the Summary window, and click the Close button to exit the Restore Progress dialog box.
22. Close the backup program and close the floppy drive window.
23. Maximize the \WINNT window.
24. Press F5 to refresh the screen.
25. Scroll down to locate the Coffee bean.bmp file that has been restored.

Oftentimes you will want to do backups at night or over the weekend when no one is around to start them. NTBackup includes an option that will allow you to schedule your backup for a future time. In order for the backup to run, it must log itself on with a user account that has the rights to back up files. You can use the administrative account, but it actually has more rights than are needed. It is more secure to create an account that is a member of the backup operators and have that account log on and back up your system. An exercise at the end of the chapter illustrates how to create a scheduled backup.

Backing Up the System State

Several critical system-related pieces of data are stored on domain controllers and should be backed up on a regular basis. If these pieces of data are damaged, the system will not function properly. The backup program allows you to back up only these critical elements without having to back up the entire server. These critical pieces of information are identified by the *System State* icon. They include—

- Active Directory files
- Boot files
- COM+ Class Registration Database
- Registry
- SysVol

Backing up these files is not as time-consuming as backing up the entire server and can be done on a regular basis, such as each evening. If your system ever crashed you could reload the Windows 2000 operating system off the CD and then use NTBackup to restore these critical files.

Backing Up and Restoring Active Directory

One of the elements in the System State backup group is Active Directory. A domain controller contains Active Directory files used by the network. When a domain controller has its Active Directory files restored, the other domain controllers in the replication group start automatically updating the Active Directory database on the restored system. However, if the Active Directory files being restored are older than the Active Directory tombstone lifetime, the backup program will not allow the restore operation. The tombstone lifetime is the amount of time an Active Directory object is allowed to exist without replication before it is marked as too old. The default tombstone lifetime is 60 days.

Another consideration when restoring Active Directory files on a domain controller is that Active Directory cannot be running when you restore the backup files. Before restoring Active Directory, the system must be placed in Active Directory restore mode. This process requires the following steps:

1. Reboot the system.

2. As the system is starting, press the F8 key to display a command window.

3. Click *Directory Services Restore Mode* and press Enter to continue booting.

4. Log on to the system using a local administrative account. You cannot log on using a domain account because Active Directory is not running.

5. Run the NTBackup program and restore Active Directory.

More options on the F8 boot menu are discussed in a following section.

Server Boot Problems

Some of the most frustrating problems to solve are boot problems. How can I fix anything if I can't even get the system to boot in the first place? Several different tools to help you resolve this type of issue exist, but you need to select the right one depending on your situation.

For a review on the boot process refer back to Chapter 2.

The Windows 2000 tools for identifying problems and fixing a server at boot time are:

- Enabling and viewing the boot logging process
- Using the recovery console
- Using the emergency repair disk

One of the first lines of defense against boot issues is the Advanced Options menu. You can access this menu by pressing F8 at the boot menu. Table 13.3 lists some of the options and what they can do for you.

T A B L E 13.3 *Defenses against Boot Problems*

Advanced Option	How It Is Used
Safe Mode	Boots a minimal system without network drivers and no network dependent services running. Can be used to diagnose network driver problems.
Safe Mode with Networking	Boots a minimal system with network drivers. Can be used to diagnose problems other than network problems.
Safe Mode with Command Prompt	Boots a minimal system without network drivers loaded and uses the command line interface to start programs. Can be used to diagnose problems with Explorer.
Enable Boot Logging	Creates a log file called ntblog.txt that will show all drivers as they load and report if they do not load. The file is located in the *WINNT* directory.
Enable VGA Mode	Boots the system in VGA mode. Can be used to diagnose problems with a video driver.
Last Known Good Configuration	Boots the system into the last configuration that was successfully logged on to. Can be used to delete changes made to the system after the last successful logon.
Directory Services Restore Mode	Boots the system in safe mode and re-indexes the Active Directory data.
Debugging Mode	Boots the system and sends debugging information through the serial port where it can be collected and viewed from another machine.

It is important, if you want to use the Last Known Good Configuration, to not log on to the system after the change is made. When a machine is booted and logged on, Windows 2000 keeps a copy of the current configuration in the registry under Hkey_Local_Machine\system\currentcontrolset. It also assumes that because you were able to boot the system and log on, the configuration is good and sets the same configuration to be the Last Known Good Configuration. If you then make a change such as loading a driver, the driver information is stored in the currentcontrolset, but it will not be copied to the Last Known Good Configuration until the next time someone successfully boots the machine and logs on. If you do not want to keep the driver, reboot the machine and click Last Known Good Configuration because it is the predriver configuration.

Exercise 10

SETTING THE BOOT LOG OPTIONS

In this lab you use the Enable Boot Logging advanced option and view the boot log. It is a good idea to run this option when your machine is functioning properly and keep a copy of the log file so you can see which drivers load and which do not. Then you will have a baseline for comparison when you have problems.

1. Reboot your machine.
2. As the computer is rebooting and when you see the boot menu, press F8 to enter the advanced options.
3. Click *Enable Boot logging*.
4. Click *Microsoft Windows 2000 Server*.
5. After the machine has booted log on as administrator.
6. Double-click *My Computer*, click your system drive, and double-click the *WINNT* directory.
7. Double-click the file named ntblog.txt. The file is opened in Notepad.
8. Look at the contents of this file and note the drivers that loaded and the drivers that did not.
9. Close the ntblog.txt file.
10. Rename the file ntblogbak.txt so it will not be overwritten the next time your machine is booted with logging enabled.

Emergency Recovery Console

A new feature for Windows 2000 is the introduction of the **emergency recovery console**. The recovery console allows access to NTFS partitions even if the Windows 2000 system will not boot. This access is possible because after it is installed, the recovery console is added as an option on the boot menu. When selected, the option will ask for the administrative password and then open a command prompt so you can perform various DOS commands to perform tasks such as copying files, or take advantage of some utilities that are especially created to help get your system back on its feet. Some of those utilities are shown in Table 13.4.

TABLE 13.4 Recovery Console Utilities

Utility	Function
Listsvc	Allows you to see what devices and services are present.
Disable	Allows you to disable a particular device or service that could be causing trouble.
Enable	Allows you to enable a particular device or service.
Fixboot	Creates a new boot sector on whichever drive you choose and sets that drive to be the bootable drive.
Systemroot	Returns you to the system root directory from wherever you may be.
Help	Reviews the available utilities that can be used in the recovery console.

It is wise to install the recovery console before issues arise with the server so it will be ready to use if needed. The install is simple. The following exercise will walk you through the steps.

If you did not install the emergency recovery console before you have a problem, you can still use it by running the setup program from the Windows 2000 Install CD. After going through some hardware inspection screens you will be asked if you want to do an install or repair. After selecting repair, you can choose to enter the recovery console.

Exercise 11

INSTALLING THE EMERGENCY RECOVERY CONSOLE

In this exercise you install the emergency recovery console, which can be done on both domain controllers. In order to install the emergency console you will need access to the I386 source files.

1. Click Start and then click Run.
2. In the Open box key **c:\i386\winnt32 /cmdcons** (you may need to substitute the location of your source files for c:\i386).
3. At the message asking if you want to install the recovery console as a startup option, click Yes.

The wizard will start up, check for necessary disk space, and copy files.

4. Click OK when you receive the message that the console has been successfully installed.

Exercise 12

USING THE RECOVERY CONSOLE

In this exercise you use the recovery console. You must first reboot your machine to use the console.

1. Click Start and then Shut Down.
2. Click *Restart* from the drop-down menu and click OK.
3. When the *Please select the operating system to start* prompt appears, use the down arrow to select Microsoft Windows 2000 Recovery Console and press Enter. Wait several moments for the console to start up. You will see a list of the Windows 2000 installations.
4. Press the number that corresponds to your installation and press Enter.
5. At the prompt key in the administrator password and press Enter. You should see a command prompt.
6. Key **Help** and press Enter to see a list of the commands available.
7. Press the spacebar to see the end of the list.
8. Key **Listsvc /?** and press Enter to view help on the listsvc command.
9. Key **listsvc** and press Enter to see the devices and services on your system.
10. Scroll through the list by pressing the spacebar.
11. Key **Exit** and press Enter to leave the recovery console and reboot your system.

Emergency Repair Disk (ERD)

Another important tool to help you recover from system problems is the **emergency repair disk** (**ERD**). The ERD is helpful when you do not know exactly what is wrong with your system but you need to return it to the state it was in when you last created an emergency repair disk. Windows NT also had an emergency repair disk, but the ERD in Windows 2000 has changed greatly. The Windows 2000 ERD is basically a boot disk that will allow you to gain access to repair utilities on the Windows 2000 Install CD. You should update your ERD each time changes are made to your system. Have a blank formatted disk available for the next exercise.

Exercise 13

CREATING AN EMERGENCY REPAIR DISK

In this exercise you create an emergency repair disk.

1. Click Start, Programs, Accessories, System Tools, and then click Backup.
2. At the Backup and Recovery Wizard click the Emergency Repair Disk button.

3. Insert a blank formatted floppy disk into the disk drive, click to put a check mark in the backup registry option, and then click OK.

4. At the message that the repair disk was successfully completed, click OK.

The registry files you chose to back up will not fit on the floppy disk but will be backed up to the directory *\winnt\repair\regback*. These files will be read if the ERD is used to repair the system, so it is important to keep them up-to-date. You therefore need to create a new ERD whenever you install new hardware or software on the server. For example, you install a new tape drive on your system and make a new ERD but you do not back up the registry files. A week later you use the ERD to repair your system. Once the system is repaired it will not know about the tape drive because the registry files used to repair the system predate the installation of the tape drive.

Exercise 14

USING THE EMERGENCY REPAIR DISK

In this exercise you use the ERD created in the previous exercise. You will need access to the source files in the *I386* folder in order to do this exercise. This exercise assumes you have a bootable CD-ROM and can boot off the Windows 2000 Install CD. If not, you can boot from another operating system but you cannot boot from the Windows 2000 system you are attempting to repair. Because your system is not actually damaged you will not see any difference after you repair it, but you will know how to use the repair disk.

1. Boot from the Windows 2000 Install CD.
2. At the Welcome to Setup screen press **R** to repair an installation.
3. At the Repair Options screen press **R** to use the ERD.
4. Key **F** for a fast repair.
5. Press Enter to indicate you have an ERD.
6. Insert your ERD and press Enter.
7. Remove the floppy disk when you are instructed to do so. The system will reboot.

Windows 2000 Setup Disks

Microsoft does not offer a disk-only setup version of Windows 2000 (which would likely consist of 300 disks). At times, however, a network administrator must use disks to boot a server. When a server fails to boot because of damaged or missing boot files, it can be fixed if the administrator can somehow boot into the server. If the Windows 2000 server hard disk has been formatted with the NTFS file system, a regular DOS or Windows 95/98 boot disk cannot be used to inspect a hard disk formatted with NTFS. To work with a hard disk formatted with NTFS, an operating system that can read this disk format must be booted. Two ways of booting an inoperable server are by using a Windows 2000 Install CD or by using Windows 2000 boot disks.

You create these Windows 2000 boot disks by running a program located on the Windows 2000 Install CD. This program, called MAKEBT32.EXE, can be run from Windows 95/98, Windows NT, or Windows 2000. This program builds a set of Windows 2000 startup disks. Once the startup disks are created, they can be used to start Windows 2000 from the disk. At that point, the recovery console can be run, which allows the administrator to inspect and repair a Windows 2000 server.

Exercise 15

CREATING WINDOWS 2000 STARTUP DISKS

In this exercise you create a set of Windows 2000 boot disks. To create a set of Windows 2000 setup disks, you will need four floppy high-density disks and access to the Windows 2000 Install CD.

1. Open the Windows 2000 Install CD and locate the *BOOTDISK* folder. The *BOOTDISK* folder will contain the following programs:

    MAKEBOOT.EXE
    MAKEBT32.EXE
    CDBOOT1.IMG
    CDBOOT2.IMG
    CDBOOT3.IMG
    CDBOOT4.IMG

The MAKEBOOT.EXE program can be run from DOS, while the MAKEBT32.EXE program can be run from Windows 95/98/NT and 2000. The IMG files are used to create the setup disks.

2. Find the program named MAKEBT32.EXE and double-click the program icon. You see the Command Prompt window.
3. Key the letter of the floppy disk drive (normally it is A)
4. You will be prompted to insert the disk and press any key. Press a key on the keyboard.

The system will copy the files for the first setup disk. When done, it will prompt you for another disk.

5. Continue inserting disks until all four setup disks are created.

Installing a Windows 2000 Service Pack

As Microsoft makes fixes and changes to Windows 2000, they issue service packs. A service pack is a set of updated files and programs that, when installed, upgrades Windows 2000. Microsoft typically makes service packs available on its Web site or through a software subscription service like TechNet or MSDN.

Of the several ways to acquire and install a service pack, one way is through the Microsoft Web site (www.microsoft.com). This site contains an automated service pack update program, which can be run while online, and a set of downloadable service pack files. If you are upgrading a single computer and you have a fast Internet connection, it is preferable to use the automated service pack update program. This program inspects the server and downloads only those elements of the service pack that are needed. This method greatly expedites downloading files. The second method, downloading the service pack files or using a service pack CD, is used when upgrading a number of network servers.

Because it is critical that network servers remain operational, and because installing service packs sometimes "breaks" a server, taking steps to make sure you can recover from installing a service pack is critical. These steps include—

- Disabling all programs and virus checking programs

- Creating a new ERD

- Performing a complete backup of the server including the registry and Active Directory files

- Making sure you have the original Windows 2000 Install CD handy

- Reading the service pack readme file to make sure that your system has enough hard drive space for the service pack and that you understand which features will be updated

This last step, verifying the hard drive space, is critical because when the service pack program installs, it saves replaced files in a folder named *NTServicepackuninstall$* on the system drive. The service pack install program also requires working space to unpack files. For example, Windows 2000 Service Pack 2, with the uninstall files, requires 710 MB of free disk space when installed from the service pack CD.

Installing from a service pack CD or from a network share containing the service pack files involves running the install program. This program is identified in the service pack readme file. For example, the file is named w2ksp2.exe. When installing from the Microsoft Web site, you will be prompted to download an update file. You should click *Run from current location*.

CHAPTER summary

➤ Monitoring and troubleshooting network servers is an important aspect of a network administrator's job. Performance monitoring can be done through several Windows 2000 tools. Task Manager is adequate for a quick overview of system performance. A more complete analysis is done using the Performance Monitor program. Windows 2000 contains a set of performance objects, each of which includes a set of counters. Information gathered through these objects can be saved as a Web page, displayed as a graph, or displayed as a report.

➤ Backing up the server is one way to avoid problems. Windows 2000 includes a backup program that can back up both data and critical system files such as the registry and Active Directory database. The different types of backups are normal, incremental, differential, copy, and daily.

➤ Boot problems are one of the major troubleshooting situations that network administrators must deal with. Windows 2000 includes the ability to log boot information, use the command line recovery console, and create an emergency repair disk.

CHAPTER terms

Alert	An object triggered by an event such as a performance counter reaching a limit.
Archive bit	A file attribute set whenever a file is modified in any way. The Windows 2000 backup program uses the archive bit to locate files for backup.
Counter log	A performance log that collects counter information.
Differential backup	Copies all files that have the archive bit set but does not reset the bit.
Directory services restore mode	Selected during the boot process and used to restore a backup copy of Active Directory.
Emergency recovery console	Selected during the boot process and used to access a server if it cannot boot.
ERD	Emergency repair disk: A specially created disk that allows recovery of the system.
Event log	A file containing event information created by applications, services, and system programs.
Event Viewer	The program used to view the event logs.

Incremental backup	Copies all selected files that have the archive bit set and resets the bit.
Network Monitor	The program used to view network data as it passes to and from the server.
Object counter	A counter associated with a performance object.
Performance object	An object that collects performance information.
Task Manager	A program used to view and manage software processes and to view CPU and memory resources.
Trace log	A log that records process and thread information.

CONCEPTS review

Multiple Choice

1. You did a full normal backup over the weekend and noticed that it took 8 hours to complete. You have a 7-hour window on weeknights to do backups. It is critical that you be able to restore as quickly as possible in the event of a system crash. Which backup plan should you choose?
   a. Full normal backup each night
   b. Full normal backup on weekends with a daily each weeknight
   c. Full normal backup on weekends with an incremental each weeknight
   d. Full normal backup on weekends with a differential each weeknight
   e. None of the above

2. Which of the following would not back up a file with the archive bit set?
   a. Normal
   b. Incremental
   c. Daily
   d. Differential
   e. None of the above

3. You are logged on to the system and load a new driver for a CD-ROM drive. The next time you reboot the system it crashes after your select the Windows 2000 Server option from the boot menu. To fix the problem you could:
   a. Press F8 at the boot menu and select Last Known Good Boot.
   b. Use your ERD to repair your installation.
   c. Start up the emergency console and disable the device.
   d. Press F8 at the boot menu and select Safe Mode.
   e. Either a or c.

4. Which of the following is not a valid emergency console command?
   a. Enable
   b. Fixboot
   c. Listsvc
   d. Repair
   e. Copy

5. From the Task Manager you *cannot* view:
   a. Memory usage.
   b. CPU usage.
   c. Virtual memory usage.
   d. A list of running processes.
   e. Hard drive usage.

6. The cache performance object is used to measure:
   a. Network performance.
   b. Memory performance.
   c. Disk read and write performance.
   d. CPU performance.
   e. None of the above.

7. When saving performance data, you view the data as:
   a. Graph.
   b. Report.
   c. Web page.
   d. None of the above.
   e. A, b, and c.

8. The trace log is used to collect information on:
   a. Memory usage.
   b. Hard disk usage.
   c. CPU usage.
   d. Cache usage.
   e. None of the above.

9. By default, the Event Viewer collects data on which log(s):
   a. Software log.
   b. Network log.
   c. System log.
   d. Hard drive log.
   e. None of the above.

10. The applications log collects data primarily from:
    a. Windows 2000 network system programs and processes.
    b. Windows 2000 application programs.
    c. The Windows 2000 security subsystem.
    d. The Windows 2000 network adapters.
    e. The Windows 2000 distributed disk.

11. The difference between a differential and incremental backup is:
    a. Differential is done each day, and incremental is done each week.
    b. Differential resets the file archive bit and incremental does not.
    c. Incremental resets the file archive bit and differential does not.
    d. Differential can only back up files that have the archive bit OFF.
    e. Incremental can only back up files that have the archive bit OFF.

12. In the NTBackup program, the System State consists of:
    a. Active Directory files.
    b. Boot files.
    c. Registry files.
    d. The COM database files.
    e. All of the above.

13. In order to back up or restore Active Directory, the following option must be selected during system boot:
    a. Active Directory Backup System.
    b. Directory Services.
    c. Directory Services Restore Mode.
    d. Active Directory Utility Mode.
    e. None of the above.

14. During booting of a Windows 2000 server, pressing the F8 key and selecting Safe Mode means that:
    a. The system boots without loading any user data.
    b. The system can be used without logging on to the system.
    c. The system can be used in single-user mode only.
    d. The system will use only 128 MB of memory.
    e. None of the above.

15. In the emergency recovery console, the Fixboot command will:
    a. Create a new boot sector on a specified drive and set the drive as bootable.
    b. Repair an existing boot sector.
    c. Overwrite an existing boot sector with a new copy of the operating system.
    d. Enable boot logging on a specified boot sector.
    e. None of the above.

Short Answer

1. What gets backed up if you select to do a System State backup?
2. Why is it important to back up the registry files when creating an emergency repair disk?
3. What are the counters for the following performance objects?

   Cache
   DNS
   Indexing Service
   Memory
   Physical Disk
   Processor
   Server

4. Briefly explain the difference between the emergency repair disk and the emergency recovery console.
5. List the performance objects you would check to diagnose a server that is running slowly.

LAB exercises

Exercise 1 – Monitoring Performance – Disk Usage

1. Open the Performance Monitor program.
2. Add the following counters for the Physical Disk performance object:

   % Disk Read Time
   % Disk Write Time
   Disk Bytes/sec

3. Display this information in a report format and write down the information for each counter.
4. Run the Stress program from a command prompt.
5. In the Stress program click item 3 (*Disk I/O*).
6. Write down the new numbers for each counter.

Exercise 2 – Monitoring Performance – Creating a New Log

1. Run the Performance Monitor program.
2. Double-click *Performance Logs and Alerts*.
3. Right-click *Counter Logs* and click New Log Settings.
4. Key the name **Memory Log** and click OK.

5. Click the Add button and add the following performance counters for the Memory performance object:

> % Committed Bytes in Use
> Available MBytes
> Pages/sec

6. Click Close to close the Add dialog box.
7. Click the Log Files tab and set the Log File type to Binary Circular File.
8. Set the log to Manually Start and to stop after 10 minutes.
9. Click the OK button to set the log.
10. After 10 minutes, click the *System Monitor* icon, click the View Log File data button.
11. Click the Memory Log file and click Open.
12. Click the Add button and add the three counters.

Exercise 3 – Monitoring Performance – Creating an Alert

1. Run the Performance Monitor program.
2. Double-click *Performance Logs and Alerts*.
3. Right-click *Alerts* and click New Alert settings.
4. For the name enter **Memory Alert** and click OK.
5. Click the Add button and, for the Memory performance object, add the counter % Committed bytes in use and then click the Close button.
6. Set the value for Over 90%.
7. Click the Action tab and click *Send a network message to*.
8. Key **administrator** and click OK.
9. Run the Stress program and try to use up memory.

Exercise 4 – Creating a Scheduled Backup

1. Using Active Directory Users and Computers, create a user in the User container with the first name and logon name of backup user and a password of classroom. Verify that the user logon name contains the correct domain. Make sure the user does not have to change the password at first login and that the password never expires. (Because it is actually a service and not a real person logging on, it is not capable of changing its password. If the password is allowed to expire the backups would cease to work.)
2. Make the user be a member of the Backup Operators group.
3. Do a quick format on your floppy to erase all files to be sure to see the results of the timed backup.
4. Follow steps 1–14 of Exercise 8 in the chapter. After step 14, click the Schedule button.
5. Click Yes to save the backup selections.
6. Save the file at the root of your system drive with the name BMPBackup and click save.

7. In the Run As box replace the name *administrator* with the name *backupuser*. Make sure the domain portion of the name is your domain.
8. Key the password **classroom** and click OK.
9. For the job name, key **Delayed Backup** and click the Properties button.
10. Schedule the job to run once in about 5 minutes and click OK.
11. Click OK to close the Scheduled Job Options window.
12. Close the Backup program.

Wait until a minute or two after the time you scheduled your job to run, then check your floppy disk for the new backup.

PROBLEM SOLVING exercises

1. You are network administrator for a three-server network and must devise a backup strategy. Server A is used as a print server, Server B contains the company database files and purchase order files, and Server C contains employee application files such as letters and memos. The data on Server A can be backed up in one hour, the data on Server B requires 26 hours for backup, and the data on Server C can be backed up in 6 hours. The data on Server B changes the most often (40 percent of the files change each day), Server C the next most often (20 percent of the files each week), and the data on Server A changes the least often.

   Create a weekly backup plan that uses the normal, incremental, differential, and daily backup options in the NTBackup program. This weekly backup plan should provide for the most security and the least amount of downtime in the event of a server crash.

2. You are a network administrator and your server starts acting strangely. It seems to slow down when performing routine tasks and spends a long time when connecting to other servers on the network. When you run an administrative program such as DNS, the program window takes two to three minutes to open. List the performance monitoring steps you would go through to diagnose the problem with this server. Explain why you did each step.

3. You are a network administrator and your server started displaying hard drive sector errors. When you tried to reboot the system, it hung and refused to reboot. List the steps you would perform to diagnose and (hopefully) fix this server.

INTERNET INFORMATION SERVICES 14

Performance Objectives

After completing this chapter you will be able to:

- Discuss the operation of a Web server
- Discuss some of the Internet protocols used with Web servers
- Create and configure a new Web server
- Create virtual directories
- Discuss routing and remote access in Windows 2000
- Configure a virtual private network
- Configure remote access services
- Install and configure terminal services

Introduction

As companies use the Internet for business, many types of Internet technologies are finding their way to business networks. Companies often set up intranets, which are internal company networks that use Internet technology. For example, a company may install a Web server that only works on the internal company network and use this server to deliver information. To make these types of network applications easier, Microsoft has included a powerful set of Web server tools with Windows 2000 called Internet Information Services (IIS). This chapter introduces you to these Web services and shows you how to use IIS to install and configure Web servers.

Windows 2000 servers can be used remotely with the remote access services. This service is installed on a server that allows users to access server resources through modem or wide area network connections. Another way to remotely access a Windows 2000 server is by using terminal services, which allow a client computer to run applications and perform administrative tasks on a server.

Web Servers

A Web server is a program running on a computer that is connected to a TCP/IP network. Web servers respond to requests from clients. For example, viewing Web pages on the Internet involves contacting a Web server. The client (your browser) sends a request for a Web page to the server and the server responds. Likewise, when you use a program like Microsoft Outlook to send and receive e-mail you are using a mail server.

A **Web server** is a computer running software that listens on the network for requests. These requests are messages in a standard protocol. A **Web page** is a document that uses the **Hypertext Markup Language** (**HTML**). The protocol used to request and deliver Web pages is called the **Hypertext Transport Protocol** (**HTTP**). This protocol is used by different kinds of browsers, such as Internet Explorer or Netscape to communicate with Web servers. The Web server software listens on IP port 80 for a client request for a Web page. When the client browser, using the HTTP protocol, contacts the server on this port, the server responds by sending the Web page across the network and back to the client. A **Web site** is a collection of Web pages with a domain name.

Another common Internet protocol is the **File Transfer Protocol** (**FTP**). This protocol is used to transfer files between a client and host, much as Web pages are transferred using HTTP. The FTP service must be running on the server. As with the Web service, the server listens for client requests on port 21. When a client uses FTP to contact the server, a connection is established between the two computers and allows files to be copied from the server to the client and from the client to the server.

Installing and Configuring IIS

Internet Information Services (IIS) is automatically installed with Windows 2000. In fact, even if you have never configured IIS on a newly installed server, you have a default Web site and an administrative Web site. You can view the default Web site by starting Internet Explorer and entering the IP address of the server in the browser's address field. The Web service part of IIS is automatically installed and started when Windows 2000 is installed on a server.

Managing IIS is done through Internet Services Manager. It allows the administrator to set options for IIS, create new Web or FTP servers, set security, and restart the Web services.

Exercise 1

USING THE INTERNET SERVICES MANAGER

In this exercise you open the IIS Services Manager and view the default Web site installed with Windows 2000.

1. Click Start, Programs, Administrative Tools, and then click Internet Services Manager. You see the window in Figure 14.1.

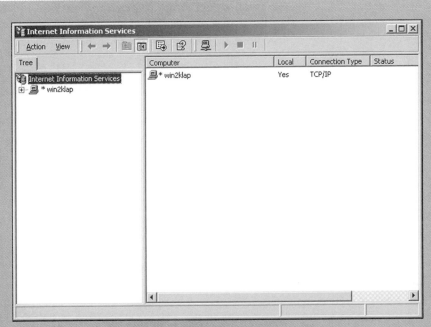

Figure 14.1

2. Double-click the server name in the right window and double-click the *Default Web Site* icon. You see the list of folders and virtual directories within the default Web site.

3. Start Internet Explorer and in the Address bar key **http://localhost** and press Enter. You see the default Web site page. Since your default Web site does not yet have a start page, the IIS documentation page and an "under construction" page is displayed. (You could also key **http://127.0.0.1**).

Creating a New Web Site

Although IIS comes with a default Web site (named Default Web Site), it can host multiple Web sites, each with its own name. Creating a new Web site involves several general tasks:

- Creating the physical Web site folders
- Configuring the Web site IP address and site name
- Configuring the Web site security
- Configuring the Web site settings

Before creating a Web site you must first create the folders to hold the site contents. When accessing a Web site, it may appear that you are viewing the contents of folders on the Web server. A Web page address may look something like—

http://www.emcp.com/files/newfile/index.htm

The index.htm file appears to be located in the *newfile* folder, which is located inside the *files* folder. However, the logical layout of a Web site does not have to reflect the physical layout. A Web site consists of a set of virtual directories. A **virtual directory** is a logical construct used by browsers to locate information on the server, but it does not have to mirror a physical folder. Virtual directories are mapped to physical folders on the Web server or to shared folders on the domain.

Once you have created the folders for the site contents, the second task when creating a new Web site is setting the Web site IP address and site name. Windows 2000 allows multiple IP addresses to be assigned to a single server. Multiple network interface cards (NIC) are not required because more than one IP address can be bound to a single NIC. When an NIC is used with IIS, a single server can host multiple Web sites, each with its own IP address. Of course, the Web site domain name must be entered as a host or alias record in a DNS server in order for the domain name to be resolved.

The third task in creating a Web site is setting the site security. The four security levels in IIS are *site-level security*, *virtual directory-level security*, *folder-level security*, and *NTFS file-level security*. Because most Web sites allow anonymous users to connect to the site and display Web pages, setting security on directories, folders, and files is extremely important.

The final task is configuring the Web site settings. These settings include the number of connections, bandwidth throttling, and other operational options.

Virtual Directories and Physical Folders

You can create virtual directories and assign them to physical folders in two ways. One way is through the Internet Services Manager program by selecting the Web site and adding virtual directories. The second way to make a physical folder a virtual directory is by setting the folder Web sharing options. This option is a property for each folder that can be set by right-clicking a folder and clicking Web Sharing. The preferred method for creating virtual directories is through the Internet Services Manager. It allows you to specify the relationship between multiple Web folders.

Exercise 2

CREATING A NEW WEB SITE AND CREATING FOLDERS AND VIRTUAL DIRECTORIES

In this exercise you create a new Web site, create a set of physical folders, and then create virtual directories for these folders.

1. Open *My Computer* and double-click the boot drive for you system.
2. Create the following set of folders by right clicking and then clicking New Folder. Make sure you correctly nest the folder structures. A folder named *Web Sites* is created under the boot drive (X). The folders named *Sales Web Site, Scripts, Applets, Images,* and *Files* are created under *Web Sites*. Continue implementing the folder structure shown in the following outline. (For example, a folder named *Main Pages* is located under the folder named *Sales Web Site* and the folder named *Sales Info* is located under *Main Pages*.)

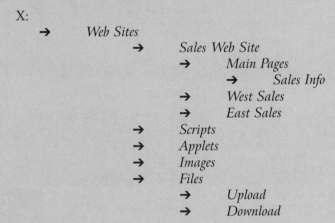

Once the physical folders have been created you will next create the virtual directories.

3. Click Start, Programs, Administrative Tools, and then Internet Services Manager.
4. Right-click the server icon, click New, and then click Web Site. You see the Create Web Site Wizard.
5. Click <u>N</u>ext to start the wizard.
6. Key the Web site description **Sales Web Site** and click <u>N</u>ext. You see the dialog box in Figure 14.2.

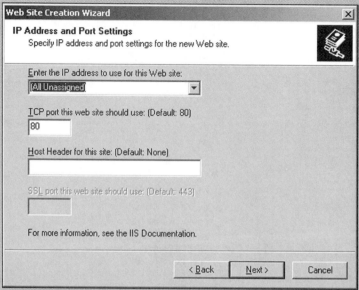

Figure 14.2

The IP address will default to the server IP address if the option *(All Unassigned)* is set. The TCP port number of 80 is the default used by browsers.

7. Click <u>N</u>ext to accept the defaults.
8. Click the Browse button and click the *Sales Web Site* folder inside the *Web Sites* folder. Make sure *Allow anonymous access* is selected and click <u>N</u>ext. You see the dialog box in Figure 14.3.

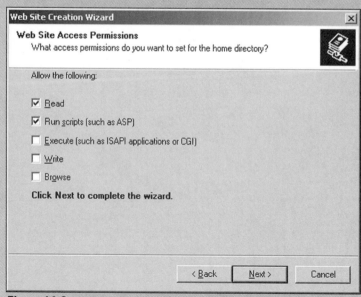

Figure 14.3

9. This dialog box allows you to set the access rights to this folder. Because users from the Internet will be accessing the contents of this folder, you should only click _Read_ and _Run scripts_ (the default). Click Next to continue with the wizard.
10. Click Finish to complete the wizard. You see the new Web site listed in the IIS window (Figure 14.4).

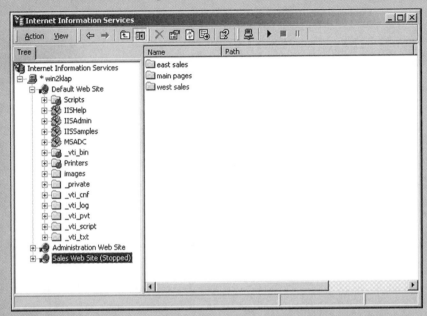

Figure 14.4

The word _(Stopped)_ displayed after the Web server name indicates that the Web server is not running because the default server is already assigned the default IP address. The folders located under the _Web Site_ physical folder are automatically added to the Web site. These folders can be accessed from a browser if the user has sufficient privileges. However, it is better to create virtual directories because if the physical folders are moved, the virtual folder can be remapped.

11. Additional virtual directories can be created within a top-level virtual directory. Right-click the _Sales Web Site_ icon, click New, and then click Virtual Directory.
12. Click the Next button to start the wizard. You see a dialog box for entering the name of the virtual directory.
13. In the Alias text box key **Scripts** and click Next.
14. For the directory, click Browse, click the folder named _Scripts_ under the _Web Sites_ folder, and then click Next.
15. Click the Execute check box option and click Next.
16. Click Finish to complete the Virtual Directory Wizard.

Exercise 3

HIDING A FOLDER AND CREATING A VIRTUAL DIRECTORY

In this exercise you hide a folder shortcut and create a virtual directory to point to the folder.

1. Open the Internet Information Services window, double-click *Sales Web Site*, right-click the *East Sales* folder and click Properties. You see the Properties dialog box for this item (Figure 14.5).

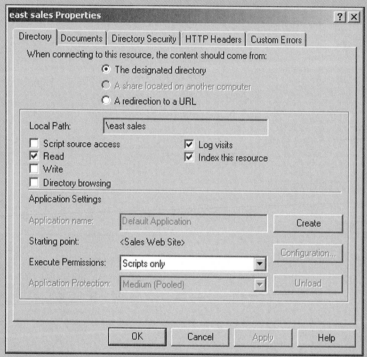

Figure 14.5

2. Clear the *Read* check box option. This command "hides" this folder from Internet browsing.
3. Click OK to close the Properties dialog box.
4. Right-click the new *Sales Web Site* icon, click New, and then click Virtual Directory.
5. Click <u>N</u>ext to start the wizard.
6. For the Alias key the name **EastSales** and click <u>N</u>ext. (Make sure the name you keyed has no spaces.)
7. Click the Browse button, click the *East Sales* folder, and then click <u>N</u>ext.

8. Accept the default permissions and click <u>N</u>ext.
9. Click Finish to complete the wizard. A new virtual directory now points to the physical folder named *Scripts*.
10. You can create virtual directories under other virtual directories to organize the Web site. In addition, multiple virtual directories can point to the same physical folder. Right-click the virtual directory you just created, click New, click Virtual Directory, and then click <u>N</u>ext to start the wizard.
11. For the Alias name enter **SalesInfo** (with no spaces) and click <u>N</u>ext.
12. Click the Browse button, click the folder *Sales Info* located under the *Main Pages* folder, and then click <u>N</u>ext.
13. Accept the default permissions, click <u>N</u>ext, and then click Finish to complete the wizard. The SalesInfo virtual directory is now located under the EastSales directory.
14. Using the preceding steps, create the following virtual directory structure mapped to the indicated physical folders:

> Sales Web Site (*Sales Web Site* folder)
> → EastSales (*East Sales* folder)
> → SalesInfo (*Sales Info* folder)
> → WestSales (*West Sales* folder)
> → SalesInfo (*Sales Info* folder)
> → Utils (*Sales Web Site* folder)
> → Images (*Images* folder)
> → Scripts (*Scripts* folder)
> → Files (*Files* folder)
> → Upload (*Upload* folder)
> → Download (*Download* folder)

Creating Web Site Content

Web site content consists of the files that will be delivered by the Web server. These files consist primarily of Hypertext Markup Language (HTML) files. Because this book does not teach Web design, you will create a simple HTML file with Notepad and save it in the Web site.

Exercise 4

CREATING AN HTML FILE

1. Open Notepad and enter the following lines of text:

```
<HTML><HEAD><TITLE>Company Page</TITLE></HEAD>
<BODY BGCOLOR = "yellow">
<P ALIGN="center"><H2>Sales Company</H2></P>
<BR>
For more information click the link to
<A HREF="info.htm">Company Information </A>
</BODY>
</HTML>
```

2. On the Notepad menu bar click File and then click Save As.
3. At the Save As dialog box change the Save As type option to *All Files*.
4. Key **INDEX.HTM** for the file name and choose the *Sales Web Site* folder. (When using Notepad it is important to save the document as an HTM file and not as a TXT file.)
5. Click the Save button, but remain in Notepad.
6. Edit the Notepad document so it looks like the following:

```
<HTML><HEAD><TITLE>Information Page</TITLE></HEAD>
<BODY BGCOLOR = "lightgreen">
<P ALIGN="center"><H2>Company Information</H2></P>
<BR>
To return to the main page:
<A HREF="index.htm">back </A>
</BODY>
</HTML>
```

7. Save this document with Save As in the *Sales Web Site* folder with the name info.htm.
8. Exit Notepad.
9. Using My Computer, open the *Sales Web Site* folder and double-click the index.htm file. If the page cannot be loaded, check the code and retype the page.
10. Using the steps outlined above, create the following files in the indicated folders:

   File Name: eastern.htm
   Save in: *East Sales*

```
<HTML><HEAD><TITLE>Eastern Sales</TITLE></HEAD>
<BODY BGCOLOR = "lightblue">
```

```
<P ALIGN="center"><H2>Eastern Sales</H2></P>
<BR>
To return to the main page:
<A HREF="..\index.htm">back </A>
</BODY>
</HTML>
```

File Name: western.htm
Save in: *West Sales*

```
<HTML><HEAD><TITLE>Western Sales</TITLE></HEAD>
<BODY BGCOLOR = "teal">
<P ALIGN="center"><H2>Western Sales</H2></P>
<BR>
To return to the main page:
<A HREF="..\index.htm">back </A>
</BODY>
</HTML>
```

11. Repeat step 9 to view both of these files.

Web Site Security

Security is a critical issue with Web servers. Allowing anonymous users from the Internet to access your Web site and your server must be done. For this reason IIS uses four levels of security:

Site-Level Security: This setting consists of securing the top-level site virtual directory and creating log files of all visitors.

Virtual Directory-Level Security: This setting indicates the type of directory access and how Windows will validate users.

File-Level Security: Done through the IIS management tool, this setting allows you to specify read and write access as well as Windows validation options on a per file basis.

NTFS-Level Security: Although set from the Windows environment, this security will be used by IIS. If a visitor to the Web site tries to access a file and the file has NTFS permissions assigned, the visitor will be asked for an account ID and password.

Exercise 5

SETTING SECURITY

In this exercise you set security on the Web site, on a virtual directory, and on a file.

1. Click Start, Programs, Administration Tools, and then click Internet Information Services.
2. Right-click *Sales Web Site* and click Properties.
3. Click the Directory Security tab to display the security options for the *Sales Web Site* folder (Figure 14.6).

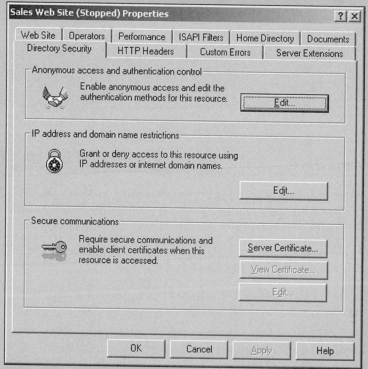

Figure 14.6

4. Click the Edit button in the Anonymous access and authentication control section.

This command displays the options available when users access resources from the Web. The first option is to allow anonymous access and is necessary for open Web sites. In fact, IIS creates a default user account on the server when IIS is installed and uses this default account.

The lower section lists the options for authenticated access. When a user tries to access restricted resources on the Web server, the listed methods for authentication will be tried (in order). Normally, you want to choose only the Integrated Windows Authentication option.

5. Click OK to leave the Authentication Methods dialog box.
6. Click the Edit button in the IP address and domain name restrictions section. You see the IP address and domain restrictions screen that allows you to grant or deny access to your Web site based on domain or IP addresses.
7. Make sure *Granted Access* is selected and click the Add button. You will add your neighbor's IP address to the restricted list.
8. Click *Single Computer*, enter your neighbor's IP address, and click OK.
9. Click OK to leave the IP address and domain name restrictions window.
10. Click the Home Directory tab. You see options for the Home Directory (Figure 14.7).

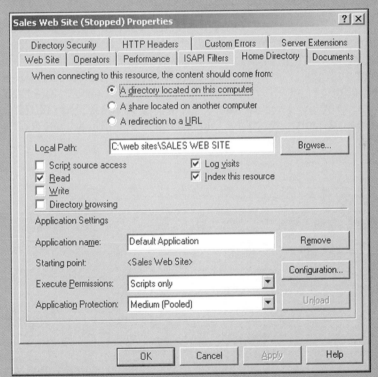

Figure 14.7

11. Click *Directory Browsing* and then click OK, which will allow users to browse the Web site directory.

12. You will be asked if you want to apply this security allowance to all virtual directories. You can set different security options for each virtual directory or repeat the one from the root Web site. Click the Select All button and then click OK.
13. In the IIS manager window, click the *Sales Web Site* folder. In the right-hand window, the index.htm and info.htm files are displayed.
14. Right-click *info.htm* and click Properties.
15. Click the File Security tab and click the Edit button in the Anonymous access and authentication control section.
16. Uncheck *Anonymous Access* and click OK. This command will force users to supply an ID and password when viewing this file.
17. Click OK to exit the Properties dialog box.

Configuring the Web Site

To this point you have created the Web site, created content, and set security. However, you cannot yet view your Web site because your computer only has a single IP address, which is used by the Default Web Site. Windows 2000 allows you to assign multiple IP addresses to a single server. When a user enters the IP address or the host name (if the IP address is in a DNS server), the Web page is displayed. In addition to setting the IP address, you must also tell IIS which file it should use by default. Entering a folder name will automatically load a default file, if the file is found in the folder.

Exercise 6

CONFIGURING THE WEB SITE

In this exercise you add another IP address and configure your Web site to use this address.

1. Click Start, Settings, and Network and Dial-up Connections.
2. Right-click the network connection and click Properties.
3. Click *Internet Protocol* and click the Properties button.
4. Click the Advanced button. You see the dialog box in Figure 14.8.

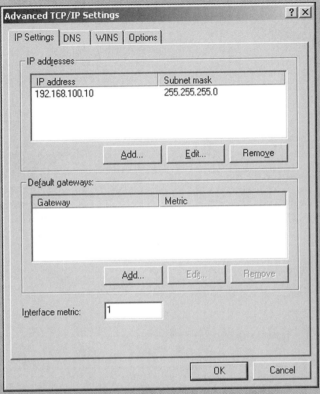

Figure 14.8

5. The upper section of this dialog box lists the IP addresses assigned to this server. Click the Add button under the IP addresses section.

6. In the IP address box enter a new IP address in the form **192.168.100.XXX**, where *XXX* is a number between 1 and 255 (you may be given this number by your instructor).

7. Click in the Subnet mask area and key **255.255.255.0**.

8. Click the Add button to add this IP address, click OK to leave the Advanced dialog box, click OK to leave the TCP/IP Properties box, and click OK to close the Connections dialog box. You have now added an IP address to your computer.

9. Open the IIS management program, right-click the *Sales Web Site* folder, and click Properties.

10. In the IP address box, click the down arrow and click the new IP address just added. Make sure the TCP port is 80.

11. You will next set the default file name. When you browse to a Web site, the server automatically loads a default file. Click the Documents tab. You see the dialog box in Figure 14.9.

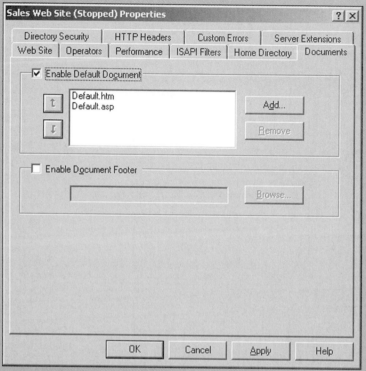

Figure 14.9

This screen displays the default document names that IIS will search for when accessing a directory. Because you have created a default document named Index.htm, you must add it to the list.

12. Click the A̲dd button, key **index.htm**, and click OK.
13. Click OK to close the Web Site properties window.
14. To start the Web site, right-click the *Sales Web Site* icon and click Start. The *Stopped* message should be removed.
15. Test the Web site by opening Internet Explorer, keying the IP address of your new Web site, and pressing Enter. You should see the starting Web page (Index.htm).
16. Click the *Company Information* link. You protected this document by removing the Anonymous access property. You should see a password screen prompting you for a user name, password, and domain. Enter **administrator**, **classroom**, and your domain name. You should now be able to view this page.

Remote IIS Administration

Most Web servers are not managed by logging on to the server itself. IIS has some powerful features that allow an administrator to manage the site remotely by connecting to the Administration Web site, which is located on a nonstandard port. During installation, IIS randomly selects a port number and assigns it to the Administration page. However, hackers can use port scanning to locate ports and potentially break into the site. A better restriction on the IIS administration site is restricting the access by IP address.

Exercise 7

REMOTELY ADMINISTERING IIS

In this exercise you examine the IIS administration site security, view the site itself, and then further restrict the site access.

1. Start the IIS management tool, right-click the *Administration Web Site* icon, and click Properties.
2. Write down the TCP port number.
3. Click OK to close the Properties dialog box.
4. Start Internet Explorer, key the following URL, and press Enter.

   ```
   http://localhost:xxx
   ```
   (where *xxx* is the port number)

You should see the administration page. You may get a warning about a nonsecure connection. The administration Web tool provides most of the management options as the IIS management program.

5. Click the *Sales Web Site* link in the right side of the screen and click the *Properties* link in the left screen to see the properties for this Web site.
6. Close Internet Explorer.
7. One way to restrict the remote administration tool is to limit access only to specified IP addresses. Open the IIS management tool, right-click the *Administration Web Site* icon, and click Properties.
8. Click the Directory Security tab and click the Edit button in the IP address section (the second Edit button). You see the dialog box in Figure 14.10.

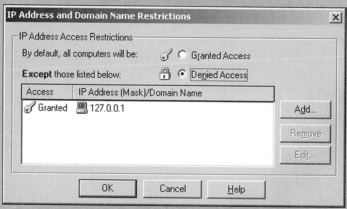
Figure 14.10

9. Click *Denied Access* to deny access to all clients except for those IP addresses listed.
10. Click the A<u>d</u>d button, click *Single Computer*, enter the IP address of your neighbor, and click OK.
11. Click OK to close the Name Restrictions dialog box and click OK to close the Properties dialog box.
12. Have your neighbor log on to your server by starting Internet Explorer and entering the following:

    ```
    http://192.168.100.100:xxxx
    ```
    (where the IP address is the address of your server and *xxxx* is the port number of the Administration Web site).

13. Your neighbor will be prompted to log on to the page with a user ID, password, and domain.

Remote Access Service

The ability to reach a network from a remote site has become increasingly important for both network administrators and users. Starting with Windows NT, a **remote access service** (**RAS**) has been bundled with the operating system. Numerous new features have been added to the version of RAS included with Windows 2000. It is now sometimes called **routing and remote access service** (**RRAS**) to reflect its new capabilities. The original implementation referred to both the client and server side of remote access as RAS. With Windows 2000, the client part is referred to as dial-up networking or DUN, while RRAS is the server part. This chapter will emphasize the server side of remote access.

In order to be able to access a local area network from a remote site, the LAN traffic must be passed over a **wide area network** (**WAN**). The different types of WANs can include **plain old telephone service (POTS)**, **integrated services digital networks (ISDN)**, and X.25 packet switching or **virtual private networks** (**VPNs**) over the Internet. RAS supports two different data link protocols that work over a WAN: **Serial Line Interface Protocol** (**SLIP**) and **Point to Point Protocol** (**PPP**). SLIP is the older protocol and is supported for outbound calls because it does not support multiple protocols or encrypted passwords. PPP is an industry standard conforming to RFC 1661 that can encapsulate and send multiple protocols, such as AppleTalk TCP/IP and IPX, over a WAN. PPP also supports error correction and various types of authentication.

Several variations to PPP include PPP Multilink and **Point to Point Tunneling Protocol** (**PPTP**). PPP Multilink allows you to combine separate physical connections to appear as one logical connection, thus giving you more bandwidth. For example, if you have two 56K modems, one on the RAS server and another on the client, both modems can be combined for a single connection. Any combination of modems and ISDN can be used with PPP Multilink. PPTP allows you to use the Internet to make a virtual private network (VPN) by encapsulating encrypted data in a standard PPP frame.

A PPP connection requires four stages: link establishment, user authentication, callback settings, and configuration. You will be able to select options for these stages as you install the protocol.

Installing Remote Access Service

The five options when installing RAS are:

- Internet connection server
- Remote access server
- Virtual private network (VPN) server
- Network router
- Manually configured server

The Internet connection server is a new option in Windows 2000. This option will allow the server to perform **network address translation** (**NAT**) between a nonroutable private internal network and a single valid IP address that has Internet access. With NAT, a client that does not have a valid public IP address will send its request to the server running NAT. The server running NAT must have a valid public IP address and connection to the Internet. The server will retrieve the desired information and return it to the client. This option does not have all the features of a dedicated proxy server, but it works well for simple environments in which a set of clients without valid public IP address wishes to connect to the Internet. This process is illustrated in Figure 14.11.

FIGURE **14.11** *Address Translation from Server to Client Computers*

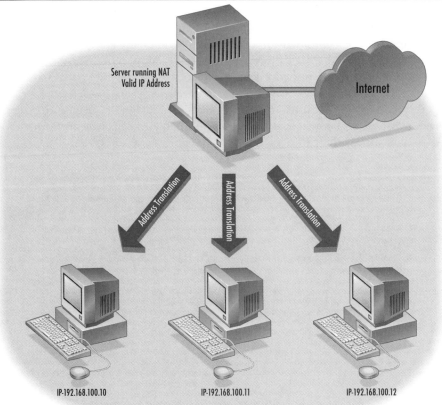

The next option, remote access server, allows users to access the network via dial-up connections. You would select this option if you have modems on your RAS server and you want clients to be able to dial directly into your RAS server.

The VPN server option allows users to connect to the server over the Internet by creating a virtual private network. The server and client in this case must both have a valid public IP address and be connected to the Internet. The data is encrypted and sent using PPTP.

The network router option is an example of why the name RAS was changed to RRAS. This option allows your Windows 2000 server to accept data from a client and be able to route that data to a different network. It can be cost-efficient for companies who previously needed to install dedicated circuits to connect their divisions. Now RRAS can inspect the data, determine where the destination is, make a demand dial connection to that site, and route the data to the appropriate remote network. This process is illustrated in Figure 14.12. Marja connects to the server in New York with a request to connect to the network in Los Angeles, while Phil connects to the server in New York with a request to connect to the network in Dallas. The server in New York is running the RRAS router option and so will, based on the data it receives from Marja and Phil, establish a dial-up connection with the servers in Los Angeles and Dallas.

FIGURE 14.12 **The Network Router Process**

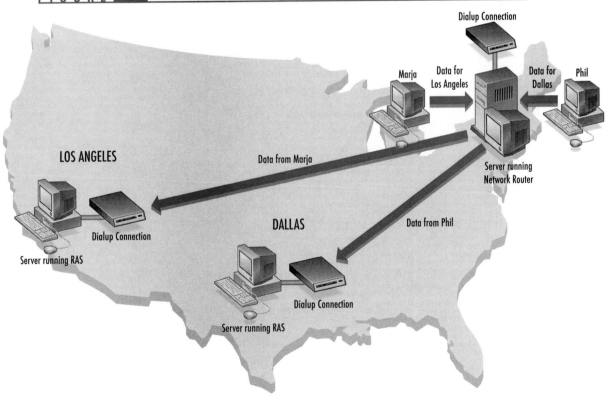

Exercise 8

INSTALLING RRAS

RRAS, or routing and remote access, is not enabled by default. In order to be used it must be installed and configured first. In the following exercise you install a VPN server and RRAS.

1. On the first domain controller click Start, Programs, Administrative Tools, and then click Routing and Remote Access.
2. Right-click your server name and click *Configure and Enable Routing and Remote Access*.
3. At the wizard screen click <u>N</u>ext. You see the dialog box shown in Figure 14.13.

Figure 14.13

4. Click *Virtual private network (VPN) server* and click <u>N</u>ext.
5. Make sure that TCP/IP shows in the list of protocols and *Yes* is selected, and then click <u>N</u>ext. You see the dialog box in Figure 14.14.

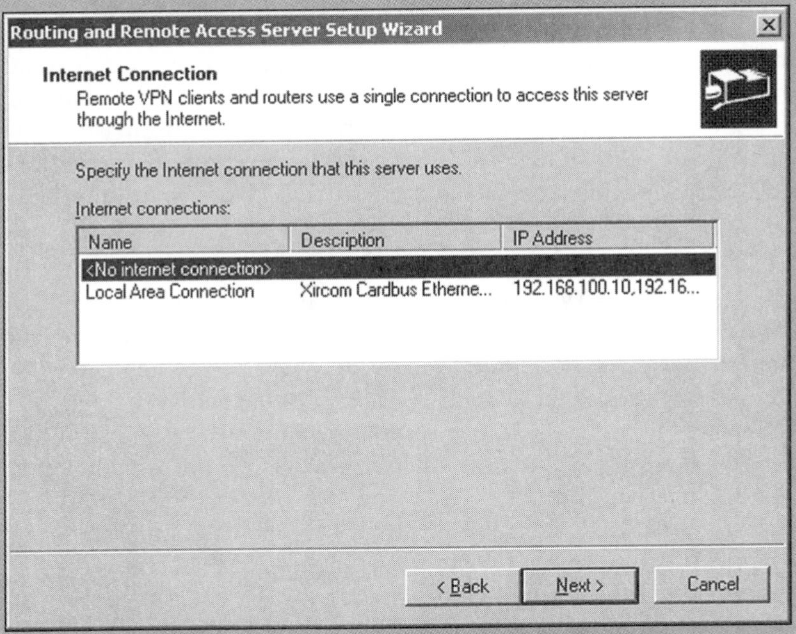

Figure 14.14

This dialog box is used to select which server connection will be used for VPN access. On a production VPN server, two network interface cards would be installed. One card would be used for the LAN connection and the other card could be selected as the VPN connection. A single connection cannot be used for both VPN and LAN access.

6. Because your server likely only has a single NIC, click *No internet connection* and click Next.
7. In the IP Address Assignment window click *Automatically* to allow your clients to obtain an address from your DHCP server. (Your other option is to have the RRAS server assign addresses from a pool.) Click Next.
8. Click OK at the window warning you that your server's address must be compatible with the addresses handed out by the DHCP server.
9. Click No when asked if you want to set up a RADIUS server.
10. Click Next to continue.
11. Click Finish to complete the wizard.
12. Click OK to acknowledge the message concerning the DHCP relay agent. The RRAS service is started.

RADIUS stands for **remote authentication dial-in user server**. In an environment with multiple RRAS servers, you may want a central point at which authentication of users should be done instead of allowing each individual RRAS server to do its own authentication. A RADIUS server is used for that purpose. Microsoft's implementation of a RADIUS server is called Internet Authentication Service or IAS. It could be installed using Add/Remove Programs. Working with a single RRAS server in this case means that a RADIUS server will not be necessary.

DHCP Relay Agent

In order to access your server using a VPN, clients must have a compatible IP address. When the RRAS was installed in the previous exercise you set the option for clients to be given an IP address from a DHCP server. When clients request an IP address, they send a DHCPDISCOVER message across the network and wait for a reply from a DHCP server. As you have learned, a DHCPDISCOVER message is a broadcast packet, and broadcast packets do not usually travel across routers. For this reason, your RRAS machine must be set up to listen for DHCPDiscover broadcast packets from the RRAS clients coming in over the WAN and pass them on to the DHCP server on the local area network. This function is called a **DHCP relay agent**, and it must be configured.

Exercise 9

CONFIGURING A DHCP RELAY AGENT

In the following exercise you will set up your RRAS server to be a DHCP relay agent. You will also view the VPN ports that were created and are waiting for user connections.

1. Open the Routing and Remote Access program from the Administrative Tools menu.
2. Double-click your RRAS server. It should now show a small green arrow because it has been started.
3. Click the plus sign next to IP Routing. The window now should look like Figure 14.15.

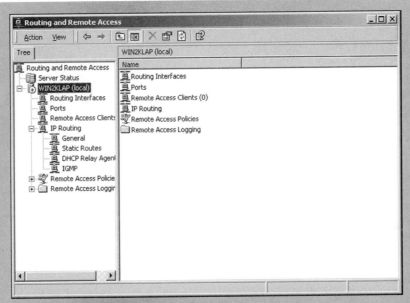

Figure 14.15

4. Right-click the *DHCP Relay Agent* icon and click Properties, which gives you the dialog box in Figure 14.16.

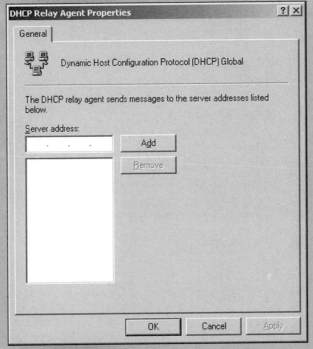

Figure 14.16

At this screen you would enter the address of your network DHCP server. The RRAS service will automatically forward DHCP messages from the clients to the server with the specified IP address.

5. Enter the address of the your DHCP server and click A<u>d</u>d. If you do not have a DHCP server, enter the IP address of your own server.
6. Click OK to finish the install.
7. To verify that VPN ports were created, double-click the *Ports* icon on the right-hand side of the screen. You should see the ports available for people creating VPN connections over the Internet (Figure 14.17).

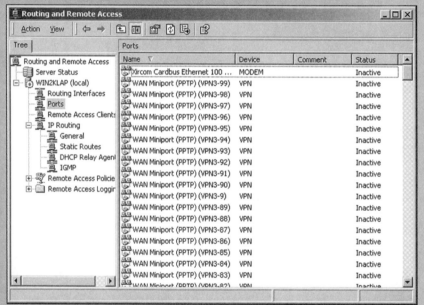

Figure 14.17

8. Double-click a port to show more information about that port.
9. Click Close to exit the Port Status window.
10. Leave the Routing and Remote Access window open for the next exercise.

Authentication

Now that the RRAS server has been set up, users will be connecting to the server remotely to gain access to your network. Before allowing anyone access to the network, RRAS needs to authenticate that they are a valid network user. PPP supports several different types of authentication, you need to configure the

RRAS server for the appropriate type. The type of authentication you select is important because both the RRAS server and the clients who are connecting to the system must be able to support the same type of authentication. Some of the possibilities are listed here.

- **Password Authentication Protocol (PAP)**: In this low-level security option clear text passwords are transmitted over the wire.

- **Challenge Handshake Protocol (CHAP)**: This industry standard uses encrypted passwords that are not passed over the wire. A random number, also called a challenge, is sent to the client machine that encrypts it using the user's password. The authenticating server can then decrypt it using its copy of the user's password. In order for this type of authentication to work, the server must store the user's password in a form that can be converted to clear text.

- **Microsoft CHAP v1**: This Microsoft version of CHAP is used for down-level clients. It uses a hashed version of the user's password instead of clear text to encrypt the challenge.

- **Microsoft CHAP v2**: This second version of Microsoft CHAP includes an additional challenge to the RRAS server to verify that it is the actual RRAS server and not an impersonator. Windows 2000, Windows NT 4 service pack 4, and Windows 98 use this version.

- **Extensible Authentication Protocol (EAP)**: This option is not a protocol itself but a method for allowing other types of authentication, such as smart cards and certificates. With this protocol selected, the client and server negotiate the authentication method during the authentication process.

Exercise 10

CONFIGURING RRAS AUTHENTICATION

In the following exercise you view the type of authentication to use with RRAS.

1. Right-click your RRAS server and click Properties.
2. Click the Security tab. You see the dialog box in Figure 14.18.

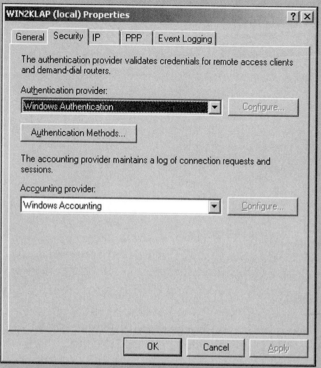

Figure 14.18

3. Click the Authentication Methods button to select the types of authentication to use, as shown in the dialog box in Figure 14.19.

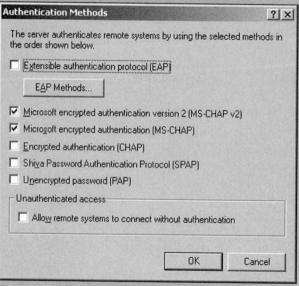

Figure 14.19

View the types of authentication available and note the default. You will not change the default value.

4. Click Cancel to close the Authentication Methods dialog box and click Cancel to close the RRAS Properties dialog box.
5. Leave this window open for the next exercise.

Remote Access Policies

In previous chapters you have used group policies. Policies can also apply specifically to RRAS and are called remote access policies. These policies differ from group policies in that they can be applied to a security group. For example, by using a remote access policy you can give a security group the ability to link VPN into an RRAS server. One policy is in place for RRAS when it is installed, which specifies anyone who has been granted dial-in access can access the server 24 hours a day, 7 days a week. You can change this specification by modifying the RRAS policy.

Exercise 11

VIEWING AN RRAS POLICY

In the following exercise you will view the default RRAS policy. If changes are desired, this policy could be modified or others could be created.

1. Click the plus sign next to your RRAS server to expand it.
2. Click the *Remote Access Policies* icon. You see a policy displayed on the right side of the window (Figure 14.20).

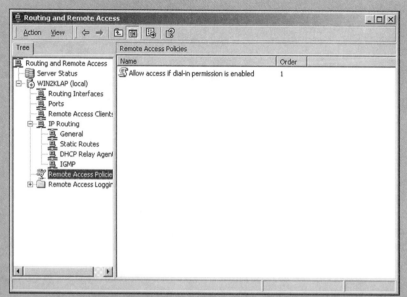

Figure 14.20

3. Double-click *Allow access if dial-in permission is enabled* on the right side of the window. You see the policy dialog box in Figure 14.21.

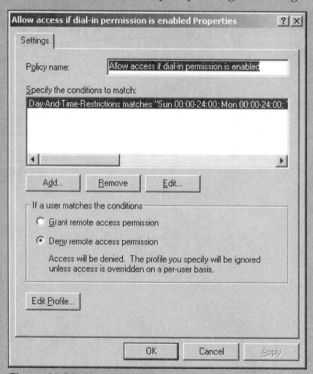

Figure 14.21

Setting RRAS Policy and Callback Options

The policy states that anyone who has permission to access the server can do so 24 hours a day, 7 days a week but, by default, users do not have permission to dial in to RRAS. An administrator must set up that privilege by giving the individual permission through their account properties or by creating a routing and remote access policy that gives a group access.

Part of the access permissions is the callback option. This option is for users who dial in to a modem to access the server. The two options are *no callback* and *callback*. The no callback option accepts incoming calls to the server modem. The callback option will, once the user has been authenticated, disconnect and call a preset number assigned to the user. The no callback option is the least secure. The *callback to a preset number* is the most secure and should be used on the administrative account if possible. In this way, if a hacker did manage to get the administrative password, he or she could not dial in remotely to use it because the RRAS server would hang up and dial back to the preset number. The *callback at number entered by the user* option is helpful for people traveling because they can have the server call them back wherever they happen to be at the time.

Exercise 12

SETTING USER ACCESS TO THE RRAS SERVER

In this exercise you will set up options for users to access RRAS, which can be done from both domain controllers.

1. Click Start, Programs, Administrative Tools, and Active Directory Users and Computers.
2. Click the plus sign next to your domain to expand it.
3. Click the *Users* folder to open it.
4. Double-click *Administrator Account* on the right-hand side of the screen and click the Dial-in tab. You see the dialog box in Figure 14.22.

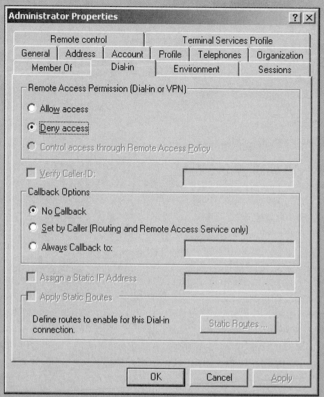

Figure 14.22

5. Click *Allow access*.

Note the callback options but leave the default of *No Callback*. This box is where you can set a phone number for the server to call back the user.

6. Click OK.
7. Close the Active Directory Users and Computers window.

Logging and Tracking Connections

Once RRAS has been installed on a server the routing and remote access MMC can also be used to track connections to the server and to set logging options. By expanding your RRAS server details in the left-hand side of the screen, you will see a *Remote Access Clients* icon. If you highlight this option you will see the connections to your machine on the right-hand side of the screen. Double-clicking an individual connection will provide more details about that connection, such as how much data have been transferred via that connection.

Your RRAS server is set up by default to send errors and warning to the event viewer. By right clicking your server clicking Properties, and then clicking the Event Logging tab, you can change which events are logged.

Terminal Services

Before personal computers, mainframe systems were accessed through terminals. A terminal normally consists of a monitor, keyboard, and a communications link. When the terminal is connected to the mainframe, applications and system administration software on the mainframe can be controlled through the terminal. Today, network servers can be accessed through personal computers that act like terminals, currently called "thin-clients."

Windows 2000 comes with a software application called Terminal Services, which consists of a server component and a client component. The server component listens for connections from clients and, when contacted, opens a connection. The client is presented with a window that appears to be a regular computer screen but displays the server. The window can be used just like a regular Windows 2000 session, but everything is done on the server and not the client.

Microsoft uses the Windows-specific Remote Desktop Protocol (RDP) to connect servers and clients. This protocol creates a virtual video display on the server, reduces the video information to a series of IP packets, and encrypts the packets before sending them to the client. On the client side, the RDP converts the packets into Win32 API calls that allow video, keyboard, and mouse interaction with the terminal window.

Terminal Services is compatible with software from Citrix Corporation called Metaframe. This software works like Windows 2000 Terminal Services but uses a different protocol called Independent Computing Architecture (ICA). Unlike Microsoft, Citrix supports non-Windows clients.

Terminal Services can be installed in either application mode or administration mode. When installed in application mode, terminal service clients can run applications such as Microsoft Word on the server. When installed in administration mode, clients can log on to the server as administrators and run the Windows administration programs. Microsoft requires terminal services client access licenses (CALs) in addition to the standard Windows server CALs when using Application mode. The reason for this requirement is that multiple clients can run the same application on the server. Licensing is not required when using in remote administration mode because only a maximum of two users can be connected at the same time in this mode.

Exercise 13

INSTALLING TERMINAL SERVICES

In this exercise you install Terminal Services and select the mode. In order to complete this exercise you need access to the Windows 2000 Install CD.

1. Click Start, Settings, and Control Panel.
2. In the Control Panel window, double-click the *Add/Remove Programs* icon.
3. Click the Add/Remove Windows Components button.
4. In the Windows Components dialog box scroll down and click the Terminal Services check box.
5. Click the Next button. You see the dialog box in Figure 14.23.

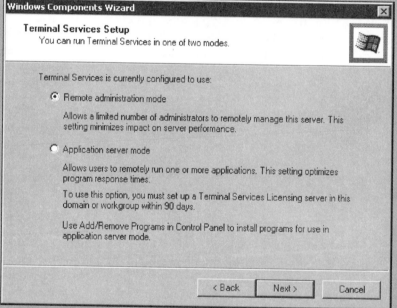

Figure 14.23

6. You must select the mode for Terminal Services during install. Click *Remote administration mode* and click the Next button to continue.
7. When the installation is complete, click the Finish button and reboot your computer.

Exercise 14

CREATING CLIENT DISKS AND INSTALLING THE CLIENT

In this exercise you create a set of client disks. These client disks are used to install the client part of Terminal Services. For this exercise you will need two blank formatted disks.

1. Click Start, Programs, Administrative Tools, and then click Terminal Services Client Creator. You see the dialog box in Figure 14.24.

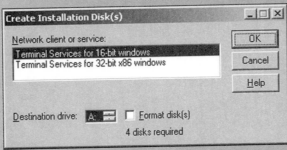

Figure 14.24

2. Click *Terminal Services for 32-bit x86 windows*, insert a blank formatted disk, and click OK. You will be prompted to click OK to start creating the disks.
3. When the disks have been created, click the Cancel button to close the Client Creator window.
4. Insert the first client creator disk in the floppy drive and double-click the *My Computer* icon.
5. Double-click the floppy disk drive and then double-click the Setup.exe program.
6. When the setup program starts, click the Continue button, enter your name and organization, and click OK.
7. Click the I Agree button to agree to licensing procedure, click the large button to start installation, and click Yes.
8. You will be prompted for the second client disk.

In most cases, Terminal Services can be used with the default settings. The most important configuration settings are security based, which means they include the encryption level applied to the RDP packets and which user accounts can be used to log on to the server. Other options include controlling the session and connection parameters.

Exercise 15

CONFIGURING AND RUNNING TERMINAL SERVICES

In this exercise you configure Terminal Services and then run the client program on your own server.

1. Click Start, Programs, Administrative Tools, and Terminal Services Configuration. You see the Configuration window in Figure 14.25

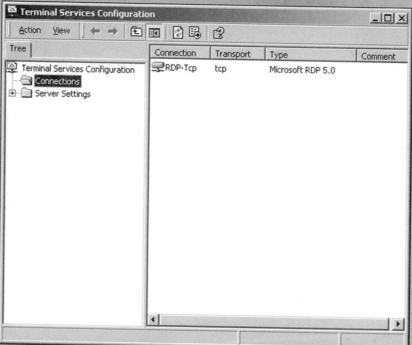

Figure 14.25

2. Click the *Connections* folder to display the existing connections.
3. Right-click the connection icon in the right window and click Properties.
4. Click the General tab and set the Encryption level to *High*.
5. Click the Sessions tab and then click *Override user settings*.
6. Set the End a Disconnected Session option to 1 hour. This setting prevents a remote administrative session from remaining active for an extended period of time.
7. Click the Permissions tab to view the list of users who have the right to log on to a server using Terminal Services.

8. Click OK to close the Terminal Services properties dialog box. You will next start Terminal Services Client and log on to your own server.

9. Click Start, Programs, Terminal Services, and Terminal Services Client. You see the dialog box in Figure 14.26

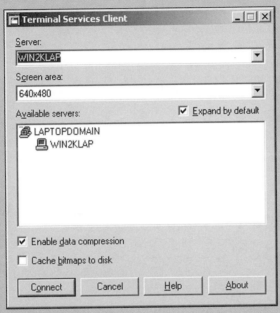

Figure 14.26

This dialog box allows you to select the server to be connected to by entering the server name or IP address. The S<u>c</u>reen area section is used to set the size of the terminal window.

10. Click the C<u>o</u>nnect button. You see a window containing a logon screen.

11. Log on as the administrator. You see the server desktop.

12. You can control a Terminal Services connection from the server by using Terminal Services Manager. In the main window (not the Terminal window), click Start, Programs, Administrative Tools, and Terminal Services Manager. If you see an error message, click OK. You see the window in Figure 14.27. The Terminal Services connection is displayed in white.

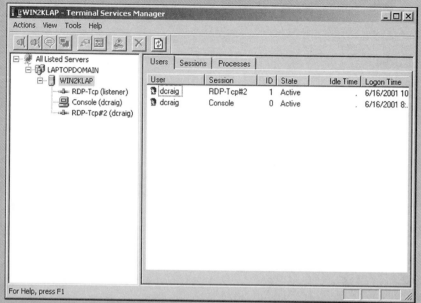

Figure 14.27

13. Right-click the user connection in the right window with the RDP session and click *Send message*.

14. In the Send message dialog box enter a message and click OK. A message appears in the Terminal window.

15. In the Terminal window click Start, Shut Down, and then click *Logoff*. Be careful not to click *Shut-down*, which will shut down the server.

CHAPTER summary

➤ The ability to remotely access networks has become an important element in network design. Windows 2000 provides several different ways to access a server. These methods include accessing Web pages on the server through Internet Information Services, remotely connecting to the server and the LAN through the remote access services, and accessing the server as a terminal.

➤ Windows 2000 comes with a built-in Web server that allows the server to host Web sites. A Web site will consist of a set of HTML pages and a set of virtual directories. A virtual directory is a shortcut through the Web server that is mapped to a physical directory. Internet Information Services hosts Web sites and can be configured to allow public or secured access to files and virtual directories.

➤ Remote access service (RAS), also known as routing and remote access service (RRAS) allows users to remotely connect to the server as network clients. RRAS software can be configured to allow dial-in connections with a modem or to allow virtual public network (VPN) connections. The RRAS software must be configured and started before it can be used.

➤ The Terminal Services program is a third way to remotely access a Windows 2000 server. This program is a service that runs on the server and listens for computers running the Terminal Services client software to connect to the server. When a client has connected, a window on the client system is used to log on directly to the server.

CHAPTER terms

CHAP	Challenge Handshake Protocol: Industry standard RRAS authentication protocol that uses encrypted password hash values to authenticate users.
DHCP relay agent	A service running on a RRAS server that will forward DHCP broadcast messages to and from a network DHCP server.
EAP	Extensible Authentication Protocol: A Windows RRAS protocol that allows the clients and server to negotiate an authentication protocol. Often used for secure card authentication.
FTP	File Transfer Protocol: A standard Internet protocol used to transfer files.

HTML	Hypertext Markup Language: A formatting language used to create Web pages.
HTTP	Hypertext Transport Protocol: A standard protocol used on the Internet to request and deliver Web pages.
ISDN	Integrated Services Digital Network: A digital network commonly used in WANs.
NAT	Network Address Translation: Translating a nonroutable IP address with a routable IP address. NAT is used on a network to share a single Internet connection with a group of clients.
PAP	Password Authentication Protocol: A low-level RAS authentication protocol that sends passwords in clear text.
POTS	Plain old telephone service: The telephone system.
PPP	Point to Point Protocol: The industry standard communications protocol commonly used for telephone connections. PPP can handle multiple network protocols, error correction, and authentication.
PPTP	Point to Point Tunneling Protocol: The protocol used to create a VPN connection by encapsulating data in a standard PPP frame.
RADIUS	Remote authentication dial-in user server: A server that will authenticate for multiple RAS servers. The Microsoft version of a RADIUS server is called the Internet Authentication Service.
RAS	Remote access service: A service that allows users to remotely access the server and network.
RRAS	Routing and remote access service: A service similar to RAS, but that also allows users to remotely access other networks.
SLIP	Serial Line Interface Protocol: An old communications protocol commonly used for telephone connections. SLIP cannot handle multiple protocols.
Virtual directory	A directory within Internet Information Services that appears on a Web site, but is mapped to a physical folder on the server.
VPN	Virtual private network: A network connection running over a public network such as the Internet.
WAN	Wide area network: A network with multiple segments that extend over a large area.
Web page	A file that uses HTML.
Web server	A computer running Web server software that delivers Web pages in response to client requests.
Web site	A collection of files, folders, and virtual directories.

CONCEPTS review

Multiple Choice

1. A Web server listens for request messages in the protocol named:
   a. Hypertext Transport Protocol.
   b. File Transfer Protocol.
   c. Kerberos.
   d. None of the above.
   e. Both a and b.

2. The Web server listens on the following IP port for Web page requests:
   a. 70.
   b. 1432.
   c. 21.
   d. 80.
   e. None of the above.

3. From a browser, you would key which of the following URLs to view the default Web site through IIS on the local computer?
   a. http://local
   b. http://127.255.255.255
   c. http://localhost
   d. http://129.0.0.1
   e. Both c and d

4. A virtual directory in Internet Information Services:
   a. Can be mapped to a physical folder.
   b. Cannot be mapped to a folder on the local server.
   c. Must be mapped to a shared folder on another server.
   d. Must be mapped to a folder with the exact name of the virtual directory.
   e. None of the above.

5. When configuring Web site security, the NTFS security is normally applied to:
   a. The entire Web site.
   b. Only virtual directories.
   c. Only shared folders on other servers.
   d. Network devices such as printers.
   e. None of the above.

6. In order to remotely administrator an IIS Web site, you need to find:
   a. The IP address of the administrative Web site.
   b. The port number of the default Web site.
   c. The port number of the administrative Web site.
   d. The IP address of the Windows 2000 server hosting the Web site.
   e. None of the above.

7. If you were using smart cards instead of a typical user name and password setup to allow users access to the network, which authentication method would you choose?
   a. PAP
   b. CHAP
   c. Microsoft CHAP
   d. EAP
   e. None of the above

8. You want to give users in the Dutch group dial-in access to the server. The most efficient way of allowing access would be to:
   a. Apply a group policy to the Dutch group permitting dial-in access.
   b. Set each individual user in the Dutch group to have dial-in access via their account properties page.
   c. Create a remote access policy giving the Dutch group dial-in access.
   d. Create a Holland OU, put the Dutch group inside, and link a group policy to that OU allowing dial-in access.
   e. All of the above.

9. Which of the following is *not* an option when installing RRAS?
   a. Network router
   b. Internet connection server
   c. Proxy server
   d. Remote Access server
   e. None of the above

10. Which of the following is not true about PPP?
    a. It can work with TCP/IP.
    b. It can work with AppleTalk.
    c. It is the basis for the Point to Point Tunneling Protocol.
    d. It requires passwords to be clear text.
    e. All are true about PPP.

11. The purpose of a RADIUS server is to:
    a. Provide a central point of authentication for multiple RRAS servers.
    b. Provide for automatic RRAS client configuration.
    c. Provide a central point of access to Active Directory for RRAS clients.
    d. Provide a central point of access to Internet Information Services.
    e. None of the above.

12. The primary purpose of a DHCP relay agent is to:
    a. Configure RAS to work over a PPP connection.
    b. Configure RAS clients to use Active Directory.
    c. Relay VPN messages to a RAS server.
    d. Relay DHCP messages to a RAS server.
    e. Relay DHCP messages to a network DHCP server.

13. By default, Microsoft Terminal Services uses the protocol:
    a. Remote Data Protocol.
    b. Remote Desktop Protocol.
    c. Remote DHCP Protocol.
    d. Remote DataLink Protocol.
    e. None of the above.

14. Terminal Services, during setup, can be configured in which two modes?
    a. Administration and remote access mode
    b. Administration and desktop mode
    c. Administration and applications mode
    d. Administration and remote control mode
    e. None of the above

15. Client access licensing for Terminal Services is:
    a. Required for administrative mode.
    b. Required for all Terminal Services modes.
    c. Not required.
    d. Required for RRAS modes.
    e. None of the above.

Short Answer

1. Briefly explain the difference between an IIS virtual directory and a physical directory.
2. List the four levels of security in IIS.
3. You have a network with five workstations that have private IP addresses and one Windows 2000 server with a valid public IP address. You want all the workstations to be able to browse the Internet. What should you do?
4. Briefly explain the purpose of a DHCP relay agent.
5. Under what conditions will you have to purchase CALs for Terminal Services?

LAB exercises

Exercise 1 – Creating a New Web Site and Setting Security

1. On your computer's system drive, create a folder named *SalesSite.* Inside this folder, create the folders named *Product, Upload,* and *Download.*
2. Click Start, Programs, Administrative Tools, and Internet Information Services.
3. Right-click the server name, click New, and then click Web Site.
4. Click Next to start the wizard.
5. Enter the Web site description *XYZCorpAdmin* and click Next.
6. Leave the IP address text box as *All Unassigned* but change the TCP port to *8080* and click Next.
7. Click the Browse button, click the *SalesSite* folder, and click Next.
8. Set the options *Read, Run Scripts,* and *Browser,* and click Next.
9. Click Finish to complete the wizard.
10. In the right-hand window, right-click the folder named *Product* and click Properties.
11. Click the Directory Security tab, click the Edit button in the Authentication section, and uncheck *Anonymous.*
12. Click *Basic Authentication.*
13. Click OK until you leave the Properties dialog box.
14. Using Notepad, create the following file and save it with the name default.htm in the *Product* folder in the *SalesSite* folder:

```
<HTML><HEAD><TITLE>ProductPage</TITLE></HEAD>
<BODY BGCOLOR=yellow>
Product page
</BODY>
</HTML>
```

15. Start Internet Explorer and enter the following in the Address field:

```
http://localhost:8080/product/
```

Exercise 2 – Backing Up IIS Configuration Data

1. Start Internet Services Manager from the Administration Tools menu.
2. Right-click the server icon, click Backup, and then click Restore Configuration.
3. Click the Create Backup button, enter the month name and year for the backup name, and click OK.
4. Click *Backup just created* and click the Restore button.
5. Click Yes when prompted.

Exercise 3 – Creating a Remote Access Policy for a Group of Users

The following exercise illustrates creating a remote access policy that applies to a group of users instead of an individual. It also exposes you to some of the settings that can be applied to a connection. Be aware that if a group is given remote access via a remote access policy but an individual of that group is specifically denied in their properties, the individual will be denied.

1. Open the Routing and Remote Access MMC.
2. Right-click the *Remote Access Policies* icon and click New Remote Access Policy.
3. For the Policy name key **Domain Users can access RRAS** and click Next.
4. Under the Conditions window click Add.
5. Highlight *Windows Groups* and click Add.
6. In the Groups window click Add.
7. Click the Domain Users group and click Add.
8. The Domain Users group should show in the lower half of the Select Groups window. Click OK.
9. Verify the Domain Users shown in the Groups window and click OK.
10. In the Add Remote Access Policy window, make sure the Conditions include the Domain Users group, and click Next.
11. Click *Grant remote access permission* and click Next.
12. Click the Edit Profile button.
13. Click the Encryption tab and remove the check mark from *No Encryption* (this option forces connections to use some type of encryption).
14. Click the Dial-in Constraints tab and set the Disconnect if idle option for 5 minutes.
15. Click the Multilink tab and allow multilink with a maximum of 3 ports.
16. Click OK to accept the settings.
17. Click Finish to finish creating the policy.
18. You should now see your policy listed on the right-hand side of the screen.

Exercise 4 – Creating a Client Connection

1. Click Start, Programs, Terminal Services Client, and Client Connection Manager.
2. In the Connection Manager window, click the File menu and then click New Connection.
3. Click Next to start the wizard.
4. Enter the connection name **remotecomp.**
5. Enter the name or IP address of your own server or your partner's server and click Next.
6. Click *Logon Automatically*, enter a valid logon name, password, and domain, and click Next.
7. Select a screen resolution and click Next.

8. Click *Enable Data Compression* and click <u>N</u>ext.
9. Click *Start the Following Program*, enter the program name **notepad.exe** in the File name text box, and click <u>N</u>ext.
10. Click <u>N</u>ext when prompted for an icon and program group.
11. Click Finish.
12. Double-click the icon for the connection just created. (You may have to enter the password.)
13. Notepad should be started. In the Terminal Services window, click the File menu for Notepad and click Exit.
14. The Terminal Services window should automatically close.

PROBLEM SOLVING exercises

1. Given the following Web site description, list the physical folders and virtual directories you feel would be needed to support the Web site. Also, list the access rights that should be given for each physical folder and virtual directory.

> XYZCorporation wishes to create a Web site to sell its products and to support the company's salesforce. The Web site will be used to sell three types of products: networking components, memory, and telephones. In addition, the company wishes to make available press releases for public viewing. The company salespeople should be able to view company memos in a special part of the Web site. The sales managers should also be able to view current sales numbers in another part of the Web site.

2. Given the following description of a small business, write a one-page proposal for implementing remote access to the company's network. For each type of remote access (IIS, RAS, or Terminal Services) indicate which is more appropriate for the types of users that will be supported.

> The XYZCorporation network will be used by internal corporate users with access to the LAN. It will also be used by salespeople who need to access the network from hotel telephones. In addition, the overseas branch of the company will be using an ISDN connection. Supplier companies will be accessing the XYZCorporation business Web site to enter and track sales orders. Sometimes, these supplier companies must log on directly to the corporate network, but must be able to do so from any type of Internet connection.

APPENDIX A: WINDOWS 2000 COMMAND LINE PROGRAMS

Overview

Windows 2000 includes a number of command line tools that can make network administration much easier. These tools and their command options are included in the Windows Help files. The following list of command line tools is not comprehensive but includes the most often used commands. For a complete list of command options use the Windows Help files. The elements enclosed in square brackets [] are optional. Vertical bars between options indicate either option, but not both, can be used.

CALCS	Displays the access control lists for files and folders on NTFS disks.
	Syntax: **CACLS** *filename* | *folder* [/t] [/e] [/c] [/g *user:perm*] [/r *user*] [/p *user:perm*] [/d *user*]

/t – changes the ACLs of the specified files, /e – edits the ACLs of the files, /g – continues on file access errors, /g *user:perm* – grants *user* the access rights R (read), C (change-write), F (full), /p *user:perm* – replaces a *user* access with *perm* R,C,F and N(None), /r *user* – revokes user access, /d *user* – denies user access

CACLS c:\afile.txt	– displays ACLs for the specified file
CACLS c:\winnt	– displays ACLs for the specified folder
CACLS c:\winnt*.* /c	– displays ACLs for all files in the winnt folder and does not stop when an access-denied error is raised.
CACLS c:\afile.txt /g jones:R	– grants user *jones* read access to the file
CACLS c:\winnt*.* /e /r jones	– revokes the user *jones* access rights to all files in the winnt folder

CHKDSK	Checks the file system on a disk.
	Syntax: **CHKDSK** [volume or drive] [/f] [/v] [/r] [/l [:size] [/x] [/i] [/c]

CHKDSK	– checks the default drive but does not fix errors
CHKDSK D: /f /v /r	– checks drive D:, fixes errors, displays file names are they are checked, and recovers all data as necessary.
CHKDSK D: /f /r /i /c	– performs a quick check of drive D: fixing errors and recovering data

CIPHER

Sets or displays the file or directory encryption

Syntax: **CIPHER** [**/e**| **/d**] [**/s:***dir*] [**/a**][**/i**] [**/f**] [**/q**] [**/h**] [*pathname* [...]]

/e – encrypts, /d – decrypts, /s:dir – performs the actions in the folder *dir* and all subfolders, /a – performs operation on selected files, /i – ignores errors, /f – performs operation on items that are already processed, /q – quiet mode, /h – displays files with hidden or system attributes.

CIPHER /e c:\filex   – encrypts filex
CIPHER /d /s:c:\myfolder /q   – decrypts all folders in myfolder in quiet mode

CONVERT

Convert a FAT or FAT32 hard drive to NTFS.

Syntax: **CONVERT** [*drive:*] /fs:ntfs [/v]

[*drive:*] – specifies the drive to convert. The current drive cannot be converted. If the drive is locked, the conversion will take place the next time the system reboots, /fs:ntfs – specifies that the volume be converted, /v – verbose mode (displays all messages)

CONVERT d: /fs:ntfs /v   – converts drive D: to NTFS and displays all messages

DISKPERF

Sets the type of disk counters that can viewed in Performance Monitor

Syntax: **DISKPERF** [**-y**[**d**|**v**]|**-n**[**d**|**v**]] [*computername*]

-y – sets both physical and logical disk counters when the system is restarted, -yd – enables checking of physical drives, -yv – enables checking of logical drives, -n – turns off all disk monitoring, -nd – turns off physical drive monitoring, -nv – turns off logical drive monitoring, *computername* – the name of the computer to set these parameters for. If not specified then the local computer is selected.

DISKPERF –y   – enables both physical and logical monitors on
                            default computer.
DISKPERF –yd \\compA – enables physical disk monitors on compA
DISKPERF –n   – turns off all disk monitoring on current system

RECOVER

Recovers readable information from a bad disk

Syntax: **RECOVER** [*drive:*] [*path*] *filename*

d*rive:* – specifies the drive, *path* – specifies the path, *filename* – specifies the name of the file

RECOVER a:\badfile   – attempts to recover data from badfile on drive A

RUNAS

Used to run a command with a permission different than the default login permission under the current session.

Syntax: **RUNAS** [**/profile**] [**/env**] [**/netonly**] **/user:***UserAccountName* **program**

/profile – indicates the name of the user's profile, /env – uses the network environment rather than the user's environment, /netonly – user information is for remote access only, /user:*UserAccountName* – specifies the user id under which to run the account in the form user@domain.xxx or domain\user, program – the command to run.

RUNAS /user:domainx@administrator cmd	– Opens a command window with administrator rights for the account "administrator" in the domain "domainx"
RUNAS /user:domainx\jwilliams "mmc admintools"	– runs the MMC named "admintools" with the rights for the user "jwilliams" in the "domainx" domain.

NET Commands   The Net commands are a series of commands following the word NET. They are primarily used to control network settings and access.

NET COMPUTER   Adds or deletes a computer from the domain database.

Syntax: NET COMPUTER \\computername {/add | /del }

\\computername – specifies the name of the computer to add or delete, /add – adds this computer to the domain database, /del – deletes this computer from the domain database.

NET COMPUTER \\systemA /add	– adds computer named systemA to the domain.
NET COMPUTER \\systemB /del	– removes systemB from the domain database.

NET GROUP   Displays and/or changes group information on a domain controller.

Syntax: **NET GROUP** [*groupname* [**/comment:**"*text*"]] [**/domain**]
 NET GROUP *groupname* {/add [/comment:"*text*"] | /delete} [/domain]
 NET GROUP *groupname username*[...] {/add | /delete} [/domain]

groupname – name of group to display or add, /comment – text to use as comment, /domain – perform operation on local domain, otherwise use local computer, /add – add to the domain or group, /delete – remove from the domain or group, *username* – names of users to add to or remove from a group

NET GROUP /domain	– displays all groups in default domain
NET GROUP newgroup /add /comment:"new group" /domain	
	– adds the group named "newgroup" to the local domain with the comment.
NET GROUP newgroup userx /add	– adds the user named "userx" to the local group named "newgroup"

NET PRINT   Display or control the print jobs to a shared printer.

Syntax: NET PRINT \\computername\sharename
          NET PRINT \\computername *jobnumber* [/hold | /release | /delete]

\\computername and sharename are used to identify the computer and printer,
jobnumber the number of the print job assigned by the server (a unique job
number is assigned to each print job on multiple shared printers), /hold – hold
the job, /release – release a held job, /delete – delete a job.

NET PRINT \\systemA\printerB   – displays print information about the
                                     printer named "printerB"
NET PRINT \\systemA 123 /hold   – put the print job 123 on hold on systemA
NET PRINT \\systemA 456 /delete   – delete the print job 456 on systemA

NET SEND   Sends a message to other users on the network.

Syntax: {*name* | * | /domain[*:name*] | /users } *message*

n*ame* – computer or user name, * – send to all members of a domain or connected
to a server, /domain*:name* – identifies the domain to which the message is send (if
name is not specified then the default domain is used), /users – sends message to
all users connected to the server

NET SEND userx "Hello there"   – sends the message to userx
NET SEND /domain "Hello there"   – sends the message to all users in
                                         the default domain
NET SEND /domain:domainx "Hello There" – sends the message to all users in
                                         domainx

NET SHARE   Displays, creates, and removes network shares

Syntax: NET SHARE *sharename*
          NET SHARE *sharename* = *drive:path* [/users:*number* | /unlimited]
                    [/remarks:*text*]
          NET SHARE *sharename* [/users:*number* | /unlimited] [/remarks:*text*]
          NET SHARE *sharename* /delete

s*harename* – the name of the share, *drive:path* – the location of the share,
/users:*number* – the number of users that can simultaneously access the share,
/unlimited – unlimited users can access the share, /remarks:*text* – remarks to add
to the share, /delete – remove the share

NET SHARE   – display all the shares on the
                                         current system
NET SHARE myfolder = c:\folderx /unlimited – shares the folder named
                                         "folderx" with the share name
                                         "myfolder" and allows unlimited
                                         users to access the share.
NET SHARE myfolder /delete   – remove the share

NET START Start a service

Syntax: NET START *service*

s*ervice* - the name of the service to be started. Refer to the Windows 2000 help files for a list of the services available.

NET START   – displays the services currently running
NET START netlogon – starts the netlogon service

NET STOP Stops a service

Syntax: NET STOP *service*

s*ervice* – the name of the service to be stopped.

NET STOP netlogon   – stops the netlogon service

NET TIME Synchronizes or displays the time on a computer

Syntax: NET TIME [*computername* | /domain[*:name*] | /rtsdomain[*:name*] [/set]
           NET TIME [*computername*] [/querysntp] | [/setsntp[*:ntp server name*]

computername – name of the computer with which to synchronize time,
/domain:*name* – specifies the domain with which to synchronize time,
/rtsdomain:*name* – specifies the reliable time server with which to synchronize,
/set – changes the local computers clock with the specified system, /querysntp –
displays the name of the network time protocol server, /setsntp:*ntp server name*
– sets the network time protocol server name

NET TIME   – displays the currently set time
NET TIME /domain:domainx – displays the time set for domainx
NET TIME \\serverA /set   – sets the local computer's time with the time on
                                serverA

NET USE Displays and sets network connections

Syntax: NET USE [*devicename* | *] [*computername\sharename\volume*]
              [*password* | *] [/user[*:domainname*]*username*]
              [/delete | /persistent: {yes | no }]
           NET USE *devicename* [/home [*password* | *]] [/delete: {yes | no}]

d*evicename* or * – the object to connect to the network resource (either a disk
drive letter or LPT1: to LPT3:) if an * is used then the next available device name
is used, *computername\sharename\volume* - the network resource to use (the
volume specifies a netware volume), *password* or * – specify a password or display
a prompt, /user:*domain\username* – specifies a different username with which to
make the connection, /delete or * – removes the network connection (if an * is
used then all network connections are removed), /home – connects the user to
the home directory, /persistent yes or no – saves the connections for next logon

NET USE X: \\systemA\shareb /persistent:yes – uses disk drive X for the share "shareb" on "systemA" and makes this a persistent share

NET USE X: /delete – removes the disk drive X share

NET USE X: \\sysA\d$ * – uses drive X for hidden share drive D on "sysA" and prompts for a password

NET USE LPT3: \\sysA\printerX – uses LPT3 for the shared printer named "printerX" on the system named "sysA"

NET USE LPT3: /delete – removes the shared printer port

NET USER Creates or removes a user account

Syntax: NET USER [*username* [*password* | *]] [/add | /delete] [/domain]

u*sername* - the name of the user to be added, *password* or * - the password given to the user or * to prompt for password, /add – add the user to the local computer or domain, /delete – remove the user, /domain – use the default domain

NET USER fsmith * /add /domain – adds the user "fsmith" to the default domain and prompts for a password.

NET USER fsmith /delete – removes the user named "fsmith"

NET VIEW Display a list of domains, computers, or resources

Syntax: NET VIEW [*computername* | /domain[:*domainname*]]
         NET VIEW /network:nw [*computername*]

computername or /domain:*domainname* – displays information about a specific computer or about the listed domain, /network:nw – displays all available computers on a netware network

NET VIEW \\systemA – displays all shares on "systemA"
NET VIEW /domain:domainx – displays all shares on the domain "domainx"

APPENDIX B: CONNECTING TO DIVERSE SYSTEMS

Many large networks include servers running a variety of operating systems. The most commonly used are Novell Netware and UNIX. Microsoft Windows 2000 includes various tools that allow Windows 2000 servers to work in an environment of diverse operating systems.

Novell Netware Clients and Servers

Several tools are available to allow Windows 2000 systems to communicate with Novell Netware systems. These are—

NWLink IPX/SPX/NetBIOs Compatible Transport Protocol   This protocol is available with Windows 2000. It is installed in the same manner as any other protocol. This protocol is only necessary if the system needs to communicate with older Netware servers running the Novell proprietary IPX/SPX protocol instead of TCP/IP. By itself this protocol does not have enough capabilities to allow file and print sharing with a Novell Machine, but would allow connection to an application running on a Novell machine that uses named pipes (such as an SQL server).

Client Services for Netware   This service comes with Windows 2000 Professional machines (not Windows 2000 Server machines) and can be installed in the same manner as any other service. By installing this service, the Windows 2000 Professional computer will receive a second logon box allowing it to logon to a Netware Server machine. The Windows 2000 Professional computer can then be used as a file and print client of the Novell server. If the Novell server it is being connected to is running IPX/SPX as its protocol, the NWLink protocol must also be installed along with the Client Services for Netware service.

Gateway (and Client) Services for Netware   This service comes with Windows 2000 servers and can be installed in the same manner as any other service. By installing this service, two extra capabilities are added to the Windows 2000 server. The first are client capabilities exactly like those found with Client Services for Netware. Second, the server can be a gateway for other clients needing access to a Netware server. This is helpful if you have multiple workstations that need occasional access to a Netware server but you do not want to load a client piece on each workstation. Data from the Novell server will appear to clients as if it is a share on the Windows 2000 server. No additional logon is required. This method is limited to occasional access because the connection between the Windows 2000 and Novell server is really a single session. The more workstations using the connection the slower response will be. Also, security is limited on the Novell data because NTFS file and folder permissions are not available. Again, if the Novell server you are attempting to communicate with is running the IPX/SPX protocol, you must also install the NWLink protocol along with the Gateway (and Client) Services for Netware service.

File and Print Services for Netware   This add-on does not come on the Windows 2000 CD but is available from Microsoft. This service causes the Windows 2000 server to appear as a Netware server to Novell clients. No additional software needs to be loaded on the Novell client for it to access this server.

UNIX Servers and Clients

The basic interoperability between UNIX and Windows 2000 (aside from DNS and other enterprise network systems) includes file access, printing, validation, and network management. Microsoft has released a set of tools named Services for UNIX that includes the following:

Server for NFS   This is a server that can be run on a Windows 2000 computer that allows UNIX NFS clients to access files. This also allows files on the Windows 2000 server to be shared and it enforces file access rights.

Client for NFS   This is a program that is run on a Windows 2000 Server or Professional computer that allows access to a UNIX system running NFS versions 2 or 3.

Telnet Server   This is a program that is run on a Windows 2000 server and that allows command line access to the system for network management.

Print Services for UNIX   This is a service running on the Windows 2000 server (LPDsvc) which runs the Line Printer Daemon. This allows UNIX clients to send print jobs to the server print queue. This also includes the Lprmon service, which allows a Windows 2000 server and it's clients to print to a printer connected to a UNIX server.

GLOSSARY

A

A record
A DNS record that include the host name and the associated IP address; Also called host records.

ACPI
Advanced configuration and power interface: A standard hardware BIOS used to control different aspects of a computer.

Active Directory
A distributed database that contains information about network users, computers, and resources.

Active Directory-integrated DNS zone
The inclusion of DNS records of a DNS server in Active Directory. DNS records are automatically replicated to other domain controllers, which provides a measure of security to DNS.

Active Directory schema
The patterns used to create network objects and attributes.

Active partition
The primary partition from which the computer will boot.

AH
Authentication header: Part of IPSec and a protocol header added to an IP packet that is used to verify the security of the packet.

Alert
An object triggered by an event such as a performance counter reaching a limit.

Allocation unit size
The smallest unit of space that can be written to, consisting of one or more sectors.

Application layer
The OSI layer that consists of application programs.

ARC path
A string found in the BOOT.INI file that is used to represent the location of a bootable operating system on a hard disk.

Archive bit
A file attribute set whenever a file is modified in any way. The Windows 2000 backup program uses the archive bit to locate files for backup.

Authentication
Verifying the identity of a user or process.

Authoritative
The ability to own and change namespace records. A DNS server is authoritative with respect to a set of DNS records if the server does not have to forward name resolution requests to another server.

B

Basic disk
Standard disk format (not a dynamic disk).

Biometric authorization
Using a physical feature such as fingerprints to authenticate a user.

BIOS	Basic input/output system: The name given to the chip-based software that is a part of the computer system. The BIOS system is used in hardware configuration and control.
Bit	A single binary digit, either zero or one.
Block inheritance	An option used in a child OU that prevents nonmandatory policies from being inherited from the parent.
Boot partition	The partition that contains the Windows 2000 system files.
BOOT.INI	A text file that contains information about the location of the operating systems on the hard drive. The NTLDR program uses this file.
Bootstrap loading	Boot process that progressively loads parts of the boot software by locating the initial boot code on a predetermined place on the hard drive.
Bridge	A network component that connects two or more similar network segments together.
Byte	A group of eight bits; also called an octet.

C

CA	Certificate authority: A trusted entity that maintains public keys and verifies ownership of these keys.
CAL	Client access license: A single user license to connect to a Windows 2000 server. In quantity, it costs about $40 each.
Certificate	A software object issued by a certificate authority that contains a verified public key for a specified user or process.
CHAP	Challenge Handshake Protocol: Industry standard RRAS authentication protocol that uses encrypted password hash values to authenticate users.
CIDR	Classless interdomain routing: A method of referring to subnet masks by appending a slash and a number indicating the number of bits designated for the network to an IP address.
Client/server	A relationship between computers on a network. The client sends requests to a server and a server responds to requests from clients.
Contradictory policy	A policy created in a child OU that is the same as an inherited policy but with different application options. A contradictory policy will override an inherited policy.
Counter log	A performance log that collects counter information.

D

Data link layer	The OSI layer that collects bits of data into a structure.

Delegating authority	Assigning the rights to control user and group accounts to users other than the administrator, normally with Organizational Units.
Device drivers	Software used by the operating system to communicate with a hardware device.
DFS	Distributed file system: Dfs. A system on Windows 2000 that allows multiple shares across the network to be linked and allows file replication between shares.
DHCP	Dynamic Host Configuration Protocol: A protocol used to automatically supply IP addresses to network clients.
DHCP relay agent	A service running on a RRAS server that will forward DHCP broadcast messages to and from a network DHCP server.
DHCPACK	An acknowledgment sent from a DHCP server to a client indicating that its request for an IP address has been granted.
DHCPDISCOVER	A broadcast message sent by a client to any DHCP server to request an IP address.
DHCPOFFER	A message sent from a DHCP server to a client requesting an IP address.
DHCPREQUEST	A request for an IP address sent from a client to a specific DHCP server.
Differential backup	Copies all files that have the archive bit set but does not reset the bit.
Directory service	A method to access information stored in a directory.
Directory services restore mode	Selected during the boot process and used to restore a backup copy of Active Directory.
Directory	A structured collection of information stored in a hierarchical format.
Distribution group	A container object used to hold name objects such as an e-mail list.
DMA	Direct memory addresses: A memory identification used by hardware to communicate with the system.
DNS	Domain Name System: A program that contains and locates names and IP addresses for network computers and resources.
DNS tree	A namespace within a DNS server.
DOD model	The network model developed by the Department of Defense that divides network communication software into four levels with each level performing clearly defined tasks and only communicating with levels above and below itself.
Domain	A resource and security boundary in a Windows 2000 network identified by a DNS record.
Domain controller	A computer that is running Active Directory.

Domain local group	A security group whose members can access resources only within the domain where the group was created.
Domain naming master	An FSMO forest-level service that controls adding and removing domains from a forest.
Driver Signing	A program from Microsoft to ensure that hardware device drivers will work on Windows 2000. A digital signature is issued to acceptable drivers and checked by Windows 2000 prior to installing the driver.
Dual booting	Installing Windows 2000 on a computer that already has Windows 95/98. A boot menu that allows selection of the operating systems on the drive is automatically added.
Dynamic disk	A method of managing disks that allows a logical volume to span physical disks.
Dynamic DNS	A method whereby domain controllers can register their IP addresses in DNS and not require the administrator to perform this task.
Dynamic IP	An IP address automatically assigned to a device by a DHCP server.
Dynamic updates	A feature of Windows 2000 DNS that allows computers to automatically update DNS records.

E

EAP	Extensible Authentication Protocol: A Windows RRAS protocol that allows the clients and server to negotiate an authentication protocol. Often used for secure card authentication.
EFS	Encrypting file system: The service used to encrypt and decrypt files.
Emergency recovery console	Selected during the boot process and used to access a server if it cannot boot.
ERD	Emergency repair disk: A specially created disk that allows recovery of the system.
ESP	Encapsulating security payload: Part of IPSec and the data part of the IP packet that is encrypted.
Event log	A file containing event information created by applications, services, and system programs.
Event Viewer	The program used to view the event logs.
Executive service	A software subsystem in Windows 2000 that performs system level tasks.
Extended partition	A logical subdivision of a disk after a primary partition has been created.

F

Fiber optic cable	A type of network cabling that transmits data through glass or plastic strands.
File/folder permissions	Access permissions set on individual files (requires NTFS).
Folder redirection	Using a group policy to automatically redirect common folders (such as My Documents) to a network share.
Forest	A group of domain trees within the same Active Directory database.
Forward lookup zone	A DNS namespace used to resolve IP addresses from domain names.
FQDN	Fully qualified domain names: A domain name that includes the object and the domain. For example, a1server.a5domain.local is an FQDN.
FSMO	Flexible single master operations: A set of services that must be done on only one domain controller per domain or per forest.
FTP	File Transfer Protocol: A standard Internet protocol used to transfer files.

G

Gateway	A network component that connects two or more network segments that do not use the same protocol.
GC	Global catalog: Part of Active Directory that contains information about each Active Directory object.
Global catalog server	A domain controller that holds a global catalog.
Global group	A security group whose members can come only from the domain where the group was created.
Group policies	A set of rights and settings assigned to domains or organizational units and applied to users or computers.
Group	A container object that holds user information.
GUID	Globally unique ID: A unique identification assigned to Active Directory objects when the objects are created.

H

HAL	Hardware abstraction layer: A software subsystem in Windows 2000 that interfaces with the system hardware devices.
HAL.DLL	Part of the Windows 2000 operating system that handles hardware interfaces. Application and operating system programs use the HAL.DLL file to access the system hardware.
HCL	Hardware Compatibility List: A list of Windows 2000-compatible hardware components and systems maintained by Microsoft.

Hive	A section of the registry that is saved as a disk file. Windows 2000 contains eight hives.
Host record	A DNS record that includes the host name and the associated IP address; also called an A record.
Host-to-host layer	The DOD layer that locates computers on the network.
HTML	Hypertext Markup Language: A formatting language used to create Web pages.
HTTP	Hypertext Transport Protocol: A standard protocol used on the Internet to request and deliver Web pages.
Hub	A network component used to interconnect a group of PCs and a server without restrictions.

I

I/O port	A number indicating where a hardware device can listen and send data to the system.
IDE	Integrated drive electronics: A type of hard drive used in personal computers.
IETF	Internet Engineering Task Force: The multinational organization that maintains RFCs and decides on the Internet standards and protocols.
Incremental backup	Copies all selected files that have the archive bit set and resets the bit.
INF file	A file that contains instructions to Windows on loading a device driver.
Infrastructure master	A FSMO domain-level service that coordinates and replicates group membership changes.
INI files	Text files that contain configuration data used with older versions of software but are not used with current operating systems.
Internet layer	The DOD layer that negotiates the data flow between computers on a network.
InterNIC	A multinational committee organized to issue IP addresses.
Interrupt	A technique whereby the CPU is caused to stop processing and respond to an event in the system.
Intersite replication	Replication that takes place within a site.
Intrasite replication	Replication that takes place between sites.
IP address leasing	The process whereby a client reserves an IP address for a specified amount of time.

IPSec	Internet Protocol Security: An IP-level security protocol that will digitally sign and/or encrypt IP packets.
IRQ	Interrupt Request: A hardware/software identification used by devices to get the attention of the CPU.
ISDN	Integrated Services Digital Network: A digital network commonly used in WANs.
ISO	International Organization for Standardization.
Iterative query	A query by a DNS server that may not return the requested IP address but rather the address of another DNS server that can provide more information.

K

KCC	Knowledge Consistency Checker: An Active Directory process that builds and maintains the replication topology.
KDC	Key distribution center: An element of Kerberos that authenticates users and distributes tickets.
Kerberos	A standard symmetrical key security protocol used by Windows 2000.
Kerberos ticket	A software object that contains user security information, which is presented by a user or process to gain access to network resources.

L

LDAP	Lightweight Directory Access Protocol: A standard directory access software system used in Windows 2000.
Linking policy	Using the same policy in different OUs and domains.
Local group	A security group for stand-alone computers.
Logical drive	A partition designated with a letter that represents a usable part of the hard drive.
LSA	Local Security Authority: A software service that is called by Winlogon.exe and used to authenticate users.

M

MAC address	Media access control: A unique number burned into an NIC that allows the computer using the NIC to be uniquely identified.
MBR	Master boot record: A data structure residing on the hard drive, used by the operating system to store disk information and to store boot programs.
Member server	A computer that joins a domain but does not host Active Directory.

Mixed mode	A mode used by Active Directory for networks that contain Windows NT servers.
msi	Microsoft Installer package file used with the group policies for software installation.
Multitasking	The ability of an operating system to perform more than one task at a time.

N

Name server record	A DNS record that indicates which servers contain DNS namespaces and can answer DNS queries.
Namespace	A group of names within a bounded area that can be resolved. For example, DNS contains namespaces for domains.
NAT	Network Address Translation: Translating a nonroutable IP address with a routable IP address. NAT is used on a network to share a single Internet connection with a group of clients.
Native mode	A mode used by Active Directory for networks that do not contain any Windows NT servers.
NetBEUI	Proprietary Microsoft networking protocol used in early versions of Windows.
NetBIOS	A method of identifying computers on a network with the NetBEUI protocol.
Network access layer	The DOD layer that formats and converts the data from binary to voltages.
Network layer	The OSI layer that negotiates the data flow between computers on the network.
Network Monitor	The program used to view network data as it passes to and from the server.
NIC	Network interface card: A card that plugs into a computer and allows the computer to be connected to the network.
No override policies	An option for policies set at the parent level that forces children to accept the policy. These policies cannot be overridden at the child level.
Nonroutable IP	An IP address that will not allow messages to be passed across a router or switch.
NOS	Network operating system: A multi-user, multitasking software application that manages network resources and users.
NT LAN Manager (NTLM) logon	The logon authentication process that uses the MSV1_0 authentication protocol.
NTFS	NT file system: The name of the file system used in Windows 2000; also used to describe the type of disk formatting.

NTLDR	Part of the Windows 2000 operating system that handles the initial boot. This program reads the BOOT.INI file.
NTOSKRNL	Part of the Windows 2000 operating system that contains the basic kernel.
ntuser.dat	The file in the user profile that contains registry settings.

O

Object counter	A counter associated with a performance object.
Object	An element in an Active Directory database.
Octet	A group of eight bits; also called a byte.
One-way hash	A mathematical method of encrypting information by use of a key such that the resulting hashed information cannot be converted back to its original source.
OS kernel	A software subsystem in Windows 2000 that contains hardware drivers.
OSI model	The network model developed by the ISO that divides network communication software into seven levels with each level performing clearly defined tasks and only communicating with levels above and below itself.
OSPF	A common routing protocol.
OU	Organizational unit: A container object in Active Directory that can contain user, computer, and other organizational unit objects, used as a security and administrative boundary within domains.

P

PAP	Password Authentication Protocol: A low-level RAS authentication protocol that sends passwords in clear text.
Parity	Using a data bit to verify other data bits when they are written to a hard disk.
Partition	A logical subsection of a hard drive, normally the section used to install operating systems and to divide them on a single hard drive.
Partition table	A data structure that contains structural information about a partition.
PDC emulator	An FSMO domain-level service used to send updates to Windows NT 4 computers in a mixed mode Active Directory network.
Performance object	An object that collects performance information.
Physical disk	The physical hard drive that is part of a computer system.
Physical layer	The OSI layer that converts data from 1s and 0s to voltages.
PING	Packet Internet Grouper: A TCP/IP utility that sends a message to a device with an IP address and waits for a reply.

PKI	Public key infrastructure: A set of security protocols that use public/private key services.
Plug and Play	A hardware standard used to automatically configure devices.
Port	A conduit through which print jobs travel to a print device.
POST	Power on self–test: A process by the hardware BIOS that initializes computer hardware.
POTS	Plain old telephone service: The telephone system.
PPP	Point to Point Protocol: The industry standard communications protocol commonly used for telephone connections. PPP can handle multiple network protocols, error correction, and authentication.
PPTP	Point to Point Tunneling Protocol: The protocol used to create a VPN connection by encapsulating data in a standard PPP frame.
Prebuilt accounts	A set of user accounts automatically created with the installation of Windows 2000.
Presentation layer	The OSI layer that formats network data.
Primary partition	A partition on a hard drive used to store boot information.
Print device	The physical printer.
Print server	A computer whose primary purpose is to receive, manage, and redirect print jobs.
Printer	The software interface between a computer and a print device.
Printer driver	The software that converts print jobs into a format understood by the print device.
Process layer	The DOD layer that formats and sends data between computers on a network.
Profile	A set of information and preferences assigned to a user and saved when the user logs off the network.
Protocol	An agreed upon method of communication between software components.
PTR record	Pointer record: A DNS record used to find a computer name when given an IP address.
Public/private keys	An asymmetrical key security protocol that uses key pairs (public/private) to encrypt and decrypt information.

R

RADIUS	Remote authentication dial-in user server: A server that will authenticate for multiple RAS servers. The Microsoft version of a RADIUS server is called the Internet Authentication Service.

RAID	Redundant array of inexpensive (or independent) disks: A multidisk configuration that allows for mirroring and disk striping.
RAS	Remote access service: A service that allows users to remotely access the server and network.
Recursive query	A query by a DNS server that will only return the final IP address of the requested resource to the resolver.
Registry	A Windows 2000 database that contains system configuration data.
Resolver	A client computer attempting to locate a network resource or computer by requesting the IP address from a DNS server.
Reverse lookup zone	A DNS namespace used to resolve domain names to IP addresses.
RFC	Request for comments: A method of creating and making changes to Internet standards.
RID	Relative ID: A code identifying a user or computer to the network. The RID is a code that uniquely identifies a security object, but without the domain information.
RID master	An FSMO domain-level service used to create security IDs that are assigned to users and computers.
Rings	A method of dividing Windows 2000 software systems so that only certain subsystems can interact with other systems.
Roaming profile	A profile that is stored on a domain controller and automatically used on each client when a user with the profile logs on.
Root key	One of six keys in the registry that does not contain any parent keys.
Router	A network device that maintains a network map and that can decide the destination of network traffic.
RRAS	Routing and remote access service: A service similar to RAS, but that also allows users to remotely access other networks.

S

Schema master	An FSMO forest-level service used to modify the Active Directory schema.
SCSI drive	Small computer system interface: A type of hard drive used in personal and large computers.
Sector	Part of the hard disk on which data is stored.
Security group	A container object that controls access to network resources.
Security Principle	A user, group, or computer that can have security settings.
Service or SRV record	A DNS record that identifies a service on a particular domain controller.

Session layer	The OSI layer that maintains connections between computers.
Share	A resource shared on the network.
Share-level permissions	Access permissions set on the share and automatically applied to all files and folders within the share.
SID	Security ID: A code identifying a user or computer to the network. The SID includes the domain of the object.
Site	A group of one or more well-connected subnets.
SLIP	Serial Line Interface Protocol: An old communications protocol commonly used for telephone connections. SLIP cannot handle multiple protocols.
SOA record	Start of Authority record: A DNS record that defines which DNS server is the primary DNS server for a domain.
Static IP	An IP address manually assigned to a device.
Stripe set	A method whereby data is written to multiple disks at the same time. It is often used in RAID.
Subnet mask	A number that, when combined with an IP address, returns part of the address not masked.
Switch	An intelligent network component used to interconnect a group of PCs and a server that can be programmed to move data from place to place.
System partition	The partition that contains the Windows 2000 boot files.

T

Task Manager	A program used to view and manage software processes and to view CPU and memory resources.
TGS	Ticket granting service: An element of Kerberos that grants tickets to authenticated users or processes.
TGT	Ticket granting ticket: A special ticket that is presented to a ticket granting service in order to get a regular Kerberos ticket.
Trace log	A log that records process and thread information.
Track	A section of the hard drive on which sectors are stored.
Transport layer	The OSI layer that locates computers on the network.
Tree	A element in Active Directory that consists of a group of related domains that share a contiguous namespace. For example, xyz.domain.local is a top-level domain and mycompany.xyz.domain.local would be a subdomain in the same domain tree.
Trusts	A relationship between domains whereby users authenticated in one domain are granted login rights in the second domain.

U

Universal group	A security group only available in native mode.
UPN	User principle name: A method of identifying users that includes the domain name and the user name in the format: domain@user.
User account	A security object in Windows 2000 used to verify access to network resources.
UTP	Unshielded twisted-pair: A type of network cable that looks like telephone wire.

V

Virtual directory	A directory within Internet Information Services that appears on a Web site, but is mapped to a physical folder on the server.
Virtual memory	A technique whereby physical memory is mapped into a disk file, allowing applications to use more memory than is physically installed in the computer.
VMM	Virtual memory manager: The software subsystem that manages virtual memory.
Volume mount point	A disk drive that is labeled as a local folder.
Volume	A logical division of a hard drive used by the dynamic disk feature in Windows 2000.
VPN	Virtual private network: A network connection running over a public network such as the Internet.

W

WAN	Wide area network: A network with multiple segments that extend over a large area.
Web page	A file that uses HTML.
Web server	A computer running Web server software that delivers Web pages in response to client requests.
Web site	A collection of files, folders, and virtual directories.
WHQL	Windows Hardware Quality Lab: A group at Microsoft that verifies third-party device drivers and issues digital signatures.
WINLOGON.EXE	The program that prompts the user with a login screen and processes the login information. After Windows 2000 has been loaded, this program is automatically executed.
WINS	Windows Internet Naming Service: A program that, when given a NetBIOS computer name, returns an IP address; only used when using NetBIOS.

Z

Zone transfer Moving a set of DNS records from one DNS server to another, which is not necessary when the DNS servers are Active Directory-integrated because Active Directory automatically reproduces DNS information.

EMCParadigm
875 Montreal Way
St. Paul, MN 55102
Toll Free: 1-800-535-6865
Email address: educate@emcp.com

YOU SHOULD CAREFULLY READ THE FOLLOWING TERMS AND CONDITIONS BEFORE OPENING THE DISC, DISKETTE, OR CASSETTE PACKAGE. OPENING THE PACKAGE INDICATES YOUR ACCEPTANCE OF THESE TERMS AND CONDITIONS. IF YOU DO NOT AGREE WITH THESE TERMS AND CONDITIONS DO NOT OPEN THE PACKAGE AND RETURN IT TO EMC/PARADIGM IMMEDIATELY.

The Publisher has developed this program and licensed its use. You assume the responsibility for the selection of the program to achieve your intended results and for the installation, use, and results obtained from using the program.

License

A. You may:
    1. use the program on any machine intended for use in conjunction with the course.
    2. transfer the program and its license to another party if the other party agrees to accept the terms and conditions of this agreement.

B. You may not:
    1. copy the program except to create back-up copies for the course instructor's use and copies of the student version in conjunction with classroom use (one copy of the program for every new copy of the text purchased), or
    2. modify or merge the program into any other program, or
    3. remove the Publisher's copyright notice from the program, or
    4. use or transfer the program, in whole or in part, except as provided by this Agreement.

IF AND WHEN YOU TRANSFER POSSESSION OF THE PROGRAM TO ANOTHER PARTY, YOUR LICENSE TO USE THE PROGRAM IS AUTOMATICALLY TERMINATED.

Term

This license is effective until terminated. You may terminate it at any time by destroying the program. It will also terminate if you fail to comply with any term or condition of this Agreement. You agree upon such termination to destroy the program.

Limited Warranty

THE PROGRAM IS PROVIDED "AS IS" WITHOUT WARRANTY OF ANY KIND, EITHER EXPRESS OR IMPLIED, INCLUDING, BUT NOT LIMITED TO, THE IMPLIED WARRANTIES OF MERCHANTABILITY AND FITNESS FOR A PARTICULAR PURPOSE. THE ENTIRE RISK AS TO THE QUALITY AND PERFORMANCE OF THE PROGRAM IS WITH YOU. SHOULD THE PROGRAM PROVE DEFECTIVE, YOU (AND NOT THE PUBLISHER OR AN AUTHORIZED DEALER FOR THE PUBLISHER) ASSUME THE ENTIRE COST OF ALL NECESSARY SERVICING, REPAIR, OR CORRECTION.

The Publisher does not warrant that the functions contained in the program will meet your requirements or that the operation of the program will be uninterrupted or error free.

However, the Publisher warrants the disc(s), diskette(s), or cassette(s) on which the program is furnished to be free of defects in materials and workmanship under normal use for a period of ninety (90) days from the date of delivery to you as evidenced by a copy of your receipt.

Limitations of Remedies

The Publisher's entire liability and your exclusive remedy shall be
1. the replacement of any disc, diskette, or cassette not meeting the publisher's "Limited Warranty" and which is returned to the Publisher, or
2. if the Publisher or the dealer is unable to deliver a replacement disc, diskette, or cassette which is free of defects in materials or workmanship, you may terminate this Agreement by returning the program.

IN NO EVENT WILL THE PUBLISHER BE LIABLE TO YOU FOR ANY DAMAGES, INCLUDING ANY LOST PROFITS, LOST SAVINGS, OR OTHER INCIDENTAL OR CONSEQUENTIAL DAMAGES ARISING OUT OF THE USE OR INABILITY TO USE SUCH PROGRAM, EVEN IF THE PUBLISHER OR ANY AUTHORIZED DEALER HAS BEEN ADVISED OF THE POSSIBILITY OF SUCH DAMAGES OR FOR ANY CLAIM BY ANY OTHER PARTY.